Unheralded Victory

The Defeat of the Viet Cong and the North Vietnamese Army 1961–1973

Unheralded Victory

The Defeat of the Viet Cong and the North Vietnamese Army 1961–1973

Mark W. Woodruff

Foreword by James L. Jones,
General, U.S. Marine Corps

VANDAMERE PRESS

Published by
Vandamere Press
P.O. Box 5243
Arlington, VA 22205

Copyright 1999
Mark W. Woodruff

ISBN 0-918339-51-0

Cover Photo: Sargeant Juan Cruz of the 1st Cavalry Division (Air-mobile) near Bong Son, South Vietnam, December 1965. Photo by Marv Wolf

Excerpted material from *We Were Soldiers Once . . . And Young: Ia Drang, The Battle That Changed the War in Vietnam* by General Harold G. Moore and Joseph L. Galloway, published by Random House, 1992 by permission of authors and publisher.

Contents

III

The Dich Van Program
Orchestrated Myths, Falsehoods, and Lies

IV

Questioning the Credibility of the Witnesses
Gaining a Fairer Verdict by History

FINAL

Foreword

In the quarter century since the end of the Vietnam War, the personal experience of those who fought there has often been at odds with the popular portrayal of the conflict. The media, the entertainment industry, and academia have frequently depicted the Vietnam War as being born of a bankrupt U.S. grand strategy, burdened by an unwieldy theater command structure, run by commanders isolated from lower level commanders in the provinces, fought by frustrated junior officers and troops in the field, and waged without regard for civilian casualties or damage.

The difficulty for many veterans of the war is that these criticisms do not ring entirely true. Memories of their experiences, while certainly burdened by the pain, loss, suffering, and frustration of combat, are balanced by the tremendous sense of camaraderie and the knowledge of, or personal witness to, extraordinary heroism on the part of their leaders, peers, and subordinates during those challenging times. Veterans recall their sacrifices with mixed emotions, but virtually all regard their effort with pride and know that they served their country honorably and to the best of their ability.

Like the author of this book, Vietnam veterans often begin to seek greater understanding of their experiences by re-examining events as they lived them—generally in small units below the battalion-level. They are naturally curious about the "what, when, where, and why" of their combat operations, and the healing power of the passing years has allowed them to somewhat dispassionately and objectively examine their time in Southeast Asia. Some veterans publish memoirs of their combat experience. Others go even further by re-examining not only their own youthful footsteps but also those of their peers in uniform as they grapple with the strategy of the war in Vietnam.

Mark Woodruff has traveled that route here, performing yeoman service for those who seek a better understanding of the Vietnam War. Like many veterans, our brief service together in Company F, 2d Battalion, 3d Marines in 1968 has grown into a lifelong friendship, and the experience and understanding of our small part in a big war serves as a common frame of reference even as we discuss today's events. Mark's post-Vietnam career took a decidedly unique path, with him eventually ending up in Australia as a psychologist and an officer in the Royal Australian Naval Reserve. His extensive social work with Australian veterans of the war has broadened his outlook on the conflict beyond that of the typical American veteran and reinforced his own need to delve deeper into its history.

Mark Woodruff understands as well as anyone that there is no such thing as a perfectly balanced or unbiased viewpoint. What has bothered him for many years is that the unspoken bias of many authors has leaned toward the North Vietnamese view for any number of reasons. Operating from the assumption that the U.S. effort in Vietnam needed to be reexamined with the benefit of the doubt going to the United States, Mark has thoroughly reviewed the official record and added important information from post-war Vietnamese sources, as well as Australian sources, to draw a clearer picture of the successes and failures of allied actions at the tactical, operational, and strategic levels of war.

Mark makes a compelling argument that American tactics and operations flowed logically from military strategy, and that we enjoyed greater success in that regard than is generally given credit by most Vietnam commentators. His thesis is simple: while the American political base at home was never solid enough to wage a protracted war in Southeast Asia, the war effort in theater was far from the quixotic venture to which many have relegated it in hindsight. Within the constraints imposed by the political environment of the day, the conflict was fought with a high degree of professionalism and competence, and the outcome was in great doubt until the United States decided to withdraw from the battlefield.

Whether or not you agree with Mark Woodruff's conclusions, the high quality of his research effort and his crisp narrative style make *Unheralded Victory* a compelling read for students of the Vietnam War. He explains American strategy in understandable terms, describes the intent of major operations, and highlights and succinctly explains relevant battles that supported both. In the end, the principal lesson of *Unheralded Victory* may be that in war you can do almost everything correctly in the field and still not end up on the winning side.

James L. Jones
General, U.S. Marine Corps

Preface

For most people, their military service, especially if it involved participation in war, is remembered as a defining moment in their lives. Many of those people who fought in the Vietnam War were in the military for only two years and in the war itself for only twelve months. Yet, those months dominate their memories and their lives in a manner all out of proportion to their brevity. As a corollary, I remember when, as a young man in the late 1960s, I observed a group of Australian veterans of World War II. Men in their mid-fifties, these Australian veterans were drinking together, swapping "war stories," and reminiscing. At the time I recall thinking that their lives after the war must have been shallow and uneventful for the war to continue to be of such interest to them, but I had missed the point entirely. No doubt they did have fruitful and full lives—raising families, working in their careers, enjoying their hobbies—but their brief exposure to the warrior culture remained a unique experience in their lives. Occasionally, those who had shared the experience wanted to share it with one another.

The Vietnam War produced another generation of warriors whose exploits fill this book. These warriors became part of a culture that honors deeds—aggressiveness against an armed foe, courage against an enemy who seeks to kill, self-sacrifice that may result in one's own death—that most people never experience. Perhaps not surprisingly, warriors tend to be more interested in actions than words. That doesn't mean they lack verbal or intellectual skills or that they don't often achieve academic success. It is a fact of life, though, that combat is a matter of actions, not words, and that those attracted to the profession of arms, especially those able to succeed in the profession, tend to be people whose focus is on action.

Because they are people of action, warriors tend not to dwell unnecessarily on the past. They analyzed the Vietnam War primarily so that they could be even more efficient in the future, as events in the Gulf War showed. Meanwhile, however, others claimed to have analyzed the war and declared that the warriors lost the war in Vietnam. This statement has not sat well with those who were there and knew better. Psychologists refer to this phenomenon as *cognitive dissonance,* an uncomfortable feeling left when beliefs and words disagree. This dissonance resounds even stronger upon hearing again the oft-quoted statement that North Vietnam ". . . lost all the battles but won the war." These warriors know that, while many wars were fought in that area of Southeast Asia over the centuries, the one in which *they fought* from 1961 until early 1973 saw North Vietnamese forces soundly defeated.

The war was a strange one. It was fought under strict "rules of engagement," intended to prevent the war from boiling over into a direct conflict with China and the Soviet Union. These rules of engagement proscribed the American military's actions and dictated the bounds of the conflict. Except for the closing days of the war, all meaningful ground combat was limited to that which took place within South Vietnam's national borders. American troops soundly won that very savage, yet very restricted, war. Sadly, American warriors acknowledge that North Vietnam did manage to win a later war against South Vietnam when that country was finally forced to fight on its own. Later still, North Vietnam even invaded Cambodia. Even later, after a falling out between the former Communist allies, North Vietnam fought a brief but bitter war against its former benefactor, China. The occurrence of all these later wars doesn't alter the fact, however, that North Vietnam's military forces were soundly defeated in their earlier war with the United States.

Perhaps at this point a distinction should be made between "defeating" the enemy and "winning" the war. Unlike games and sporting events, wars are not neatly and cleanly defined with a clear winner at the end. It is often difficult to declare that one side or the other "won" a particular war. Historians continually reevaluate history, and with the passage of time and change of perspective, the significance of particular events changes. The clear impact of any event in history may take years or decades to be fully understood. Even apparently clear and total victories such as that won by the coalition forces in the Gulf War have been called into question by those who looked at Sadam Hussein's continuing rule, and at the domestic political defeat of George Bush and Margaret Thatcher. Some of them now ask: "Who really won the war?" Despite this questioning by some, however, it seems entirely reasonable for history to state that Iraqi forces were totally and absolutely defeated in that war. So, too, can the military outcomes of the Vietnam War be viewed. This book therefore deals with a narrowly defined "victory." It exclusively examines the purely military defeat of one side by the other and does not address the follow-on political happenings or later military events.

Also, it must also be acknowledged that there is real wisdom in the belief that resort to war is everyone's loss and there can be no winner. Certainly, the grieving families of those killed would not consider themselves winners, despite whatever political, military, or geopolitical outcomes might be touted by experts.

Because of its focus on the combat actions of the Vietnam War, this book has an overwhelmingly male emphasis, which may seem somewhat out of place now. The readers should remember that this book is about a war in the 1960s and 1970s. Women, of course, did participate in noncombat roles, mainly as nurses and other medical personnel; twelve American servicewomen died there. Good accounts of their involvement include several books recently published, included in the bibliography, but outside the scope of this account.

Because of their similarity of language and culture and my own long residency in Australia, the Australians and New Zealanders too are included. I hope my inclusion of their valuable contribution helps rectify the usual manner in which they are ignored in American histories. This book makes no real attempt, however, to chronicle the contribution of many others, including the South Koreans, Thais, and Cambodians. This exclusion is regretted but, frankly, there was simply too much material for everything to be included. Similarly, the story of the South Vietnamese people fighting for their own survival is a fascinating, but different, account from this one. Their role is only touched upon. Instead, *Unheralded Victory*, chronicles the sacrifice of thousands of young Americans and Australians who faced no direct personal threat should they have failed to act. It chronicles those young men who left the safety of their own faraway homes to fight alongside a people of different race, culture, and country.

In this book, I refer to the *Republic of Vietnam* as South Vietnam. The *Democratic Republic of Vietnam* is referred to as North Vietnam. Referring to them by their official names is confusing because they are too similar. Also, the differentiating word, Democratic, which distinguishes North Vietnam from South Vietnam is clearly misleading as the North was certainly no more democratic than the South.

I use primarily western terminology in this book for several reasons. First, this book is written in English and aimed at western readers who are already familiar with terms like, "North Vietnamese Army." Changing this terminology is pointlessly confusing. Also, direct quotes from those years typically use that terminology and, as a matter of writing style, I prefer to keep terminology consistent in the text. Finally, the Communist terminology appears a worse alternative. Their highly emotive terms, referring to the South Vietnamese Army as "puppets" and American pilots as "pirates," continue to seem inappropriate. Probably the most questionable is my use of the term, "Viet Cong." In brief, I do so because most observers and participants (even the Communists) used that term.

The reader will note that I split the war into two distinctive campaigns: that waged against the Viet Cong in Part I and that against the North Vietnamese Army in Part II. In the case of the battles with the North Vietnamese Army (Khe Sanh, for instance), this division is fairly easy. The battles with the Viet Cong are less easily divided because of the fact that, filling their depleted ranks with Northern troops, so-called "Viet Cong" units were mainly made up of North Vietnamese Army soldiers by the early 1970s. Nonetheless, a convincing case exists for seeing it as two separate, but contiguous, campaigns. The distinct nature of this difference is perhaps best illustrated by their different roles and missions during the Tet battles of 1968. For those who like analogies, it is somewhat like a history of World War II wherein the Allied campaigns against the Germans and Italians in North Africa are treated in separate sections.

In countless conversations with friends who did not go to Vietnam, I have been constantly frustrated by the inability to use a common language. I found that, on almost any aspect of the Vietnam War, from body counts to soldierly skills, the discussion was so tainted by false assumptions that discourse proved very difficult. Because of these misperceptions, I ask the reader to approach this account of the war with an open mind. The myths themselves are dealt with at some length in Part III. Part IV then looks at how these myths came to be.

Unheralded Victory is written specifically for those who fought in Vietnam, for those whose loved ones fought there, and for all those who would like to know what really happened there.

☙

Soon after the United States became involved in Vietnam, the Assistant Secretary of Defense for International Security Affairs, John T. McNoughton, outlined a (Draft) Plan for Action for South Vietnam. It attempted to summarize what had already been started and what needed to be done. McNoughton wrote, *"It is essential—however badly [South East Asia] may go over the next 1–3 years—that the U.S. emerge as a 'good doctor.' We must have kept promises, been tough, taken risks, gotten bloodied, and hurt the enemy very badly"*[1]

For over 12 long years, the United States and a handful of good friends from Australia, New Zealand, South Korea, Thailand, and Cambodia kept their promises as "guarantor" to their South Vietnamese ally. The United States was, indeed, the "good doctor." It acted with toughness, time and again. It took risks, both on and off the battlefield. The grieving families of its young troops killed there can attest to having been bloodied. The United States proved beyond doubt that it would do everything reasonable, and perhaps then some, to stand by its various allies. By doing so, it sent a clear message throughout the world that America was no paper tiger and that any potential foe would not succeed without struggle.

The military involvement in South Vietnam began in earnest in 1961. By the time it had fully withdrawn its armies in 1973, U.S. troops had totally eliminated the Viet Cong, the force it had been first sent to fight. Along the way, U.S. forces had also defeated the armies of North Vietnam fighting in South Vietnam and, for good measure before it withdrew, inflicted serious damage on the North's future ability to wage war. In fulfilling its aim of being the "good doctor," the United States had indeed hurt the enemy very badly. It had, in fact, soundly defeated it and had achieved a notable victory before its forces returned from the battlefield. It wasn't a victory for which it would receive its due public credit, though. Even 30 years later, an account of the actions of America and its allies in South Vietnam would remain that of an *Unheralded Victory.*

THE EARLY HISTORY
207 B.C.–1961

1

Two Different Countries, Many Different Wars

Most Americans seem accustomed to using the term "the Vietnam War" to describe the period of American involvement there. In so doing, Americans ignore the centuries of conflict before America became involved and the decades of continuing conflict after America withdrew in 1973. In fact, the recorded history of what is now known as "Vietnam" began in 207 B.C. when a Chinese warlord named Trieu Da established the kingdom of Nam Viet, extending from the area now known as Da Nang northward to southern China. In 111 B.C., the Chinese under Han emperor, Wu Ti, laid claim and ruled for the next thousand years. The separate kingdom of Champa lay to the south running from Nam Viet to the Mekong Delta.[1]

While the Chinese dominated the northern kingdom of Nam Viet, the southern kingdom of Champa was Hindu and influenced by India. Further to the west, and also on the extreme southern tip, lay another Hindu kingdom, Funan, conquered by the Mon-Khymer people of the Cambodian empire in the 6th century.

The southern kingdom of Champa was often at war with the northern kingdom of Nam

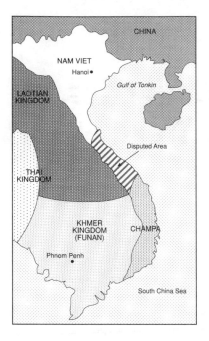

Viet, but maintained a separate identity until being conquered by Nam Viet in 1471. Saigon and the Mekong Delta were taken from Cambodia during the period 1700–1760. Although nominally ruled by the Le dynasty, this area, which occupies the rough geographical boundaries known today as "Vietnam," continued to be divided, ruled by the Trinh family in the north and the Nguyen family in the south.

Throughout the 17th century, the animosity between the people of the north and the people of the south was so great that a long and bloody war ensued between them. Between 1627 and 1673, the aggressive Trinh emperors of the north tried seven different times to invade the south, but each time they were stopped by the Nguyens' defenses. The southerners had constructed two 20-foot-high walls, one of them six miles long and the other twenty miles long at the point where the coastal plain was at its narrowest: the 17th parallel. In the late 1700s, the northerners briefly prevailed but a survivor of the southern family, Nguyen Anh, occupied Saigon and the Mekong Delta. After a 14-year struggle, the southerners seized Hue and Hanoi with French military aid. In 1802, Nguyen Anh assumed the throne as Emperor Gia Long of a united Vietnam.

Gia Long's successors, however, distrusted the French and, more specifically, their Christianity and, by 1820, they were expelling French missionaries and imprisoning or executing Vietnamese converts to Christianity. The French responded militarily and, with Napoleon III on the French throne, set about establishing French colonial rule. This French intervention superseded domestic, north-versus-south, politics for over 100 years, commencing in 1847. Although occupied by the Japanese in World War II, the French quickly reestablished control at the end of the war. The Communist Viet Minh forces, which had fought against the Japanese, now turned their attention to the French.

Weapons captured by the Communist Chinese in Korea began to flow to the Viet Minh in the early 1950s. The French and their Vietnamese allies fought a see-saw battle with the Viet Minh forces. In France itself, the French

Communist Party was a major political force committed to the support of the Viet Minh. America, concerned about the Soviet threat to Europe and keen to have a strong, non-Communist France, increasingly financed the French effort but stayed out of direct involvement.

The French eventually tired of the struggle, disheartened by their defeat in the battle of Dien Bien Phu, which took place deep in the north of the country. A cease-fire was signed in Geneva in 1954, establishing the 17th parallel, that same narrow stretch of coastal plain where the Nguyens had built their defensive walls and previously fought the northerners, as the border separating the southern Republic of Vietnam (South Vietnam) and the northern Democratic Republic of Vietnam (North Vietnam). Elections were scheduled to be held in two years.

While the French had tired of the struggle and no longer backed the fight, the Communists, too, had suffered massively in their battles. Nikita Khrushchev's memoirs make it clear that the Communist troops were at the point of exhaustion and needed the cease-fire in order to regroup and rebuild. Even their own official history, written in 1970, makes reference to the fact that the Communists were not then strong enough to seize the whole of Vietnam.[2]

Ho Chi Minh's government was installed in North Vietnam, while the government of one-time emperor (1925–1945) Bao Dai was installed in South Vietnam. While it is often said that Ho Chi Minh could have won an election in 1954, when South Vietnam was in chaos and he was riding a crest of popularity from having ousted the French, the situation changed quickly. Within a few weeks, 850,000 people fled from North Vietnam to South Vietnam, most of them Catholics and small landowners fearful of the Communists. Only some 80,000 people went to the North, almost all of them guerrilla cadres who had fought the French.[3]

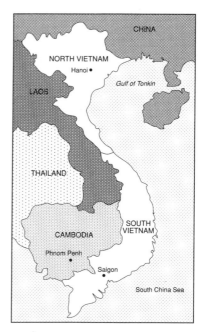

The actual effect of this massive population shift was never tested at the polls. The elections were not held. South Vietnam, which had not signed the Geneva Accords, did not believe the Communists in North Vietnam would allow a fair election. In January 1957, the International Control Commission (ICC), comprising observers from India, Poland, and Canada, agreed with this perception, reporting that neither South nor North Vietnam had honored the armistice agreement. With the French gone, a return to the traditional power struggle between north and south had begun again. At the 15th Meeting of the Party's Central Committee in May of 1959, North Vietnam formally decided to take up arms against the government of South Vietnam.[4]

The war against South Vietnam was fought by the Hanoi-backed, southern-born Viet Cong as well as directly by the North Vietnamese Army itself. The goals of the Viet Cong and North Vietnam were parallel but not identical. The Viet Cong sought to achieve power in South Vietnam; the North Vietnamese sought to annex the South and "unify" Vietnam. Viet Cong Minister of Justice, Truong Nhu Tang, summed up the Southern viewpoint by saying that historically ". . . there were substantial economic, social, and cultural distinctions between North and South (let alone the ethnic minority regions) that argue for a regional rather than a centralized approach to unity." But North Vietnam, despite its protestations at the time, sought to have both North and South Vietnam ruled under the North Vietnamese flag. The two forces' "marriage of convenience" would last only briefly; but, while it did, they would mount savage attacks on South Vietnam.[5]

Unlike the French previously, the United States in the 1960s did not seek colonies or an empire. Rather, the United States *was* committed to backing any nation that opposed Communism. The Korean War was still fresh in American memories and only an uneasy truce had stopped the fighting there. Soviet tanks had crushed the Hungarian revolution only five years before and now sat poised to launch an attack against western Europe. Tensions in Europe were at their peak. Within months these tensions would result in building the Berlin Wall dividing Communist East from democratic West. With this backdrop of global military confrontation between the superpowers, President John F. Kennedy viewed the situation in South Vietnam with increasing concern as spring turned to summer in 1961.

THE DEFEAT
OF THE VIET CONG
1961–1971

2

The Advisor Period

By 1961, the threat to South Vietnam's continued existence had become extremely serious. For the two previous years, neighboring North Vietnam had poured money and weaponry into the southern Viet Cong forces.

In 1960, the Communists had created a political body, the National Liberation Front (NLF), to control their southern activities. The NLF then created its own armed forces, the Peoples Liberation Armed Forces (PLAF), which soon shortened this title to Liberation Forces. The non-Communist government of South Vietnam referred to them simply as the Viet Cong and, within a few years, even the Communists themselves used the term to describe their own troops.[1]

The Viet Cong consisted of three types of combat units by 1961: full-time Viet Cong Main Force units, as well as paramilitary troops, split into the Viet Cong Regional Forces and the Viet Cong Local Forces. In addition, there remained the political structure (NLF) which soon became known as the Viet Cong Infrastructure (VCI). These VCI personnel were the political officers entrusted with the mission of ensuring the political correctness of the fighting units. They were also the administrators and tax collectors who kept the machinery running in the Communists' shadow government.

Of the combat units, the Viet Cong's Main Force units consisted of relatively large numbers of troops, usually organized in 2,000-man regiments. These troops were full-time soldiers and made no attempt to pretend they were civilians. Generally they operated out of base camps hidden in mountain areas or along remote stretches of the border. Main Force units were well equipped with assault rifles, machine guns, antitank weapons, and mortars. They were recruited from the length and breadth of Vietnam and posted to wherever their Main Force unit happened to be deployed at the time. Many of these troops, at least in the early 1960s, were South Vietnamese who had gone to the North in 1954 and then, after undergoing military training in North Vietnam, were sent back to South Vietnam.

Viet Cong Regional Force units were more likely to be of smaller size, generally organized into 500-man battalions. They were recruited from the same province (roughly equivalent to an American county) in which they served. Although they were full-time soldiers, these Regional Force units tended to have lower standards of training and poorer equipment than the Main Force units. Like their Main Force comrades, the Regional Force troops operated out of the more remote and secluded areas of their particular province. In many ways, they were the local militia of the Viet Cong.

Viet Cong Local Forces were recruited from the same villages in which they served. They were usually organized into squad-sized units of 10 to 12 men and were often armed with a motley array of weapons. These Local Force units were part-time soldiers. Often farmers by day, Local Force troops were detailed to plant mines and boobytraps, take potshots at passing convoys, and gather intelligence about Allied troop movements. They were often used as guides and porters for Regional Force and Main Force units when these big units passed through their areas.

Together, these forces, consisting of the VCI and their Main Force, Regional Force, and Local Force combat troops, threatened to topple the government of South Vietnam. President John F. Kennedy reacted to the deteriorating situation in South Vietnam by sending Vice President Lyndon Johnson to Saigon on May 12, 1961, with a mission to reconfirm America's solidarity with that country. On October 11, President Kennedy dispatched his personal military adviser, General Maxwell D. Taylor, together with Kennedy's aide, Dr. Walt W. Rostow, to South Vietnam to study the situation. After lengthy discussions with his various advisers, President

Kennedy offered American military assistance. The President of South Vietnam readily accepted.[2]

The Americans and South Vietnamese both realized that in order to destroy these Viet Cong Forces, they would need to employ multiple strategies. While the VCI and the Local Force Viet Cong guerrillas were best countered by an antiterrorist force, modern conventional forces equipped with helicopters and armored personnel carriers would be needed to deal with the Viet Cong's Regional and Main Force units.

America offered equipment and technical help to deal with the more conventional aspects of the conflict. On December 11, 1961, 33 U.S. Army H-21C Shawnee helicopters and the 400 men necessary to fly and maintain them arrived in South Vietnam. Their numbers were quickly swollen by more pilots and crews from other units.

America also offered help in training and advisory personnel. President John F. Kennedy had foreseen a need for special tactics and forces and, as a direct result of his enthusiastic support, the Army's Special Forces, or Green Berets as they came to be known, had been created. Originally intended to organize guerrilla forces behind enemy lines, they were already being used, but in very small numbers, in a counterguerrilla role in Vietnam. With their knowledge of guerrilla tactics and their ability to organize and assist indigenous troops, the Special Forces assisted South Vietnamese Army troops to track down and destroy the Viet Cong. By the end of 1961, with the Cold War nearing boiling point, American advisory strength in Vietnam was increased substantially. In February 1962, the Military Assistance Command Vietnam (MACV), was formed to coordinate these activities. By June 1962, the authorized number of U.S. military advisers was increased from 746 to more than 3,400. In August, the first 30 Australian soldiers, the forerunners of the much-decorated Australian Army Training Team, arrived in Vietnam.[3]

The battle to defeat the Viet Cong would not be a conventional one like that fought in World War II against the Germans or the Japanese. While the Viet Cong's Main Force Units would stand and fight occasionally, their Regional and Local Force units were very reluctant to engage in stand-up battle. The Local Force units in particular, small handfuls of a dozen or so troops who would gather together only once every few weeks to attack an outpost or murder a village official, by their nature avoided head-to-head fights. So the war against the Viet Cong in these early days was characterized by thousands of small, daily actions between the opposing forces. This period in the very early 1960s became known as "the adviser period" because of the influx and the impact of these American and Australian advisers. Ostensibly there solely to make suggestions to their South Vietnamese allies, the advisers often assumed a more active role in the actual heat of combat.

The advisers made a solid contribution to the South Vietnamese fighting capability and their physical presence "on the ground" helped stiffen the resolve of the units to which they were assigned. The advisers, together with the technological advantages provided by the American-supplied armored personnel carriers (APCs) and helicopters, helped save the South Vietnamese Army from the defeat President Kennedy had feared.

World focus shifted to Cuba in October 1962, when the United States and the Soviet Union went to the brink of nuclear war during the missile crisis. That crisis appeared to confirm the threat of world Communism and the need for constant vigilance. In Europe, the Berlin Wall remained an imposing daily reminder of the threat of invasion from the east and kept American military priorities centered there. In South Vietnam, meanwhile, American forces assisted in countless successful military actions against the Viet Cong. Communist forces also won the occasional fight, of course, such as the January 1963 firefight with the South Vietnamese Army outside the little village of Ap Bac, an event which was widely reported in the United States. Overall, however, by the time of President Kennedy's tragic assassination in 1963, the tide had turned against the Viet Cong.

The Viet Cong's backers in Hanoi also noted this trend and became increasingly displeased with the progress of the war, concluding that the Viet Cong lacked the skill and experience to defeat the South Vietnamese Army in the sort of stand-up, conventional battle that would be necessary to topple the South Vietnamese government. By the middle of 1964 Hanoi responded by posting Northern-born troops to Viet Cong units and also by supplying these units with communications experts, ordnance technicians, political commissars, and even combat commanders.[4]

In the early 1960s, the Viet Cong had been equipped with a variety of French, Chinese, American, and even Japanese weapons. This lack of standardization would cause acute problems in ammunition and weapons resupply if the Viet Cong forces were to be increased in size. In 1964, therefore, Hanoi decided to convert Viet Cong forces to a standard family of modern small arms using one caliber of ammunition. Hanoi issued a weapons system based on the fully automatic AK-47 assault rifle. This system not only standardized ammunition and spare parts, it also provided Viet Cong forces with a dramatic increase in firepower, easily outgunning South Vietnamese forces still armed with World War II-era weaponry. The decision to issue fully automatic weapons on such a huge scale was an

Viet Cong troops of a Main Force Unit. Their NVA-supplied weaponry and equipment, courtesy of the Soviets and the Chinese, made the VC a formidable foe but led to a total reliance on Hanoi for resupply.
Credit: Democratic Republic of Vietnam

important one, as it obliged Hanoi to thereafter send large quantities of ammunition and weaponry southward into the war zone. It also sealed the Viet Cong's dependence on North Vietnam.[5]

With this massive assistance from the North, Viet Cong regiments were combined to form even larger combat formations. In 1964, the Viet Cong fielded their first 10,000-man, division-sized Main Force unit. The war was entering a dramatic new phase.[6]

3

Fighting The VC Main Force

By the end of 1964, America's direct involvement in the war against the Viet Cong had proceeded for three years. Meanwhile, the North Vietnamese had continued to pour men and material into the southern war at ever-increasing rates. Most ominously of all, North Vietnam had begun moving its own conventional army, complete with tanks and artillery, into positions that threatened a direct attack against South Vietnam. America responded by deploying its own combat troops to South Vietnam.[1]

On March 8, 1965, the U.S. Marines of Battalion Landing Team 3/9 (BLT3/9) waded ashore at Da Nang, South Vietnam, while their sister battalion (BLT1/3) began landing at Da Nang airport, having flown in from Okinawa. At first, the Marines were used in a purely defensive capacity, that is, defending the airfield at Da Nang and by their presence countering the threat of a direct North Vietnamese invasion. Strict "rules of engagement" initially even prevented the Marines from shooting at Viet Cong troops outside the airbase's barbed-wire perimeter. Not until mid-April 1965, and after intensive two-day negotiations with the South Vietnamese, did the Marines increase their area of responsibility by four square miles. Little by little, the Marines' numbers also grew until, in mid-May, BLT3/3 arrived from their base at Okinawa, bringing Marine infantry strength in Vietnam to seven battalions.[2]

The arrival of these American combat troops would see a new phase in the war. Large-scale offensive actions against the Viet Cong Main Force units now became a possibility. Whereas South Vietnamese troops had generally lacked the mobility needed to fight battles in the remote areas in which the Viet Cong sheltered, the Americans were able to attack the Communists in their own backyard and thereby seize the offensive.

In mid-August, intelligence reports, including information supplied by a Viet Cong defector, indicated that the 1st Viet Cong Regiment, a full-time Main Force infantry unit, had established itself in fortified positions on Van Tuong Peninsula, only 15 miles south of the Marines' airstrip at Chu Lai near Da Nang. The 1st Viet Cong Regiment was arguably the best of their Main Force units, responsible in May for the total annihilation of one battalion of South Vietnamese troops and the mauling of at least one more at the battle of Ba-Gia. Both the battle and the 1st Viet Cong Regiment that had fought it, were said to have acquired "heroic significance" to the Viet Cong forces as a result.[3]

The 1st Viet Cong Regiment consisted not only of their own 60th and the 80th Viet Cong Battalions, but also of reinforcements for this occasion, the 52nd Weapons Battalion, heavily armed with antitank weapons and heavy mortars supplied by North Vietnam. A Viet Cong deserter, who fortuitously appeared on August 15, told the Marines that the Communists, flushed with confidence from their recent victories against the South Vietnamese Army, were readying themselves for an attack on the Marine base. This lucky bit of information, plus the good fortune of the arrival of Regimental Landing Team 7 (500 Marines from the 1st Battalion) plus the nearby Special Landing Force (another 500 Marines from BLT 3/7), presented an opportunity the Marines couldn't resist. The Marines quickly reinforced Regimental Landing Team 7 with two additional battalions (2/4 and 3/3 with a combined total of 1,000 Marines), bringing it up to authorized strength. In one of those strange twists of war, the Marines, sent to counter the North Vietnamese regiments, would fight their first battle in South Vietnam against a Viet Cong regiment. The battle would be closely watched by both sides, eager to see how the Americans would fare against such a seasoned foe.[4]

Within only three days the Marines had planned and organized the highly complex operation, code named Operation Starlite, to begin on the

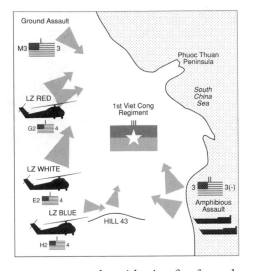

Ground Assault

M3 | 3

Phuoc Thuan Peninsula

South China Sea

LZ RED

1st Viet Cong Regiment

G2 | 4

LZ WHITE

E2 | 4

LZ BLUE

HILL 43

3 | 3(-)

Amphibious Assault

H2 | 4

morning of August 18. Combining an assault from land, air, and sea, the Marines planned to trap the Viet Cong on the peninsula and then destroy them.

The 500 or so men of the 3rd battalion, 3rd Marines, stormed ashore from the south in a classic amphibious landing, the first wave charging out of the surf in eleven 40-ton amphibious tractors known as amtracs. Led by Lieutenant Colonel Joseph E. Muir, they were soon met by withering fire from the entrenched Viet Cong. "Machine guns opened up on us as we ran across the beach," Muir observed, "but our Marines knocked out the gun, and we began to push." The Marines of Lima Company attacked uphill into the Viet Cong positions so swiftly that the Viet Cong were forced to retreat, taking with them only their weapons and leaving behind their packs, their food, and even their civilian clothing. The six-inch guns of the USS *Galveston*, cruising offshore, were brought to bear upon the enemy bunkers and trenches. Even before the smoke had cleared, the Marines assaulted again, only to be met by yet another withering barrage of fire. Eventually, after several hours of combat, including hand-to-hand fighting, the Marines had seized the vital hillside that dominated the terrain.[5]

Meanwhile, the heliborne troops were also involved in savage fighting. Three landing zones were designated: code-named Landing Zones (LZs) Red, White, and Blue. The 100 Marines of Hotel Company 2/4, landing on LZ Blue, landed almost on top of the 500 troops of the 60th Viet Cong Battalion. To the north, on LZ White, Echo Company 2/4 landed on a ridgeline overlooked by a second ridge occupied by entrenched Viet Cong troops. Fierce battles were fought, with the Marines charging up the slopes into the enemy positions and naval gunfire from offshore providing support. Meanwhile, the Viet Cong, forced to stand and fight, fought tenaciously. By August 24, though, the 1st Viet Cong Regiment had been destroyed. Six hundred fourteen Viet Cong troops had been killed and nine prisoners taken. American losses were listed as 45 dead. The Marines had given the Viet Cong a masterful demonstration of the subtlety of their mobility, mixed with the brutal effectiveness of their courage and firepower. In their first "stand-up fight" with American troops, the best unit that the Viet Cong could field had been thoroughly defeated.

General William Westmoreland, ground commander of all U.S. forces, would increasingly use his American units to aggressively "search for and destroy" the enemy's Main Force units. In doing so, American troops would provide a shield behind which the South Vietnamese Army could deal with issues of pacification and the counterguerrilla war.

The Australians: The Battle at Long Tan

On August 3, 1962, Australian military advisers arrived in Vietnam. Like their American counterparts, these advisers had helped train and often led their South Vietnamese allies in battle. Like their American allies, the Australians soon became aware of the increasing numbers of North Vietnamese troops on the battlefield and so chose to counter this move with the introduction of their own regular army units. On May 25, 1965, the 1st Battalion, Royal Australian Regiment, and its various support units arrived in South Vietnam.

The Australians were heavily influenced by their recent experiences in counterguerrilla operations in Malaya. American and Australian strategies were therefore quite different, leading to different tactical methods of operating. The Australians patrolled constantly to find and counter the enemy reconnoitering their positions; the Americans used patrols to invite confrontation. The Australians were slow and methodical; the Americans preferred quick-in, quick-out methods to unsettle the enemy.[6]

Upon arrival in South Vietnam, the Australians were integrated with an American unit, however, soon creating problems. For their first few months in Vietnam, the Australian battalion was attached to the two battalions of the 173rd Airborne Brigade near the Bien Hoa Air Base. The Australians were restricted by Australian Government policy to defensive operations around the base. They were not allowed to participate in actions in other parts of III Corps, much less even consider accompanying the Americans on their general duties as a reserve to be employed anywhere in the country.[7]

Australian Lieutenant General Sir John Wilton was very wary of Australians fighting alongside American units. He felt that American units in Vietnam took extremely heavy casualties. The simple fact of the matter was that Australia could not afford to be as generous with its soldiers' lives as could the Americans. While the loss of a battalion would be a setback to the Americans, it would be a national catastrophe to Australia's small army.[8]

On July 28, General Westmoreland was forced to replace the Australians with another U.S. battalion so that the 173rd Airborne would have its full complement of three battalions for an operation 56 kilometers from Bien Hoa. Only after much political wrangling was a compromise effected so that the Australians would accompany the Americans, but no further than one adjacent province.[9]

Many of these differences were finally put to rest when the Australians decided to increase their military efforts in Vietnam. By the end of June 1966, they had put in place an entirely independent fighting force, the 1st Australian Task Force (1ATF) built around two infantry battalions with supporting artillery and armor. No longer a part of an American division, the Australians were an independent force reporting directly to the Corps Commander. They were now able to pursue strategies and tactics best suited to their own experience and training.

One of many differences found in the Australian force was related to their replacement policy. Whereas an American soldier would be posted to a unit in Vietnam and simply join an existing unit, the Australians instead took a group of men and trained them together as a unit in Australia before

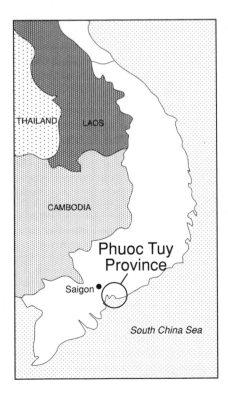

moving them as a unit to Vietnam. The Australians believed this policy led to better unit cohesion, since the men had trained together and knew they would serve the whole year together. This method had many advantages, but an unfortunate outcome of the Australian unit-rotation system was that the experienced 1RAR (1st Battalion, Royal Australian Regiment), which fought alongside the Americans for a full year, returned to Australia en masse and was replaced by two fresh battalions, 6RAR and 5RAR, which completed their movement to Vietnam on June 9, 1966.[10]

Settled in Phuoc Tuy Province on the southern approaches to Saigon, the Australians were allowed a unique role. Unlike the Americans and Koreans, whose primary task was to find and engage the enemy Main Force units, the Australians' role was to establish a permanent base near the town of Nui Dat and attempt to keep the local guerrilla forces away from the civilian population. Thus, the Australian involvement was more akin to that of the South Vietnamese Army: one of "pacification" and specifically intended to keep it out of America's battles with Main Force units. General Wilton still saw these actions as "a bit of a meatgrinder."[11]

The primary enemy unit operating daily in Phuoc Tuy Province, and the one the Australians soon became familiar with, was D445 Provincial Mobile Battalion with an estimated strength of 550 men. These troops, being Regional Force units, were recruited from the hamlets and villages of the province and operated only within the provincial boundaries. They were armed with a motley collection of bolt-action rifles and captured Korean War vintage carbines. Another 400 Local Force guerrillas, in units ranging in size from 5 to 60, operated out of their home villages.[12]

Against this unit, the Australians would use the lessons they'd learned in Malaya. They would patrol slowly and methodically, avoiding trails and preferring instead to hack their way through the jungle. Also, the Australians were very lightly armed by American standards. The riflemen carried only 60 rounds of ammunition compared to the American infantryman's 300 rounds. Similarly, the Australians carried only 200 rounds of ammunition for each machine gun in contrast to the standard load of 500 rounds for the Americans.

As promised, the Australians had outstanding success against these guerrilla forces. Trinh Duc was a ranking Viet Cong cadre at the time. He recalls his unit being ambushed several times and stated that, "The Australians were more patient than the Americans, better guerrilla fighters, better at ambushes." By the middle of 1966, the Australian presence had become a real concern to the local Viet Cong. In desperation, it was decided to teach the Australians a lesson, one that the local villagers would also understand and would get them to rally to the side of the Communists. They would use one of their Main Force units against the Australians.[13]

Lurking in the hinterlands and available for just such strong-arm missions was the 5th Viet Cong Division, consisting of 274 Regiment (2000 personnel) and 275 Regiment (1850 personnel). Holed up in the May Tao mountains to the northeast, these Main Force troops were well trained and equipped, responsible for the three adjoining provinces.[14]

To teach the Australians their lesson, the Communists threw at them the entire 275 Main Force Regiment, who were guided and assisted by the troops of D445 Battalion and further bolstered by a 100-man company of

North Vietnamese Army regulars sent by Hanoi to shore up the indigenous Viet Cong Forces. The Viet Cong's other Main Force unit, 274 Regiment, lay in wait along the nearby highway to ambush the nearby American unit should they be called in to the fight. While neither prepared nor armed to wage battle against this type of Main Force unit, the Australians demonstrated their flexibility by standing toe to toe with the enemy in three hours of brutal combat, outnumbered ten to one.

The Battle of Long Tan Begins

Commencing at 2:43 A.M. on August 17, 1966, the Australians' sprawling base at Nui Dat was hit by approximately 60 rounds of mortar fire. Twenty-two Australians were wounded, one fatally. One New Zealander was wounded. The men of D Company, engrossed in a board game at some distance from the rounds' impact, were unsure whether it was incoming or outgoing and continued their game. The Australian artillery fired counter-battery fire and eventually the mortaring ceased.

At daybreak, the Australians decided to send a patrol out to search for the enemy mortar teams in the unlikely case they were still lingering in the area. B Company 6 RAR spent the day scouring the area and then settled into positions a short way from the base. The next morning, 48 of its men returned to the base for their rostered turn on leave to the nearby resort beach at Vung Tau, leaving only 32 men of B Company to continue the search.

At approximately 11:00 A.M., D Company began moving through the base's defenses to relieve B Company, now much reduced in strength. D Company, consisting of three platoons, numbered in the Australian way, 10, 11, and 12 Platoons, had a strength of 108 men, all of them recent arrivals in Vietnam. They proceeded east toward the nearby rubber plantation. As they met up with B Company at about 1:00 P.M., the troops could hear the drumbeat and musical refrain being pumped through the loud-

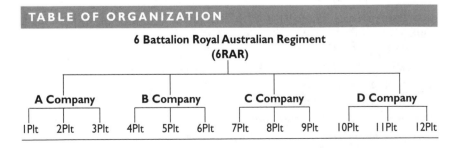

TABLE OF ORGANIZATION

6 Battalion Royal Australian Regiment
(6RAR)

A Company			B Company			C Company			D Company		
1Plt	2Plt	3Plt	4Plt	5Plt	6Plt	7Plt	8Plt	9Plt	10Plt	11Plt	12Plt

speakers at their base camp as a band warmed up in preparation for that afternoon's concert starring "Col" Joye and Little Pattie, two popular Australian entertainers. The troops then took a meal break and later B Company began moving off in the direction of the music, back to their base camp. By about 3:00 P.M., D Company was ready to continue on its way to the rubber plantation.

After proceeding only 200 meters, the track forked; one branch led to the northeast, the other almost due east. 10 Platoon followed the northeast track on the left, and 11 Platoon followed the right-hand track, which led straight through the middle of the plantation. At 3:40 P.M., 11 Platoon spotted a group of enemy troops and opened fire, apparently wounding one of the enemy before they disappeared into the trees, leaving one AK-47 assault rifle behind. While perhaps the modern assault rifle should have warned them that these men were not from D445, the Australians continued with their mission. Major Harry Smith ordered 11 Platoon to proceed in extended line, virtually an assault formation, and the platoon moved out at a brisk pace to catch the enemy. A little after 4:00 P.M., 11 Platoon, still moving ahead with the men stretched abreast over a frontage of 200 meters, came across a hut that had been searched earlier that same day by the men of B Company. Believing he heard sounds emanating from it, Second Lieutenant Sharp ordered his men to assault through the area but found no enemy troops. By now, 11 Platoon was still moving forward on line and had increased the distance between itself and 10 Platoon on its left. The two platoons had lost sight of each other, separated by some 300 meters in the rubber trees.

The Australians continued their advance, 11 Platoon on the right and 10 Platoon on the left, separated by several hundred meters. Some distance behind followed 12 Platoon and the headquarters group, covering the area that separated the two lead platoons but some distance behind them. They, too, advanced in a line-abreast formation in order to cover this middle ground.

At 4:08 P.M., the men of 11 Platoon began to take heavy fire from their front and left and they immediately dropped to the prone position. Soon they had taken several casualties from the section on the left. The buildup of enemy fire increased quickly and soon 11 Platoon estimated that at least a company of enemy soldiers confronted them. At that same time, a monsoonal downpour of rain began falling.

An Australian who had fought in the battle recalled that, "The reaction of all the soldiers in 11 Platoon was disbelief as a battle such as this had never been envisaged by anyone." He recalled that, "The training in Australia had been focused on short, sharp clashes against an enemy who would fall back as soon as he was sighted."[15]

Lieutenant Sharp immediately called for artillery fire, saying, "It's bigger than I thought it was. *They're* going to attack *us!*" Soon after, Lieutenant Sharp was killed by a bullet when he raised himself up to observe the fall of the artillery rounds. At the same time, 10 Platoon on the left was also taking fire. Mortar rounds began falling to the right of them and the troops pulled back to the left, away from the exploding rounds and back closer into their platoon headquarters area. 10 Platoon quickly established a defensive perimeter and began digging shallow foxholes. 12 Platoon and the headquarters group, some distance behind, also began receiving mortars to their right and so they, too, pulled back to their left, away from the rounds' impact.[16]

The Company Commander, Major Smith, ordered 10 Platoon to form up for a flanking attack, approaching the beleaguered 11 Platoon from the left. With two sections up front and one following in trace, 10 Platoon proceeded at a walk through the pouring rain toward the sound of the gunfire. About 200 meters along, they were surprised to see an assault line of enemy troops passing by in front of them on their way to continue the attack against 11 Platoon. The Australians immediately opened fire, wiping out the right hand portion of the assault line and causing the survivors to give up the attack. They proceeded another 30 meters before coming under heavy fire themselves, which destroyed their radio and forced them to take whatever cover they could.

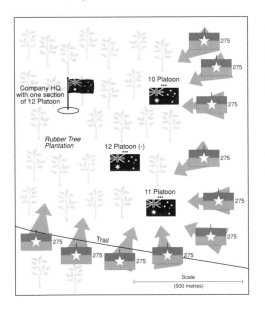

At their base camp at 4:30 P.M., the Battalion Commander, Lieutenant Colonel Colin Townsend placed A Company, just back from a three-day patrol, on standby to go to D Company's aid. At the same time, he told Lieutenant Adrian Roberts' 3 Troop of APCs to be prepared to move out. Also, the depleted B Company, which had stopped on its movement back to the base when it heard the gunfire, was told to turn around and attempt to reinforce D Company.[17]

By 5:00 P.M., 11 Platoon's situation, some short distance away, could hardly be worse. They had been under constant attack for almost an hour. Their Platoon Commander was dead, along with several of the soldiers. They had lost radio communication, the antennae having been shot away.

At 5:02 P.M., Major Smith requested a resupply of ammunition by helicopter. Brigadier O.D. Jackson, the Task Force Commander, in turn asked the Royal Australian Air Force (RAAF) commander for helicopters to deliver the ammunition. The RAAF refused, citing the requirement that the landing zone must be ". . . relatively secure where enemy resistance is not expected." He was not prepared to risk his few helicopters in such bad weather with so much enemy ground fire. Brigadier Jackson sent for the US Army Aviation Liaison Officer who offered that, ". . . my guys can help out," and that he could have American helicopters there in 20 minutes. As it turned out, they wouldn't be needed.[18]

At Nui Dat, Lieutenant Roberts brought the seven APCs of 3 Troop, augmented by three APCs from 2 Troop, to Headquarters 6RAR soon after 5:00 P.M. In very sketchy orders, he was told to load up the men of A Company and proceed to D Company's rescue.

Back on the battlefield, Major Smith began shifting his Headquarters Group and 12 Platoon closer toward the battle raging with 10 and 11 Platoons. In order to properly control the heavy volume of artillery fire being called in, he held up not far from the edge of the rubber plantation. Keeping one section back for security, at 5:15 P.M., he ordered Second Lieutenant David Sabben and the rest of his 12 Platoon to proceed on to 11 Platoon's position.

12 Platoon advanced toward the sound of the battle, but after having progressed only 500 meters they were forced to stop by large groups of enemy soldiers advancing from the north and smaller groups attempting to encircle them. 12 Platoon's commander, Lieutenant Sabben, overheard on the radio that Major Smith was going to throw colored smoke to guide the resupply helicopters into the battle. The helicopters were about to arrive, and he decided to throw yellow smoke himself in the hopes that the men of 11 Platoon might see it.

Coincidentally, at that same moment, Sgt. Bob Buick, having taken over command of 11 Platoon from the fallen Lieutenant Sharp, decided that their position was untenable and that there was no option but for the survivors to withdraw. Warning the dozen or so survivors of the plan, he yelled out for them to move, and they sprinted off to the west, taking more casualties in the process. They spotted the yellow smoke and, thinking it was company headquarters, made a dash for it. Soon they were within the little defensive perimeter of 12 Platoon and, after re-grouping for a moment, Sabben gave the order to withdraw.

At the base camp, the men of A Company were aboard the APCs by 5:45 P.M. After some problems departing through the base's defensive wire and being ordered to send two vehicles back to pick up the Battalion Commander and his group, the rescue party and its eight remaining APCs cleared the task force area at 6:00 P.M. and headed out to relieve D Company.

Even though they had conserved their ammunition and used aimed, semiautomatic fire, D Company was suffering the consequence of having entered the battle with such a light battle load. The company was down to its last 100 rounds, approximately one bullet per man.[19]

Faced with the prospect of an American helicopter unit doing what they refused to do, the RAAF commander ignored his instructions about the use of helicopters in a hostile environment and gave the order to go ahead. At 6:00 P.M., Flight Lieutenants C.M. Dohle and F.P. Riley forever endeared themselves to the Australian Army as they hovered over the rubber trees, dropping ammunition to the beleaguered infantrymen of D Company at Long Tan.[20]

The APCs, loaded with the men of A Company, had progressed to the swollen Suoi Da Bang creek, now almost two meters deep. Lieutenant Roberts was ordered to halt his advance there and await the arrival of the Battalion Commander but Roberts could hear on his other radio the plight of D Company and decided to disobey this order. Leaving one vehicle behind for security at the crossing, the remaining seven APC commanders successfully swam their vehicles across; several were spun around in full circles to eventually wallow up the other bank. Once across, Lieutenant Roberts was again ordered to hold his advance and again ignored this order.

By 6:10 P.M., Major Smith had all three of his D Company platoons together for the first time in the battle. They now occupied a position only 1,000 meters from where they had taken a meal break with B Company earlier that same day. They occupied a slight depression in the ground so that the troops faced slightly uphill, the ground cresting some 60·meters away. This position made the enemy rifle and machine gun fire pass harmlessly over their heads. Major Smith organized the distribution of the ammunition and placed the much-depleted 11 Platoon, fifteen of its men missing, on the northwestern portion of the perimeter where a nearby hill and stand of bamboo made it an unlikely avenue of attack. His stronger platoons completed the circle.

At 6:20 P.M., D Company's position began receiving machine gun fire from the east and southeast. A few moments later, they saw movement in the trees some 150 meters distant and, hoping it was a rescue party, the Australians momentarily held their fire. When they realized it was the enemy, sporadic shots were fired but the Australians soon ceased firing, knowing the enemy was too far away for their fire to be accurate.

At approximately 6:30 P.M., the APCs entered the edge of the rubber plantation and soon spotted a company of enemy troops, over 100 in number, advancing across their front in an assault formation on their way to join the attack on D Company. The APCs opened up with their .50-caliber machine guns and a number of the Australian infantry exited the carriers, forming up a skirmish line to take the enemy under fire. While one APC took the wounded back to the base camp, the infantry remounted the remaining six carriers and the APCs pushed through the enemy. Proceeding on another 200 meters, the APCs came upon small groups of enemy withdrawing to the east and opened up with a broadside of machine gun fire. The Viet Cong fired back with antitank weapons, halting the APC assault for approximately five minutes before proceeding again.

The enemy, finally able to locate and isolate the Australians of D Company, began forming up into assault waves. By 6:35 P.M., to the sound of whistles and bugles, the enemy began their assault. Well-spaced, proceeding at a fast walk, the first wave was within 150 meters. The reserves, their job to exploit the successes of the first wave, followed 100 meters further behind.

At this point the Australians' artillery began raining down on the enemy again, totally wiping out the reserve wave, but the first wave continued their advance. Because of the terrain, the Australians were shielded from the enemy fire until they came over the little crest some 60 meters away. The terrain, however, also prevented the Australians from delivering effective fire on the enemy until they closed within that 60-meter range.

The battle continued to rage, the Australians being assaulted again and again by disciplined waves of enemy soldiers. Private Harry Esler thought, "it was just like a kangaroo shoot. They were coming in waves. They were blowing bugles off to the left, in front, and across to the right. I remember thinking, '*By Christ I wish I had a set of bagpipes here. I'd put the fear of Christ up these blokes'!*"[21]

As darkness approached, Major Smith sent another message: "If you don't come within half an hour, don't worry about coming for us."[22]

Closing in on D Company's position, the three APCs on the left, raked by machine gun fire that inflicted casualties on their crews, ground to a halt.

The three APCs on the right were unaware of this and continued on, reaching D Company's cheering survivors. In addition to their powerful .50-caliber machine guns, the APCs jerked and swerved, using the crushing weight of the vehicles to plow through the massed Viet Cong. Suddenly aware that three APCs remained behind, the vehicles looped back to their stranded comrades. They met up some 300 meters to the southeast and were quickly joined by three additional APCs, which had brought Lieutenant Colonel Townsend to the battlefield. With six vehicles abreast, and the three recent additions forming a second wave, the APCs assaulted forward again, sweeping past D Company's position and beyond them for another 500 meters before turning northwest and entering D Company's position at 7:10 P.M. At about the same time, the 31 men of B Company finally made it into D Company's position. They had been harassed along the way with mortar fire but had suffered no casualties.

The Australians organized their defenses, now bolstered by the nine APCs and the infantrymen of A and B Companies. At 8:50 P.M., the Australians decided that they didn't have the troops necessary to secure the battlefield and decided to withdraw the force to a position where the dead and wounded could be evacuated by helicopter. D Company, and the dead and wounded, were loaded onto the APCs and withdrew from their battlesite at 10:45 P.M. with A and B Companies leaving on foot some 45 minutes later.

At their new location on the edge of the rubber plantation, the APCs formed a square and illuminated the makeshift landing zone by leaving their hatches open and their internal lights on. At 12:00 midnight, a U.S. Army helicopter swooped in and loaded the three most badly injured. Moments later, six Australian helicopters completed the medical evacuation. Throughout the night, the men of D Company agonized over their mates of 11 Platoon left behind on the battlefield. Artillery continued to pound the area, but specifically avoided the areas where Australian dead and wounded might remain.

At 8:45 the next morning, the Australians returned to the battlefield in strength. The Australians discovered that the area was littered with hundreds of enemy dead. They also discovered two of their own men, whom they had thought dead, had survived the night. One, shot twice through the chest, had lain face down in the mud throughout the battle. The other, shot through the mouth and leg, was found leaning against a tree, waving weakly in recognition. At 11:00 A.M., they found the bodies of the remaining 13 Australians. They were found lying side by side in prone position, their rifles to their shoulders in firing position and fingers on the triggers. The body of Lieutenant Sharp was with them, his hands still clutching the

AK-47 they had captured earlier. A total of 17 Australians had been killed; 19 were wounded.

The Australians had killed 245 of the enemy by actual body count. It was later found that most of these came from the Viet Cong's 275 Main Force Regiment, with a handful from D445, which had played only a minor role in the battle. The Australians also collected an enormous haul of enemy weapons from the battlefield, over 10,000 rounds of ammunition and 300 grenades. Three wounded prisoners were taken. One was from D445 Battalion; the others were North Vietnamese who believed themselves to be in 45 Regiment. In fact, they were in 275 Regiment but hadn't been told that their unit changed names when operating in South Vietnam.[23]

275 Regiment had taken the brunt of the casualties at Long Tan. The regiment was forced to retire and lick its wounds. Learning from their experience, the Australians henceforth required infantrymen to carry a minimum load of 140 rounds and machine guns to have 500 rounds. They also ensured that a standby-reaction force would be on call whenever there was a company out on patrol. With these modifications, the Australians returned to the anti-guerrilla war at which they were experts.

The pattern of American success in Operation Starlite and the Australian victory at Long Tan would be repeated again and again. Operation Attleboro would take place in October 1966 and leave over 1,100 Viet Cong

Marines under fire attack Viet Cong positions during Operation Harvest Moon, December 1965. Aggressive American tactics such as this kept the enemy off balance and forced the Viet Cong onto the defensive.
Credit: National Archives and Records Administration

troops killed when U.S. troops attacked their base camp in War Zone C to the northwest of Saigon. In January 1967, Operation Cedar Falls in the Iron Triangle north of Saigon would result in 700 Viet Cong killed and 200 captured. Another 500 Viet Cong deserted and then surrendered. The four-month long Operation Junction City in February of 1967 would again hit the Communist stronghold of War Zone C and cost the Viet Cong another 2,700 killed. With the availability of highly mobile American troops to attack the Viet Cong in these remote strongholds, Communist casualties would become so high that replacement with Southern-born troops would soon become impossible. Increasingly, the ranks of Viet Cong units would be filled instead by Northern-born conscripts.[24]

4

TET 1968

With the arrival of American and allied ground troops in 1965, the Communists' fortunes continued to worsen at an accelerated pace. The southern Viet Cong battalions continued to be decimated in battle, and even North Vietnam's own conventional Army (NVA) had been resoundingly defeated several times by the Americans. The first defeat was at the battle of Ia Drang in November of 1965 when the NVA attempted to invade from the western border. The NVA was defeated again in Operation Hastings in July 1966 when they attempted to invade southward through the demilitarized zone (DMZ).

In May 1967, Hanoi's Politburo met to discuss the course of the war and decide future plans. They acknowledged that their continuing debilitating losses called for a change of strategy and drastic action. Increasingly disenchanted with their Soviet and Chinese backers, Hanoi also concluded that the Communist superpowers were not prepared to risk a direct confrontation with the United States over the matter of Vietnam and that they must act on their own.[1]

In July 1967, the Thirteenth Plenum was held in Hanoi. The decision was made that it was nearing time for what Communist theorists proclaimed as the final stage of their revolutionary warfare: the General Offensive/General Uprising. The Southern-born faction, which included General Nguyen Chi Thanh, remained hopeful that they had the support of the people of South Vietnam. The Northern-born faction, including Defense Minister Vo Nguyen Giap, argued strongly against launching this final stage plan of action, believing the time was not yet right for the popular uprisings upon which it was based. However, once it was accepted over his arguments to the contrary, Giap appeared to dutifully set about to put it into action. The plan called for three phases.

In Phase I of the plan (October–December 1967), the North Vietnamese Army would use their large regular units in major attacks along the Cambodian border and along the DMZ. While the Americans were engaged in these battles, the Viet Cong would surreptitiously infiltrate their smaller guerrilla units from the surrounding areas into the cities themselves.[2]

In Phase II of the plan (January–March 1968), the General Offensive/General Uprising itself would be launched. Hanoi knew that the planning and execution for this event had to be perfect if it were to were work. The attack was timed to coincide with the Tet holiday, the most significant holiday to the Vietnamese people. The Vietnamese people regarded Tet as Westerners might regard Christmas, New Year, and their own birthdays, all rolled into one. It was an occasion when an attack would be least suspected. Surprise was of the essence, and the attacks had to be widespread and simultaneous if they were to be successful. Plans were immediately put into place by the various pro-Communist student unions and youth organizations to stage mass Tet celebrations on the evening of February 4. "Student" demonstrations were to be held in front of the Presidential palace and in Saigon's Tao Dan public gardens. Hopeful of getting a crowd numbering in the tens of thousands, the organizers planned to incite the crowd, urging them to occupy the palace and the radio station once they were seized by specially trained Viet Cong commandos (referred to as "sappers").[3]

Pham Chanh Truc, secretary of the Saigon Youth League, was responsible for the demonstrations throughout Saigon. He began conducting daily rehearsals on December 20, 1967. The Viet Cong cadre had ". . . prepared the people throughout the city to show their support for the attacking units in the target areas."[4]

Phase III of the plan would be launched as soon as the cities, including the airports, radio stations, municipal buildings, and police stations, were in the hands of the Viet Cong and their "popular demonstration" supporters. At that moment, North Vietnamese Army troops would come pouring through the DMZ, overrunning the American forward bases at Khe Sanh and Con Thien and spilling into the populated areas to the south.

During the latter half of 1967, the Viet Cong watched from the sidelines as the North Vietnamese Army launched their Phase I attacks along the country's borders and American troops rushed to counterattack them. Then, on November 17, 1967, the Viet Cong announced they would observe an extended truce over the Tet holiday: a seven-day cease-fire from January 27, 1967, to February 3, 1968. The seven-day period was critical for the Communist attack plan for two reasons. First, it would require several days for their troops to actually make their way to their assigned targets; such travel would be far less likely to be spotted under the reduced security brought about by a cease-fire. Second, it was important to suitably prepare and assemble the people if they were to "spontaneously" rise up and join the attackers. Hanoi was confident that U.S. politicians, eager to start peace negotiations and hopeful that the cease-fire was a precursor to such negotiations, would immediately accept. As predicted, when Hanoi announced the cease-fire on November 17, 1967, American politicians were indeed quick to accept the offer. It never occurred to the political generals in Hanoi, however, that America's purely military generals might thwart the wishes of their political masters for the sake of their troops' safety. If America's generals did alter the cease-fire arrangements, the changes could prove fatal to the Viet Cong.

TET: The Battle Begins

In the closing days of 1967, much of the U.S. military's attention was focused on the buildup of NVA forces along the DMZ separating North and South Vietnam. The small U.S. Marine outpost there, Khe Sanh, reported two NVA divisions, some 20,000 enemy troops, in the immediate vicinity and another two divisions within striking distance.

On January 5, 1968, troops of the U.S. 4th Infantry Division captured a five-page plan outlining specific details of upcoming enemy attacks planned for Pleiku Province in the northern half of South Vietnam. This plan and other concerns caused General Westmoreland to approach the South Vietnamese Army Chief of Staff, General Cao Van Vien, on January 8.[5]

Meanwhile, Lieutenant General Frederick Weyand, whose troops were operating closer to Saigon, met with General Westmoreland on January 10.

General Weyand, a former chief of U.S. Army Intelligence, was concerned because American attacks against Viet Cong strongholds deep in the jungle to the west of Saigon were not drawing the same response they had in the past. Further, radio intercepts picked up more and more Viet Cong radio traffic, and most of it closer and closer to Saigon. He told General Westmoreland of his concerns and asked for permission to redeploy his troops back into the Saigon area. With General Westmoreland's approval, General Weyand began shifting 27 U.S. Army maneuver battalions back within 30 miles of Saigon. He also put his armored cavalry squadrons on alert and ordered huge "Rome plow" bulldozers to clear great strips of vegetation away from likely targets so as to expose any attackers.[6]

On January 16, the South Vietnamese Army Chief of Staff and General Westmoreland, without informing U.S. Ambassador Bunker of their intention, met with South Vietnamese President Thieu and successfully argued for a reduction in the cease-fire from seven days down to only 36 hours and a total cancellation of the cease-fire in I Corps. Also, while the South Vietnamese had planned to grant leave to all their troops over this period, they now agreed to keep one-half of them at their duty stations.[7]

While the battle of Khe Sanh was unfolding along the DMZ and NVA forces began throwing themselves at the Marine defenders of the base, American forces throughout South Vietnam were put on full alert on January 24. General Weyand's officers formed a betting pool, trying to guess when the Communists would attack. Most thought it would occur after dark on January 30.[8]

The Communists

The American military's decision to reduce the cease-fire from seven days to only 36 hours, done to the surprise and consternation of American politicians, caused catastrophic problems to the Viet Cong. The revised cease-fire now expired at 6:00 A.M. on January 31, not on February 3 as they had planned. The timing of the Viet Cong attacks had to be moved forward dramatically and the planned demonstrations had to be canceled. Any "popular uprising" would no longer be the carefully orchestrated one the Communists had planned.

Even worse, when Defense Minister Giap drew up the plans for Tet, he simply ordered the attack to occur "on the first day of the Lunar New Year" instead of following usual military custom and specifying the day, month, and year. There were, however, two different calendars in use: the older version in Giap's northern areas and a revised one being used in the south.

Using the northern calendar, the lunar new year fell on January 31, but on the revised southern calendar, it fell a day earlier on January 30. The resulting confusion would cause some provinces to attack on January 30, while others would wait until January 31. In many other cases, Viet Cong sappers would seize a target only to discover that the Main Force battalion, which should have immediately reinforced them, was still a day's journey away.[9]

I and II Corps: The Northern Provinces

At 12:35 A.M. on January 30, the Viet Cong opened the attack with six 82-mm mortars fired at the Vietnamese Navy Training Center. All six rounds missed their target. Almost an hour and a half elapsed before the Viet Cong followed up with their ground attack. The defenders, fully alerted, caught the 18-B North Vietnamese Regiment as it moved toward the town and stopped it cold, inflicting heavy casualties. Local Viet Cong forces, attacking several targets within the city, managed only to enter the province chief's headquarters and a logistics headquarters briefly before being killed in counterattacks. Almost the entire Nha Trang Viet Cong force, including the ranking Communist Party political officer, Huynh Tuong, was captured. Other attacks occurred in the two most northern corps of South Vietnam. The commander of Viet Cong troops in these provinces ordered his men into the attack on January 30, a full day ahead of those in the southern zones.

III, IV, and V Corps: The Provinces Further South

Concerned by the attacks in the northern provinces, U.S. forces were placed on heightened alert. At the American Embassy, an extra U.S. Marine stood guard, bringing the guard detail to three. No American combat units were in Saigon itself. As a point of national pride, the South Vietnamese were solely responsible for their country's capital city. The only American "troops" were 500 or so lightly armed military policemen of the 716th M.P. Battalion.

Meanwhile, in the early morning hours of January 31, everything was quiet at the American Embassy. Four Vietnamese policeman were on guard outside; only three of the four policemen carried weapons. One side gate allowed vehicular access to the embassy compound itself. This access was guarded by two U.S. Army military policeman: 23-year-old Specialist Fourth Class (Spec4) Charles L. Daniel of Durham North Carolina and 20-year-old Private First Class (PFC) William E. Sebast of Albany, New York.

Lightly-armed Military Policemen (MPs) of the 716th MP Battalion—seen here along-side Australian, Korean, and South Vietnamese MPs as they prepare to start another shift—were primarily responsible for keeping American servicemen in order. The actual defense of Saigon itself was in the hands of the South Vietnamese Army.
Credit: US Army Military History Institute

Inside the vast embassy compound itself, which contained various buildings and garages, three U.S. Marines stood guard. Corporal George Zahuranic and Sergeant Ronald Harper, both 20 years of age, stood guard inside the embassy building itself. Twenty-five year old Marine Sergeant Rudy Soto was posted on the roof of the six-story building.

The five-man guard detail seemed more than adequate on that dark morning in 1968. After all, the American Embassy, like all embassies all over the world, was by protocol and agreement safe from attack. Even during the darkest days of World War II, the Germans and the Japanese honored the sanctity of foreign embassies. But that was all soon to change.

Action At the Embassy (Saigon)

Shortly after midnight on January 31, a 19-man team of hit-and-run sappers from the Viet Cong's C-10 Battalion met at a small automobile repair work-shop at 59 Phan Thanh Gian Street. For the first time, the Viet Cong unit was briefed on its mission: an attack on the American Embassy. Either by mistake or by plan, the two leaders, known as Bay Tuyen and Ut Nho, did not brief their troops on the plan of action once the outer wall had been breached.[10]

Just before 3:00 A.M., the sappers piled into a small Peugeot truck and a taxicab and headed off to the embassy. As they approached the embassy, they opened fire on the two M.P.s with AK-47 assault rifles, spraying their guardpost with bullets. The sappers then did a quick left turn, the two M.P.'s return fire whistling around them, and came to a halt in front of the embassy compound itself. The Vietnamese police on duty there ran from the scene, the senior policeman fleeing to the nearby First Precinct station house. The two American M.P.s quickly sent the coded message, "Signal 300," indicating the compound was under attack, and then stepped into the compound, closing and locking the steel gate behind them.

Two M.P.s on patrol in a jeep nearby, 24-year-old Sergeant Jonnie Thomas and 20-year-old Spec4 Owen Mebust, heard the coded signal and raced to the aid of their colleagues. Within seconds the sappers detonated a 15-pound explosive charge against the compound wall, blowing a small hole in the eight-foot-tall concrete wall. As the Viet Cong scrambled through the hole, the two M.P.s inside the compound turned to face them and opened fire, killing Bay Tuyen and Ut Nho, the first two Viet Cong through the wall. Spec4 Daniel screamed into his radio, "They're coming in! They're coming in! Help me! Help me!" before being shot in the head himself. His partner, PFC Sebast, was also killed in the gunfire.

At the first sound of gunfire, Corporal Zahuranic immediately went to the telephone just behind the Marine guard desk inside the embassy building to sound the alert. Meanwhile, Sergeant Harper, outside the building at the rear of the compound when the shots first rang out, sprinted back inside through the back door and then past his fellow Marine to the heavy teakwood front doors. He grabbed the terrified, unarmed Vietnamese guard, pulled him inside, and then slammed the heavy doors shut before bolting them secure.

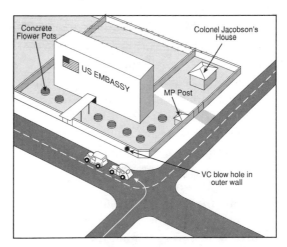

Mission Coordinator George Jacobsen, asleep in the upstairs bedroom of his house, situated within the embassy compound just behind the embassy building, was awakened by the shuddering explosion and the crackle of gunfire. Jacobsen, a retired U.S. Army Colonel, had seen no need to possess a weapon in his job as a diplomat. The only weapon in the house was one solitary hand grenade he discovered in a desk drawer. The half-dozen clerks and other personnel on duty in the embassy's upper floors gathered up whatever weapons they had, generally .38-caliber revolvers, and locked themselves inside the relatively secure code room on the fourth floor.

M.P.s Thomas and Mebust, speeding down the boulevard toward the embassy in their jeep, were met with a fatal fusillade of bullets fired by the Viet Cong, still outside the compound, lining up to crawl through the hole in the wall. Up on the embassy building's roof, Sergeant Soto, armed only with a pistol and a shotgun, saw the heavily armed Viet Cong scrambling through the hole in the compound wall and, realizing it was futile at that distance, nonetheless fired all six .38-caliber revolver bullets at the invading enemy.

Inside the embassy building, Sergeant Harper sprinted down the hall to the Marines' meager arsenal, consisting only of shotguns and pistol-caliber weapons. The Viet Cong opened fire through the grilled windows beside the door. Thirty seconds later, they fired a rocket-propelled grenade at the embassy door, hitting the Seal of the United States and penetrating through the brick wall to explode near the receptionist's desk inside. The explosion seriously wounded Corporal Zahuranic with shrapnel and destroyed the radio links with the outside. Two more rockets quickly followed, and then the Viet Cong lobbed a grenade through the shattered window. Sergeant Harper, by now armed with a shotgun, could hear the Viet Cong just outside and assumed they would come bursting in at any moment. Fully believing he was about to die, he nonetheless waited in the lobby, prepared to make the Viet Cong pay dearly.

George Jacobsen crouched in the upstairs hallway of his two-story house, listening to the gunfire and speaking on the telephone to Ambassador Bunker and other embassy officials. Unfortunately, he was unable to communicate with the adjacent embassy buildings, still defended by Sergeant Harper, or the various M.P.s and Marines outside the compound.

Armed with more than 40 pounds of C-4 explosives, which could have easily blown the door apart, and faced by a lone U.S. Marine guarding the lobby, the leaderless Viet Cong unit made no concerted effort to enter the embassy building. Instead they milled about aimlessly before eventually taking refuge behind the circular concrete planter boxes on the front lawn. Meanwhile, Americans on the rooftops of buildings outside began firing at the hapless, disorganized Viet Cong on the Embassy's front lawn.

The Marine in charge of security, 36-year-old Captain Robert O'Brien, had been at the Marines' living quarters five blocks away when the shooting started. He quickly gathered up the rest of his men and made his way to the embassy. As they approached the side gate, they discovered it was locked. They were on the outside and the Viet Cong were inside. Captain O'Brien discreetly called out to the M.P.s to open the gate but was greeted instead by half-a-dozen Viet Cong who spun around and fired in his direction. One of the Marines, Sergeant Raymond Reed, returned fire through the steel bars and then the Marines pulled back.

At 4.20 A.M., the Headquarters of the 716th Military Police Battalion was told to secure the embassy compound as a first priority effort. The M.P.s in turn requested helicopters and armored vehicles for the assault. In the meantime, the M.P. lieutenant in charge at the embassy decided not to risk his men fighting their way into the compound in the dark, a problem made even more difficult because they had not yet discovered the hole through which the Viet Cong had entered. The M.P.s apparently reasoned that the compound perimeter was secure; no one could enter or leave and, at daylight, they could easily mop up the remaining Viet Cong.

A 20-year-old Marine, Corporal James Marshall, climbed on top of the roof of a small adjoining building and was thus able to fire over the wall at the Viet Cong. The Viet Cong wounded him with a rocket-propelled grenade fired in reply but he continued to pour fire into their midst for half an hour before eventually being fatally wounded by gunfire.

Sporadic gunfire continued to ring out for the next two hours. The Viet Cong were pinned down in the front courtyard, taking refuge behind and inside of the planter boxes, while the Americans attempted to fire at them over the high wall surrounding the compound. Because of its proximity to the luxury hotels where the correspondents and journalists stayed, the site soon teemed with media people. The high concrete wall safely shielded them from any Viet Cong gunfire, but it also made it impossible to see anything of the events in the embassy compound. Confused and often outlandishly fabricated dispatches and reports soon emanated from the media personnel, flashing across the airwaves worldwide. A United Press International (UPI) report claimed that ". . . a Viet Cong suicide squad stormed the U.S. Embassy Wednesday and occupied the first five floors for several hours." A few minutes later, another UPI dispatch added that the Americans had fought back ". . . with small arms and grenades through the carpeted offices" of the embassy, despite the fact that the Viet Cong had failed to even enter the building.[11]

As daylight began to dawn, Jacobsen, from his upstairs hallway vantage point, could see fresh blood and footprints on the floor below. He telephoned across town to another diplomatic mission and, speaking in a hushed voice, asked the Marine who answered to relay a message to the troops outside the embassy. He told the Marine of his situation and then lay down on the floor of the hallway, preparing to roll his sole grenade down the stairs.

At first light, the M.P.s on the outside blew the lock off the gate and crashed a jeep through. They charged into a sight of dead and dying Viet Cong sappers littering the compound's garden. At the same time, a helicopter landed on the roof of the embassy building and paratroopers began making their way down the stairs, checking room by room to ensure no Viet Cong had entered the building. None had entered; the three Marines and two M.P.s had seen to that.

Other M.P.s and Marines closed in on Jacobsen's house and exchanged shots with the Viet Cong inside. A tear gas grenade was lobbed into the house and, as the house began filling with smoke, Jacobsen realized that the Viet Cong down below would soon be forced upstairs. He quietly made his way to a back room and then yelled out through the window for the troops to toss him up a gas mask and a weapon.

Moments later, Jacobsen crouched low around the corner of the hallway. He was now armed with a .45-caliber pistol tossed up to him through the window by an obliging M.P., while the Viet Cong intruder stealthily climbed the stairs. Reaching the top, the Viet Cong fired a long burst from his assault rifle, spraying the hallway with bullets. George Jacobsen leaped to his feet and killed the intruder with his .45 pistol.

Of the 19 Viet Cong, 17 were dead and the other two, Nguyen Van Sau and Ngo Van Giang, were taken prisoner. Except for the one Viet Cong who had staggered into Jacobsen's nearby house, the attacking force had died on the Embassy's front lawn, sheltering behind the ornamental planter boxes, only meters from the hole in the front wall through which they had entered.

Government Radio Station (Saigon)

While their colleagues attacked the American Embassy, another unit of the C-10 Sapper Battalion, dressed in South Vietnamese uniforms but with red linings sewn into the cuffs of their pants for identification, were assigned to attack and seize the government radio station. Led by Dang Xuan Teo, who had been ordered in November 1967 to train a 14-man squad for the "once-in-a-lifetime" assignment, the attackers were told to seize the building and hold it for two hours, at which time a Main Force unit of Viet Cong troops would relieve them. Accompanied by a North Vietnamese radio technician, the intruders planned to play tapes calling for a general uprising and announcing the liberation of Saigon.

The Viet Cong were unaware that the director-general of the station, Lieutenant Colonel Vu Duc Vinh, had arranged the day before to take the station off the air should it be seized. As the Viet Cong attacked, a technician inside the studio signalled the transmitter site 14 miles away to shut the lines down and the studio went off the air. Meanwhile, an alternative site continued to play music throughout the night.[12]

The Viet Cong remained at the now-useless radio site for six hours, their relief nowhere to be seen, venting their frustration by destroying the equipment they were unable to operate. By daylight the building was surrounded by South Vietnamese Army troops and the Viet Cong were trapped inside. The only Viet Cong survivor of the ensuing firefight was the unit's leader, Teo, who had earlier fled from the scene after his unit had suffered six casualties.

South Vietnamese Armored Command School (Saigon)

The 101st Viet Cong Regiment, including a contingent of troops specially trained to operate tanks, attacked the headquarters of the South Vietnamese Armored Command, planning to seize the unit's tanks. Half of the vehicles were then to be used for an attack on Westmoreland's headquarters and the South Vietnamese Joint General Staff. The other half would support the attack against Tan Son Nhut Air Base. When they arrived at the school on January 31, the Viet Cong discovered that the tanks had been moved out of Saigon two months previously.

Tan Son Nhut Air Base (Saigon)

General Cao Van Vien, chief of the South Vietnamese Joint General Staff, had only two battalions of reserve troops. He'd originally promised them to the embattled cities of the northern provinces but through a problem in transport and what would turn out to be a stroke of incredibly good luck they had been unable to leave. He parceled out one of those battalions to the defense of various key sites around Saigon. The remaining four companies were still sitting in the terminal at Tan Son Nhut in full battle gear.[13]

Tan Son Nhut Air Base itself was suddenly attacked from three sides at approximately 3:00 A.M. on January 31. Two battalions of Viet Cong managed to breach a minefield and then destroy a South Vietnamese Army guard bunker with a B-40 rocket. The Viet Cong stormed into the sprawling base.

An urgent message was quickly dispatched to Colonel Glenn Otis's 3rd Squadron, 4th Armored Cavalry, part of the 25th Infantry Division under Weyand's command near Cu Chi. The cavalry's orders were simple: to proceed as quickly as possible to Hoc Mon on the outskirts of Saigon where higher command would take control. Colonel Otis had only one unit in reserve: Charlie Troop under the command of Captain Leo Virant. The unit was quickly dispatched. The situation was very unclear with reports of North Vietnamese Army and Viet Cong attacks all around them. Within minutes, Charlie Troop's orders were changed, and they were told to go directly to Tan Son Nhut. Disregarding the obvious danger, the three tanks and ten APCs of Charlie Troop "took off like a bat out of hell for Tan Son Nhut."[14]

At Tan Son Nhut, U.S. Air Force security troops fought back. General Cao Van Vien sent two companies of his fortuitously present airborne troops to counter-attack, temporarily stalling the Viet Cong thrust at the expense of their own heavy casualties. While the battle raged, the little force of American Cavalry under the command of Captain Virant raced to their rescue. Knowing full well that the enemy would have ambushes in place along the roads and also knowing how vulnerable the noisy armor was at night, the battalion commander, Colonel Glenn Otis, prudently ordered his men to avoid the roads and, instead, to head out "across country." Flying overhead in his command helicopter, Colonel Otis scouted the path for his unit and dropped flares to illuminate their way.

At daybreak, the leading Viet Cong elements were being taken under fire by helicopter gunships. Charlie Troop of the Armored Cavalry arrived about the same time, crashing into and through the rear elements of the attackers, effectively splitting the Viet Cong force in two. Supported by helicopter gunships, the armor wreaked great damage on the Viet Cong and turned the battle's focus to this action just outside the base's gate. The Viet Cong, however, heavily outnumbered the Americans and were well equipped with antitank weapons. They quickly knocked out the lead tank and several APCs. Within minutes, Charlie Troop had suffered heavy casualties; many of its 13 vehicles were on fire and the handful of survivors were managing only desultory return fire.

Back at Cu Chi, Colonel Otis monitored the battle and hurriedly dispatched two more troops of his cavalry to Tan Son Nhut. Alpha Troop was hit by a unit of NVA and pinned down. Bravo Troop, spread out along Highway 1 guarding bridges, was ordered to speed down the highway, now illuminated by the early morning sun, and use its speed and firepower to punch through the enemy.

Colonel Otis immediately flew to Tan Son Nhut, losing a helicopter in the process, but managing to crash-land safely at the air base. While waiting for his cavalry to arrive, he commandeered a replacement helicopter and used the time to ferry ammunition to the scratch group of Air Force personnel holding the base's perimeter. When that helicopter too was lost in the action, he managed to acquire a third one just in time to direct the actions of Bravo Troop as it arrived around 10:00 A.M.

With the survivors of Charlie Troop scattered along Highway 1 and just inside the base's gate, Otis directed Bravo Troop to proceed within 2,500 meters of the beleaguered unit before ordering the lead tank to perform a 90-degree, right-hand turn, to lead the column off the Highway. Once the last vehicle had done so and the relief column was stretched out 90-degrees to the highway and facing west, he ordered them to halt. He then ordered Bravo Troop to do a left flank maneuver, each of the giant armored vehicles spinning to the left so that they were on line, their weapons now aimed at Charlie Troop's attackers some 2,500 meters away in the distance. Otis then gave the order for Bravo Troop to "attack on line," sending the armored vehicles roaring into the exposed left flank of the Viet Cong. "The troop commander carried out this entire maneuver with superb reactions," Colonel Otis noted. "With Bravo Troop attacking the flank of the regiment and Delta Troop and other air assets attacking from overhead, the Vietnamese regiment was caught in a tremendous trap. They could not move to the east because of Charlie Troop and its remnants defending the air base. They were being attacked from the north by Bravo Troop, and they were effectively in a complete box. The attack was a complete success."[15]

Bravo Troop engaged the enemy in a dry rice paddy. The Viet Cong, caught in the open by Bravo Troops flanking maneuver, sought whatever cover they could find. Many of them sought shelter behind and even within the many bundles of rice stalks scattered throughout the paddy, which proved no defense whatsoever from the firepower weighed against them.

The few surviving Viet Cong withdrew to the nearby Vinatexco cotton mill with Bravo Troop taking fire from the factory's upper-floor windows. Colonel Otis called for an air strike, which silenced the enemy. Two days later, when it was searched by troops from another battalion, 162 dead Viet Cong were found in the heavily damaged mill.[16]

South Vietnamese Navy Headquarters (Saigon)

As the battle at Tan Son Nhut was unfolding, a 12-man sapper unit of the C-10 Battalion blew a hole in the wall of a sentry post outside the nearby South Vietnamese Navy Headquarters. Ten of the twelve attackers were killed within the first five minutes. The captured survivors, when questioned later, said they had been told to seize the headquarters and await the arrival of two battalions of Viet Cong troops from just across the Saigon river. The two battalions never materialized.[17]

Hoc Mon Bridge

North Vietnamese Army Major General Tran Do specifically targeted the Hoc Mon bridge for destruction. This vital link, over which American reinforcements would flow into Saigon, was to have been destroyed early in the battle. The Viet Cong assigned to the task never arrived.

Chi Hoa Prison (Saigon)

The 6th Battalion of the 165-A Viet Cong Regiment was assigned to attack Saigon's Chi Hoa Prison on January 31, planning to free and arm its 5,000 inmates and then turn them loose on the police. The unit's local guides were killed by the police on the outskirts of Saigon. Having been briefed that the prison was located in a rubber plantation, the Viet Cong troops searched in vain for the distinctive trees. Unknown to the Viet Cong, General Weyand had bulldozed them away only days previously. Disoriented, the Viet Cong eventually milled around in a small village, home for many widows and dependents of South Vietnamese soldiers. Alerted to the enemy's presence, the American troops attacked, sending 10-ton APCs from the 9th Infantry Division roaring into them, supported by infantry from the 199th Light Infantry Brigade. The Viet Cong unit was quickly destroyed in the one-sided battle; the unit died in a brief battle in a cemetery nearly a mile from the prison.[18]

South Vietnamese Artillery Command Headquarters (Saigon)

Elements of the 101st Viet Cong Regiment attacked the South Vietnamese Artillery Command planning to seize the weapons and turn them against the South Vietnamese and the Americans. The men of the Artillery Command foiled the Viet Cong plan by removing the breechblocks, rendering the weapons useless, before withdrawing from the compound. [19]

The South Vietnamese Presidential Palace

Three vehicles, including a truck loaded with TNT, brought a sapper unit consisting of thirteen men and one woman to the Presidential Palace in the early morning hours of January 31. Their attack, directed at the palace's side gate was quickly repelled. The Viet Cong fled across the street, taking refuge in an apartment block still under construction.

American television crews, arriving from their nearby luxury hotels, filmed the ensuing firefight. While the action to finally root out these "holdouts" was of no consequence militarily, CBS aired a one-minute broadcast of the "Presidential Palace gunbattle." NBC aired a two-minutes broadcast, and ABC, whose Vietnamese sound recordist was wounded on-camera, aired three full minutes.[20]

Assassinations in Saigon

The Saigon-Cholon Security Section of the Viet Cong had orders to assassinate President Thieu, Ambassador Bunker, General Linh Quang Vien (Chief of South Vietnam's Central Intelligence), Brigadier General Nguyen Ngoc Loan (Chief of National Police), and Lieutenant Colonel Nguyen Van Luan (Chief of Saigon Police). The Viet Cong also planned to capture Premier Nguyen Van Loc, take him to the government radio station, and force him to order the South Vietnamese troops to lay down their weapons. All of these plans failed. One Viet Cong team got lost and another got separated from its cache of weapons.[21]

While unsuccessful in attempts to assassinate General Nguyen Ngoc Loan, the Viet Cong did manage to break into the home of one of his best friends, a colonel in the National Police. They murdered the colonel, then turned their rage on his family, slitting the throats of the colonel's wife and six young children, several of whom were General Loan's godchildren. South Vietnamese Marines captured one of the Viet Cong at the site. The man was armed with a pistol, indicating he was the leader of the unit. He

was brought to General Loan, standing near the An Quang Pagoda, headquarters of militant Buddhists and Viet Cong and the command post for the
attack on Saigon. When General Loan asked where the man had been captured, the Marines replied. The Viet Cong agent then gained media immor-
tality as General Loan, unconcerned by the clicking of the photographers'
cameras around him, abruptly put a pistol to the killer's head and summarily executed him.[22]

Terror in Hue (I Corps: Northern Provinces)

Security for the 140,000 residents of the city of Hue was primarily the
responsibility of the police. With the exception of a hundred-or-so reconnaissance troops of the South Vietnamese Black Panther Company billeted
in the city, the nearest combat troops were located about five miles to the
northwest. North Vietnamese Army troops under the command of the
6th North Vietnamese Army Regiment had managed to enter the city surreptitiously during the days preceding Tet, assisted by Viet Cong troops of
the 12th Sapper (Commando) Battalion. On January 31, they signaled their
occupation with a mortar and rocket barrage against South Vietnamese
troops and had virtual control of the city, including the province headquarters, the jail, the public utilities, the hospital, the university, and almost
all of the old imperial fortress known as the Citadel. Except for a few isolated pockets of resistance, the city was in the sudden control of the Communists. Reinforced with troops including the Viet Cong 416th Battalion,
U.S. intelligence later identified 16 North Vietnamese Army battalions (all
under the operational control of the 6th North Vietnamese Army Regiment) eventually in and around Hue.[23]

A long and bloody battle raged for control of the city. At its peak, the
battle pitted three understrength battalions of U.S. Marines and 13 South
Vietnamese battalions against this North Vietnamese Army force. Little by
little, the North Vietnamese were forced to fall back, withdrawing into an
ever-shrinking pocket and eventually holding up in the thick-walled Citadel
where resistance finally ceased.

While the North Vietnamese Army was locked in battle with the U.S.
Marines in Hue's outskirts, the Viet Cong were allowed sway over the city
itself. Local sympathizers provided detailed lists of the residents, including
where they lived, who they worked for, even their likely movements. The
Viet Cong soon acted on this information, targeting government workers,
foreigners, and other "reactionaries".

Stephen Miller, an American civilian, was one of those on the lists. A 28-year-old Foreign Service officer, he was in the home of Vietnamese friends when he was taken by the Viet Cong. They led him away to a field behind a nearby Catholic seminary, bound his arms, and then shot him to death.

Dr. Horst Gunther Krainick, a German pediatrician, and his wife Elisabeth thought that they would be safe as civilian medical workers and German nationals. So too did Drs. Raimund Discher and Alois Altekoester. When the Viet Cong came to take them away, Elisabeth Krainick was heard to scream out in English, "Keep your hands off my husband." The four were later found shot to death, their bodies dumped in a shallow grave in a nearby field.[24]

Father Urbain and Father Guy, French priests, were similarly led away by the Viet Cong. Father Urbain's body was later found, bound hand and foot, where he had been buried alive. Father Guy, his cassock removed, lay with a bullet hole in the back of his head. In their common grave were the remains of 18 other victims.

Father Buu Dong had long ministered to everyone within his parish, including the Viet Cong. Ironically, he kept a portrait of Ho Chi Minh in his room as a tangible symbol that he took no side in the war. Taken away during the Communist occupation of Hue, his body was found 22 months later in a shallow grave in the coastal sand flats along with the remains of 300 other victims.

On the fourth day of the occupation, the Viet Cong went to the home of Pham Van Tuong. Tuong was on the list because of his "crime" of being a part-time janitor at the government information office. When they ordered him to come out of hiding, he emerged with his three-year-old daughter, five-year-old son, and two nephews. The Viet Cong immediately gunned down all five of them, leaving their bodies to be found by the rest of his family when they emerged moments later.

Mrs. Nguyen Thi Lao, a 48-year-old widow, who eked out a meager living by selling cigarettes from a street stand, was led away without explanation. She was found later in a common grave at the local high school, having been buried alive, arms bound behind her. Later explanations suggest she may have been mistaken for her sister, a government clerk.

On the fifth day of the Communist occupation, the Viet Cong came to Phu Cam Cathedral and gathered together 400 men and boys. Some were identified by name from their lists, others because they were of military age, and still others simply because they looked wealthy. They were last seen being marched away to the south. Two years later, three Viet Cong defec-

tors led troopers of the 101st Airborne Division to a creek bed in the dense
jungle ten miles from Hue. Spread out for a hundred meters were the bones
of the men and boys of Phu Cam. The number murdered was later confirmed as 428. About a hundred of that number had been soldiers, another
hundred had been students, and the rest had been civil servants, government workers, and just ordinary citizens. Some had been shot, others had
been clubbed to death. Among those murdered was Nguyen Ngoc Ky, a
leader of the Vietnam Nationalist Party, described as anti-Communist but
also anti-U.S.[25]

The bloodletting continued for days until the North Vietnamese Army
commander learned of the Viet Cong's actions and put a stop to it. A total of
2,810 bodies were eventually found in shallow mass graves; 1,946 people
remained unaccounted for. On February 24, Hue was back in the hands of
the South Vietnamese Army; the city's residents gladly helped to identify
and locate any Viet Cong still alive.[26]

Tet 1968: The Viet Cong Defeat

Most of the Saigon-based journalists, stunned and confused at their first up-
close and personal view of combat, quickly declared the Tet Offensive a
Communist victory even before the smoke had cleared. Cooler, more reasoned appraisals assessed it differently: a total catastrophe for the Viet Cong.
Even General Giap himself privately conceded that it had been a staggering
military defeat. The Viet Cong Main Force units had been broken. In the
two weeks between January 29 and February 11, a total of 32,000 Communist troops were killed and another 5,800 captured. Perhaps even worse for
the Viet Cong was that their secret operatives and spies, a network which
had taken years to build, had come out into the open during the attacks.
Many of these agents had already been killed during the offensive and those
remaining were now exposed and being rigorously pursued by South Vietnam's police and security forces.[27]

The Tet Offensive also showed the clear distinction between the forces
of the Viet Cong and those of the North Vietnamese Army. Hanoi assigned
entirely separate missions, targets, and objectives to the southern battalions.
The casualties borne during the failed offensive fell disproportionately upon
the Viet Cong units, which would never recover from these losses. Despite
all of Hanoi's efforts in the past four years to train and reequip them, events
in the Tet Offensive proved that the Viet Cong units had failed to achieve the
military skills, such as those of "command and control," necessary to win a
"stand-up battle" against American or even South Vietnamese forces.

South Vietnamese forces themselves provided a surprise to the Communists. They proved generally resolute in the defense of their cities. The civilian population clearly rejected the Communist plea to rise up against the South Vietnamese government. Further, as stories emerged about what had occurred in Hue, both civilian and military personnel alike feared the reprisals that now seemed inevitable should the Communists seize control. This strengthened their anti-Communist resolve.

5

The End of
the Viet Cong

With the military failure of the Communist Tet Offensive, the war in Vietnam had changed dramatically. Not only had the Viet Cong been decimated, but also the North Vietnamese Army had been defeated in their battles in the northern provinces of South Vietnam. The NVA suffered heavy casualties at Hue, and the provincial capital was again back in the hands of the South Vietnamese Army. Meanwhile, those Hanoi troops which had encircled Khe Sanh, and survived the rain of B-52 attacks, were withdrawing, battered and bloody, back into the safety of North Vietnam.

In spite of these facts, the American news media continued to trumpet the Communist "successes" of the Tet Offensive and hail the "wily" skills of the Viet Cong. However, the troops pitted against them continued to prove more than a match for the Communist enemy. Typical of these encounters occurring daily in the aftermath of Tet was an otherwise obscure action, involving a unit of U.S. Marines, that occurred in mid-March, 1968.

On March 15, 1968, the 100 men of Fox Company, 2nd Battalion, 3rd Marines had engaged in a brief and violent firefight with a mixed group of Viet Cong regulars and North Vietnamese Army troops. The Marines' target in their mission were holdouts and survivors of the attacks on nearby Hue only a few weeks before during the Tet Offensive. The Marines cornered the Communist troops on a sandy peninsula and proceeded in parallel columns, separated by 200 meters of rolling sand dunes, with 1st Platoon on the left and 2nd Platoon on the right. The Viet Cong suddenly opened fire on 1st Platoon from concealed positions. While 1st Platoon immediately returned their fire, 2nd Platoon instinctively hit the deck at the sound of the gunfire before rising up and attacking on line, charging through the sand hills to the aid of their buddies. When the smoke cleared, the Marines had inflicted heavy casualties on the enemy but had also taken casualties, including their much-respected hospital corpsman, "Doc" George Riordan.[1]

The next day, Fox Company dispersed into even smaller platoon (25-man) groups to search for any enemy survivors of yesterday's action. As 2nd Platoon filed through the sandy terrain, it skirted the perimeter of an old cemetery. The point element warily followed the trail where it veered off to the right. Soon after having turned the corner, perhaps another 30 meters along the trail, the point Marine found himself staring at two Viet Cong sentries, idly sitting atop one of the mounds in front of him. The Marine got off a quick burst from his M-16, hitting one of them as the "wily" Viet Cong attempted to sprint away into the cemetery mounds. Unfortunately for the sentries, however, they took a course that paralleled the remainder of the Marine platoon. The two Viet Cong had soon taken multiple wounds from the Marines' accurate rifle fire. One lay dead and the other raised his arms in surrender as the Marines first disarmed him and then "cleared" his jammed rifle with the well-placed heel of a boot. Unsure of the size of the Viet Cong unit, the Marines maintained a wary vigilance while treating the wounded man's injuries before transporting him by helicopter to their medical facility at Phu Bai.

Once they ensured that the area was secure, the Marines smiled and joked about the incompetence of these two Viet Cong sentries. The Marines, products of arguably the best military training in the world, had taken the two Viet Cong sentries completely by surprise. They learned that, while the Viet Cong were a dangerous enemy because of their local knowledge and the fact that they often had the advantage of well-prepared and concealed positions, they were no match for the Marines when it came to military skills. And now, the Tet Offensive had forced the Viet Cong out into the open.

Former senior Viet Cong Trinh Duc similarly recalls the aftermath of Tet. "First of all, casualties everywhere were very, very high, and the spirit

of the soldiers dropped to a low point." The South Vietnamese troops reoc-
cupied posts they had abandoned years ago. Then the Americans and their
Australian allies began aggressively hunting down the remaining Viet Cong.
"I would send units out on supply missions," he recalled, "and they would
disappear. People would be killed while they were cooking or going for
water. Sometimes I could find out what happened to them, sometimes I
couldn't."[2]

While the Tet Offensive had broken the enemy's back, it was in countless small-scale actions, like the one which took place in the cemetery that
sunny March 1968 day, that the Viet Cong were gradually being ground into
extinction. The process continued for several months as the Viet Cong survivors of Tet were relentlessly hunted down. By mid-1968, the Viet Cong
forces were all but finished. Soon their defeat would be total as American
and allied forces increasingly took the fight to enemy areas that had previously been sacrosanct, cleaning out the last bastions of the Viet Cong.

An example of this pursuit occurred in the village of Chanh Luu, in
Ben Cat District, Binh Duong Province. Chanh Luu served as a supply and
staging base for the NVA and Viet Cong for the Tet Offensive of 1968.
Hence, the units there had avoided the destruction wrought upon most
Communist units in the first half of 1968. Three companies (C-61, C-62,
and C-301) of Viet Cong Local Force troops were permanently stationed
there. Four battalions (K-1, K-2, K-3, K-4 of the Dong Nai Regiment) of
Main Force troops operated within a 12-kilometer radius of the village.[3]

In August 1968, U.S. forces decided it was time to eliminate these
Viet Cong troops. The job to be done was given to Colonel George S. Patton,
son of the famous World War II General, who commanded the 11th
Armored Cavalry Regiment. Colonel Patton began by deceiving the Communists into believing he planned to attack the nearby village of Bien My.
He conducted aerial reconnaissance of Bien My, usually the precursor to
an American attack. He also allowed the enemy to eavesdrop on misleading
radio transmissions, which suggested Bien My as the target. He even planted
phony maps that showed American avenues of approach to Bien My.

Just before midnight on August 8, having traveled for many hours in
the direction of Bien My, the 11th Armored Cavalry abruptly spun around
and headed for its real target, the village of Chanh Luu. The Americans
quickly surrounded the village and fired illumination rounds all night,
lighting up the sky and preventing escape. At 7:00 A.M. the next day, the 5th
South Vietnamese Army Battalion was helicoptered directly into the village.
A Vietnamese interpreter later recalled that, "The confused enemy were running up and down the village carrying AK-47s and small arms." Following

a brief firefight with the disorganized Viet Cong, the South Vietnamese Army troops began a systematic search of the village. One small group of Viet Cong was captured almost immediately. The task of the South Vietnamese Army was made easy by their prisoners' willingness to lead them to the hiding places of other Viet Cong troops.[4]

By the end of the three-day operation, 125 Viet Cong troops had been captured and 18 had been killed. An additional 10 VCI were also detained. Increasingly, the Viet Cong realized that their only hope for survival was to avoid combat altogether. In some areas of South Vietnam, the Viet Cong sought sanctuary from the powerful Americans by hiding in deep underground tunnels.

Death In the Tunnels

To the west and north of Saigon, the Communists constructed an elaborate system of tunnels in an attempt to hide from searching American and South Vietnamese troops. Forced to live below ground while the Americans moved freely on the surface, the Viet Cong would occasionally fire at the patrolling Americans. It was only some time later that the Americans appreciated the size and scope of the tunnel complex, estimated to be at least 30 kilometers in length.[5]

At first, the Americans tried using explosives to collapse the tunnels and suffocate the occupants. Later, they experimented with gases pumped into the tunnel complexes by huge fumigating machines. Later, they would send men, stripped to the waist and armed only with a knife and a pistol, down into the tunnels. These "tunnel rats" would take the fight to the enemy, pursuing him to the furthest recesses of the tunnel system.

Attitudes about the threat posed by the tunnels varied. General Fred Weyand, who commanded the 25th Infantry Division when it first established its base at Cu Chi, was not worried by their presence. General Weyand observed, "They were there, they'd always been used by these people to protect themselves and to move about, but I never viewed them as anything that was a major threat to the division." The 1st Infantry Division, operating out of Lai Khe further to the north and across the Saigon River, paid them more attention. The division organized teams of volunteers, usually drawn from men of small stature, to go down into the tunnels to flush out the Viet Cong.[6]

The Communists saw the tunnels as important to their survival. The political commissar of the Viet Cong's Military Region IV, Mai Chi Tho, interviewed in 1978 by British historians, commented, "They were especially valuable after the offensive failed to achieve its objectives." Captain Nguyen Thanh Linh, the local commander of Viet Cong forces, crept back to the tunnels of Cu Chi after the disastrous Tet Offensive. He and three of his men were the only survivors. "When the Americans counterattacked, we had no good men left," he recalled. "We were nearly out of ammunition. Our food reserve was being used up day by day. Between four men, we had just 50 grams of rice a day. We ate fish from the Saigon River and plenty of rats." He summed up the situation: "You could say that the Americans were winning tactically, if not strategically."[7]

Many of the Viet Cong saw their cause as hopeless after Tet 1968 and turned themselves over to the South Vietnamese. Many of these defectors, known *as hoi chanhs*, went even further and actively assisted the southern troops. A particularly effective *hoi chanh* was Nguyen Van Tung from An Tinh near Cu Chi. While serving as the village's Communist Secretary, he had ordered the execution of a fellow Viet Cong soldier for the crime of rape. When he subsequently discovered the rapist was the nephew of a high-ranking Communist official, he feared for his own safety and turned himself in to the South Vietnamese Army. He told them everything he knew of the tunnels and their occupants, leading to the arrest of more than 300 Communist sympathizers and the capture of the secret headquarters of sapper troops which that attacked Saigon during Tet 1968. Following an artillery barrage, South Vietnamese troops entered the tunnels, led by a *hoi chanh* guide, and killed or captured every single one of its occupants. In the headquarters, they found newspaper clippings of their various Tet attacks as well as a directory of 60 of their agents living secretly in Saigon. This information was passed on to the Special Branch in Saigon, which arrested 50 of them. For the rest of the war, there were no more major terrorist attacks or acts of sabotage in Saigon.[8]

While American "tunnel rats" had made life difficult for the Viet Cong, things got even worse for them as the Americans used bulldozers to strip away the foliage in tunnel-infested areas. Captain Linh recalled having to be careful they didn't leave a single footprint on the cleared paths, lest the constantly patrolling Cobra attack helicopters of the 25th Aviation Battalion might spot them. "They had two gunners—blacks," he recalled, "who were excellent sharpshooters. Just a glimpse of us and they swiveled their gun pods to shoot and kill instantly; many of our soldiers died. They flew low and fast and were deadly accurate." Captain Linh was captured in 1970.[9]

Tran Nhu, a filmmaker sent to Cu Chi to make propaganda films, gives some suggestion of the short life span of a Viet Cong guerrilla. He notes that, if a soldier had done something noteworthy, they had to film him that very same day ". . . in case, with all that continuous shelling, he was hit before we had filmed him."[10]

One outcome of President Johnson's decision to end the bombing of North Vietnam on October 31, 1968, was to make many more American planes available for use in the South. Many of these were unleashed on the tunnel complexes of Cu Chi. Major Nguyen Quot, a veteran of the tunnels, observed that "a five-meter hole could be sufficient to destroy a tunnel." He lamented that, "B-52 bombs made holes twelve meters deep." Even if the tunnel did not collapse on its occupants, air ducts were blocked by falling debris. When the tunnel system was blocked in several places, the air could no longer circulate. Death by suffocation became commonplace.[11]

In 1971, the Communist writer, Vien Phuong, was ordered to return to Cu Chi from the relative safety of Cambodia. "There were only about four guerrillas left in each village; there were no other people," he recalled. "The guerrillas ate leaves to survive and washed their wounds in salted water." The destruction of the Viet Cong continued. Not even the dank and gloomy tunnels of Cu Chi could provide a safe haven from the relentless Americans.[12]

Phung Hoang, Eliminating the Viet Cong Infrastructure

The clandestine element of the Viet Cong had shown itself to be a particularly difficult enemy to defeat. Known as the Viet Cong Infrastructure (VCI), this clandestine element was different from the full-time military units that moved from province to province to do battle, such as the 1st Viet Cong Regiment destroyed by the U.S. Marines in Operation Starlite in August 1965. Instead, this clandestine element of the Viet Cong was composed of Local Force units, the part-timers who only occasionally took up weapons in a terrorist strike or planted a land mine. It also consisted of the informers who ostensibly worked for the South Vietnamese government, sometimes even the army itself, but who gave information and aid to the Communist enemy. Finally, this element also included the noncombatants: the tax collectors and bureaucrats of the Communist machinery. Defeating such an enemy required a well-coordinated and effective counterespionage force. In the early years, the South Vietnamese counterespionage effort was, in the words of one expert, ". . . splintered, badly led, poorly financed and understaffed."[13]

In late 1966, an experimental anti-infrastructure program was started, entirely staffed and run by the South Vietnamese themselves under the guidance of an American Central Intelligence Agency (CIA) adviser. This program was called the Phung Hoang Program, named after the bird of Vietnamese mythology. The Phung Hoang was one of four sacred animals in Vietnamese mythology. It represented grace, virtue, peace, and concord, and appeared only in times of prosperity disappearing when bad times approached. It was chosen by the Vietnamese because it was meant to symbolize the coming of peace and prosperity but American advisers privately joked that it represented the South Vietnamese troops who fled into hiding at the first sign of trouble. This patronizing humor eventually turned to a profound respect, however, when the Phung Hoang Program began making its devastating inroads into the formerly safe recesses of the Viet Cong infrastructure.[14]

While similar programs had been in existence for some time, it was only after the Tet Offensive of 1968 that they became strongly supported. They did so for several reasons. For one, South Vietnamese President Thieu was deeply shaken by the number of Viet Cong agents who had come out into the open during the fighting, stirring him into vigorous action. Second, the Phung Hoang's new chairman, South Vietnamese Premier Tran Van Khiem, was a potential political opponent of Thieu who was as cunning a politician as his American counterparts. He felt it was better to openly support the program rather than let Khiem take credit for its potential success.[15]

Two misconceptions about the program still persist: its functions and its ownership. First, the Phung Hoang Program was not an American program. Robert Komer, Director of Civil Operations and Revolutionary Development Support (CORDS), states, "Like all pacification programs, it was run by [South Vietnam]; U.S. support was confined chiefly to advisory support on improved identification, collation, and measurement techniques." This American contribution to the Phung Hoang Program was officially born on December 20, 1967, under the operational name, "Phoenix," the nearest American equivalent of the South Vietnamese bird of mythology.[16]

The second misperception is that Phung Hoang and its Phoenix advisers were not the actual instrument used for attacking the VCI. Instead, the program merely *coordinated* the efforts of the local intelligence committees (usually the village council chairman, hamlet chiefs, full-time police staff, and local paramilitary personnel) to make them more effective. It was precisely this coordination, both through the Phung Hoang and its American Phoenix advisers, which had been missing previously. Once these local committees identified local Viet Cong sympathizers, plans were developed and then carried out by Vietnamese military forces or, in some special cases, by U.S. Navy commandos known as SEALs.

Interestingly, many Americans were critical of the Phung Hoang Program and believed it was unsuccessful against the higher echelon of the VCI. They noted that, ". . . three out of four people killed, captured, or defected in both 1970 and early 1971 were from the lowest levels of the organization." They also stated that, "the pattern continued throughout 1971 and may have been the norm for the program."[17]

The real problem was that the Americans continued to think of the VCI as a highly centralized organization. In fact, it encouraged units to operate autonomously, relying on low-level, often part-time, obscure personnel. The CIA was reluctant to accept rank-and-file National Liberation Front (NLF) members, sympathizers, occasional workers, or tax collectors as real VCI and therefore thought the program was failing even as it killed or captured so many Viet Cong, more than 13,000 in 1968.[18]

The Viet Cong themselves had no doubts about the effectiveness of the program. In the words of one former Viet Cong, the program in some locations ". . . was dangerously effective. In Hau Nghia Province, for example, not far from our old base area, the Front infrastructure was virtually eliminated."[19]

The district Viet Cong companies and the regular Viet Cong battalions, which had previously served as "enforcers," were wiped out during the Tet Offensive of 1968. Many of the hamlets officially listed as under Viet Cong ownership in IV Corps in February 1969 were actually held by only half a dozen guerrillas. A combination of the Phung Hoang Program, which specifically targeted these local forces, plus the extra resources put into South Vietnam's own local forces, the Regional Force (RF) and Provincial Force (PF), made a dramatic difference. These RF/PF units, sometimes referred to as "Ruff-Puffs" by the Americans, were expanded by 100,000 men in 1968 and numbered more than half a million troops by 1973. Without the full-time forces to bolster them when attacked, the clandestine Viet Cong were progressively eliminated.[20]

Communist Headquarters

The Central Office of South Vietnam (COSVN) was the headquarters for most of the Communist forces in South Vietnam and a prime target of the Americans. In spite of wartime propaganda to the contrary, former NLF Minister Truong later acknowledged, "American intelligence had located

COSVN rather precisely. To B-52 pilots flying the secret bombing raids of 1969 and 1970, it was known as 'Base Area 353' (code named 'Breakfast')."[21]

The first of these American raids comprised 48 B-52s, dropping their bombs in a "box" two miles long and half-a-mile wide on top of the area known as "Breakfast" on the morning of March 18, 1969. General Phillip Davidson ordered a helicopter-borne patrol of elite Studies and Observation Group (SOG) commandos into the area as soon as the last bombs had fallen. The SOG troops observed a number of secondary explosions, probably enemy ammunition caches, and they received heavy ground fire from alert Viet Cong Main Force security troops. The SOG patrol leader described the scene as, ". . . like somebody had kicked over a hornet's nest." To General Davidson, the situation confirmed he had hit the jackpot, knowing it ". . . is precisely the defensive reaction one would expect from elite troops guarding a high-level headquarters complex." In the next 14 months until May 1970, the United States hit the six border area base camps with a total of 108,823 tons of high explosives.[22]

The Viet Cong were often warned of these attacks by Soviet trawlers equipped with sophisticated electronic monitoring equipment, cruising off of the coast of Guam. Whenever the Soviets detected the B-52s taking off, they would relay a warning to the Viet Cong that the big bombers were on their way. However, even when their Soviet-aided warning system worked and the Communists were able to flee to safety, they would later return to find their headquarters, in the words of a senior Viet Cong official, ". . . utterly destroyed: food, clothes, supplies, documents, everything. It was not just that things were destroyed," he continued, "in some awesome way they had ceased to exist."[23]

Generally flying in threes for the attack, each B-52 would disgorge more than 100 750-pound bombs within 30 seconds, cutting a swath through the jungle one quarter of a mile wide by a mile long. In the words of that same Viet Cong leader, "There would simply be nothing there, just an unrecognizable landscape gouged by immense craters."[24]

When they received insufficient warning to flee the area, the Communists would retreat into their shelters deep underground and be able to withstand B-52 strikes as near as 100 meters, but the concussion was still shattering. Once, a visiting Soviet delegation to COSVN in the Mimot Plantation of the Fish Hook was caught on short notice. When they emerged after the attack, the Viet Cong noted that the Soviets trembled uncontrollably and had emptied their bladders all over the fronts of their trousers.[25]

Much was done in an attempt to conceal it at the time, but it is quite clear that in July 1967, Hanoi's commander in South Vietnam, General

Nguyen Chi Thanh (the Communist equivalent of General Westmoreland) was seriously wounded in a B-52 raid and died of those wounds shortly afterward in a Hanoi hospital. At the time, Hanoi attempted to deny that he had been killed and claimed Thanh had died of a heart attack. British researchers, who interviewed Communist leaders in 1978, found that the cause of his death had mysteriously changed to "death by cancer." A dozen years later, the Communists were claiming he died of "heart disease."[26]

The attacks on COSVN also included helicopter-borne infantry assaults. On March 30, 1970, NLF Minister Nhu Tang Truong suddenly heard explosions bursting around his bunker and could hear the sound of helicopters landing nearby. The South Vietnamese had launched a surprise attack on COSVN. Truong watched as his bodyguards fired through the gunslits at the attacking forces. With the Cambodian Army attacking from the east down Route 7 and the South Vietnamese from the west, COSVN personnel were forced to flee when the battle eased as darkness approached. While the 5th Viet Cong Division tried to hold back the Cambodians and the 9th Viet Cong Division tried to prevent the South Vietnamese from breaking through, the Viet Cong's COSVN leadership fled through a narrow corridor protected by a third Viet Cong Division, the 7th Division. All the while, American jets strafed the fleeing Viet Cong. Forced to abandon their headquarters and run barefoot in ankle-deep mud, the Viet Cong leadership fled virtually nonstop for five days.[27]

The Demise of the Viet Cong

Historian Stanley Karnow, revisiting Vietnam after the war, met with Dr. Duong Quynh Hoa. She was one of the many Viet Cong agents who shed their cover and joined in the abortive attack on Saigon in Tet 1968. He noted that she ". . . bluntly denounced the venture as a 'grievous miscalculation' by the Hanoi hierarchy, which . . . had wantonly squandered the southern insurgent movement."[28]

A brief high point, from the Viet Cong's point of view, had been the January 1963 battle of Ap Bac, in which a South Vietnamese Army unit had performed poorly. They had been soundly defeated by the 514th Viet Cong Battalion (also known as the "Gironde Battalion"). The situation changed dramatically by 1968, however. The commander of that same Viet Cong battalion, Hai Hoang, commanded the Long An Province troops during the Tet Offensive in 1968. He was killed near Minh Phung Street at the hands of allied troops conducting what General Tran Van Tra, one of the senior Communist generals at the time, referred to as "insane counterattacks."[29]

General Tran Van Tra recalled the period immediately after Tet in 1968: "The Americans sent additional troops to Vietnam, stepped up shipments of all kinds of weapons and ammunition, attained their highest troop level during the war, and insanely counterattacked us. The Americans and [South Vietnamese Army] continuously attacked, and carried out very fierce sweeping and pacification operations." He further admitted that, "Many infrastructures were lost and many comrades were lost, especially in the areas adjacent to cities and the highly populated areas which were important strategically."[30]

In April 1968, Colonel Tran Van Dac, a Viet Cong political officer with responsibilities equal to an American general, gave himself up. He was soon followed by the regimental commander of the elite 165th VC Regiment. Both men said they viewed the war as hopeless and believed the Communists could not win.[31]

Former senior Viet Cong Trinh Duc recalled the enormous casualties the Viet Cong took in 1969 and 1970. "There was no way we could stand up to the Americans. Every time they came in force we ran from them." Often, however, the Viet Cong didn't get away. "During those years I had to reorganize my unit three times," he recalled. "Twice, the entire unit was killed. Each time I reorganized, the numbers were smaller. It was almost impossible to get recruits."[32]

Even back in 1969, the Institute of Strategic Studies in London confirmed another serious problem the Viet Cong were facing. They stated, "The Viet Cong also experienced increasingly serious recruiting difficulties during 1969. They had been forced in 1968 to abandon much of their rural base, in the form of territory under their control, in order to launch the assault upon the cities. That assault having failed, they found in retreat that their rural base, once neglected, had begun to crumble."[33]

Adding to the Viet Cong's recruitment problem was the demographic change occurring in South Vietnam. Traditionally linked to agrarian peasants, the population movement to urban areas eroded the Viet Cong's recruiting base even further.

General Tran Van Tra described Tet: "We suffered large sacrifices and losses with regard to manpower and materiel, especially cadres at the various echelons, which clearly weakened us. Afterwards, we were not only unable to retain the gains we had made but had to overcome a myriad of difficulties in 1969 and 1970 so that the revolution could stand firm in the storm."[34]

Lieutenant Colonel John Paul Vann was one of the first Americans to note the significance of the Viet Cong's Tet losses. Not only had their troops taken massive casualties, but also they had lost the best of their battalion and company-grade officers as well as most of their noncommissioned officers. Previously, northern replacements had been able to integrate with the Viet Cong units because they were under southern leadership. By late June, however, 70% of the officers and men in regular and local force battalions in III Corps were North Vietnamese. These soldiers were trained in conventional warfare and had difficulty adapting to the guerrilla warfare tactics previously used by the southern Viet Cong.[35]

Because of the catastrophic casualties, Communist battalions had an average strength of only 300 to 400 troops by the end of 1969, down from an average strength of 500 to 600 previously in the war. By 1972, even "Viet Cong" Battalions were mainly made up of North Vietnamese Army troops, filling the void left by their dead southern comrades. The once-famous Viet Cong 316 Company, described as a "first-class unit" which operated about 48 kilometers south of Saigon, had a peak strength of some 300 troops. By 1971 this unit was *down to three soldiers,* all of them North Vietnamese.[36]

The effect was clear to see by the early 1970s. When the Australians had first arrived in Phuoc Tuy Province in 1966, for example, a major combined force of Australians and Americans was required to make Route 15 safe for the newly arriving 9th US Army Division to travel to their new base. By 1971, however, the war against the Viet Cong had been so successful that civilians from Saigon and families of western diplomats were driving down Route 15 without fear just to reach the holiday port of Vung Tau. The Australians' main nemesis, the Viet Cong's D445 Battalion, had been reduced to a total strength of only 80 men. Split into five groups, these stragglers hid out in the most remote areas, merely growing their own food and attempting to avoid battle.[37]

Dr. Duong Quynh Hoa told historian Stanley Karnow that "We lost our best people" in 1968-69. She then went on to elaborate that the indigenous southerners had borne the brunt of the fighting in the Tet Offensive of 1968 and had suffered the heaviest casualties. The Phung Huang Program then "badly battered" the South Vietnamese Communist political organization. So, their places were filled by Northerners who rebuilt the movement and then remained after the war to manage it. These Northerners, despite their abstract commitment to "national" unity, clung to their Northern identity. Many South Vietnamese viewed them as doctrinaire, alien, and even carpetbaggers. Dr. Hoa openly loathed them, saying, "They behave as if they had conquered us." [38]

Epilogue

When South Vietnam collapsed in 1975 at the hands of the North Vietnamese Army, the final humiliation occurred. As Senior Viet Cong official Nhu Tang Truong observed the victory parade in Saigon, he watched as all the various North Vietnamese Army units, with their Soviet-built tanks, passed by and then, in his words, ". . . the Vietcong units finally appeared. They came marching down the street, several struggling companies, looking unkempt and ragtag after the display that had preceded them. Above their heads flew a red flag with a single yellow star—the flag of the Democratic Republic of North Vietnam."[39]

A few months later in mid-July, the North Vietnamese Politburo Member in charge of the south, Pham Hung, addressed the collected leadership of the NLF, the Provisional Revolutionary Government (PRG), and the Alliance of National, Democratic, and Peace Forces. This group included every significant player in the Viet Cong insurgency. Pham Hung made it clear they had no role to play in the new government. When a member of the NLF remarked that it was like the funeral of the Viet Cong, victorious Northern leaders decided to formalize the event and hired the Rex Dance Hall, described as a "sleazy former pleasure land," for the "Viet Cong funeral celebration."[40]

The Viet Cong, destroyed on the battlefields of the 1960s and early 1970s by the Americans and their allies, was formally laid to rest in 1975 by the North Vietnamese.

THE DEFEAT OF THE NORTH VIETNAMESE ARMY 1965–1973

6

A Different Struggle, Battling the North Vietnamese Army

America had shown time and again in the early 1960s that it did not want to commit ground combat troops to the Vietnam War. While it had provided huge *financial* support to the French in the early 1950s, America had carefully avoided the use of its own troops. Later, when the French withdrew, America responded by supplying advisers to assist the South Vietnamese in their fight against the Viet Cong. It still resisted committing its own ground troops.[1]

Why did the United States suddenly change its mind in 1965 and send ground troops to South Vietnam after President Johnson's statement that "American boys shouldn't have to fight Asian boys' wars?" Referring to that time in early 1965, when the United States decided to send in its first ground combat troops, Secretary of State Dean Rusk observed that there "... was no change of mind. There was a major change in the *situation* in Vietnam." The North Vietnamese had invaded South Vietnam with whole regiments of its troops and was "... threatening to cut the place in two. And the shape of the struggle became very different. We had to consider whether we got out under those circumstances or try to resist the North Vietnamese and the decision was made to try to resist it."[2]

North Vietnam's Two-fold Invasion

North Vietnam undertook a two-fold invasion of its southern neighbor. Beginning in 1959, it sent troops southward to flesh out Viet Cong units. This process continued throughout the war. A more dramatic step was taken in 1964 when Hanoi decided to alter radically the nature of the conflict by sending entire units of its own conventional army to fight in South Vietnam. This task was made easier by the fact that, while the border dividing the two countries was at that same narrow point where the southerners had thrown back seven different invasion attempts in the 1600s, no longer would the north be restricted to attacking on such a narrow front. South Vietnam's western neighbors, Cambodia and Laos, were now ruled by so-called "neutral" governments, which allowed Hanoi's troops to use their countries for supply lines and staging bases. While American and South Vietnamese troops were entitled technically under international law to attack these North Vietnamese "sanctuaries," American fear of antagonizing China and the Soviet Union prevented these attacks. China had already shown in the Korean War some 10 years previously that she was prepared to use her massive army to intervene should a friendly state's borders be "violated." Wary American political leaders believed this threat grew even more ominous when, on October 16, 1964, China exploded its first nuclear device.[3]

While the American decision to confine its military actions to those within South Vietnam's borders may well have prevented a wider Asian war, it also allowed the North to enter anywhere along South Vietnam's 800-mile western border at the time and place of their choosing.

Strengthening the Viet Cong Battalions

Having privately reached their decision in January, North Vietnam's leaders formally decided, at the 15th meeting of the Party's Central Committee in May 1959, to take control of the war in South Vietnam. As a result of that decision, southern-born troops were infiltrated back to South Vietnam and the tempo of the war increased. Communist General Tran Van Tra confirmed the significance of this date in his history of the war, referring to May 1959 as "the birthday of the [Ho Chi Minh] trail."[4]

NVA General Tran Do felt that the Vietcong guerrillas lacked the skill and experience to wage the conventional war the Communist leadership then foresaw. By the middle of 1964 NVA troops were filling the Vietcong ranks and strengthening them with commanders, political commissars, communications experts, ordnance technicians, and other specialists.[5]

NVA Captain (later promoted to Colonel) Huong Van Ba left North Vietnam to fight in the South on May 24, 1964. He was second in command of a 45-man artillery unit, which went south as an intact group. The weapons themselves were transported separately. Having trained in civilian clothes to avoid any suspicion, the unit was transported to the Vietnam-Laos border in covered trucks to further disguise the action. Captain Ba remembers that, after a brief rest, ". . . we traded in our North Vietnamese army uniforms for black pajamas, to give us the appearance of southern peasants. We were asked to make sure we weren't carrying anything related to North Vietnam or to other Communist countries. We were invading, but we did our best to disguise ourselves as native liberators." By June 1968, fully 70% of the officers and men in "Viet Cong" regular and local force units in III Corps were NVA.[6]

Strengthened by NVA replacements and armed with more sophisticated weapons provided by North Vietnam, 1964 saw the formation of the first 10,000-man, division-sized unit of Viet Cong Main Forces. This unit, based in Tay Ninh Province west of Saigon, was known as the 9th Viet Cong Division, formed around the nucleus of the 271st and 272nd Viet Cong Infantry Regiments.[7]

Differences existed between the southern-born Viet Cong and their NVA replacements. To begin with, their accents were as different to a Vietnamese ear as a "Georgia drawl" and a "New York twang" might be to an American. Further, the NVA soldiers appeared rigid and doctrinaire to the southerners. The NVA, on the other hand, thought the southerners to be slow and unsophisticated. The experience in III Corps, where the Australians operated, is interesting in this regard. D445 Viet Cong Provincial Battalion had been their main nemesis. Then in 1967, the Communists formed another battalion, D440. Rather than being recruited from the local population, however, this unit was composed mainly of NVA. Arguments immediately occurred between the northerners and the southerners, with orders and counterorders being issued and general dissatisfaction noted throughout. As one Australian veteran observed, "Internal trouble began almost at once, since the NVA regarded allocation to a local unit as a lowering of status. They had come south to join their own formations, to take part in decisive battles."[8]

NVA soldier Nguyen Danh remembers his unit (the 301st NVA Division) setting off on a secret mission: the surreptitious invasion of South

Vietnam. Before crossing the Ben Hai River into South Vietnam, they had to leave behind everything that could identify them as NVA. "This simple necessity turned out to be a major problem," he recalled, "especially for me. If you looked at the *boi doi* [NVA soldiers], everything about him came from the North, from his pith helmet to his uniform to his belt, shoes, flashlight, and cigarettes."[9]

During the war, the Communists insisted that the Viet Cong were simply a revolutionary indigenous group with no links to North Vietnam. This claim was thoroughly aided and abetted by support from America's antiwar movement and celebrities like Jane Fonda who publicly promoted that view. After the war, however, Hanoi finally admitted the truth. Northern Communist Party Historian Nguyen Khac-Vien, interviewed in 1975, said: "The [Viet Cong] was always simply a group emanating from [Hanoi]. If we [the North Vietnamese] had pretended otherwise for such a long period, it was only because we were not obliged to unveil our cards."[10]

Conventional Warfare with Northern Divisions

North Vietnamese Army Colonel Bui Tin made the trek southward in late 1963 to learn something firsthand about the progress of the Viet Cong. For the past four years, Hanoi had been sending its troops to reinforce Viet Cong units. He found that the Viet Cong were poorly organized and lacking in leadership. He believed it would be impossible to train the Viet Cong for a larger conflict and that the only answer lay in sending in whole North Vietnamese units. After five months in South Vietnam, he returned to Hanoi, told the leadership of his findings, and, within months, the invasion began in earnest.[11]

In August 1964, the 808th North Vietnamese Army Battalion was sent south. Its primary mission was to prepare the way for other troops soon to follow. Also in August, orders were issued for the three regiments (95, 32, 101) of the 325th NVA Division based in Vinh in North Vietnam to prepare for the move south. The 95th North Vietnamese Army regiment arrived in Kontum Province, South Vietnam, in December 1964. By February 1965, they were joined by the 32nd and 101st North Vietnamese Army regiments. The 6th North Vietnamese Army Regiment moved into Quang Tri Province at the same time.[12]

Australian intelligence was able to provide advance warning of these troop movements. Its first clue was a report in North Vietnam requesting large numbers of handcarts to move baggage. This report was followed up by Australian agents on the ground, who then tracked the 325th NVA Division as it moved into Laos and later into South Vietnam.[13]

Thus forewarned, General Westmoreland was able to counter these moves by landing elements of the U.S. Marines at Da Nang on March 8, 1965. Later, he deployed the U.S. 1st Infantry Division to Lai Khe, north of Saigon. He put the 25th Infantry Division to the northwest of Saigon. He sent the 4th Infantry Division into Pleiku in the Western Highlands and the 9th Korean Division into Tuy Hoa. The 1st Cavalry Division (Airmobile) was in the coastal plains of Binh Dinh.[14]

In October, three entire North Vietnamese Army Regiments assembled in Cambodia and western Pleiku Province in anticipation of driving eastward to the sea, cutting South Vietnam in two. The American 1st Cavalry Division (Airmobile) was sent in to counter their attempt.[15]

7

Ia Drang

During the summer of 1964, the North Vietnamese acknowledged the problems facing the Viet Cong and decided to escalate the war dramatically. The decision was taken to send three of their regular army regiments (320th, 33rd, and 66th) south through Laos and Cambodia to attack the Central Highlands area of South Vietnam. The attack itself was scheduled for October 1965 after the monsoonal rains ended. The attack would begin with a siege on the U.S. Special Forces compound and its 400 Montagnard tribesmen at Plei Me. This action was really just a diversion to lure the South Vietnamese relief column into an ambush. Once this relief force was destroyed, freeing them to take Pleiku, the NVA planned to proceed along Route 19 to the coastal city of Qui Nhon, effectively cutting South Vietnam in two.[1]

By the time the NVA were ready to launch their attack the situation had changed dramatically. To counter the introduction of these enemy forces, the United States began committing its own ground combat troops. The process began with the Marines' landing at Da Nang in March 1965 and, by August, the Marines had already grabbed the world's headlines by defeating a Viet Cong regiment in Operation Starlite.

The Marines weren't the only American unit in Vietnam. Their arrival was quickly followed by others, including the innovative 1st Cavalry Division (Airmobile). Known affectionately as "the Cav" or as the "1st Air Cav," the 1st Cavalry Division was a product of President John F Kennedy's desire to resist Communist aggression. Like his other creation, the "Green Berets," the 1st Cavalry Division was specifically intended to fight in the smaller wars on America's frontiers. The unit was born as the 11th Air Assault Division (Test) at Fort Benning, Georgia, in February 1963. It proved itself quickly and was officially designated the 1st Cavalry Division (Airmobile) in July.

The NVA attacked the Plei Me Special Forces base as planned in late 1965, but South Vietnamese intelligence had already deciphered the scheme and dispatched an armored column to fight its way through to their relief. The NVA found themselves too weak to deal with the surprisingly aggressive South Vietnamese Army and were forced to withdraw. The 1st Brigade of the 1st Cavalry Division, which included Lieutenant Colonel John B. Stockton's 1st Squadron, 9th Cavalry Regiment, was sent to Camp Holloway at Pleiku to deal with this NVA force. On November 1, helicopter gunships in his command spotted small groups of NVA troops between Plei Me and the Cambodian border. Lieutenant Colonel Stockton sent in his troopers to investigate and quickly captured the field hospital of the 33rd North Vietnamese Army Regiment. Fifteen NVA soldiers were killed and 44 captured in the quick, one-sided battle. Also captured were huge stocks of weapons, food, and medical supplies. The enemy counterattacked a few hours later and the cavalry, reinforced with another battalion, killed 250 of the enemy at a cost to themselves of 11 killed and 51 wounded.[2]

Captured documents and prisoner interrogations revealed that the 33rd NVA Regiment had suffered badly. Forty percent of its men, including two of the three battalion commanders, had been killed. The 1st Battalion of the 33rd NVA Regiment, which had conducted the attack on the Plei Me Special Forces Camp, was down to 100 men. The Regiment had lost almost all of their mortars and their antiaircraft machine guns. Although replacements would help the 33rd to maintain some semblance of combat function, the NVA would now pin all of their hopes on the newly-arrived 66th NVA Regiment, which had taken no part in the previous battles.

On November 3, Lieutenant Colonel Stockton's men were ordered into the Ia Drang valley in a "reconnaissance in force" to observe and intercept enemy units crossing in from Cambodia. Stockton's men quickly established three platoon (30-man) ambushes, one on a trail two miles from the Cambodian border. The Americans, lying in wait along the trail, observed a reinforced company of the 66th NVA Regiment, numbering over 100 men, approach to within 120 yards and then come to a halt, taking a lengthy rest break. A few minutes after 9:00 P.M., they resumed their approach. The troopers let the front of the column pass by, waiting for the heavily laden, crew-served weapons section to enter the trap. Then they simultaneously fired eight claymore mines into the enemy. A split second later, this action was followed by a roar of rifle and machine gun fire into the kill zone. The commander of the troopers, Captain Charles Knowlen, ordered all of his ambush parties back to their defensive perimeter, and within half an hour, they were under attack by a large force of NVA, which threatened to overrun his position. Quickly reinforced by another company, the troopers eventually beat off their attackers.[3]

The search for the NVA continued for the next two weeks. The 1st Battalion, 7th Cavalry, had been looking for the enemy to the east but with no success. The 7th Cavalry was one of the more colorful units, tracing its lineage to the unit that fought at the Little Big Horn under George Armstrong Custer. The unit was very proud of its history and traditions, including its regimental marching song, the Irish drinking ballad "Garry Owen." The troops characteristically greeted each other with a hearty "Garry Owen" and, when saluting officers, replaced the usual "Good morning, sir" or "Good afternoon, sir" with the 7th Cavalry greeting of "Garry Owen, sir." But the 7th Cavalry wasn't having much luck in its search for the NVA. It was a "dry hole" in the words of Colonel Tim Brown. "We're just wearing out the troops," was Lieutenant Colonel Hal Moore's summary. After a quick consultation, General Dick Knowles and his two commanders agreed that the hunting would be better to the west in the Ia Drang Valley area near that where Lieutenant Colonel Stockton had been. They couldn't have been more correct.[4]

According to NVA General Chu Huy Man, the spot where the cavalry was about to land was "right in the middle of three of our battalions of the 66th Regiment, our reserve force. It was the strongest we had. [At] full strength the battalions each had about four hundred fifty men. Also there was a headquarters battalion. The regiment's total strength was about sixteen hundred men."[5]

All of Lieutenant Colonel Moore's companies were understrength, as usual, with most of them numbering about 100 men. Altogether, he could count 450 men in his battalion. Worse still, though, was the fact that there were only 16 Huey "slick" transport helicopters available to ferry his troops. Because of the small load capacity and the weight of the fuel, the helicopters would be able to carry less than 80 men on their first trip. They would then need to fly the 15-mile journey back to pick up more troops and then return, thus taking 30 minutes before returning with the second group. Factoring in their need to refuel, Colonel Moore estimated it would take more than four hours to get all of his men together in the landing zone.

On the morning of November 14, 80 cavalry troopers boarded the sixteen helicopters en route to "setting up shop" right in the center of the enemy's fortress defended by over 1600 NVA soldiers. Because of the small landing zone, the 16 helicopters would land, only moments apart, in two eight-helicopter groups. With them in the first wave was their battalion commander, Colonel Hal Moore, and UPI correspondent, Joseph Galloway, one of the rare journalists who actually went with the troops and spent significant time with them.

After first hitting the LZ with artillery and rockets from helicopter gunships, the first wave of eight helicopters touched down on LZ X-Ray at 10:48 A.M. Within moments, the next wave of eight helicopters landed. The 80 cavalry troopers immediately disgorged from the helicopters and began fanning out in groups

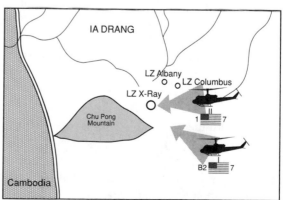

of three or four to secure the area around the LZ, which was about the size of a football field. Sergeant John Mingo spotted an NVA soldier sitting on the ground. The startled NVA attempted to escape, but Sergeant Mingo tackled him and took him prisoner. Colonel Moore quickly questioned the prisoner with the help of an interpreter; the shaken soldier said, "there are three battalions on the mountain who want very much to kill Americans but have not been able to find any."[6]

Colonel Moore had to wait until 12:10 P.M. for the arrival of the next wave bringing the rest of Captain Tony Nadal's Alpha Company. Their arrival allowed him sufficient troops to secure the LZ. Colonel Moore realized that, vastly outnumbered, he would need to take the fight to the enemy located up on the mountain rather than fight it out on the LZ. The enemy could threaten the cavalry's lifeline of helicopter resupply at the LZ and prevent him from bringing in the rest of his men. A sprinkling of gunfire was already coming from that direction, and he ordered Bravo Company to move out in the direction of the mountain. Captain John Herren ordered his men to attack with two platoons abreast, a third platoon following a short distance behind as a reserve. Meanwhile, the Weapons Platoon's solitary mortar would fire what support they could with their 40 rounds of mortar shells. By 12:30 P.M. the scattered gunshots increased in intensity.

Within moments, 1st Platoon, on the left, spotted a column of NVA soldiers walking down the mountain, nonchalantly carrying their weapons on their shoulders. After quickly confirming that there were no South Vietnamese troops in the area, the cavalry opened fire on the column. A few moments later, 1st Platoon itself was attacked by the khaki-clad enemy, well-armed with automatic rifles.

When 1st Platoon radioed back to Captain Herren that they were pinned down, 2nd Platoon, commanded by 2nd Lieutenant Henry T. Herrick, was ordered to move up on the right, tying in with 1st Platoon and taking some of the pressure off them. The aggressive troopers of 2nd Platoon soon reached their comrades in 1st Platoon, but spotting a group of the enemy further to the right of them, Lieutenant Herrick asked permission to pursue them. Captain Herren radioed back, "Fine, but be careful. I don't want you to get pinned down or sucked into anything."[7]

3rd Platoon, commanded by Lieutenant Dennis Deal, came up on the left of 1st Platoon and linked in with it. But Lieutenant Herrick's 2nd Platoon, continued to chase after the fleeing enemy, losing sight of the other two platoons as they disappeared into the trees to the right. 2nd Platoon continued to advance for another 100 yards, crossing a small waist-deep stream and then forming up, two-squads abreast to climb a gentle ridge on the stream's other side. It was here that they were suddenly confronted by about 50 NVA hurtling down the trail in their direction. The cavalry troops quickly took them under fire and sent one squad around to the right to carry out a flanking attack on the enemy, who had quickly spread out and taken cover. This move took the enemy by surprise. The flanking squad killed scores of the enemy before an even bigger group of enemy suddenly dashed out of the trees and directly into the L-shaped "ambush" of the cavalry's position. Sergeant Savage, leader of the flanking squad recalled that, "We had one hell of a firefight for three or four minutes and we hadn't lost anyone. We killed a lot of them. I hit a lot of them. I saw them fall. They tried to put a machine gun up on our right and we shot the gunner and two men with him."[8]

Within moments, however, an even larger force of NVA had moved between Lieutenant Herrick's 2nd Platoon and Lieutenant Devney's 1st Platoon. 2nd Platoon was cut off and isolated. An entire NVA battalion was rushing down the mountain into the attack on 2nd Platoon.

At 1:32 P.M., the fourth lift of the day saw two waves of eight helicopters land, bringing in the rest of Alpha Company and the lead element of Charlie Company. Alpha Company quickly took positions 75 meters from the LZ, tying in to the left of Bravo Company and forming a defensive arc swinging from due north around to the southwest. The newly arrived Charlie Company, under Captain Edwards, took up defensive positions to the south. Colonel Moore took a calculated gamble and left a huge gap in the defenses, an arc sweeping all the way from due north around to the east. The cavalry now had 250 men on the ground. The cavalry called down an avalanche of artillery, airstrikes, and rocket-firing helicopter gunships onto the area to the south and west.

While 1st and 3rd Platoons of Bravo Company formed up on line and attacked toward the cut-off 2nd Platoon, Alpha Company to the left was moving to a dry creekbed that ran across their front. Suddenly Lieutenant Bob Taft's 3rd Platoon of Alpha company ran headlong into 150 NVA troops barreling their way toward them along the creekbed and its sides. Lieutenant Taft's men quickly dropped their packs, formed up abreast, and assaulted into the much larger NVA force. The troopers of 3rd Platoon attacked on the trot and within five minutes every man in the lead squad had been hit. Lieutenant Taft was killed by a bullet to his throat. Captain Nadal observed that, "The enemy on the mountain started moving down rapidly in somewhat uncoordinated attacks. They streamed down the hill and down the creekbed. The enemy knew the area. They came down the best-covered route."[9]

Though badly hit, Lieutenant Taft's platoon stood firm, now led by Sergeant Lorenzo Nathan, a veteran of the Korean War. The NVA boiled around to the left, hoping to outflank them and ran right across the front of Lieutenant Marm's platoon, rushing up to assist. Eighty NVA soldiers were caught entirely by surprise by the hail of rifle and machine gun fire unleashed by the thirty or so men of 2nd Platoon, Alpha Company. Captain Tony Nadal described it as not much of a fight: "2nd Platoon just mowed them down." Staff Sergeant Les Staley said, "Fifty NVA came right across my front and were cut down almost immediately and they did not turn and return our fire." The NVA survivors fell back to the creekbed where the two platoons of Bravo Company lay waiting.[10]

Lieutenant Herrick's platoon, meanwhile, continued its running battle about 100 yards to the north. Lieutenant Herrick was able to organize a defensive position on a small knoll. One of his machine gun crews was gone, their position swarmed by massed NVA attacks. Lieutenant Herrick, organizing the defense, received an agonizing bullet wound to the hip. He told the medic, Specialist Fifth Class Charles Lose, to tend to the others. His last words, said to Sergeant Ernie Savage, spoke volumes for an ethos some in his country would never understand: "If I have to die," Lieutenant Herrick said, "I'm glad to give my life for my country." He died within moments of being hit. It was now 2:30 P.M.[11]

Of the 29 men of Alpha Company's 2nd Platoon, eight were dead and another 13 wounded. They continued to hold their little 25-yard perimeter. Command was transferred from Lieutenant Herrick to Sergeant Carl Palmer who, while lying wounded, was killed by an NVA soldier who had tossed his grenade and then stood laughing at the dead American. Specialist 4 Michael Patterson stopped the laughter with a long burst of M-16 rifle fire directly into the NVA soldier's stomach and noted, "I swear I saw daylight through him before he went down." Command was passed to Sergeant Robert Stokes who himself was soon killed. Sergeant Savage now took over.[12]

Sergeant Savage's small band gathered up weapons and ammunition from the dead, and then burned the platoon's maps and signals codes lest they fall into enemy hands. Captain Herren radioed to them, describing the attempts of the others to reach them. Shortly after 2:30 P.M., the fifth wave of helicopters arrived at the LZ. As before, coming in two groups of eight, the first wave was hit by withering fire, much of it at point-blank range. Onboard one of those helicopters, Captain Ray Lefebvre, commander of Delta Company, saw his radio operator killed next to him before either one of them had even exited the helicopter. Several of the helicopters were hit, but all managed to limp away to safety. Colonel Moore radioed the remaining eight helicopters to move away to the safety of Plei Me until the LZ was better secured.

The newly arrived men of Charlie Company joined their brothers in the defensive arc, filling in what had been a gap on the southern side of the perimeter. Just as they settled into position, they were confronted by the massed soldiers of the 7th Battalion of the 66th NVA Regiment who thought they were approaching an undefended area. They were thrown back violently. At the same time, the 9th Battalion of the 66th NVA Regiment was attacking Alpha Company to their right, trying to find the gap between the two cavalry companies. A party of 30 NVA had found the gap and were about to flank Alpha Company when Captain Lefebvre arrived in the gap with his handful of men and stopped them.

In the relative lull caused by the enemy's defeat at the hands of Charlie Company, Colonel Moore was able to call in the last of his battalion airlifts, which arrived at 3:20 P.M. With these troops, the cavalry was able to establish a full-round defense of their perimeter and even designate a reserve platoon, Lieutenant James Rackstraw's Reconnaissance Platoon. The NVA fell back, dragging their dead and wounded with them.

By 2:45 P.M., Colonel Moore had three rifle companies on the ground fighting an NVA force of three battalions. The cavalry's supporting arms were performing miracles. Colonel Moore recalled, "No matter how bad things got for the Americans fighting for their lives on the X-Ray perimeter, we could look out into the scrub brush in every direction, into that seething inferno of exploding artillery shells, 2.75-inch rockets, napalm canisters, 250- and 500-pound bombs, and 20mm cannon fire and thank God and our lucky stars that we didn't have to walk through *that* to get to work."[13]

At 4:20 P.M., Captain Nadal's three platoons of Alpha Company tried yet again to reach their comrades of 2nd Platoon, Bravo Company. He gave his men a brief "pep talk," telling them, "We've got an American platoon cut off and we're going after them!" His men's replies were enthusiastic: "Let's go get them," and "Gary Owen." [14]

The men were instructed to fix bayonets and then the assault began. It had not progressed more than 50 yards when, in the words of Lieutenant Deal, "the whole world exploded," as the enemy opened up on the troopers. Many of them were killed in the initial burst but the rest pressed on. Specialist Fourth Class Bill Beck, firing a machine gun in the assault, still recalls a memorable sight: "A tall, thin sergeant bayoneting a North Vietnamese in the chest. It was just like practice against the straw dummies: Forward, thrust, pull out, move on. One, two, three."[15]

At 5:00 P.M., 13 more Huey's were approaching the LZ, bringing reinforcements from Captain Myron Diduryk's Bravo Company from the 2nd Battalion, 7th Cavalry Regiment. As they approached, some of the men saw troops running around in khaki uniforms whose color resembled the Americans' parade ground uniform. Sergeant John Setelin momentarily thought, "We must really be desperate if we're bringing guys just back from R and R without giving them time to change into their fatigue uniforms." Then he noticed that the men in khaki were shooting at him.[16]

In the din of the shooting, Ukranian-born Captain Myron Diduryk rushed to Colonel Moore's "command post" beside a large termite mound. "Garry Owen, Sir!" he shouted. "Captain Diduryk and Bravo Company, 2nd Battalion, 7th Cavalry, a hundred and twenty men strong, reporting for duty!"[17]

By 5:40 P.M., it became clear to Alpha Company's Captain Nadal that he would not be successful in breaking through to Bravo Company's 2nd Platoon. He requested permission to fall back. Under a barrage of white phosphorous shells landing right in their midst, the cavalry troopers pulled back, dragging their dead and wounded with them.

Bravo Company's Captain Herren informed his 2nd Platoon of their unsuccessful attempts and advised them of the need to hold on until morning. Colonel Moore then ordered two platoons of the newly arrived men of Captain Diduryk to strengthen the defenses on the northeast. He ordered Diduryk's 2nd Platoon commanded by Lieutenant James Lane to reinforce the 120-yard length of the line held by Charlie Company.

Captain Nadal's Alpha Company had by now lost three of its five officers and 31 of its 115 enlisted men. Captain Herren's Bravo Company had lost one of its five officers and 46 of its 114 enlisted men. Charlie Company was by far the strongest, still having all five of its officers and 102 of its 106 enlisted men. In addition, Charlie Company was now further strengthened with the newly arrived men.

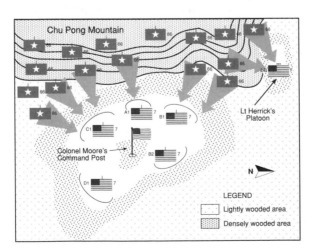

Just after 9:00 P.M., two helicopters approached the cavalry's LZ, bringing in a resupply of water and ammunition. As they approached the LZ, they could see a trail of signal lights, 300 yards wide and half a mile long, coming down from the mountainside. The NVA were pouring down from the mountain to attack the cavalry. The NVA knew their lights could not be seen from the LZ but hadn't counted on the helicopters. Artillery strikes were called in on these lights and, shortly after midnight, the mountain erupted from "secondary explosions" caused by the enemy's own munitions exploding.

Out in the area of Bravo's 2nd Platoon, artillery was being walked all around the platoon's position. Sergeant Savage called the artillery in so close that the men were lifted off the ground from the shuddering impact and then covered with dirt and debris. Galen Bungum recalled that the NVA would crawl to within ten yards of their position ". . . and many times just stand up and laugh at us. We would mow them down. It begins to work on your mind: What are they laughing at? I couldn't believe it." At other times, Sergeant Savage would hear the enemy moving through the bush and would call artillery onto them, the sounds of their shouts and screams confirming the artillery's accuracy.[18]

Throughout the night, the NVA launched three separate 50-man attacks at Bravo's 2nd Platoon. Each was thrown back by the platoon's seven men, assisted by some of the 13 wounded, including Sergeant Ruben Thompson, who was shot through the chest but continued to fight. Nine troopers lay dead beside them.

For the 7th Battalion of the 66th NVA Regiment, things were not working out as planned. Their attack against the American LZ, scheduled for 2:00 A.M., had been delayed for hours. The airstrikes, combined with some of their men getting lost, had resulted in the "night attack" being planned for dawn.

At first light the cavalry sent out reconnaissance patrols of four men from each platoon. Within moments, though, the patrol from 2nd Platoon, Charlie Company, came running back to the perimeter. One of the men yelled, "They're coming Sarge! A lot of 'em. Get ready!" Sergeant Robert Jemison readied his men, cautioning his machine gunners to hold their fire.[19]

Ten minutes later, at 6:50 A.M., waves of NVA came surging out of the waist-high grass. They were wearing pith helmets, screaming at each other and the cavalry troopers and firing their assault rifles. They hit in the area of Charlie Company in a ferocious struggle of close-range combat. Within minutes Charlie Company had taken heavy casualties, including two platoon commanders killed and the company commander wounded. The NVA swarmed over the dead and wounded defenders. Specialist Arthur Viera Jr recalled, "The enemy was all over, at least a couple of hundred of them walking around for three or four minutes; it seemed like three or four hours. They were shooting and machine gunning our wounded and laughing and giggling."[20]

Twenty-six-year-old Air Force Forward Air Controller, Lieutenant Charlie Hastings, was with Colonel Moore at the LZ. He saw what was happening and radioed the code word, "Broken Arrow," which told his fellow airmen that an American unit was about to be overrun. This call brought every available fighter-bomber to their rescue. Aircraft were soon "stacked" 28 high, one on top of the other at 1,000 foot intervals, waiting patiently for their turn to deliver bombs and napalm on the NVA.[21]

While the artillery and airstrikes were effectively killing the enemy's reserves and preventing reinforcements from joining the fight, the NVA assault troops were already safely within the ring of steel. Colonel Moore dispatched Sergeant George McCulley's "platoon" of 16 men from Alpha Company to sprint across the LZ to reinforce Charlie Company. They lost two killed and two wounded just getting there, but managed to plug the gap in Charlie Company's position.

To the left of the battle raging with Charlie Company, a newcomer to the battle was committed, the H-15 Main Force Viet Cong Battalion. Fresh troops, these men were easily distinguishable from the others by their black uniforms. They were about to launch themselves at Delta Company at 7:15 A.M. Delta Company's 75-yard front provided better visibility than Charlie Company's and was well prepared for attack. They not only had their own six machine guns, but also were reinforced by three additional ones from the Reconnaissance Platoon. Each of the nine machine guns had a four-man crew who were well-supplied with ammunition: 4,000 rounds per gun. The H-15 Battalion attacked but were stopped cold. Specialist Willard Parish's M-60 machine gun alone accounted for more than 100 of the enemy who lay dead, scattered in a semicircle around his gun.

At 9:10 A.M., reinforcements arrived in the form of Alpha Company, 2nd Battalion, 7th Cavalry. They quickly leaped out of their helicopters and rushed into the Charlie Company sector, killing scores of the NVA. By 10:00 A.M., the NVA admitted defeat and began withdrawing. Worst hit was Charlie Company. Of the 111 men of Charlie Company, who had begun the battle that morning, 42 had been killed: two lieutenants, 16 sergeants, and 24 troopers. Another 20 men were wounded.

Later, when the cavalry moved back into the area where Charlie Company had fought, they found the evidence of the vicious struggle. Some suggestion of the battle's ferocity was the discovery of an American and an NVA soldier, both dead, the American's hands still locked around the NVA's throat. Many of the American wounded had been murdered by the NVA, shot in the head. Colonel Moore noted that, had the NVA been better disciplined and better led, they wouldn't have paused to kill the wounded and loot the dead Americans' belongings. If so, they would have had the chance to sweep right through the LZ and attack his command post. Their momentary orgy may have cost the NVA their lives and the battle.[22]

Lieutenant Colonel Bob Tully's 2nd Battalion, 5th Cavalry, marched overland to LZ X-Ray early in the morning. After a brief firefight with fleeing NVA, they arrived at the LZ shortly before noon. Their line of approach brought them through that sector held by Delta Company. As they approached, they were stunned at the damage done by the defenders' nine machine guns, having had to step over piles of bodies for the last 30 minutes of their approach.

Shortly after 12:00 noon, for the first time ever, B-52s were being used tactically on the battlefield. Sixteen B-52s from Guam arrived over NVA Lieutenant Colonel Nguyen Huu An's Regimental headquarters on Chu Pong Mountain, delivering their payload. Also shortly after noon, John Herren's Bravo Company, 1st Battalion, guided and joined two companies of the newly-arrived 2nd Battalion, 5th Cavalry, on a mission to rescue their separated platoon. They moved slowly and cautiously, killing several NVA along the way, and reached the platoon by 3:00 P.M. The 2nd Platoon had suffered nine killed and 13 wounded; only seven were uninjured. The dead and wounded were helicoptered out, and the cavalry prepared for its second night on the LZ. The 1st Battalion, 7th Cavalry, was now down to a total of eight officers and 260 men, but were reinforced with the fresh men of the 5th Cavalry.

The cavalry did everything they could to prepare themselves for the attack they knew would come. Fortunately, the NVA let them prepare for almost four hours, uninterrupted. While the 5th Cavalry manned the eastern half of the perimeter, Colonel Moore's now much-depleted 7th Cavalry manned the western half, the scene of Charlie Company's desperate struggle. At the precise section that Charlie Company had defended, however, Moore shifted his Bravo Company, 2nd Battalion, 7th Cavalry, which had suffered only relatively light casualties.

Lieutenant Rick Rescorla commanded 1st Platoon of Bravo Company, 2nd Battalion, 7th Cavalry. British by birth, Lieutenant Rescorla was a veteran of the British Army in Cyprus and the Colonial Police in Rhodesia. He placed his men in an arc 50 yards back from the line Charlie Company had been forced to hastily defend earlier. This move allowed his men to have an open stretch of ground to their front, an open area any attacker would need to traverse in order to attack them. With several hours to prepare themselves, his men were able to dig deep, three-man foxholes and carefully emplace their machine guns for maximum effectiveness. Just before dusk, a specially designated team of troopers reconnoitered the area far to their front, emplacing trip-flares and booby-trapped hand grenades along likely avenues of approach.

Just before 4:00 A.M., the defenders of LZ X-Ray were alerted by trip-flares 300 yards to their front. The enemy was on their way again. The 7th Battalion, 66th NVA Regiment, their numbers filled with fresh replacements, was about to do battle again. Approximately 100 NVA rushed toward the lines of Lieutenant Rescorla's Bravo Company, but within 10 minutes, they were cut down in a storm of artillery, rifle, and machine gun fire. After a lull of some 20 minutes, the NVA poured down out of the mountain in even greater strength. To the sound of whistles and bugles, the NVA came screaming toward the Americans but were again destroyed in an avalanche of shells.

In between NVA assaults, Lieutenant Rescorla urged his men to talk to their fellow troopers in nearby foxholes to keep their spirits up. As a further measure, the young, British-born officer sang choruses of the Australian bush ballad, "Wild Colonial Boy"; its slow and measured cadence helped to steady his young cavalrymen. Lieutenant Rescorla chose this ballad, which celebrated an Australian outlaw named Jack Doolan. Even though outnumbered three to one, this outlaw preferred to fight rather than surrender. Lieutenant Rescorla's British-accented voice rang out eerily in the silence between the attacks:

> "Jack drew a pistol from his belt
> And waved it like a toy
> 'I'll fight but not surrender,' cried
> The Wild Colonial Boy."

Although heavily outnumbered, Lieutenant Rescorla's American cavalrymen held firm.

At 5:03 A.M., the NVA, still looking for a weak point, hurled themselves at the right-hand portion of Bravo Company's line. Sergeant John Setelin's men lay in wait for them, alerted to their approach by trip-flares. Sergeant Setelin told his squad to hold their fire until the enemy emerged into the open ground to their front. The cavalry did so, in spite of the bullets coming in their direction. "Then," Sergeant Setelin recalls, "they stepped into that open area. The flares were burning, they were lit up, and it was easy. We opened up and picked 'em off." Within 30 minutes, the attack had been thrown back.[23]

At 6:27 A.M., the NVA commander decided to launch an all-or-nothing attack. Private First Class John Martin remembers that, "It was like a shooting gallery; waves of NVA were coming in a straight line down off Chu Pong Mountain." That, together with the airbursts of 105-mm artillery and 81-mm mortar, threw the enemy back in less than 15 minutes. The attack had failed totally. Unlike the night before, when the NVA had managed to close with Charlie Company before effective fire could be brought to bear, the cavalry's artillery was this time able to dilute the attacking waves of enemy sufficiently for the defenders. Hundreds more NVA bodies were added to the hundreds already there from the previous night's fighting. Total cavalry casualties for the whole night were only six wounded, none seriously.[24]

At 9:30 A.M., Lieutenant Colonel Robert McDade's 2nd Battalion, 7th Cavalry, began marching overland to LZ X-Ray from LZ Colombus, three miles to the east. Shortly after 10:00 A.M., after a massive series of airstrikes, the cavalry on LZ X-Ray pushed out from their perimeter, killing another 27 enemy, ending all NVA resistance.

Just before noon on November 16, the men of the 1st Battalion, 7th Cavalry, as well as their attached companies of Alpha and Bravo 2nd Battalion, 7th Cavalry, began helicoptering out of LZ X-Ray back to the rear for reorganization and rest. By 3:00 P.M., the process was finished and the last helicopter lifted off, carrying Colonel Moore. The LZ was now in the hands of the 5th Cavalry and those members of the 2nd Battalion, 7th Cavalry, who had marched in from LZ Colombus.[25]

The bloody battle had cost the enemy dearly. The NVA left 634 bodies in the immediate vicinity of the battle and another 1,215 some distance away, killed by artillery and air attacks. Six enemy soldiers were captured. The cavalry lost 79 killed and 121 wounded.

The Move to LZ Albany

In stark contrast to the fury of the previous nights, Tully and McDade's newly arrived cavalry battalions spent a quiet night on the battlefield. The following day, November 17, with B-52 strikes against the foot of the Chu Pong planned to arrive within two hours, the two battalions were ordered out of LZ X-Ray. With no helicopters available to lift them, the troops would have to march overland to two nearby clearings some few kilometers away. They moved off to the east for two kilometers, at which time the 5th Cavalry units proceeded the short distance to a clearing called LZ Columbus. The 7th Cavalry units branched off to the north on their way to another clearing called LZ Albany. Lieutenant Colonel Robert Tully's battalion made it into LZ Colombus at 11:38 A.M. and had a hot meal waiting for them.

At 11:57 A.M., while their fellow cavalrymen were already enjoying a hot meal at LZ Colombus, Lieutenant Colonel Robert McDade's 7th Cavalry troopers en route to LZ Albany surprised two NVA soldiers lying in the grass and took them prisoner. Unknown to the cavalry, a third NVA soldier escaped to raise the alarm. The column was halted, just short of LZ Albany, for perhaps 30 minutes while the prisoners were interrogated. Then Lieutenant Colonel Robert McDade called his commanders forward. The company commanders brought their radio operators and, in some cases, their first sergeants and artillery forward observers with them. Captain George Forrest, Commander of Alpha Company (A/1/5), had traveled 600 yards from the tail of the column to attend the meeting. He brought with him his two radio operators.

Meanwhile the NVA, alerted by the escaped sentry, were rushing toward the cavalry troopers. In the immediate area were the soldiers from the 8th Battalion, 66th NVA Regiment; the 1st Battalion, 33rd NVA Regiment; and the HQ of the 3rd Battalion, 33rd Regiment. While the others had been bloodied at Plei Me, the only losses suffered by the 8th Battalion had been the loss of most of its Heavy Weapons Company at the hands of Stockton's cavalry troopers two weeks ago; with new replacements, they numbered 550 men. As soon as they sighted the cavalry, they began firing. The fighting commenced at the head of the column and then roared along its length, with NVA firing at the troopers from trees and large termite hills as they swept in from the east. At the first sound of gunfire, Captain Forrest took off at a sprint to rejoin his men at the rear of the column. In the gauntlet of fire, both of his radio operators were killed but he made it through unscathed. He formed his men into a defensive perimeter.

Charlie Company, in the middle of the column, was led by Executive Officer Lieutenant Don Cornett in the absence of Captain Skip Fesmire, who had gone up to the front of the column. Lieutenant Cornett yelled, "Follow me!" and led his troops into the attack, attempting to roll up the right flank of the enemy. The company ran head on into the 66th Regiment's troops and Lieutenant Cornett was soon killed. A bloody battle ensued in the tall grass. Charlie Company started the day with 112 men; by the next morning, they suffered 45 killed and 50 wounded.[26]

The NVA managed to cut the column in half. A defensive perimeter was formed up at LZ Albany at the front of the column, and another one at the rear where Captain Forrest formed up his Alpha Company. In the 700 yards intervening lay the remains of two rifle companies, a headquarters company, and a weapons company who would fight it out with the enemy in little groups of twos and threes. The NVA moved amongst the American casualties, killing those who cried out for help. Later, Captain Buce Tully, Commander of Bravo Company, discovered the bodies of troopers with their hands tied behind their backs and fatal bullet wounds to the back of their heads.

Lieutenant Larry Gwin at LZ Albany climbed atop a huge termite mound and, from its elevation, could clearly see NVA soldiers wandering around in the tall grass to the south. Lieutenant Gwin picked them off one by one with his M-16, killing ten to fifteen of them, not knowing at the time that they were looking for wounded Americans to kill. The NVA commander Nguyen Huu An recalled: "My commanders and soldiers reported there was very vicious fighting. I tell you, frankly, your soldiers fought valiantly. They had no choice. You are dead or not. It was hand-to-hand fighting."[27]

The two defensive perimeters at the head and the tail of the column were receiving strong ground attacks. The first effective support came in the form of U.S. Air Force A-1E Skyraiders, propeller-driven fighter-bombers, which napalmed and machine-gunned the NVA. Lieutenant Pat Wayne, the Reconnaissance Platoon leader recalled: "You could see a large number of North Vietnamese, fifty or a hundred, quite a number, within fifty or seventy-five yards of us—massing to attack—when one of the Air Force planes dropped the napalm on a direct hit on them. We began to cheer."[28]

Back at Camp Holloway, Bravo 2/7, hardly recovered from their ordeal at X-Ray, were told to prepare for a night assault into a hot landing zone. The cavalry rode to the rescue again, arriving at LZ Albany at 6:45 P.M. The fighting continued throughout the night. When the fighting finally ended the next morning, the surviving NVA withdrew from the battlefield, leaving behind 33 light machine guns, 112 rifles, four mortar tubes, 2 rocket launchers, and three heavy machine guns. The NVA lost 403 in battle and an estimated 150 wounded. The cavalry suffered 155 men killed and 120 wounded.

A postscript to the battle occurred late on the afternoon of November 20, when the South Vietnamese Airborne Brigade made contact with General Man's troops as they attempted to withdraw to the safety of Cambodia. The NVA had been slow to withdraw, impeded no doubt by their casualties and by American airstrikes. The South Vietnamese paratroopers had been inserted to cut them off. The American advisers gleefully described the "enemy in the open" target to the 24 artillery pieces on nearby fire bases. The American artillery ripped the NVA apart, leaving 127 bodies on the field. One of the advisers, then-Major Norman Schwarzkopf, described the enemy as ". . . tired and beaten and almost home free." The NVA were clearly surprised by a South Vietnamese force on their retreat route and Schwarzkopf recalls: "When we opened up with small arms and artillery they threw down their guns and ran for it"[29].

General Harry Kinnard, Commander of the 1st Cavalry Division, wanted to pursue the enemy into Cambodia and eliminate them forever but permission was denied. Colonel Hal Moore notes that soon after the battle of Ia Drang, "Orders came down . . . that we were never to speculate or suggest to any reporter that the North Vietnamese were using Cambodia as a sanctuary or that they were passing through Cambodia on their way to South Vietnam."[30]

General Giap is sometimes quoted as saying that he learned how to fight the Americans at Ia Drang. General Kinnard responds to this with typical Cavalry bluntness: "When General Giap says he learned how to fight Americans and our helicopters at the Ia Drang, that's bullshit! What he learned was that we were not going to chase him across a mythical line in the dirt."[31]

Privately, to his other generals, Giap acknowledged the soldierly skills and firepower of the Americans and conceded that the lesson of the Ia Drang was that it would require from seven to nine of his battalions to defeat one American battalion. Now, however, by the closing months of 1965, the southern Viet Cong were under enormous pressure. Their best unit, the 1st Viet Cong Regiment, had been thoroughly defeated by a U.S. Marine force only three months before. It was clear that the Americans were adopting more aggressive tactics. While still hoping to maintain some autonomy, the Viet Cong continued to plead for more of Hanoi's battalions. Giap moved warily, but he now felt safe in the knowledge that American political restrictions prevented Westmoreland from attacking his forces in Laos and Cambodia. Giap knew this restriction gave the NVA a tremendous advantage, which helped to offset their relative inferiority. They could safely marshal their forces in their Cambodian and Laotian base camps and then, at the time and place of their own choosing, cross South Vietnam's borders and attack its cities. Hanoi could thus set the tempo of the war. Although he might adopt aggressive *tactics* in fighting his individual battles in South Vietnam, General Westmoreland was left no option except to assume a strategically *defensive* posture in his conduct of the war at large. So Giap's armies continued to flow southward.[32]

Meanwhile, although hamstrung by these political restrictions, General Westmoreland's forces also continued to grow in numbers. He still lacked the troop strength necessary to form a fully impregnable defensive line along the Cambodian and Laotian borders to the west. Still, he had learned many things about how the Communists fought their battles. By the middle of 1966 after a year of fighting them, Westmoreland noted that North Vietnamese Army commanders were capable planners at the tactical level and always organized their attacks in three successive steps. First, they formulated a plan which invariably emphasized deception and/or some sort of trap. Second. they always undertook comprehensive reconnaissance of the selected battleground and the opposing forces in that area. Third, they always prepared for the battle by building up caches of weapons and supplies nearby. While preparing for the battle, their assault forces undertook meticulous rehearsals, using sand table maps and even practicing attacks on similar terrain. Only when all three steps had been completed did the NVA attack. General Westmoreland also knew that, if the NVA's plans and movements were discovered and parried before they could attack, their inflexible approach required them to start all over again from step one. Because of this "set-piece" approach to operations, General Westmoreland knew that the North Vietnamese Army, far more than other opponents, was hurt by aggressive preemptive operations known as "spoiling attacks," which disrupted their plans.[33]

Using this line of reasoning, General Westmoreland formulated his plan of battle. Rather than assuming a defensive posture around the coastal population centers as preferred by some, including the Marines, Westmoreland adopted a more aggressive approach. He established a loose screen of lightly defended outposts along South Vietnam's borders, which served as "trip wires" alerting him to the presence of NVA activity. The spoiling attacks and battles that he subsequently launched would be fought by the relative handful of American combat units available for such offensive actions and referred to as "maneuver battalions." These maneuver battalions, largely made up of the infantry battalions of the Army and the Marines, with a field strength of about 500 men each, represented a tiny portion of overall American strength. Even at its peak strength, America

Troops of the 4th Marine Regiment storm the high ground during Operation Hastings which blunted an attempt by Hanoi to invade directly southward through their mutual border. The NVA's 324B Division suffered 882 known casualties on this 28 day Operation which began on July 7, 1966.
Credit: National Archives and Records Administration

only fielded about 100 of these maneuver battalions. They would bear the brunt of the war as they attacked the North Vietnamese aggressor.[34]

Throughout 1966, American and allied forces successfully conducted a number of these spoiling attacks. In July, the Marines launched Operation Hastings in response to an attempt by the North Vietnamese 324B Division to move southward through the DMZ. Battered and bruised and suffering from the loss of almost 900 killed, the NVA were forced to withdraw by the end of the month. Much further south, in an area northwest of Saigon along the Cambodian border, a combined VC/NVA force attempted to deploy in October but suffered 1,100 casualties when U.S. Army and allied troops launched Operation Attleboro in reply.[35]

The war appeared to settle into this routine, with continuing North Vietnamese attempts to launch attacks against South Vietnam from within their "safe sanctuaries" in Laos and Cambodia and even the DMZ. While occasionally scoring very local wins in the opening moments of these attacks, Hanoi's troops invariably suffered badly at the hands of the Americans. In every single battle they were beaten, even by their own admission. Communist casualties soared. Nonetheless, Hanoi continued to throw its troops into battle.

8

Battles Along the Borders

The village of Khe Sanh is in the extreme northwest corner of South Vietnam in close proximity to the Laotian border and the DMZ, separating North and South Vietnam. Situated along Route 9, a major east-west roadway, Khe Sanh also lies astride a valley running roughly north-south through which flows the Rao Quan River. These two avenues, the roadway and the valley, provided ideal paths through which the North Vietnamese sought to move their troops into the South Vietnam battlefront.[1]

Three and one-half kilometers north of the village on a small plateau overlooking the river lay the Khe Sanh Combat Base, its dirt airstrip recently surfaced with aluminum matting to allow it to take both helicopters and fixed-wing aircraft. The little airstrip was defended by the hundred or so men of Bravo Company, 1st Battalion, 9th Marines.

In early 1967, the North Vietnamese were well on their way with the planning of their winter-spring offensive, which had as its ultimate goal the capture of Dong Ha, Quang Tri City, and Hue. One of their first obstacles was this small base at Khe Sanh. The NVA planned to first isolate the base through artillery attacks upon Khe Sanh's nearby fire support bases such as Camp Carrol, Con Thien, and Gio Linh. At the same time, the NVA planned to attack the helicopter and supply bases of Dong Ha and Phu Bai and also to cut Route 9, preventing reinforcements from coming to Khe Sanh overland from Cam Lo. The nearby Special Forces Camp at Lang Vei would also be attacked as a diversion. The coup de grace was to then be delivered by a regiment-sized ground assault by a unit from the 325C NVA Division, sweeping down through the valley, seizing the Khe Sanh Combat Base and its airfield. On April 24, 1967, a patrol from the Khe Sanh garrison prematurely

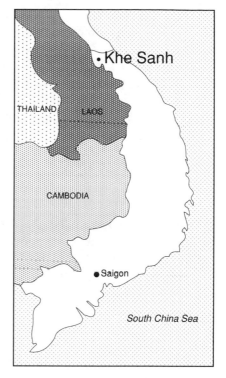

triggered the attack when it became engaged with an NVA force northwest of the base.

The Hill Fights

The Marines knew they would have to push the NVA off the dominating hill features that overlooked the airstrip. These hills, named after their height in meters, lay a short distance to the northwest of Khe Sanh itself. Coincidentally, two of the hills were of the same elevation. The Marines distinguished between the two by calling one of them 881 North (881N) and the other 881 South (881S); the third hill was Hill 861.

The assignment to seize these vital hills went to two battalions (the 2nd and 3rd Battalions) of the Third Marine Regiment. The Marines planned to attack the hills in sequence, the 2nd Battalion seizing Hill 861 first, then the 3rd Battalion would follow "in trace" before wheeling to the west and attacking 881S from the northeast. Meanwhile, the 2nd Battalion, its objective secure, would stand by as reinforcement. Once these first two hills were taken, the Marines of the 2nd Battalion would attack their third objective, 881N.

The first part of the operation went according to plan with the Marines' 2nd Battalion meeting only sporadic resistance while taking the high ground of Hill 861; its defenders were knocked senseless by the close air strikes conducted by the 1st Marine Aircraft Wing. But the attack on 881S was slowed when the NVA threw into its defense those troops earmarked for the attack on the Khe Sanh base. The battle raged for days until eventually, on May 2, Lieutenant Colonel Wilder's 3rd Battalion secured the hilltop. Lieutenant Colonel De Long's 2nd Battalion then pushed on to 881N. The NVA counterattacked on May 3, but the Marines bulled their way through to the crest and secured their final objective on the afternoon of May 5, 1967.

While the thousand or so Marines of the two battalions suffered 155 killed and 425 wounded, the NVA lost 940 confirmed killed in the battle, lost the strategic hills that overlooked the Khe Sanh Combat Base, and lost the very troops earmarked for the ground attack on the base. The Khe Sanh airstrip and its surrounding hills remained in American hands.

Dak To

By late 1967, intelligence reports confirmed that the 1st North Vietnamese Army Division, consisting of three infantry regiments (the 32nd, 66th, and 24th) as well as the 40th NVA artillery regiment, was occupying positions near Dak To in the central highlands of South Vietnam. This enemy force totaled some 4,300 troops.[2]

On November 2, 1967, Lt Colonel James H. Johnson's Fourth Battalion (4/503) of the 173rd Airborne Brigade was ordered into the attack. Reinforced with other battalions from the 173rd, heavy fighting took place around Hill 823 for a week before the 66th NVA Regiment was forced to retreat. While the 66th NVA Regiment (soon joined by the 32nd NVA Regiment) withdrew to its Cambodian safe sanctuary, the 2,000-strong 174th NVA Regiment took up positions to cover the withdrawal. A key feature of their defense was their fortified position atop Hill 875.

For the two previous days, the paratroopers of the 2nd Battalion (2/503) of the 173rd Airborne had moved along the jungle-covered hills of that part of the Cambodia-Laos border, uncovering enemy base camps. On November 19, Charlie, Delta, and Alpha Companies (Bravo had previously taken heavy casualties and its survivors had been scattered through the three remaining companies) began its move up Hill 875. They paused at its base, noting the steps cut into the hill. Charlie and Delta Companies assaulted the hill from two sides with Alpha following behind. In the ensuing firefight, the paratroopers of Delta Company took several casualties in nearing the summit. Their buddies of Alpha Company moved back down the hill to chop out a clearing for helicopters to remove the wounded. Before they could begin their mission of mercy, Alpha Company was attacked by a large force of NVA. The

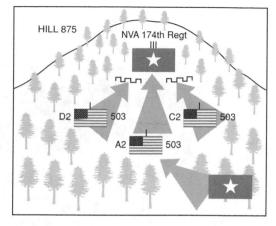

paratroopers near the hill's summit established a perimeter defense and Alpha company withdrew back up the hill. PFC Carlos Lozada and Spec4 John Steer covered their retreat with machine gun fire. They killed 20 of the enemy before PFC Lozada was killed and Spec4 Steer critically wounded. Their action allowed Alpha Company to join the others and establish a defense atop the hill.[3]

The paratroopers soon discovered that they had penetrated through the enemy's defensive line of heavy bunkers. It wasn't until Monday night that another battalion of paratroopers (4/503) was able to fight their way through the enemy's bunker system and reach them. On Tuesday, the NVA fired from the safety of their bunkers at the Americans, only 100 meters away. They also pounded the paratroopers with 82-mm mortars. Calamity also struck in the form of an errant U.S. Air Force bombing run that fell on American troops.

By late Wednesday, a landing zone at the base of the hill had finally been cut, and 140 of the wounded were evacuated while the much-needed supply of food, water, and ammunition arrived. Brigadier General Leo Schweiter also gave his paratroopers an unexpected offer. He asked them whether they would like to finish the assault themselves or prefer to withdraw and let a nearby unit from the 4th Infantry Division take over. The surviving paratroopers insisted on continuing the attack themselves. A witness recalled that the resupply seemed to put new life into the men and observed that the paratroopers ". . . talked eagerly of a final assault on the enemy bunkers." That evening, the Americans brought up flamethrowers and, finally, the 4th Battalion (4/503) of the 173rd Airborne Brigade succeeded in clearing out the NVA on Hill 875 on Thanksgiving Day, 1967.[4]

An NVA soldier surrenders to Marines of Alpha Company 1st Battalion, 9th Marine Regiment during Operation Prairie II which took place about 2,000 meters below the DMZ. The 46 day Operation in 1967 also resulted in 693 known NVA casualties.
Credit: National Archives and Records Administration

The 2nd Battalion suffered particularly. Of its 16 officers, eight were dead and another eight wounded. Of its 13 medics, only two were still alive. General Westmoreland described the fighting as ". . . exceeding in numbers, enemy losses, and ferocity even the Ia Drang campaign of 1965." Two-hundred and eight paratroopers died in the fighting, and more than 1,000 North Vietnamese Army soldiers were killed.[5]

The enemy had intended to draw American troops away from the population centers and defeat them in head-to-head battles. They accomplished neither objective. Hanoi had not fully comprehended the strategic mobility of American troops, which allowed them to rush to the borders, defeat the NVA, and then quickly redeploy back to their bases in the interior of the country. The North Vietnamese Army was badly defeated, losing several thousand of its best troops. Communist Colonel Tran Van Doc later defected, describing these border battles as ". . . useless and bloody."[6]

9

The Generals Argue

The Communists split along North-South lines on a number of matters. Typically, they split along these same lines concerning how to pursue the war. The bitter debate raged within the military hierarchy of North Vietnam for some years. On the one side was Defense Minister General Giap, Pham Van Dong, and Truong Chin, the very man who had converted Giap to Communism many years before. All were born in the North and, during the war with the French, duties kept them in the northern half of the country. They favored the building of a strong socialist economy in North Vietnam as a first priority. The struggle in South Vietnam, they believed, should be dealt with mainly by the southern Viet Cong until the time was eventually right for large scale North Vietnamese intervention.[1]

On the other side there was the Viet Cong commander in the South , General Nguyen Chi Thanh; his political ally, Le Duan, the most powerful Southern-born man in North Vietnam's Politburo, and Le Duc Tho. All of these men had been born in the South and, during the war against the French, served in the South. With all of them now deposed from their Southern

93

homes, they sought a quick end to their struggle. General Thanh, under constant attack by the armies of South Vietnam and America and forced to conduct his war in primitive conditions along the western border, was especially outspoken. These three argued that the first priority was to seize power in South Vietnam. To do so, they sought as much direct help from Hanoi as possible, including the use of conventional North Vietnamese Army divisions.

In 1958, Hanoi's Politburo had begun tilting toward direct intervention. This focus was confirmed as early as January 1959 when the Central Committee decided to launch its war. In July 1959, North Vietnam began infiltrating its Southern-born, Northern-trained troops into South Vietnam. In September 1960, North Vietnam publicly announced its support of the Communist insurgency in South Vietnam.[2]

The argument between Generals Thanh and Defense Minister Giap continued, with Giap dragging his feet and General Thanh urging direct confrontation. The argument became public by 1966 when the two of them chided each other's views on radio and in the newspapers using the most transparent of references to each other. The pro-Giap spokesman, who used the pseudonym "Cuu Long" (Mekong River), claimed that Thanh ignored the Viet Cong's part-time guerrillas in favor of conventional warfare with the Main Force Viet Cong units. He rebuked Thanh's belief that the guerrilla units were there simply to "provide services" rather than engage in combat. Thanh, under the guise of an authoritative military writer with the pseudonym of "Truong Son" (Long Mountain Range), berated Giap for his "bookish" approach to the war removed from the battlefield in the safety of Hanoi.[3]

Because of the superior firepower, mobility, communications, and training of U.S. troops, Giap estimated that NVA units needed to outnumber an American unit by a ratio of perhaps nine-to-one in order to win a given battle. North Vietnamese Army Colonel Huong Van Ba later recalled that Thanh argued ". . . that if we needed a division to fight against each American battalion we ought to just quit fighting the Americans because we'd never have enough men for it."[4]

General Thanh felt he was defeating the South Vietnamese Army in conventional battles in the early 1960s. When American troops arrived in large numbers in 1965, General Thanh felt he could continue to use similar tactics against the Americans and still win. But battles such as "Operation Starlite." in which his best regiment was thoroughly defeated by the U.S. Marines, forced him to reconsider. To continue to wage conventional battles, Thanh concluded, he would need the direct involvement of North

Vietnam's Army. Giap, though, was fearful of an American invasion into North Vietnam itself and was reluctant to allow his army too deep into South Vietnam for fear that they would be unable to return in time to defend his own national borders.[5]

Giap had good reason to be fearful. General Westmoreland had finalized plans to invade North Vietnam but was consistently refused permission to do so. With a different American president about to be elected, though, that permission might soon come. To prepare for it in August 1967, Westmoreland ordered the airstrip at Khe Sanh, a natural jumping-off point, to be improved so that it could take the cargo and troop transport aircraft he would need.

Westmoreland's invasion plan also called for an amphibious attack on North Vietnam. The U.S. Marines kept their skills honed for this eventuality by carrying out 23 amphibious assaults along the South Vietnamese coast in 1967. The average number of enemy killed in each of these operations was only 100, hardly worth the effort. These assaults, though, ensured that the Marines would be ready for the big attack should it ever be approved. For many years after, Marines would continue to speculate on what might have been. A U.S. Marine Colonel, wounded at Hue and awarded the Navy Cross, would later describe the possibility of ". . . landing a Marine Division, under massed naval gunfire and carrier air, north of the 17th parallel." He noted whimsically that, "There would have been the thunder of sandals going back *up* the Ho Chi Minh Trail."[6]

Tri-Thien-Hue

While the overall conduct of the war was run from Hanoi, the day-to-day responsibility for the war in South Vietnam was vested in the Central Office of South Vietnam (COSVN) and its military commander, General Thanh. In April 1966, however, the Communists transferred the responsibility of South Vietnam's two most northern provinces out of their Region Five headquarters in the central highlands and placed them into Region Four, which included provinces in the southern area of North Vietnam. The responsibility was effectively taken out of the hands of COSVN and placed directly under Hanoi's control. It was believed to be a part of North Vietnam's plan to annex the two provinces as part of a bargaining point in any future negotiations.[7]

These two provinces, Quang Tri and Thua Thien, would form the NVA's Tri-Thien-Hue front. From the city of Hue northward, the war was run directly by Hanoi with no Southern mediation whatsoever. In the words

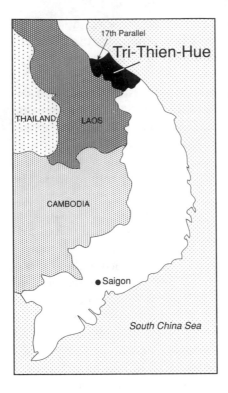

of Vu Ky Lan, the political commissar of the 164th NVA Regiment which fought near the DMZ: "Near the demilitarized zone, fighting did not depend on the local Party Committee. Only the Supreme Command in Hanoi had any say in the matter." In spite of the pleas of General Thanh, Defense Minister Giap argued against the large-scale deployment of NVA units to COSVN-controlled areas. Giap preferred to keep them closer to his border to quickly return to the defense of Hanoi if needed.[8]

Some analysts reduce the Thanh-Giap disagreement to one in which Thanh argued for conventional war and Giap argued for guerrilla war. A closer inspection, however, will show that Giap had no hesitancy to wage pitched, conventional battles. His Red River Delta campaign against the French, as well as the battle of Dien Bien Phu, show his willingness to fight conventional battles. Similarly, after 1966, Hanoi's Tri-Thien-Hue front was notable for its heavy and recurring use of North Vietnamese regulars in pitched battles. Giap was reluctant to use his troops in this manner in the more southern provinces, though, telling Thanh that he must use his own troops there. The essence of the Thanh-Giap argument was really, therefore, one of *how far south Hanoi was prepared to deploy the bulk of its conventional army divisions.*

In May 1967, the Politburo met again to discuss their war plans. The Communists were very concerned about the war's progress and reluctantly concluded that neither the Chinese nor the Soviets were prepared to risk a direct confrontation with the United States. They decided that their fate lay entirely in their own hands and they could expect little outside help. At the urging of the Southern faction, who were especially concerned about the continuing Viet Cong losses, they decided that the time had come for the General Offensive/General Uprising, which their ideology claimed to be the final stage of revolutionary warfare. They were prepared to gamble that the people of South Vietnam would rise up and turn against the South Vietnamese Government and their American allies if the offensive were launched.[9]

General Giap, however, had previously burned his fingers badly on this same matter when, in 1951, he'd been convinced that the time for the General Offensive/General Uprising against the *French* had come. Events soon proved, though, that he had underestimated French strength. Giap was subsequently soundly defeated by the French at the battles of Vinh-Yen, Mao-Khe, and Ninh-Binh, which were part of that premature offensive. Giap's forces suffered over 9,000 killed in those battles and the war against the French had been set back by years.[10]

No doubt influenced by this experience against the French in 1951 and by his current concerns about a possible American invasion, Giap now argued against the Southern proposal, saying that the time was not yet right for a head-to-head clash with the Americans throughout South Vietnam. In spite of his protests, though, the Southern faction had the numbers and won, no doubt to the delight of General Thanh. At last he would be able to throw the big Northern divisions against the Americans.

Defense Minister General Giap dutifully, though reluctantly, set about drawing up the plans as General Thanh suggested. In July, however, General Thanh died of wounds he'd received from a B-52 attack on his headquarters in the South. His death cleared the way for Giap to modify Thanh's original plan.[11]

Giap, forced to organize and implement a plan in which he had little faith, changed it to suit his own orthodoxy. He would proceed with the General Offensive/General Uprising attacks on the cities and civilian institutions, including airports and radio stations, using Viet Cong troops. In addition, though, in the Tri-Thien-Hue front which he controlled directly, he would implement a complementary plan with more limited objectives: the seizure of two provinces, about which he had more faith. Giap himself later described his plan that first required him ". . . to move a larger force toward Khe Sanh." The purpose of that force? Giap continued, saying that, "The force was going to be used for the third phase of the winter/spring offensive, called 'Second Wave.'" This attack force, which he assembled near Khe Sanh, would consist of his best divisions, heavily armed with artillery and tanks. Once this force was in position near Khe Sanh, he would then use other units to seize the city of Hue, capital of Thua Thien Province and a historic seat of government, and declare it the capital of a "neutral" southern-based government. Once Hue was successfully occupied, he planned to quickly proceed with the "Second Wave" attacks, in which his heavily-armed troops would pour through the DMZ and flood into the populated areas to the south, linking up with his units holding Hue. With the mountains to the south of Hue forming a natural defense line against counterattacks from the south and with thousands of U.S. troops held as hostages to prevent U.S. retaliatory air strikes, he would be ideally placed to begin negotiations.[12]

Giap drew up the plans and soon announced a seven-day Lunar New Year cease-fire from January 27 until February 3. Before long, though, confusion reigned when General Westmoreland reduced the cease-fire to 36 hours, forcing Giap to move the attack date forward. Because of the different calendars then in use, some Communist units believed they should attack on January 30, while other units interpreted Giap's orders to indicate January 31. Hanoi's official history admits that, "Those that started a day late faced troops who were already alerted, and had a more difficult time." Hue, though, was too important for a mistake and Giap was crystal clear to the commander there. Tran Bach Dang, who planned the attack on Saigon, observed that Hanoi gave the order to attack Hue, *specifying that they should do so according to the revised calendar,* and therefore ". . . got Hue to jump the gun by attacking eighteen hours before the designated time."[13]

Giap thus planned to attack Hue with nine full NVA battalions already inside the city by the early hours of January 31. Almost simultaneously, the whole country of South Vietnam would erupt with a thousand different and noisy Viet Cong attacks. The Viet Cong risked being slaughtered in their thousands but would cause chaos and confusion.

There was only one more item to be dealt with: Giap needed to have his troops massed near the DMZ in order to pour south . . . and he needed to deal with the small blocking force of U.S. Marines that stood in his way.[14]

10

Operation Scotland: The Battle for Khe Sanh

The 3rd Marine Regiment, which had seized the hills surrounding Khe Sanh back in May 1967, had moved on to other battlefields. Now the defense of the Khe Sanh area was in the hands of two battalions of the 26th Marine Regiment. To defend the Khe Sanh airstrip, they emplaced troops on Hills 881S and 861, hills the 3rd Marines had previously fought so hard for. They also placed a small security detachment on Hill 950 to protect the communication relay equipment there.[1]

On August 12, 1967, Colonel David E. Lownds took command of the 26th Marine Regiment, but the very next day, in response to the relative quiet in the Khe Sanh area, two of Lownds' companies (Kilo and Lima) were transferred to the 9th Marines for action elsewhere. Three weeks later, the remaining two companies of that battalion were also dispatched, leaving Colonel Lownds with only one battalion under his command.

The understrength Marines used their time well, improving the defenses of the base and its hill outposts. The task proved especially difficult on the hills. When the downpours of the monsoon rains struck, the trenchline encircling Hill 861 was completely washed away on one side of the hill and caved in on another in the ensuing flood. Because of the poor soil and the hill's steep slope, the new bunkers were constructed above ground; all materials had to be helicoptered from the base below. The Marines attempted to obtain logs from the canopied jungle surrounding them but this proved unsuccessful; the trees were so filled with shrapnel from the battles in May that chainsaws proved unworkable. Eventually, however, the Marines managed to provide every position on both 881S and 861 with overhead cover.

At the same time, the decision was made to upgrade the base's airstrip. Consisting simply of aluminum matting placed atop the bulldozed earth, the matting routinely buckled when the ground below it turned to mud in the monsoon rains. General Westmoreland wanted to upgrade the airstrip for two reasons. First, to improve the ability to resupply the Marines who defended that part of the country, but also for a planned attack into Laos and North Vietnam itself, once permission had been granted. Colonel Lownds closed the airstrip on August 17, and with heavy equipment,

Hill 861, one of Khe Sanh's hill outposts which formed the outer defense perimeter, 28 July 1967. These hill outposts were the scene of bloody hand-to-hand fighting as the Marines threw back NVA attacks bent on seizing this vital high ground which looked down upon the Khe Sanh base.
Credit: National Archives and Records Administration

including three 15-ton rock crushers, established a quarry one and one-half kilometers southwest of the base. Meanwhile, the Air Force, using parachutes and newly developed low-altitude extraction systems, delivered 2,350 tons of construction material. On October 27, the Seabees (Navy Construction Battalions) and Marine working parties completed their task and the airstrip was re-opened, now able to land huge cargo aircraft throughout the wet season.

Combat action remained relatively quiet in the area; fighting during that time from mid-July through the end of October resulted in 113 NVA and 10 Marines killed. In November, Major General Rathvon Tompkins took command of the 3rd Marine Division and visited the base, an occurrence that would soon be on an almost daily basis.

U.S. intelligence learned in late November that major NVA units were heading south through North Vietnam. Intelligence identified the 325C, the 304th, and the 320th NVA Divisions plus a regiment of the 324th moving toward South Vietnam.[2]

In December, enemy activity began to increase again, with the arrival of two of these divisions in the immediate vicinity of Khe Sanh. The companies on the hill outposts began receiving increasing amounts of sniper fire. NVA units began probing the perimeter defenses of the outposts and even of the base itself. Especially worrying was the NVA practice of cutting the defensive barbed wire in the outer defenses and then camouflaging and concealing the break, obviously in preparation for some future attack.

Before long, the North Vietnamese deployed their 325C Division in the area north of Hill 881N. A newcomer, the 304th NVA Division, an elite home guard unit from Hanoi and a veteran of Dien Bien Phu, crossed over from Laos and established positions southwest of Khe Sanh. In the DMZ within striking distance to the northeast was the 320th NVA Division. Supporting these divisions and also in the vicinity of Khe Sanh were elements of the 203rd NVA Armored Regiment, the 68th Artillery Regiment, and elements of the 164th Artillery Regiment. The Communists brought in 27 tanks, heavy 122-mm field guns, and at least one communication relay site.[3]

The Marines Reinforce Khe Sanh

With two enemy divisions in the immediate vicinity and two more within striking distance, the decision was made to bring the 3rd Battalion, now commanded by Lieutenant Colonel Harry Alderman, back to the Khe Sanh area. For the first time since August, Colonel Lownds was now able to mount a battalion-sized offensive operation. On December 21, the newly arrived battalion conducted a sweep of the area out to about five kilometers. While the five-day operation didn't result in contact with the enemy, the Marines found ample evidence, including freshly-dug foxholes and well-used trails, to confirm that the NVA were moving into the area in force.

One of the features of the Marine's defense was their use of "listening posts" to detect enemy movement. These listening posts typically consisted of only two or three Marines, the task taken in turns by the Marines defending that sector. Those assigned to the listening post would proceed out beyond the wire soon after darkness to a prearranged, but constantly changed, location to detect any enemy movement. Their assignment was not so much to engage the enemy but rather, to act as a "trip wire" to their parent unit. Such listening posts were typically placed in likely avenues of attack, such as along valleys or roads, to give an early warning of approaching danger.

At approximately 8:30 in the evening of January 2, Marines manning one such listening post just outside the main perimeter of the Khe Sanh base west of the airstrip reported that six unidentified persons were approaching the defensive wire. The six intruders made no attempt to hide their presence, but instead walked around brazenly "as if they owned the place." Second Lieutenant Nile Buffington led a squad of Marines (from Lima Company 3rd Battalion, 26th Marines) out to investigate. As the Marines cautiously approached, they could see that the six visitors were dressed as Marines. While no friendly patrols were supposed to be in that area, Lieutenant Buffington challenged them in English just to be on the safe side. Lieutenant Buffington thought he saw one of the six reaching for a hand grenade and the Marines opened fire, killing five of the unidentified men in the initial volley. The sixth man, though wounded, appeared to take some papers from a mapcase on the body of one of those killed and then disappeared into the darkness. The Marines, using a sentry dog, followed the blood trail for some distance in the direction of the nearby rock quarry but eventually gave up the chase.

Later, the Marines were astonished to discover that all five men they had killed were NVA officers, including a communications officer, an operations officer, and an NVA regimental commander, the enemy equivalent of Colonel Lownds himself. Colonel Lownds realized full well that the NVA would never risk officers of this seniority on a mere diversion. It suggested that there was something big in the offing and that, whatever it was, it would happen soon.[4]

In response to these events, Khe Sanh was reinforced by a third battalion (2/26) under the command of Lieutenant Colonel Francis Heath, Jr.

For the first time, Colonel Lownds now had all three battalions of his regiment under his operational control. It also marked the first time they would fight together since the battle of Iwo Jima in World War II.

The Khe Sanh Defense

Realizing full well that the dominating hills that surrounded the base and its airstrip were the key to the base's defense, Colonel Lownds immediately set about occupying several key features as well as reinforcing the ones already held. By January 21, he had deployed approximately two-thirds of his infantry strength to these key hill outposts that blocked the enemy's avenues of approach to the base. These five outposts, named after the height of the hills on which they were situated, were defended by small units ranging in size from the platoon (approximately 30 men) on Hill 950 to the three reinforced companies (approximately 400 men) who defended Hill 558.[5]

The remaining one-third of his infantry formed a perimeter defense encircling the base itself. Inside that perimeter, he could call on the support of four howitzer batteries, one battery of 4.2-inch mortars, five M-48 tanks, and two platoons of Ontos antitank vehicles. Because Khe Sanh was his logistic and administrative base for the battle, about 80% of the total personnel under his command were at the base itself. The big 175-mm guns at Camp Carrol and the Rockpile had sufficient range to also be used in Khe Sahn's defense.

Hill 881N

The next phase of the battle for Khe Sanh began unfolding when, on January 17, a Marine reconnaissance team operating on a ridgeline 700 meters southwest of Hill 881N clashed with an NVA unit. In the ensuing firefight, the team leader and the radio man were both killed. While their bodies were recovered, the radio and the coded frequency card were missing. Two days later, a platoon from nearby Hill 881S was sent to the area to search the area for the missing items. Taken under fire by an NVA platoon, the Marines returned fire and then pulled back, allowing artillery to pound the NVA positions.

The next morning, January 20, the Marines occupying 881S dispatched a much stronger force under the command of Captain William Dabney. Included on the patrol was another reconnaissance team, planning to conceal their movement back onto the ridge by the ruse of simply tagging along on the patrol and then discreetly fading into the bush when they reached the site and then staying there when the rest of the patrol withdrew.

Captain Dabney's men moved off Hill 881S, descending into a valley, before beginning the climb back up onto 881N. Two ridgelines led up the slope, separated by about 500 meters. Captain Dabney planned to send one of his platoons up the right-hand ridgeline while the other two proceeded up the one on the left. After some initial slow-going caused by dense fog, the two elements began ascending the hill. Pausing partway up the hill to consolidate, the Marines fired a precautionary salvo of artillery ahead of them before moving on to the next terrain feature, a stretch of high ground with four small mounds running from left to right directly in front of them. Third Platoon, on the right, was suddenly struck by a withering barrage of rifle, rocket-propelled grenade (RPG), and heavy machine gun fire from the mounds up ahead. Captain Dabney ordered them to hold up their advance while he rained artillery on the enemy while simultaneously moving the two platoons on the left forward to get their flanking fire onto the enemy. They soon discovered that those innocent-looking mounds were a small part of a heavily fortified defensive line and, taking fire from them and from other positions hidden in nearby hills, the Marines soon had taken 20 casualties themselves.

Meanwhile, the platoon on the right charged forward as soon as the artillery had lifted and, urged on by their platoon commander, Second Lieutenant Thomas Brindley, took the crest of the hill. In the course of the brief battle several Marines were killed, including Lieutenant Brindley. By the time the objective was taken, the senior man in the platoon was its radio man, a corporal, who temporarily assumed command. Captain Dabney realized this summit was vital. So, leaving one platoon on the left to serve as a base of fire, he led the other platoon back down the ridge and then proceeded back up the right-hand ridgeline to join the Marines at the top. Having cracked the NVA defensive line, the Marines added the weight of artillery, mortar fire, and recoilless rifle fire from their base on 881S and from Khe Sanh itself. The battle raged throughout the afternoon, claiming the commander of 2nd Platoon, Second Lieutenant Michael Thomas, among those killed.

Meanwhile, back at the Khe Sanh Base, sentries observed an NVA soldier brandishing an AK47 assault rifle in one hand and a white flag in the other off the eastern end of the runway at about 2:00 P.M. Under the watchful eyes of fellow Marines, a team of Marines went out to accept the soldier's surrender. The soldier turned out to be the commanding officer of the 14th Antiaircraft Company, 95C Regiment, 325C NVA Division. Immediately questioned, the officer showed no reluctance in telling everything he knew of the NVA plans. He explained that the NVA planned to initiate their assault on Khe Sanh with attacks on Hills 881S and 861 scheduled for that very same night. Once these objectives were seized, the NVA would be able to fire directly down onto the base below, pinning its inhabitants down. The plan then called for diversionary attacks on the northern and western sector of Khe Sanh's defenses while the main thrust came from the east. The terrain in this eastern sector dropped away sharply to the river below. While the NVA would have to attack uphill, the steep slope was heavily wooded and would allow them to be almost on top of the Marines' positions before they were detected. This assault was to be conducted by a regiment of the 304th NVA Division. They would seize the airstrip, and they believed, the Marine defense of Khe Sanh would then collapse.

While the NVA officer was being interrogated, the Marines fighting their way up 881N knew that the balance had tipped in their favor and asked for reinforcements to finish off the enemy. Colonel Lownds, alerted to the impending attacks scheduled for that night, refused the request and ordered the Marines to break off the attack and return to their defensive positions on Hill 881S. The three platoons had suffered seven killed and thirty-five wounded but they had killed 103 NVA. Reluctantly, the Marines trudged back down the ridges and then back up into their positions on 881S.

Back at their defensive positions, the Marines on Hills 881S and 861 were placed on full alert in their trenches and their bunkers, awaiting the enemy attack. As forewarned, shortly after midnight, the NVA commenced a mortar barrage on Hill 861 that lasted half an hour. Next came a salvo of rifle, machine gun, and rocket-propelled grenades. Preceded by specially trained sappers, whose job it was to breach the defensive wire with long pole-like explosives called bangalore torpedoes, approximately 300 NVA assaulted the Marines positions. In brutal close range combat, the Marines were able to stop the NVA completely, except for one sector where the NVA were able to overrun and penetrate the Marines' lines. Throughout the battle, the NVA assault commander could be heard screaming out for his reserves, frantically trying to get them to exploit the opportunity his assault troops had created. The reserves never appeared.

Colonel Lownds, leaving the NVA assault troops to be dealt with by the hills' own defenses, marshaled his artillery and airstrikes onto likely areas from which the NVA would assemble their reserve units. While the NVA assault troops were dying at the hands of Marine riflemen, the NVA reserve troops were being crushed under an avalanche of artillery and bombs in the near distance. With no reserves with which to exploit their momentary success in breaching the Marine wire, the NVA were soon subjected to a punishing Marine counterattack, reestablishing their lines and then eliminating the NVA intruders.

Four Marines were killed defending their positions on Hill 861; 47 NVA bodies lay strewn over the hill they had sought to seize. Countless other NVA bodies lay out in the jungle surrounding the hill; the stench from their decaying corpses was so strong that, for several days, the Marines on Hill 861 were forced to wear gas masks.

The attack on Hill 881S never happened. A combination of the casualties inflicted by Captain Dabney's men on the NVA that afternoon, plus the effect of Colonel Lownds' artillery concentrations, were the probable explanation. For whatever reason, this situation left the men on 881S free to assist their comrades fighting on Hill 861. The mortar section, for example, fired 680 rounds of 81-mm mortars against the attackers of Hill 861.

Bombardment of the Base

Soon after the battle at Hill 861 ceased, the NVA unleashed a massive artillery, mortar, and rocket attack onto the base itself. This attack caused extensive damage, including a "lucky hit" on the base's largest ammo dump. The explosions wreaked enormous destruction; the resulting fire caused rounds to "cook off" and explode even 48 hours later. Simultaneously, the NVA launched an attack on the nearby Khe Sanh village. Guarded only by a local militia unit and a Combined Action unit, the defenders managed to beat off two major attacks by the 304th NVA Division. With artillery support from the base and supporting airstrikes, the NVA suffered heavy casualties. The American adviser counted 123 NVA bodies on or around the barbed wire. Colonel Lownds decided to evacuate the village to the relative security of the base. Later that same evening, along the western sector, a platoon of NVA was observed crawling toward the defensive wire encircling the base. The Marines opened fire, killing 14 of the enemy and forcing the others to flee.

With three full NVA divisions identified in the area, General Westmoreland conferred with Marine General Cushman. They both agreed that the position at Khe Sanh must be held. First, it allowed the Marines to block any major NVA thrusts into South Vietnam. The Marines, lacking the helicopters to support more mobile operations, had little option except to maintain a fixed position there. Second, as Westmoreland noted, the NVA's ". . . emergence from hiding afforded an opportunity to bring to battle a foe for whom elusiveness was the name of the game." Elsewhere throughout

Vietnam, much time and energy were spent trying to locate the enemy in order to attack him. Here, the enemy was present in huge numbers and, especially when he massed his troops to attack one of the Marine positions, provided ideal targets for air and artillery strikes.[6]

Another battalion (1/9) of Marines was dispatched to Khe Sanh on January 22 to further strengthen the base's defenses. Colonel Lownds was still concerned about the western sector, where the NVA officers had been killed while reconnoitering and where, only days ago, a platoon of NVA had tested the defenses. Lownds placed this newly arrived battalion in position to block any attacks on Khe Sanh from that direction. They moved overland to the nearby rock quarry and set up a kidney-shaped defensive perimeter around it. The battalion commander, Lieutenant Colonel John Mitchell, established his command post on a small hill. This battalion, while forming a separate defensive perimeter to that of Khe Sanh itself, effectively blocked any approach from the west.

Five days later, Colonel Lownds also gained the 318 men of the 37th South Vietnamese Army Ranger Battalion. Mindful of the intelligence report from the NVA deserter that the main assault was to come from the wooded area to the east, Colonel Lownds instructed his Marines to prepare positions for the new arrivals 200 meters outside the existing Marine lines in the eastern sector. The South Vietnamese Army Rangers thus formed an outer defense in that area. Any NVA coming from that direction would now need to penetrate two lines of defense.

Meanwhile, far away in a labyrinth of U.S. Army offices, Lieutenant Bruce Jones, an Army intelligence officer, noted fresh reports of a heavy traffic of radio transmissions coming from a site just over the border in Laos believed to be the headquarters of the NVA forces besieging Khe Sanh. One strike of B-52s was ordered against the site. Then, because a second flight of B-52s suddenly became "available" and because Jones knew a sec-

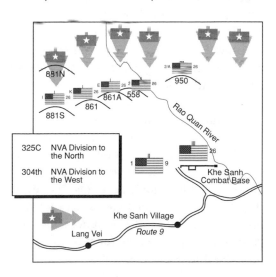

ond strike was not the usual way the U.S. operated, he urged an additional attack just in case the NVA escaped the first one and attempted to "set up shop" again. On January 30, the radio signals abruptly stopped after B-52s dropped an additional 1,350 tons of bombs on the NVA headquarters. The next day, while Tet erupted with a fury up and down the country, Khe Sanh remained quiet.[7]

Most worrisome of the Tet attacks was the Communists' seizure of Hue City just to the south. Early reports were confused, but it began to look like the Communists were very intent on holding it. That battle was of vital interest to the Marines at Khe Sanh, and it soon held a very personal interest to Colonel Lownds. His son-in-law, Captain George R. Christmas, would lead a company of Marines in the attacks against the Communist troops there.

The Hill Outposts . . . Again

In the early morning hours of February 3, a battalion of the 325C NVA Division tried again to knock the Marines off of Hill 861A. Echo Company received the brunt of the attack with a barrage of 82-mm mortars raining down on the hill while rocket-propelled grenades sought out the crew-served weapons defending the hill. Under cover of this barrage, NVA sappers crept up to place bangalore torpedoes, blowing laneways through the hill's barbed-wire defenses. The NVA then swarmed over 1st Platoon's positions, forcing them to pull back to a secondary line of defense. Captain Breeding ordered the hill to be saturated with tear gas to disorient the attackers, but this failed to have the desired effect. The NVA apparently had fired themselves up with drugs prior to the attack. Instead of pursuing their momentary advantage, though, the NVA went on a souvenir hunt, focusing their attention on paperback novels and magazines in the Marines' bunkers and trenches.

While the NVA hesitated, the Marines organized a hasty counterattack to reclaim their positions. Captain Breeding, who had come up from the ranks and was a veteran of the Korean War, threw his Marines into both sides of the breach. The young Marines poured over the NVA, launching into them with rifles, bayonets, and their trademark "Ka-bar" fighting knives. When fighting at close range in the dark, a favorite technique was for the Marines to toss their grenades forward, then turn away from the blast, hunch up, and allow the shrapnel to be absorbed into their armored flak jackets. The fight went on for about a half an hour. Captain Breeding said later that the NVA ". . . didn't know how to cope with it . . . we walked all over them." As the NVA retreated, they were taken under fire by 106-mm recoilless rifles on Hill 558. The NVA officers managed to rally their troops for another attempt, but it was quickly stopped altogether.

While the Marine riflemen, with the support of their fellow Marines on the nearby hills, dealt with the attackers, Colonel Lownds again directed the bulk of the artillery concentrations and radar-directed bombing missions onto those areas where the NVA were marshaling their reserve troops in anticipation of a follow-up attack.

The fight on Hill 861 left seven Marines killed and thirty-five wounded. The NVA suffered 109 known to be killed, with many bodies still scattered around the Marine perimeter.

Lang Vei

Just eight kilometers to the west of Khe Sanh lay the American Special Forces compound at Lang Vei, manned by 22 Americans and 400 South Vietnamese. Before the NVA moved into the area in such force, the compound served as a base for Special Forces reconnaissance missions along the Ho Chi Minh Trail. Now, with 40,000 NVA soldiers in the surrounding area, the Special Forces' lightly armed troops were almost entirely dependent on the support of nearby Khe Sanh.

On February 7, the NVA tried another ploy in their attempt to take the Marine base at Khe Sanh. Using nine Soviet-built PT-76 tanks, flamethrowers, and tear gas, a battalion of the 66th Regiment, 304th NVA Division, launched an attack on the Special Forces compound at Lang Vei. As confirmed by documents found on an NVA officer killed in the battle, the NVA planned to destroy the base and ambush any relieving Marine force, drawing them into an ambush far from their fortified positions.

When the Communists attacked, the defenders at Lang Vei managed to knock out at least one, and probably two, of the Soviet-built tanks. Soon, however, the NVA were swarming over the compound. As two NVA tanks rumbled toward the command center, Lieutenant Colonel Daniel F. Schungel , who was visiting the base on an inspection tour, charged toward the tanks armed only with hand grenades. He deposited the grenades under the belly of the lead tank and, seconds after his grenades exploded, the tank was also hit by a shoulder-fired antitank rocket. Flames shot forth from the tank's hatches. The crew of the other NVA tank, now stalled, crawled out of their vehicle and were killed one by one by the defenders. In spite of this spirited defense, the NVA were soon in virtual possession of the compound. Within two hours, the surviving defenders were forced to seal themselves into their bunkers and request artillery fire onto their own compound.[8]

While it was no doubt an agonizing decision for Colonel Lownds, there appeared to be no viable rescue option available. To go to the relief of Lang Vei using Route 9 would have been suicidal, just what the NVA were hoping for. Going overland through the mountains would have taken too long. Also, the NVA had placed their armor onto the only landing zones suitable for a helicopters. A helicopter assault onto a defended landing zone in the face of enemy armor was clearly not feasible. Overriding the whole matter was the simple fact that the NVA greatly outnumbered any forces available to Colonel Lownds. Although he saturated the Lang Vei area with a massive artillery barrage as requested, Colonel Lownds did not dispatch a relief force of ground troops.

At first light, the survivors of Lang Vei managed to work their way 500 meters to the east where, later that same day, Marine helicopters picked them up while gunships circled overhead. Those indigenous troops who couldn't get onboard the helicopters marched overland to the Khe Sanh Base.

Action Near the Rock Quarry

While the battle at Lang Vei was happening, a reinforced battalion, perhaps 500 men, of the 101D Regiment, 325C NVA Division, launched a ground attack against the 30 or so Marines manning a small outpost near the 9th Marines' positions around the rock quarry. Pinning the nearby 9th Marines down with some 350 rounds of mortar fire, the NVA breached the outpost's barbed wire by throwing canvas over the top and then throwing themselves on top of the wire, or by using explosive charges to blow laneways free. The NVA then poured into the Marines' positions, attacking them with satchel charges and RPGs. The Marines at the outpost, led by their platoon commander, Second Lieutenant Terence Roach, counterattacked down their trenchline, attempting to throw the NVA off their hill. The outnumbered Marines were pushed back and Lieutenant Roach was mortally wounded in the action.

At 7:30 the next morning, the commander of Alpha Company, Captain Henry Radcliffe, personally led another platoon in a frontal assault against the NVA battalion to retake the hill. With massive fire support including 90-mm tank fire and air strikes on the hill's reverse slopes, it took only 15 minutes for the Marines to reclaim the summit. Twenty-one Marines had been killed defending the outpost and twenty-six were wounded. NVA losses numbered 150 killed. Back at the base, five Marines had been killed and six wounded.

Incoming and Outgoing

In addition to the large numbers of smaller 60-mm and 82-mm mortars ranged against them, the Marines faced large numbers of 122-mm rockets and heavy NVA artillery, 130-mm and 152-mm guns. These heavy artillery pieces, operating from caves in Co Roc mountain just over the border in Laos were out of the range of Khe Sanh's batteries. Some of the NVA artillery was mounted on railway tracks so that they could be wheeled out of their protective caves, fired, and then wheeled back into safety. Also, the NVA maintained another artillery battery at a location 305 degrees west-northwest of Khe Sanh near a supply artery.

The rockets were particularly interesting. Because of their flight characteristics, they were quite accurate in not missing to the left or right of where they were aimed. On the other hand, their arcing trajectory often caused them to overshoot or undershoot a target. Because of this inaccuracy, and because the main target was the base's airstrip, the NVA were forced to use their rockets so that they be launched somewhere along the long axis of the runway. Since the runway ran from west to east, the NVA were therefore forced to locate their batteries to the east or west of Khe Sanh. Placing the rocket launchers to the east would have put them within range of the 175-mm batteries from Camp Carroll. The NVA therefore had little choice but to locate them to the west of the base. While Hill 881S provided the best vantage point to the west, the Marines were claiming it as their own. The NVA were forced to use Hill 881N as their rocket site, emplacing hundreds of launchers there. Although Hill 861 blocked their view of Khe Sanh, the NVA nonetheless fired off about 5,000 122-mm rockets at the Marine base throughout the battle.

The Marines on Hill 881S also helped the Khe Sanh Base by warning them of enemy rocket and artillery attacks. The Marines were able to observe directly the rockets arcing up from the reverse slope of Hill 881N, and they could often see the muzzle flashes coming from the guns on Co Roc mountain. While they couldn't see the guns firing from "305," they could hear the rounds roaring overhead on their way to the base and so could still give advance warning. When they saw or heard the firing, the Marines on Hill 881S radioed through to Khe Sanh where a signal (a truck horn mounted on a pole) would be sounded giving the base from 5 seconds to 18 seconds warning before the shell would crash home. While their bunkers were protection against the mortar rounds, the available materials prevented the Marines from building anything sufficient to stop the bigger shells. At one point, Colonel Lownds decided to build a new command bunker. He asked the engineers what would be required to withstand a 122-mm rocket. Taking no chances, Lownds doubled the roof strength. The day before he was to occupy the bunker, it was hit by a 152-mm round from Co Roc which penetrated right through its roof. Some of the NVA shells were so large that even "dud" shells, which failed to explode, penetrated four feet into the ground.

Hill 881S was so important that it received the lion's share of enemy shells, especially the heavier caliber ones. Forty Marines were killed and 150 wounded on Hill 881S. A nearby enemy position, referred to as the "Horseshoe" was particularly troublesome to the men on Hill 881S. The NVA most likely used a technique they had used at Dien Bien Phu where they constructed mortar positions deep underground and fired the rounds through long shafts, sometime as long as 50 feet, leading to the surface. These positions could not alter their point of aim because of limitations imposed by the angle and deflection of the long shaft. This technique worked well for small, stationary targets, however, and the terrain of Hill 881S forced the Marines into such a compact area.

In spite of the enemy shelling, Khe Sanh's defenders continued to give better than they got. For every round of incoming fire , the Marine gunners fired ten in reply. Throughout the whole battle, only three of Khe Sanh's 46 artillery pieces were destroyed. The Marine artillery was especially effective against NVA ground attacks. The Marines' Fire Support Coordination Center controlled a highly complex and effective defensive fire plan. When the NVA attacked, the Marines cut off the lead battalion by massive artillery barrages on either side and on the rear of the attackers. Meanwhile, a fourth artillery battery walked its barrage up and back this three-sided box, creating a pistonlike action. To deal with any reserves, the Army's big 175-mm artillery batteries directed their fire 500 meters on either side of this box, rolling their barrage into the primary box and then back out again in an accordionlike movement. Meanwhile, continuous airstrikes hit the rear or "third side" of this box, preventing any escape.

During the day, the sky over Khe Sanh was filled with Navy, Marine, and Air Force F-4 Phantoms; Marine and Navy A-6 Intruders, A-4 Skyhawks, and F-8 Crusaders; and Air Force F-105 Thunderchiefs and F-100 Super Sabers. South Vietnamese A-1 Skyraiders could also be seen. Often the traffic was so heavy that the planes were put into holding patterns extending up to 35,000 feet. The planes queued up to drop their bombs and napalm under the direction of a tactical air controller who circled the area in a spotter plane.

No doubt one of the most impressive and awesome sights was that of the B-52 attacks called "arc-light" missions. With each B-52 carrying a 27-ton payload consisting of a mixture of 108 mixed 500-pound and 750-pound bombs, a flight of several bombers was able to do massive damage to the enemy. Directed onto target by radar while flying at 30,000 feet, the first sign of their presence was the sound of the huge bombs crashing to earth. Knowing that once the bombing stopped, any surviving NVA typically emerged from their bunkers and staggered around the area for several minutes, stunned and bleeding from the concussion, the Khe Sanh artillery batteries frequently put a massed artillery barrage into the strike area ten minutes to fifteen minutes after the B-52s had gone.

The Marines, while admittedly absorbing some punishing blows from the NVA, were certainly meting out a far more devastating counterpunch, but this fact was rarely reported in the United States. The frustration caused by this lack of favorable reporting was summed up by a U.S. Marine Colonel at nearby Da Nang interviewed during the battle. He had just read a letter from his wife and was flushed with anger. His wife wrote that some neighbors and stateside editorial writers couldn't understand why Marine Corps units hung on at Khe Sahn, getting pounded day after day by artillery, mortar and rocket fire. "Damn it," said the colonel. "For every round they drop on us, we drop a whole planeload of bombs on them." That wasn't the message the journalists were giving to their audiences and it was clearly frustrating to the Marines.[9]

The Marines' counterpunch was not limited to air strikes and artillery, however. Their ground defense of the base was also lethal. Typical of this was the instance when Second Lieutenant Daniel McGravey led a platoon (from D/1/26) of Marines in assaulting an NVA antiaircraft position too close for the Marines' comfort. The Marines killed several of the NVA and captured both the NVA gunner and his antiaircraft gun.

NVA Command Headquarters

While the fighting at Khe Sanh raged, the NVA established a headquarters in the limestone caves of the DMZ, just northwest of the Marines' base. U.S. intelligence observed heavy vehicular traffic in the vicinity and a bank of antennas at the cave's entrance. Captured Communist soldiers reported General Giap was there, directing the war personally and no doubt planning to be present for his hoped-for victory. Hit by American bombers repeatedly during February, the Seventh Air Force managed to close off the cave's entrance briefly with falling rocks and debris, effectively sealing the NVA high command up for a period of time.[10]

Commenting on the speculation about whether General Giap had entered the battle area to direct the fighting, General Phillip Davidson concedes that history may never know. Noting several supporting clues, such as Giap's absence from public view which coincided with the allegations of his presence near the battle, General Davidson concludes that, ". . . the best guess is that Giap was in the cave."[11]

Supplying the Marines

The airborne resupply mission to keep Khe Sanh and its hill outposts supplied throughout the battle were truly Herculean. While official figures vary, the Air Force claims to have delivered over 12,000 tons of supplies to Khe Sanh during the battle. Approximately two-thirds of this total was delivered by parachute or low-altitude extraction, the plane skimming the runway while the cargo was pushed out the ramp with a small parachute acting as a brake on the pallet. Also, Marine helicopters from the 1st Marine Aircraft Wing carried over 4,600 tons of cargo. The supplies delivered by helicopter direct from Dong Ha to the hill outposts, estimated to account for about three-fourths of the helicopter tonnage, was not included in this total.

The 9th Marine Regiment was responsible for the security of the parachute drop zone after Colonel Lownds moved it out of the base itself for fear that the falling debris would cause accidental casualties among his men. While engineers swept the area for mines or boobytraps the NVA may have established during the night, the 9th Marines patrolled the periphery of the zone to flush out any enemy who might want to disrupt the collection of the paradrops.

In addition to the rumblings of bombs striking their foes and the warm feeling of food in their bellies, the Marines occasionally received other reminders of the support given them by the Navy, Marine, and Air Force pilots overhead. On one occasion, Marine defenders looked up to see Major William Loftus parachuting down to them after bailing out of his battle-damaged A-4 fighter-bomber, which crashed into the surrounding jungle in a huge fireball. The major, unhurt, sheepishly accepted the help of Lieutenant Dillon and his men in extricating him from the barbed-wire in which he'd become entangled.

The Final Attempt

Further south at Hue City, Hanoi's troops were being forced into an ever-shrinking defensive pocket. Their commander asked for permission to withdraw, but Hanoi refused the request. With their troops at Hue clearly unable to hold on for much longer and the monsoons about to end, the NVA at Khe Sanh tried a desperate gamble. Even though they had failed to knock the Marines off their hill defenses, the NVA decided to proceed with the next phase, a direct ground assault on the base itself.

Shortly after noon on February 21, the NVA fired 350 rounds of artillery, mortar, rocket, and recoilless rifle fire into the eastern sector, manned by the 37th South Vietnamese Army Rangers. Approximately 100 NVA then probed the lines of the Rangers but made no concerted attempt to get close. Presumably, they were only testing the defenses. They then withdrew by 3:00 P.M. Results of this action were unclear. The Rangers believed that, together with the Marines' supporting artillery, they may have killed 20 to 25 of the enemy.

On February 29, intelligence indicated that the NVA were moving large numbers of troops into attack positions, especially into the eastern sector where the enemy probe had recently occurred. Khe Sanh's Fire Support Coordination Center used every weapon available to it, from artillery and mortars through to B-52 bombers, to saturate the enemy's attack routes. At 9:30 P.M., a battalion of the 304th NVA Division attempted a ground assault against the eastern sector but was cut down by the massive firepower arrayed against it, even before it got to the barbed-wire defenses. The NVA launched a second attempt with another battalion two hours later, and a third at 3:15 A.M. the next day. Both of these also failed to reach the wire. The next day, a cursory search of one small section disclosed 78 NVA bodies, huddled in three successive assault trenches, their bodies riddled with holes from artillery airbursts.

As before, the real carnage took place in the distant jungle, however. Local Montagnard tribesmen later told of finding groups of NVA dead, in formations of 200 to 500 at a time, stacked in rows along the various avenues of approach to the Khe Sanh base. Whole units of NVA troops were destroyed on the march.

The Enemy Withdraws

By mid-March, Marine intelligence noted that the Headquarters of the 325C NVA Division had withdrawn to Laos. Soon the 95C and the 101D

Regiments also withdrew. Before long, the 304th NVA Division withdrew several kilometers to the southwest.

While Khe Sanh's artillery fired some 158,891 rounds during the battle, at times they had too much ammunition and safe stowage became a problem. One such time occurred in mid-March. The decision was made to use up the ammunition rather than leave it lying around where it could pose a hazard. So on March 17, St. Patrick's Day, grinning Marines fired 90 rounds of harmless green smoke projectiles onto known positions, such as 881N, where the luckless NVA still remained. The serious business of settling old scores would happen soon enough.

On March 30, the Marines launched a daring raid against a 700-meter-long series of NVA trenches, bunkers, and fighting holes. This NVA position, less than a kilometer from Khe Sanh and occupied by a full battalion of enemy troops, held special significance to the Marines. On February 25, a patrol of Marines from Bravo Company 1/26 happened on this complex and suffered 26 killed in the ensuing firefight. Now, at 8:00 A.M. one month later, Captain Pipe was about to lead an attack by that same Marine company against the same NVA battalion. The attack was closely coordinated with the artillery units and used a variation of their defensive plan.

The enemy position was hit by a barrage of Marine artillery behind and to the right and left, again forming a three-sided box. Meanwhile, a secondary box, consisting of airstrikes and rolling barrages from Army 175-mm artillery ensured the enemy would receive no assistance from supporting units. The Marines moved into assault positions and then advanced, directly behind a rolling barrage. While they advanced, the entire "box" advanced as well. The Marines then shifted their artillery fire to suppress any possible NVA artillery or mortar fire. The two platoons of Marines, bayonets fixed, then assaulted the final few meters into the NVA defenses. The stunned NVA were taken completely by surprise and, while one Marine platoon kept the enemy pinned down with rifle and machine gun fire, the other Marines used flamethrowers and explosives to attack the enemy bunkers and trenches methodically. The Marines blasted and burned the enemy positions, one by one, for the next three hours, killing 115 of the enemy.

The battle for Khe Sanh, known to the Marines as Operation Scotland, concluded on March 31. A total of 1,602 enemy bodies were actually counted in the immediate defensive areas, but estimates of the total enemy casualties in the surrounding area were between 10,000 and 15,000. The NVA had been prevented from seizing the base and then pouring through the DMZ to relieve and reinforce their comrades at Hue. Two of the best NVA divisions had been destroyed in the process.

The following day, an NVA soldier managed to surrender to the Marines on Hill 881S. Captain William Dabney described the soldier as ". . . an impressive man, almost six feet tall, healthy looking, and of imposing physique." But a Marine jet suddenly roared overhead and Captain Dabney was shocked by the man's sudden transformation. "He literally lost control of himself—his muscles, his eyes, even his bowels—and fell in a quivering heap to the bottom of the trench." The man had been psychologically destroyed by the terrible destruction wrought on him and his comrades by American aircraft during the preceding weeks.[12]

The combined Army-Marine mission to relieve Khe Sanh, dubbed Operation Pegasus, commenced on April 1. The 1st Cavalry Division (Airmobile) as well as two battalions of the 1st Marine Regiment and one battalion of the 3rd Marine Regiment arrived in the region. The operation concluded on April 16, 1968. In that two-week period, an additional 1,304 NVA were killed and 21 captured. Fifty-one Marines were killed; 41 U.S. Army troops were killed; and 33 South Vietnamese troops were killed.

On March 31, President Johnson had announced an end to air strikes into North Vietnam above the 20th parallel (about 250 miles north of the DMZ), enabling thousands of NVA troops previously assigned to road repair to shift their efforts further south. These NVA engineers soon constructed a network of arteries that effectively bypassed the base at Khe Sanh. The Marines couldn't hope to counter each of these new arteries with fixed defenses since these countermeasures were deemed neither efficient nor desirable. The arrival of the Army's 1st Air Cavalry Division and 101st Airborne Division increased air mobility and allowed General Cushman to use the more mobile tactics he'd always preferred. Because of these factors, on June 11, General Westmoreland approved the recommendation of Generals Rosson and Cushman to raze the Khe Sanh base.

While abandonment of the base was queried and debated by the public, it made little difference to the Marines. It had always been just another assignment. Khe Sanh's commander, Colonel David Lownds, later expressed this indifference. "Marines have one funny habit," he said. "That is that they do what the Hell they're told to do. If the decision is made by people above me that it [a permanent base at Khe Sanh] is not required, I don't have any feeling about that either way. I was told to go there; I was told to stay there. I went there; I stayed there. When they told me to come out, I came out."[13]

While fully agreeing that Khe Sanh had lost its previous tactical importance, the blood spilled in its defense ensured that the Khe Sanh Combat Base would always have an emotional significance to the U.S. Marine Corps. Before finally closing the base the Marines ensured that Hanoi's troops would never be able to walk among its ruins or, worse, later take posed, postbattle propaganda photos of their troops in the Marine positions. When elements of the 1st Marine Regiment were handed this assignment, they worked methodically, from June 16 to July 6, destroying old bunkers, filling in trenches, and removing the equipment and debris of battle. Finally, the Marines leveled the entire area with bulldozers so that, when they departed in July, ". . . it was level and smooth as a ballfield."[14]

11

Hue

Hue, the third largest city in South Vietnam, had a population of some 140,000 people. It was the seat of government for the province of Thua Thien. Hue was located about 10 kilometers from the coast and about 100 kilometers south of the DMZ. With the Perfume River running through its center, Hue was like two different cities linked by the Nguyen Huoang Bridge. On the northern bank of the river was a three-square-kilometer section known as the Citadel, surrounded by massive walls and deep moats and constructed with French help in the 1800s. On the southern bank of the river was a newer, residential area. Highway 1, crossing the Phu Cam canal just south of the city, led down to the American base at Phu Bai further to the south.[1]

As 1968 began, Hue was fortunate to have been spared from the war; both sides respected its historical and cultural significance. There were no combat troops in the city itself, with the exception of one company of South Vietnamese reconnaissance troops. Headquarters and garrison troops of the South Vietnamese Army occupied a small area in the northern half of the city.

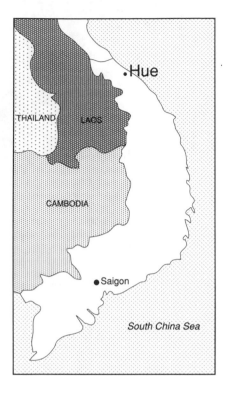

Just across the bridge to the south, the American Military Assistance Command, Vietnam (MACV) compound consisted of several two- and three-story buildings that housed the American and Australian advisers.

In late January 1968, intelligence reports advised that there were two enemy regiments building up some 40 kilometers to the west of the city. Although half of his troops were on leave for the Tet holiday, South Vietnamese General Ngo Quang Truong took the precaution of ordering all his headquarters staff to spend the night inside the headquarters compound, tucked inside the northern corner of the Citadel's massive walls, and remain on 100-percent alert. His combat troops, minus those away on leave, were deployed south of the city, prepared for the most likely scenario: defending against a Communist attack on nearby Phu Loc.

The peaceful nature of Hue and its environs was in stark contrast to the fighting taking place only 100 kilometers further north along the DMZ. North Vietnamese Defense Minister Giap, however, was about to change all that. He moved his troops into attack positions surrounding Khe Sanh and now planned to seize the city of Hue.

On the night of January 30, about four kilometers southwest of the city of Hue, a South Vietnamese reconnaissance company was in position near the river bank. Commanded by 1st Lieutenant Nguyen Thi Tan and accompanied by Australian adviser, Warrant Officer Terry Egan, the 38 men of the company sat silently in the darkness, watching and listening. At 10:00 P.M., they heard an exchange of gunfire as an NVA unit attacked a South Vietnamese militia unit to the east, back in the direction of Hue. Spotting enemy soldiers running through the trees, the reconnaissance team immediately radioed a warning to General Truong at his headquarters in Hue.

Unlike the noisy Tet Offensive actions erupting all over South Vietnam, the seizure of Hue was quiet, surreptitious, and virtually total. Many of the Communist troops were already in Hue, waiting in civilian clothes, in the city's tearooms and bars until midnight when they simply donned their uniforms and took up their weapons. Other Communist troops, like those spotted by the reconnaissance company, quickly rushed in from the surrounding countryside to join them. The Communists soon controlled all the northern half of Hue, except for the small South Vietnamese Army Headquarters. In the southern half, they controlled the provincial headquarters, the jail, the hospital, and the public utilities. Only the small MACV compound remained outside their control.[2]

In total, nine battalions were committed to the Hue battle on the first day (804th, K4B and K4C Battalions of the 4th NVA Regiment; 800th, 802nd, and 806th Battalions of the 6th NVA Regiment; 810th NVA Battalion; and 12th and Co Be Sapper Battalions). These troops were soon joined by five more (416th Battalion of the 5th NVA Regiment, 4th and 6th Battalions of the 24th NVA Regiment, and 7th and 8th Battalions of the 90th NVA Regiment).[3]

At 3:40 A.M., the Communists signaled their occupation of the city by firing a dozen 122-mm rockets at the MACV compound just south of the river. One hit a building, killing and wounding several men; another hit a jeep inside the compound; the rest missed their targets entirely. Intelligence later discovered that one of the NVA rockets hit one of their own assault companies, causing many casualties and delaying their attack. The Americans quickly grabbed rifles and ammunition and took up defensive positions on the surrounding walls. About five minutes later, 40 NVA from the 804th NVA Battalion dashed from the surrounding buildings and charged at the walls, firing their rifles wildly. An American Army soldier in an unfinished wooden observation tower opened fire with a machine gun, killing six of the attackers before his tower was hit by an antitank rocket. Momentarily delayed, the NVA regrouped and then proceeded toward the compound's gate, which was guarded by a group of Marines in a bunker. The Marines opened fire on the NVA, delaying them for several more minutes until they too were hit by an antitank rocket.[4]

Two American majors and their Australian roommate, armed with rifles and grenades, used the moments thus gained to rush to the top floor of the building . The three of them could see, 40 feet below, the remaining 16 NVA, armed with satchel charges and still trying to get through the main gate. Major Frank Breth sprayed the NVA with M-16 fire, while the other two men lobbed grenade after grenade at the enemy. Within moments, the NVA lay dead, sprawled around the compound's front gate.

Simultaneously with the attack on the MACV compound, the 800th NVA Battalion launched an attack on the South Vietnamese troops within the Citadel in the north of the city. The elite Black Panther Reconnaissance Company was the only South Vietnamese combat unit within the Citadel. Deployed around its small airfield, this unit unleashed a barrage of shoulder-fired light assault antitank weapon (LAAW) rockets and small arms fire at their attackers, causing severe casualties to the NVA. Meanwhile, the 802nd NVA Battalion attacked the headquarters itself but was eventually repulsed by the 200-man staff of clerks and administrative personnel whom General Truong had wisely kept on alert at the headquarters.

Around the American MACV compound, NVA troops began moving into the surrounding buildings but there were no more direct attacks on the compound itself. The combined force of U.S. Army and Marine personnel, augmented by the handful of Australians, prepared to defend the compound against further attacks. The five-minute delay, from the time the rockets hit until the NVA began their ground attack, allowed the Americans to man their defenses better. It had saved the compound. The NVA had made an early mistake.

Back at Marine Headquarters in Phu Bai, the situation was very unclear. The whole country had erupted in the Tet Offensive and battles raged throughout the land. Marine Brigadier General Foster C. LaHue knew only that the MACV compound at Hue was under attack and that he was to send reinforcements. Most of his scattered units had reported battles with the enemy. All up and down Highway 1, the NVA had tried, unsuccessfully, to attack the various bridges leading to Hue. The only troops immediately available to him were the eighty or so Marines of Alpha Company, 1st Battalion, 1st Marine Regiment (Alpha 1/1). Captain Gordon Batcheller, commander of Alpha 1/1, was simply told that "something was up" and that he was to get his men together and link up with South Vietnamese troops just outside Phu Bai and then to proceed up Highway 1 to attack the enemy. To make matters worse, though, his company was seriously undermanned; one of his platoon commanders was in Da Nang and the other two had become stranded in Quang Tri along with a small contingent from his first platoon.[5]

With two sergeants and a corporal taking over command of their respective platoons, Captain Batcheller boarded his men onto the trucks at 8:30 A.M., five hours after the initial NVA assault and, armed with an Army truck-mounted quad-fifty four-barreled machine gun at the front of the convoy and another at the rear, set out to link up with a South Vietnamese Army unit. When the South Vietnamese Army unit failed to appear, Captain

Batcheller was ordered to head his men up Highway 1 through Hue and link up with another group of South Vietnamese Army troops north of the city.

Along the way, the Marines happened upon another small convoy that had been escorting some equipment to its new destination when Tet erupted. This group consisted of four Marine M-48 tanks, a jeep, and a mobile crane. While the tanks packed an awesome firepower, they were extremely vulnerable to close-in attack unless defended by infantry. At the same time, Captain Batcheller was well aware that his badly understrength infantry company lacked any real hitting power on its own. The two units immediately decided to join forces, thus forming an armor/infantry team that multiplied their separate strengths, and proceed together.

Captain Batcheller then received another change of orders: proceed directly to the MACV compound. Speed was suddenly of the essence. The little convoy proceeded as quickly as it could, taking sniper fire along the way. Soon they had crossed the An Cuu Bridge, the vital access to the city, and observed the NVA's unsuccessful attempts to destroy it with explosives. It appeared that the NVA had used shaped charges but had emplaced them incorrectly. While these charges had blown holes in the bridge's concrete, they'd failed to knock it down. The NVA had made another mistake.

Once over the bridge, the Marines saw that the road led directly between two rows of closely packed two-story houses. The convoy ground to a halt before proceeding further. To many of the young Marines, the narrow street and the architecture of the buildings reminded them of a scene from a western movie. There was no sign of movement. The Marines knew it was an ideal ambush site, but they also realized that the MACV compound, which needed their help, lay beyond it. Captain Batcheller's men warily left their trucks and boarded the tanks, which then took off at top speed to run the likely gauntlet. As expected, enemy fire immediately began pouring from the buildings. The Marines, clinging to the tanks, returned fire as best they could with their M-16s. The NVA then began firing their RPG antitank rockets, scoring direct hits on the tanks and peppering the Marines with shrapnel and knocking them to the ground with their concussion. Eventually, the tanks made it to the end of the street into a small traffic circle where the Marines dragged their wounded to relative safety. The Marines then poured 90-mm tank fire and volumes of .50-caliber fire from the quad-fifty machine guns into the enemy. They proceeded only a few meters further before being stopped. Captain Batcheller was seriously wounded, a corpsman was dead, and the radio operator's foot was all but severed, attached to his leg by only a string of flesh. The Marines could proceed no further and could only hope to consolidate their hastily established defensive position.

US Marine tanks among the rubble of Hue. Captain Batchellor's relief force ran a gauntlet of fire from the two-story houses which lined the streets.
Credit: US Army Military History Institute

At about noon, the Marines back at Phu Bai became aware of the fate of Captain Batcheller's Alpha Company. The battalion commander, Lieutenant Colonel Marcus J. Gravel, immediately organized a rescue party. Using troops loaned to him from another battalion (Golf 2/5), Colonel Gravel gathered up the men of his headquarters group, including a chaplain, and went to the aid of their fellow Marines. The Marines clambered aboard trucks and headed north.

Once over the canal, they came across the battered trucks, tanks, and men they had been sent to rescue. The chaplain, Lieutenant Richard Lion, crawled from man to man administering last rites and then, his anger getting the better of him, grabbed an M-16 from among the dead and wounded Marines and fired a long burst in the direction of the NVA. The Marines, firing furiously, managed to load the wounded onto the back of one of the trucks. One of them leaped behind the steering wheel but was immediately hit by the NVA fire. While other Marines quickly bandaged him and heaved him into the back of the truck with the other wounded, another Marine grabbed the wheel and accelerated.

Withering fire still poured out of the buildings on either side of them. A sharp-eyed Marine spotted a small concrete building from which crackled the muzzle flashes of AK-47s. Three Marines, firing their M-16s as they ran, charged the position. Blowing the door open with grenades, the Marines burst in and killed the startled NVA at point-blank range.

Part of the rescue column pushed through, proceeding towards the MACV compound. Eventually, after destroying an NVA position across the street that had been hammering the compound, the front element of the rescue column made it to the MACV compound and told them of their efforts. A group of volunteers from the compound then jumped into a civilian truck and headed back to the pinned-down Alpha Company and loaded its wounded onto the trucks. With Golf Company in the lead, the Marines made it to the compound. The MACV survivors cheered the arrival of the tanks, the Army quad-fifties, and the two companies of U.S. Marines.

Similarly, at South Vietnamese Army headquarters within the Citadel, General Truong ordered reinforcements drawn from his infantry, armor, and airborne units positioned outside the city. One by one, his various battalions punched narrow corridors through the NVA's formidable defenses and managed to fight their way into their besieged headquarters in the Citadel. They gave and received heavy casualties in the process.

The Americans and South Vietnamese quickly decided that the responsibility for the recapture of the city of Hue was to be split. The Marines were to be responsible for the southern half, launching out from their MACV compound. The northern half, including the Citadel, was to be the responsibility of the South Vietnamese Army. National pride required them to retake their imperial capital.

The arrival of the Marine rescue party at the beleaguered MACV compound on the very first day of the battle marked the beginning of the end for the NVA. The Marines, using their toehold at the MACV compound, soon began bringing in reinforcements. Using a nearby soccer field as a helicopter landing zone, two Marine battalions eventually joined in battle to free the southern half of Hue.

Captain G.R. Christmas, son-in-law of Khe Sanh's commander, Colonel David Lownds, commanded the 100 men of Hotel Company, Second Battalion, Fifth Marines, who entered the battle on February 2. He soon found that the NVA had fortified the city with various strong points every few blocks. These strong points were typically based around a three-story building with a walled courtyard surrounding it. The NVA put their snipers in the upper stories and emplaced their machine guns in the lower floors. Around the building, the NVA laced the courtyard with one-man spider-hole fighting positions. Each NVA soldier in these spider-holes was armed with both an AK-47 assault rifle and an RPG antitank weapon.[6]

In addition to this series of strong points, the NVA placed snipers and antitank teams in the various buildings between the strong points. It was a truly formidable defense, predicated on the belief that the counterattacking force would be a South Vietnamese armored force consisting of tanks and armored personnel carriers that would approach along Lei Loy, the main street paralleling the river. The NVA had cleverly prepared themselves to allow the South Vietnamese to enter the heavily defended street, then cut it off at either end, and destroy it in a well-planned trap. However, the relieving force was not South Vietnamese; it was a force of U.S. Marines. The Marines didn't approach by vehicle down the main street; instead, they came in a house-to-house infantry attack. By doing so, the Marines gained the advantage of a coordinated attack, one unit covering another.

Even so, the NVA resisted stubbornly. At first, the Marines used the standard tactics they had learned in training. Before crossing a defended street, the Marines would first toss smoke grenades to conceal their movement. But the NVA, well equipped with automatic weapons and realizing the purpose of the smoke screen, responded by firing blindly but furiously into the smoke at preregistered firing points killing and wounding several Marines in the process. The Marines quickly adapted, however, and invented new techniques. Realizing that the NVA assumed the billowing smoke was concealing a Marine advance, the Marines used that assumption to locate the enemy. A favorite technique, one apparently never figured out by the NVA, was first to toss a smoke grenade into the street to draw the enemy's fire. Having thus located the source of the gunfire, the Marines would then quickly poke a 106-mm recoilless rifle partially into the street and blast a round in the enemy's general direction. While the NVA were preoccupied ducking for cover, a team of Marines would streak across the street, concealed in the dust and smoke of the weapon's backblast. Once across these open areas, the Marines used explosive charges to blow holes in the walls and the courtyards. The Marines cleared out each building, working their way room to room and house to house. At first, the NVA attempted to withdraw from the buildings under attack, virtually running out the back of the building into new fighting positions as the Marines entered the front. The Marines quickly countered this tactic, too. Before attacking a strongpoint, they fired a barrage of mortars to the rear and either side of the building, effectively cutting off the enemy's avenues of retreat.

While the Marines were fighting inside Hue City, troopers from the U.S. Army's 1st Cavalry Division (Airmobile) were engaged in bitter fighting just to the west. In order to cut off NVA reinforcements to the city, the 2nd battalion of the 12th Cavalry, the only unit that could be spared from heavy fighting elsewhere, helicoptered into an LZ about ten kilometers northwest of Hue and began attacking southward toward Hue. They would eventually be joined by three more Cavalry battalions and see fierce fighting, including at least one regimental-size, 1500-man, attack on one of their units.[7]

Because of the significance of the city, the rules of engagement prohibited any bombing or artillery in the city's environs. Only very late in the battle were the rules finally lifted and the Marines allowed to use artillery and air support. Even though they had to fight with just the weapons they could carry into battle, the Marines were able to recapture their southern sector of the city within 10 days. But the South Vietnamese Army, which was responsible for ejecting the NVA from the northern sector, was having difficulty with the NVA who had occupied the Citadel.

Once the South Vietnamese gathered their forces inside their headquarters, they began launching attacks intended to eject the NVA from the Citadel. As the Marines were experiencing to their south, the South Vietnamese soon found that the NVA were well equipped, well emplaced, and able to continually reinforce and resupply their troops from the western approaches to the city. Further, most of the South Vietnamese Army troops had families living in the city, and they were often forced to destroy their own homes in order to drive the NVA out. A South Vietnamese artillery observer with the South Vietnamese 1st Army Division was ordered to bring artillery fire onto his own home and his family sheltering inside it. An Australian Army adviser standing nearby recalled, "I watched him give the fire order with tears streaming down his face." Two days later, he was killed by the NVA and the same Australian commented that, "I daresay he was glad to die."[8]

The South Vietnamese Army troops fought bitter, desperate battles; seizing ground only to have the NVA counterattack and recapture it. The 4th Battalion, 3rd South Vietnamese Army Regiment, made seven unsuccessful attacks against the Citadel's walls. A cavalry unit had entered the battle with 12 armored personnel carriers; eight were quickly destroyed by the NVA who were well supplied with antitank weapons. The South Vietnamese Air Force was given permission to bomb within the Citadel. After a week of heavy fighting, however, the morale of the South Vietnamese cracked. They ceased the attack and chose to withdraw into the safety of their headquarters to assume a defensive posture.

Major Wayne R. Swenson, the liaison officer, fought in the initial battles at the MACV compound and then helicoptered to his post in the South

Vietnamese Army compound some days later. While he had great respect for General Truong and his regimental commanders, and he had seen the South Vietnamese fight well on several occasions, he sadly noted that this time their performance was poor. He said, "Although many South Vietnamese were killed and others fought extremely well, beyond day four of the offensive, their casualties were low and their tempo of operations can be characterized as 'remain in place, don't take more casualties.'" [9]

Although he would have preferred to retake the Citadel with South Vietnamese troops alone for the sake of national pride, it was apparent to General Truong on February 9 that he would not be able to do so. He therefore requested American troops to join the battle north of the river. At about the same time, the North Vietnamese Army divisions attacking Khe Sanh further north were discovering it to be a much tougher objective than they had planned. The Marines at Khe Sanh were obstinately blocking the valley through which Giap planned his troops to pour south, linking up with those already occupying Hue. Unless reinforced soon, the Communist troops in Hue could not hold out long enough. On February 10, Hanoi was forced to shift five battalions, approximately 2,500 troops, from the Khe Sanh attack, leaving their heavy weapons and tanks behind and moving circuitously through Laos and then entering the city from the west, in order to reinforce Hue. [10]

With two battalions of Marines (1/1 and 2/5) wrapping up the battle south of the river, a third battalion of Marines was ordered in. On February 10, the 1st Battalion, 5th Marines, situated at nearby Phu Loc, was committed to retake the Citadel from the NVA. With the Army's 101st Airborne taking over their Phu Loc base camp, the Marines helicoptered and trucked into the Marine base at Phu Bai. General LaHue met with the battalion commander, Major Robert Thompson, and made it clear that he was to take orders only from Colonel Hughes, the commander of the Marines already in Hue, not from the South Vietnamese command.

While part of one company (B 1/5) helicoptered directly into the South Vietnamese Army Headquarters in the Citadel, the rest of the battalion trucked from Phu Bai up to the MACV compound in southern Hue. They then boarded U.S. Navy landing craft and steamed down the Perfume River, following its twisted course northward where it formed the eastern boundary of the Citadel. The Marines disembarked at a quay north of the Citadel, crossed the moat, and with Major Thompson in the lead, began pushing through the fields and houses toward the South Vietnamese Army Headquarters. Suddenly, several South Vietnamese civilians came running toward the Marines, waving their arms and speaking in broken English.

They were able to make themselves understood well enough to explain to Major Thompson that the NVA were lying in wait up ahead, ready to spring an ambush on the Marines. The Marines were unsure of any other route into the South Vietnamese Army Headquarters but the civilians offered to lead them. Taking a back road, the Marines were safely escorted to the back gate of the South Vietnamese Army Headquarters, to be met by a party of South Vietnamese officers and the Marines of Bravo Company who had helicoptered in earlier. The Marines soon attacked southward, squeezing the NVA against the Perfume River and their fellow Marines in the southern half of the city. Having received South Vietnamese permission, the Marines were now able to employ artillery and airstrikes against the enemy.

On February 16, the NVA commander of forces north of the river was killed by artillery. His replacement requested permission to withdraw his battered troops but the request was refused by Communist high command outside the city. The fighting continued. On February 21, four battalions of the U.S Army's 1st Cavalry Division (Airmobile) attacked the NVA command and supply base in the La Chu Woods west of the city. Hitting the base with artillery, fixed wing and helicopters, and following up with an infantry assault, the Air Cavalry eliminated the support available to the few remaining NVA still alive in the city. The NVA commander was finally given permission on February 23 to withdraw from the city of Hue. Attempting to break through the South Vietnamese Army forces to the west, the retreating NVA were further battered by artillery.[11]

By Saturday, February 24, the Marines had retaken virtually the whole of Hue. Only the Imperial Palace was left. As the Marines prepared to charge through the 200 yards of open ground and attack the palace's walls, word came down that the South Vietnamese would do so instead. With their adviser, U.S. Marine Captain James J. Coolican, at the front, the Black Panther Company fearlessly charged through the open ground, carrying ladders, screaming, and firing their rifles. Soon they scrambled over the wall while others ran through holes left by previous firing. The surviving NVA had already pulled out. A short while later, the Black Panthers pulled down the Communist flag and replaced it with the flag of the Republic of South Vietnam. The battle of Hue City was over.

Gradually, the Marines learned that, while they and the NVA were locked in battle, the Viet Cong had held sway over the city's terrified citizens, murdering anyone even vaguely associated with the government. Joined by a handful of students from the university, the blood-letting had continued unabated for days until the NVA Commander eventually heard about it and put a stop to it.[12]

A patrol of weary Marines from the victorious 1st Battalion, 5th Marine Regiment in Hue, February 29, 1968. The Communists who seized Hue suffered approximately 5,000 casualties in their month-long unsuccessful battle to hold the city.
Credit: National Archives and Records Administration

The Communists lost an estimated 5,000 soldiers within the city of Hue and another 3,000 in the surrounding clashes. They had held on tenaciously, waiting for the flood of troops through the Khe Sanh valley that would never come.[13]

12

The Offensive Is Stopped
A Retrospective Look at the
NVA's Role in the Tet Offensive

Defense Minister Giap intended that his seizure of Hue would be successful, and by the early hours of January 31, defended it with nine full battalions. The chaotic Viet Cong attacks throughout South Vietnam occurred almost simultaneously. While these attacks were soundly defeated within days, they diverted attention from Giap's Tri-Thien-Hue battles. Typical of this was the case of the four companies of South Vietnamese paratroopers sitting on the tarmac at Tan Son Nhut Airport in Saigon. Awaiting transport to join the fight in Hue, they were diverted to the defense of Tan Son Nhut itself.[1]

In contrast to the battles occurring elsewhere, the North Vietnamese Army troops in Hue did everything they could do to conceal their real strength, tempting some to believe it was similar to the other attacks occurring throughout the country and thus no more or less important. So successful was this strategy that, by the end of the first day, South Vietnamese High Command estimated that Hue was held by a 30-man platoon of Communist troops rather than the thousands of NVA actually there. [2]

The situation was much different in the other, COSVN-controlled, provinces. Like a thousand little pinpricks, the Viet Cong in those provinces attacked and seized government buildings and sites as ordered, but within hours they were killed or forced to flee. The promised reinforcements never arrived. In Giap's Tri-Thien-Hue Front, in contrast, nine full battalions of North Vietnamese troops seized Hue and were reinforced a week later by another five battalions.

General Westmoreland had long been concerned that Giap planned to annex the two northern provinces of the Communists' Tri-Thien-Hue Front. He realized that Hue would have made the ideal capital for such an "annexed state" with the mountains to the south of Hue forming a natural defense line against counterattacks from the south. NVA Colonel Mai The Chinh, who was involved in the attack against Hue, confirms this intention. He recalled that, "The aim was to annihilate the enemy so that we could control the northern provinces." This opinion was confirmed in an a order directly issued by Hanoi's Politburo, which detailed the progress of the war and noted that the northern provinces ". . . will be completely liberated during the 1967–1968 winter-spring campaign."[3]

Giap came very close to success. Against all odds and at great cost, however, the small relief force of Marines managed to get through to the MACV compound in Hue. Quickly seizing the nearby soccer field, the Marines began ferrying in troops by helicopter. Able to attack from the inside out, the Marines were able to evict the North Vietnamese in three weeks of bitter fighting. Full credit must be given to the NVA battalions at Hue for continuing to hold on, waiting for the planned "second wave" that never came.

Further north, at Khe Sanh, the Marines proved more difficult than Hanoi planned. Also, Giap could be forgiven for not predicting that America would use the greatest bombing campaign in the history of warfare against his hapless troops. With the attack through the DMZ stalled, on February 10, Giap was forced to reinforce his troops in Hue with five battalions of infantry, their artillery and armor left behind, drawn from the Khe Sanh battle and sent circuitously through Laos to enter Hue from the west. General Creighton Abrams, a year after the battle, would observe that, had the NVA instead been able to reinforce Hue with a division in early February, "We would still be fighting there." Finally, on February 24, Giap was forced to admit defeat and gave the order for the survivors of the battle of Hue to attempt a withdrawal.[4]

NVA Colonel Mai The Chinh's 500-man battalion was sent into Hue in the first few days of Tet and fought for several weeks. His unit was named a "heroic unit" by Hanoi. Later, he recounted that, ". . . eventually the Americans drove us out and we retreated into the western jungle. There were a hundred of us left." Starving, unable to shoot wild game for fear of disclosing their position, constantly bombed by American aircraft, with no protection from the pouring rain, he summed up his unit's situation as ". . . starving in the rain in the mountains." Within weeks of ordering the withdrawal from Hue, Giap began withdrawing his troops from around Khe Sanh. Hanoi's big gamble had failed.[5]

Another Chance

Hanoi was amazed and delighted that its unsuccessful Tet attacks were being portrayed as Communist victories in America. Senator Eugene McCarthy, a presidential hopeful on the Democratic ticket, trumpeted the successes of the Communists. He cited their seizure of "a section of the American Embassy" and of the city of Hue as evidence that the Communists were winning the war. On February 27, while enemy shells were still hitting Khe Sanh, Walter Cronkite, without doubt the most trusted and popular of American television newscasters, dealt a body blow to American troops. In a half-hour television special, he asked: "Who won and who lost" in the great Tet Offensive? He then answered his own question by saying that, while the Communists didn't win "by a knockout," neither did the Americans. He then predicted that, "Khe Sanh could well fall with a terrible loss of American lives, prestige and morale." He said that, at best, the American military in Vietnam was "mired in a stalemate."[6]

Hanoi reacted with surprise and delight. Always carefully attuned to political developments in the United States, Hanoi elected to capitalize on this unexpected "political" victory the western press was saying they had won at Tet. Thus encouraged, the NVA would continue their attacks in the hopes of a decisive military victory which would shift the balance of power at any future negotiations which now seemed increasingly likely.[7]

Another, more sinister, outcome of the media's misreading of the Tet Offensive was the deaths it later caused among American troops fighting the war. Hanoi increasingly directed its efforts toward the American media and the antiwar movement and soon sought *American* casualties as their main objective. In contrast to the Tet Offensive where, except for the Marines blocking their path at Khe Sanh, the Communists primarily attacked South Vietnamese military and civilian targets, Hanoi would now attempt to inflict heavy *American* casualties because of their effect on American politics.[8]

Even though the southern faction's spokesman, General Thanh, had been killed by the Americans, they still controlled the Politburo. Direct head-to-head clashes with the Americans would therefore continue regardless of the Tet Offensive's horrendous casualties and continuing opposition by Defense Minister Giap. Changes had to be made, however. The guerrilla war needed to be abandoned altogether; the southern Viet Cong no longer existed as a viable force. There would be a very brief lull on the southern battlefield while Hanoi conscripted and trained new replacements for their own Tet dead. Regrettably, from the Communists' viewpoint, the training of these new troops would be only perfunctory if they were to return quickly to the battlefield.

13

Foxtrot Ridge

The 304th NVA Division had been badly mauled by the 26th Marine Regiment at Khe Sanh and their supporting B-52 strikes, code-named Niagara. The division had been forced to withdraw back to North Vietnam in March 1968 to reequip and await reinforcements. In early May, they reentered the fray, their numbers now bolstered by fresh conscripts. Many of the new conscripts had first put on the green North Vietnamese Army uniform only two months before and their rifles were still shiny and new.[1]

On May 14, 1968, elements of the 304th NVA Division struck a convoy taking supplies from Ca Lu to Khe Sanh. Three days later, they attacked a convoy of Marines from the 1st Marine Regiment on Route 9 to the west of Khe Sanh, halfway to the abandoned Special Force Camp with rusting Soviet-made tanks still in its perimeter. On that same day, a battalion of the 4th Marine Regiment began a two-day battle with elements of the 304th NVA Division just west of Khe Sanh in the vicinity of Hills 689 and 552. Two days later, a battalion of Marines (2/1) engaged a battalion of the 304th NVA Division along Route 9, a mile east of Khe Sanh.

In a move to counter this menace, the Marines decided to place a rifle company, approximately 100 men, atop a low ridgeline that overlooked Route 9 to the north and the Laotian border to the west and south, effectively screening the road from the enemy.[2]

Commanded by 24-year-old 1st Lieutenant James L. Jones Jr. of Kansas City, Missouri, the 88 men of Foxtrot Company, Second Battalion Third Marine Regiment, were assigned the mission and moved overland, climbing the gentle slope of the ridgeline on May 25, 1968. They immediately began establishing their defensive positions. The ridgeline was perhaps 150 meters long, too big an area for one understrength company to defend entirely. But the ridgeline had a slight dip or saddle near the eastern end. The Marines were able to place their main defense around the bulk of the ridgeline, a size equivalent to two basketball courts laid end to end, and place a dozen men on the smaller bump of high ground to the east and separated from their main perimeter by perhaps 40 meters. The Marines soon dubbed this key secondary feature "the crows nest."[3]

By the next day, the Marines' position began proving its value. Just after 7:00 P.M., they spotted a small group of NVA soldiers on a nearby ridgeline. The NVA were wearing packs and Soviet-style steel helmets. The Marines directed artillery and air strikes onto the enemy, killing five of them and disclosing fifteen freshly constructed enemy bunkers. Only an hour later, the Marines spotted a whole column of NVA soldiers snaking their way across another open ridgeline. The Marines called in artillery and mortars, killing seven of the enemy and scattering the rest.

The next 24 hours remained fairly peaceful. The Marines, whose usual activity was to move 15 or more kilometers a day carrying heavy packs in difficult terrain, were happy with their relative inactivity. They spent their time digging in deeper, running short patrols around the area, and seeking whatever shade they could find in the sun's searing heat.

In addition to the Marines in "the crows nest" on the eastern tip of the perimeter, other small teams of Marines took turns spending their nights on "listening post" duty. These little groups of three or four Marines would quietly slip out of the perimeter just after dark. Proceeding a short distance into likely avenues of approach an enemy might use, the Marines would then quietly sit and wait, listening for any noises in the pitch black of night that might suggest an approaching enemy.

As darkness approached on the evening of May 27, Private Donald Schuck and three other Marines from 1st Platoon prepared for their turn on the listening post. They took little gear with them: only their rifles, ammunition, and a few grenades. Before going out, they checked their equipment to ensure nothing rattled or made noise and then slipped down off the ridgeline, disappearing into the darkness. Their destination was a spot on the gentle grassy slope about 50 meters out, leading up to the southwestern portion of the perimeter. Shortly before 3:00 A.M., the Marines up in the "crows nest" position on the eastern tip of the ridge, using the newly invented "starlight" night vision scope, spotted approaching enemy soldiers. The Marines repelled this attack, using fragmentation grenades and mortar fire.

A few minutes later, Private Don Schuck, sitting well outside the Marines' defenses on the grassy slopes leading up the western end of the ridge, reported over the radio something about "boocoo gooks" coming up the slope toward the four-man listening post. The Marines out on the listening post threw a volley of grenades at their attackers and prepared to run back to the main perimeter. But two NVA soldiers, armed with explosive "satchel" charges, managed to jump into the midst of the four Marines on the listening post. The NVA immediately detonated their charges, killing themselves and wiping out the Marines' forward position in the process.

A green flare suddenly shot skyward from out of the darkness in front of the Marines on the ridgeline. A full NVA battalion, perhaps five hundred men, swept past the dead and wounded at the listening post position and assaulted all up and down the southern and western slopes of the ridge. In their attack they were supported by other NVA troops on nearby ridgelines who fired at the Marines with rocket-propelled grenades (RPGs). The NVA loosed off a volley of 40 RPGs in the initial attack. 1st Platoon's machine gunners tried to fire into the waves of NVA soldiers trotting up the grassy slope but, after only a few short bursts, and their resulting "one of every fifth round" red tracer, an RPG round would slam into their position. In one case an RPG round detonated directly under the barrel.

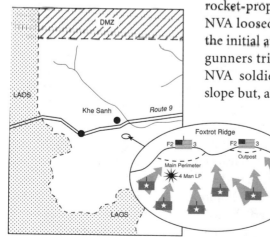

The machine gunners were courageously doing precisely what they were trained to do, but they were killed almost immediately for doing so.

Lieutenant Jones, having observed that the enemy had commenced the attack with a *green* flare, decided to fire a *red* one himself to see what the enemy would do. He aimed the flare pistol skyward and fired, sending the flare streaking through the starry sky. The NVA, still coming up the slope, reacted with a sudden confusion and abruptly slackened the momentum of their attack. They had the initiative and were about to capitalize on it, but instead they were bewildered by the red flare, their pre-arranged signal to break off the attack, and the night was filled with the hoarse cries of NVA officers and noncommissioned officers (NCOs) as they attempted to restore the momentum of their attack.

Vital moments were lost, however, while the NVA equivocated. In those moments, the Marines' artillery and mortars were called in. As the NVA resumed their assault, the night was filled with the roaring explosions of shells, the pounding impacts and blinding flashes of their detonations. The voices out in the darkness were drowned by the crashing of shells into their midst, but the NVA leaders were able to regain order and again surged forward against the Marines.

The Marines' mortar team could hear the NVA talking and taunting the Marines: "Marines you die!" The Marines responded by throwing grenades and firing at the enemy, stopping three different assaults on their position and then crawling out to the area in front of them in the momentary lull to strip weapons and ammunition from the enemy soldiers they'd killed before the next wave approached.

Eventually, by sheer weight of numbers, the NVA were able to penetrate the Marines' defense and soon swarmed inside their defensive perimeter. Second Lieutenant Ray Dito, commander of 1st Platoon, immediately called for the survivors of his platoon to fall back toward the center of the ridgeline and establish a new line of defense some meters back. Foxtrot's commander, Lieutenant Jones, quickly ordered his other platoons to tie in with 1st Platoon, effectively cutting themselves off from the NVA who were now occupying the area vacated by 1st Platoon.

Sixty or more NVA continued on, passing through 1st Platoon's old position and occupying a small clearing, which the Marines had used as a helicopter landing zone. Lieutenant Jones recalls that the NVA ". . . were acting as though they were under the influence of some medicine or narcotic or something." He remembers them ". . . babbling incoherently, yelling, laughing, screaming, smoking, anything that you might imagine."[4]

Although some survivors of 1st Platoon were still out there on the other side of the little landing zone, Lieutenant Jones had no choice but to call in artillery onto his own position. Assisted by the artillery Forward Observer, the fire was immediate, accurate, and deadly. Within seconds, it had cut short the laughter of the milling NVA, killing 20 of them and forcing most of the others back down the slope.

While the whole southern half of the perimeter was being assaulted, the NVA were also attempting to knock the 12 Marines on the crows nest off their key position. Elevated slightly from the main position, its height allowed the Marines to look down on their fellow Marines on the ridge below. Once the NVA soldiers occupied 1st Platoon's old foxholes, the Marines up on the crows nest immediately brought accurate machine gun fire onto them, wreaking havoc on the NVA. The NVA mounted attack after attack on the crows nest, but the Marines beat back each attack with grenades and rifle fire. At one point, it appeared the NVA would break through. Private First Class (PFC) Lawrence Kenneth Arthur, undaunted by the hail of incoming grenades and bullets, moved to the weak point and heaved a volley of grenades, turning the tide of battle. Moments later, he was wounded by an NVA grenade, but he continued, regardless, to fire at the enemy for another 15 minutes until his rifle jammed. An NVA soldier suddenly loomed up out of the grass and the grievously wounded PFC Arthur, now armed only with a bayonet, leaped onto the enemy and killed him. A short time later, PFC Arthur died of his previous grenade wounds.[5]

Another Marine in the crows nest position was 22-year-old Corporal Kevin Howell, a Canadian citizen born in Kingston, Ontario. On the very day of his honorable discharge after four years' service as a military policeman with the Royal Canadian Air Force, Corporal Howell had driven south to Buffalo, New York and fulfilled his childhood ambition of joining the U.S. Marines. He enlisted only after extracting a guarantee from the Marines that he would be put into the infantry and sent to fight in Vietnam. Now, just over one year later, the recruiter's promises were fully realized as Corporal Howell found himself in a fight to the death with the NVA. At one point in the battle, he joined several other Marines in a counterattack to clear a nearby gully of 20 or so enemy soldiers who sheltered there to lob grenades at the crows nest. In the ensuing melee, Corporal Howell was bayoneted in the arm, both hands, and also in the mouth. After successfully evicting the enemy and eliminating this threat, he and the other Marines returned to the crows nest. Corporal Howell was later hit by fragments of an enemy grenade which exploded so close to him that it caused his shirt and trousers to catch fire; he somehow survived.[6]

The 1st Platoon corpsman, Hospitalman Frank Sarwicki, was cut off from the main body of Marines when they were overrun and forced to pull back. He spent the night with his wounded Marines, keeping them alive for several hours. One of the Marines in his care eventually groaned, however, and the NVA located the corpsman and his wounded patients. The NVA then moved among the wounded Marines, murdering each with a bullet to the back of the head. They also put a rifle to Sarwicki's head; the bullet penetrated his helmet but miraculously only grazed his head and knocked him unconscious.[7]

For the next two hours, the Marines in the main defensive perimeter held on, beating back wave after wave of NVA attackers. It was touch and go with the Marines. By any conventional logic, all the advantages lay with the numerically superior enemy. Reading the concern on one of his men's face, Lieutenant Jones put his hand on the Marine's shoulder and, smiling, said: "Just think, twenty years from now we can look back on this and proudly say that we were in the thick of it in South Vietnam." At 4:15 A.M., an AC-47 "Spooky" gunship arrived over head, adding its 6,000 round-a-minute gatling guns to the Marines' defense. The NVA weren't intimidated, however, and fired back at the gunship with .51-caliber machine gun fire of their own.[8]

After another hour, the enemy fire began to slacken off noticeably. Sergeant Joseph Quinn, who had taken command of 2nd Platoon, was amongst the first to sense that the tide of battle had turned in the Marines' favor and that they would be able to hold on. Over the continuing blast of artillery and grenades, he yelled out, "We've got 'em beat! We beat them!" Then, in real euphoria, he yelled out, "Come on everybody. I want the gooks to hear us laughing at them! I want them to know we beat them!" Sergeant Quinn roared with a burst of maniacal, mocking laughter. The other Marines immediately joined in with a roar of guttural howls.

Most of the Marines knew only a smattering of the Vietnamese language. Perhaps predictably, most of the words they knew were swear words and obscenities. As daylight began to break, they continued to taunt the NVA, yelling out in broken Vietnamese, swearing at *them* and at Ho Chi Minh. The obscene taunts and the chorus of Marine laughter enraged the NVA; they fired volley after volley of rocket-propelled grenades at the Marines on Foxtrot Ridge, an estimated 400 rounds in all.

Groups of enemy soldiers could be seen in the near distance, gathering up their dead and wounded onto stretchers and carrying them off to the southwest toward the Laotian border. Their actions were taken under the protective fire of other NVA soldiers, who continued to fire rocket-propelled grenades at the Marines. The Marines braved the fire regardless of the risk, rising up in their foxholes to fire at the fleeing enemy soldiers and swear and laugh at those who remained. Soon after daylight, helicopter gunships arrived overhead along with a spotter plane. The spotter plane's pilot radioed back that "NVA bodies litter the area around Company F's position."

Finally, just before noon, the Marines of Echo Company, 2nd Battalion, 3rd Marines, reached the beleaguered Marines of Foxtrot Company, who had held on doggedly to their position for almost nine hours of continuing attacks by an enemy force that outnumbered them by five to one.

The 88 Marines of Foxtrot Company had suffered 13 killed and 44 wounded but had killed 230 of the enemy. Echo Company, which relieved them and now held the ridgeline, was attacked the following night, but the dispirited NVA were driven off, leaving another 96 dead on the battlefield. On the next day, May 31, the Marines engaged in a daylight battle with the NVA on a nearby ridge, killing another 44 of the enemy.

The Marines boldly positioned themselves on a ridgeline and blocked the NVA from attacking Route 9 from their Laotian sanctuary. In spite of repeated and costly attempts, they were unable to force the Marines to quit their vantage point.[9]

Perhaps the most notable thing about the defense of Foxtrot Ridge was that there was nothing "special" about it. It was not a deciding battle, not a turning point, and remains only a footnote in most histories. Yet, it was in battles like these, fierce battles fought at the 100-man company level that were so typical of the war and of the defeat of the NVA. Just about every infantryman of the 1960s, whether they be Marine or soldier, can tell of similar incidents from their own experience. Repeated thousands of times over, they *were* the Vietnam War.

The month of May 1968 was a time of intensive fighting throughout South Vietnam. The Australians, too, went on the offensive, dramatic change from their small unit actions against Viet Cong guerrillas. The Australians set up base camps in areas the enemy previously thought safe. The Australians fortified their fire bases, Balmoral and Coral, with artillery and their British-made Centurion tanks forcing the enemy to attack. In the heaviest fighting of the entire war for the Australians, 267 NVA/VC troops lay dead around their perimeter. Another 60 enemy bodies were thought to have been dragged away.[10]

Destruction of the Northern Army, the Situation by Mid-1968

General Thanh continued to pursue his strategy of full-scale, bloody, pitched battles in spite of the Americans' inflicting defeat after defeat on his troops. Evidence suggests he was personally reproached by Giap for his failure to achieve the promised military victory against the Americans in his 1965-1966 dry season offensive. Later, in the Tet Offensive of 1968, it was Giap's turn to be defeated on a score of battlefields. Then, buoyed by hopes of the effect upon American domestic politics, Hanoi continued the attack throughout May 1968.[11]

A listing of the operations and battles of those days gives some sense of the enormity of Communist casualties. Halfway through 1968, General William Westmoreland compiled the following list of operations and battles that resulted in 500 Communist casualties or more.[12]

- The U.S. Marines in Operation Starlite killed 700 troops from the VC 1st Regiment (18–21 August 1965).
- The 1st Cavalry Division (Airmobile) dealt the enemy 1,771 known enemy casualties (23 October–20 November 1965) on Operation Silver Bayonet.
- The 101st Airborne Division along with ARVN troops on Operation Van Buren killed 679 enemy soldiers (19 January–21 February 1966).
- 1st Cavalry Division (Airmobile) along with ARVN and South Korean troops and U.S. Marines killed 2,389 enemy troops on Operation Masher/White Wing/Thang Phong III (24 January–6 March, 1966).
- U.S Marine Corps and ARVN troops on Operation Utah/Lien Ket 26 killed 632 enemy troops (4–8 March, 1966).
- U.S. Marine Corps/ARVN/Vietnamese Marine Corps inflict 623 known enemy casualties on Operation Texas/Lien Ket 28 (20–24 March 1966).
- 25th Infantry Division along with ARVN forces killed 546 enemy soldiers on Operation Paul Revere/Than Phong 14 (10 May–30 July 1966).
- 101st Airborne Division and ARVN troops killed 531 enemy during Operation Hawthorne/Dan Tang 61 (2–21 June 1966).
- 1st Infantry Division and ARVN troops inflict 855 known casualties on VC 9th Division on Operation El Paso II (2 June–13 July 1966).
- Marines killed 507 enemy troops on Operation Macon (4 July–27 October 1966).
- U.S. Marine Corps/ARVN/Vietnamese Marine Corps killed 882 NVA soldiers from the NVA 324B Division during Operation Hastings/Deckhouse II (7 July–3 August 1966).

- 1st Cavalry Division (Airmobile) and ARVN troops killed 809 on Operation Paul Revere II (1–25 August 1966).
- U.S. Marines killed 1,397 soldiers from NVA 324B Division on Operation Prairie (3 August 1966–31 January 1967).
- U.S. Marines and ARVN troops killed 674 enemy on Operation Colorado/Lie Ket 52 (6–21 August 1966).
- Elements of the 1st Cavalry Division (Airmobile) inflicted a total of 849 enemy casualties on Operation Byrd (26 August 1966–20 January 1968).
- 196th Light Infantry Brigade, joined by 1st Infantry Division, elements of the 4th Infantry Division as well as the 173 Airborne Brigade inflicted 1,106 enemy casualties on Operation Attelboro in the biggest operation in the war to that date (14 September–24 November 1966).
- 1st Cavalry Division (Airmobile) as well as ARVN and South Korean troops on Operation Irving killed 681 enemy soldiers from the NVA 610th Division (2–24 October 1966).
- 4th Infantry Division along with element of the 25th Infantry Division and 1st Cavalry Division (Airmobile) on Operation Paul Revere IV killed 977 enemy troops (18 October–30 December 1966).
- 1st Cavalry Division (Airmobile) on Operation Thayer II killed 1,757 enemy troops (25 October 1966–12 February 1967).
- One battalion from each of the 1st, 4th, and 25th Infantry Division, later taken over by the 199th Light Infantry Brigade, along with ARVN troops killed 1,043 enemy troops on Operation Fairfax (30 November 1966–14 December 1967).
- On Operation Sam Houston, the 4th and 25th Infantry Division killed 733 enemy soldiers (1 January–5 April 1967).
- At least 570 enemy soldiers killed by the 9th Infantry Division on Operation Palm Beach (6 January–31 May 1967).
- Operation Cedar Falls, conducted by the 1st and 25th Infantry Divisions, the 173rd Airborne Brigade, 11th Armored Cavalry Regiment, and ARVN troops killed 720 enemy (8–26 January 1967).
- U.S. Marines on Operation Prairie II killed 693 NVA soldiers (1 February–18 March 1967).
- In a lengthy pair of operations called Pershing and Pershing II first directed against the NVA 610th Division and then shifting attention to I Corps, the 1st Cavalry Division (Airmobile) killed 5,401 NVA soldiers.

■ Operation Enterprise, conducted by the 9th Infantry Division along with ARVN troops as well as Regional and Popular Forces, resulted in 2,107 enemy dead (13 February 1967–11 March, 1968).

■ Junction City, the largest operation to date (22 February–14 May, 1967) conducted by 22 U.S. battalions drawn from the 1st, 4th, and 25th Infantry Divisions, 196th Light Infantry Brigade, 11th Armored Cavalry Regiment, and 173rd Airborne Brigade inflicted 2,728 enemy casualties.

■ Republic of Korean troops killed 831 Communist troops on Operation Oh Jac Kyo I (7 March–18 April 1967).

■ 4th Infantry Division troops on Operation Francis Marion killed 1,203 enemy troops (5 April–12 October 1967).

■ U.S. Marines killed 865 enemy in Operation Union (21 April–17 May 1967).

■ Operation Kole Kole by the 25th Infantry Division killed 645 enemy (14 May–7 December 1967).

■ U.S. Marines on Operation Union II killed 701 enemy soldiers (25 May–5 June 1967).

■ Operation Buffalo conducted by the U.S. Marines killed 1,281 enemy troops (2–14 July, 1967).

■ U.S. Marines killed 1,117 enemy troops in Operation Kingfisher (16 July–31 October 1967).

■ Operation Swift by U.S. Marines resulted in 517 enemy dead (4–15 September 1965).

■ Republic of Korea troops killed 541 enemy soldiers in Operation Dragon Fire (5 September–30 October 1967).

■ 1st Infantry Division killed 956 enemy troops on Operation Shenandoah II (27 September–19 November 1967).

■ In the ongoing Operation MacArthur which started on 12 October 1967, the 4th Infantry Division killed 4,944 enemy soldiers by the end of June 1968.

■ Operation Scotland conducted by the U.S. Marines resulted in 1,562 enemy casualties (1 November 1967–31 March 1968).

■ By 30 June, U.S. Marines on Operation Kentucky in the Con Thien area killed 2,658 NVA soldiers (commenced 1 November 1967, ongoing)

■ Operation Wheeler/Wallowa, conducted by two brigades from the Americal Division killed 8,689 enemy soldiers by 30 June in an operation which started on 11 November 1967.

- The 25th Infantry Division's Operation Yellowstone (8 December 1967–24 February 1968) resulted in 1,254 enemy dead.
- A simultaneous operation by the 25th Infantry Division, Saratoga, (8 December 1967–11 March 1968) resulted in 3,862 known enemy casualties.
- Operation Uniontown (17 December 1967–8 March 1968) resulted in 922 enemy casualties inflicted by the 199th Light Infantry Brigade.
- Republic of Korean troops killed 749 enemy soldiers in Operation Maeng Ho 9 (17 December 1967–30 January 1968).
- The Americal Division killed 1,129 enemy soldiers in Operation Muscatine (19 December 1967–10 June 1968).
- Operation McLain by the 173rd Airborne Brigade resulted in 637 known enemy dead by 30 June in a continuing Operation (commenced 19 January, 1968).
- The 1st Cavalry Division (Airmobile) killed 614 enemy troops on Operation Pershing II (22 January–29 February 1968).
- In a subsequent operation, dubbed Jeb Stuart, the 1st Cavalry Division (Airmobile) killed 3,268 enemy soldiers (22 January–31 March 1968).
- During the Battle of Hue, U.S. Marines and ARVN troops inflicted 5,113 enemy casualties (31 January–25 February 1968).
- South Vietnamese Marine, Ranger and Airborne troops killed 953 enemy soldiers on Operation Tran Hung Dao (5–17 February 1968).
- Republic of Korean troops killed 664 enemy soldiers in Operation Maeng Ho 10 (16 February–1 March 1968).
- A further 713 enemy troops were killed by South Vietnamese Marine, Ranger and Airborne troops in Operation Tran Hung Dao II (17 February–8 March 1968).
- In the continuing Operation Napoleon/Saline, U.S. Marines killed 3,127 NVA soldiers by the 30th of June 1968 (commenced 29 February, ongoing).
- Elements of the 1st, 9th, and 25th Infantry Divisions, along with ARVN troops killed 2,658 enemy soldiers in Operation Quyet Tang (Resolve to Win), (11 March–7 April 1968).
- Continuing operations by the 9th Infantry Division killed 1,251 enemy troops by 30 June in Operation Duong Cua Dan (People's Road) which started on 17 March 1968.

- Operation Pegasus/Lam Son 207, conducted by the 1st Cavalry Division (Airmobile) along with U.S. Marine and ARVN troops, killed 1,044 NVA soldiers (1–15 April 1968).
- The 101st Airborne Division, along with a brigade from the 82nd Airborne Division and ARVN troops, killed 2,100 NVA soldiers on Operation Carentan II (1 April–31 May 1968).
- A total of 42 U.S. battalions from II Field Force along with 37 ARVN battalions killed 7,645 enemy troops in the Capital Military District in Operation Toan Thang (Complete Victory) in the followup to the Tet Offensive (8 April–31 March 1968).
- In the continuing Operation Burlington Trail, troops from the Americal Division killed 577 enemy soldiers by 30 June 1968 in an operation which started on 8 April 1968.
- The U.S. Marines' continuing operations around Khe Sanh known as Operation Scotland II (commenced 15 April 1968) resulted in 2,053 known enemy dead by 30 June 1968.

NVA soldiers of the 8th Battalion, 90th North Vietnamese Army Regiment, who surrendered to these American soldiers after a battle in South Vietnam's northern provinces during Operation Carentan II.
Credit: U.S. Military History Institute

- Operation Delaware/Lam Son 216 by the 1st Cavalry Division (Airmobile), 101st Airborne Division, and elements of the 196th Light Infantry Brigade, along with ARVN units killed 869 NVA soldiers (19 April–17 May 1968).
- In a continuing operation known as Allen Brook which commenced on 4 May 1968, U.S. Marines killed 871 enemy soldiers by 30 June 1968.
- Operation Jeb Stuart III, which commenced on 17 May 1968, resulted in 843 enemy dead inflicted by the 1st Cavalry Division (Airmobile) by the end of June 1968.
- Nevada Eagle, an operation which began on 17 May 1968, resulted in 1,024 enemy dead through the actions of the 101st Airborne Division by the end of June 1968.
- The U.S. Marines on 18 May 1968 commenced Operation Marmeluke Thrust, which by the end of June 1968, resulted in 576 known enemy dead.

Also by mid-1968, Hanoi noted the declining strength of the American antiwar movement in party politics. Peace candidate Senator Eugene McCarthy was soundly defeated in the Democratic primaries and staunchly anti-Communist Richard M. Nixon looked certain to be the next American president. Hanoi turned away from its previous policy of aiming for high American casualties for its effect on American domestic politics.[13]

Faced with the realities of their continuing failures on the battlefield and the massive casualties they were taking, the Politburo finally tilted in favor of the northern faction. Now under Giap's direction, the aggressive big battles of the earlier 1960s were no more. Hanoi would gradually wind down its military effort in South Vietnam. Little by little, the war would recede. Communist attacks would be limited to small-scale sapper attacks on airfields and bases, intended largely for their media coverage and nuisance value. American and South Vietnamese casualties would still occur, but nowhere near the numbers to this point.

In June 1968, General Westmoreland left Vietnam to become Chief of Staff of the U.S. Army and was replaced by General Creighton Abrams. Except for sporadic battles, almost exclusively caused by aggressive American attacks into the NVA's previously safe areas, the war began inexorably to wind down.[14]

14

Operation Dewey Canyon
A Few Good Men Raid the Enemy's Sanctuary

In early January 1969, Major General Raymond G. Davis' 3rd Marine Division was enjoying its quietest month of the war since it first entered Quang Tri Province in July 1966. Under his command, much had changed. The Marines now had an improved version of their CH 46 helicopter and could lift almost three times the number of troops. Also, there was now an abundant supply of helicopters from nearby U.S. Army units to draw upon. This increased airlift capacity made the Marines more mobile and no longer tied to static defenses. Instead, they regularly and routinely carried out aggressive missions against the enemy.[1]

The Marines' main antagonist, the NVA 320th Division, had been defeated for the third consecutive time in late 1968 and had withdrawn to North Vietnam yet again to lick its wounds. This NVA division had been replaced by elements of six independent NVA regiments (138th, 270th, 84th, 31st, 27th, and the 126th Naval Sapper) operating along the DMZ. A short distance further south in Quang Tri Province, the three battalions of the NVA 812th Regiment, also badly defeated in the battles of early and mid-1968, had withdrawn to their jungle sanctuaries in the A Shau Valley for resupply and replacements. The total enemy strength in the DMZ and Quang Tri Province was estimated at 36,800 troops, half of which were combat troops.

Slightly further south, in Thua Thien Province, which included Hue and Phu Bai, most enemy units had been withdrawn into Laos. What few units remained, such as elements of the 4th and 5th Regiments, were forced to confine most of their efforts to rice-gathering and mere survival in the foothills. Enemy strength in Thua Thien Province was estimated at 15,200 troops.

While combat activity was down, the NVA weren't totally inactive. On November 1, 1968, President Johnson called a halt to all bombing of North Vietnam in return for several concessions from Hanoi, including their promise that they would not move troops southward through the DMZ. With this halt to the bombing of North Vietnam, NVA engineers, who had previously been employed repairing roads and bridges in the North, were now available for work on routes elsewhere. One of these projects was the recently reopened Route 922, which went south through Laos and then entered South Vietnam where it linked up with Route 548 in the A Shau Valley. This traditional Communist staging area, known to the Americans as Base Area 611, was the enemy's warehouse and storage area, where equipment was stockpiled in preparation for battles further east on Route 548: the areas of Hue and Phu Bai.[2]

Colonel Robert H. Barrow, a regimental commander with the 3rd Marine Division, knew that standard NVA practice in preparing for battle was first to move all the necessary food and equipment of war into position from the sanctuaries in North Vietnam or Laos, an activity that could take weeks or possibly even months. Then, when everything was in position, the enemy would rush his troops into position, marry up with the cached equipment, and do battle. Colonel Barrow later remarked: "We must do everything we can to find that stuff, wherever it exists and obviously destroy it. And if we miss any of it, we must attempt by vigorous patrolling, radio intercept, signal intelligence, recon team inserts, and whatever else, to find out when any troops were moving in."[3]

Beginning in January, Marine and Air Force reconnaissance aircraft began reporting a tremendous increase in traffic down Route 922, at times sighting more than 1,000 trucks per day. Intelligence reports noted that NVA units, thought to be the 6th and 9th NVA Regiments, together with the 65th Artillery and the 83rd Engineer Regiments, had crossed over from Laos. Reconnaissance also noted a heavy volume of antiaircraft fire, a sure sign that something was happening.

In early January 1969, First Lieutenant Justin Martin, a former infantry commander, was sitting in the observer's seat of a tiny O-1 Piper Cub, a propeller-driven spotting plane, cruising slowly at treetop level as he followed the twists and bends of the Da Krong Valley. Lieutenant Martin was acting on a report from a Marine reconnaissance patrol down on the ground, which had reported vehicle sounds emanating from the jungle. Suddenly, looking out the small plane's window, he caught sight of a glistening string of light, in reality a long section of communication wire strung through the treetops which, covered with dew, caught the sun at just the right angle for him to notice it. Like an arrow, the wire guided him southward down the valley until it met a well-worn path, which he later realized was a part of Route 922 in Laos. The sighting of the communication wire, as well as other intelligence reports, confirmed to the Marines that the North Vietnamese Army had moved from Route 922 into the valley. General Davis requested permission from XXIV Corps to conduct an operation to block this threat. On January 14, plans were drawn up for the operation, scheduled to begin on January 22.[4]

Colonel Barrow's 9th Marine Regiment was given the task of attacking in this valley area. Not only would his men again be outnumbered, operating in the enemy's very backyard, but also this time they would be totally dependent upon helicopters for resupply more than 50 kilometers from their nearest base. The latter was all the more dangerous because the monsoonal conditions made flying weather uncertain, and the Marines would be operating in an area where the NVA were well-supported by heavy artillery and antiaircraft batteries. However, the bad weather gave the Marines one advantage: the NVA would not be expecting an attack.

The plan of the attack called for the Marines first to seize a series of abandoned artillery positions north of the suspected enemy base camp and then quickly emplace their own 105-mm howitzers. From these hilltop artillery positions, the Marines would then launch ground attacks southward, seizing new hilltop positions onto which they would leapfrog their artillery and then repeat the process, driving deeper and deeper into the enemy's base camp.

On January 18, the Marines began the campaign by reopening three previously established fire support bases, placing their 105-mm artillery atop positions they now named Shiloh, Tun Tavern, and Henderson. The attack itself, code-named Dewey Canyon, began on the morning of January 22 with Lieutenant Colonel George C. Fox's 2nd Battalion. He sent half of his troops (Echo and Hotel Companies) to assault a 600-meter hilltop about eight kilometers distant from the nearest fire base, Shiloh. Meanwhile, he sent the other half (Foxtrot and Golf) to secure a landing zone further to the southwest. The initial attacks met little resistance and by the evening of January 23, a battery of 105-mm artillery was in place in the new position named Razor. On January 25, the Marines attacked three landing zones on a 1,100-meter-long ridgeline six kilometers to the southwest of Razor. By January 28, the Marines had leapfrogged their artillery from Tun Tavern and Shiloh and had also brought in 155-mm howitzers from Ca Lu. Their new position, Cunningham, could now provide artillery support to a distance of eleven kilometers, covering an area almost to the limit of the Marines' plans.

On January 24 and 25, the Marines began moving out of these newly constructed firebases to secure their flanks. They soon discovered a sophisticated four-strand communication line, strung between trees with porcelain insulators, running from Base Area 101 into Laos. Prepared for just such a discovery, the Marines had brought along a specially trained intelligence team who immediately tapped into the line, quickly breaking the NVA code. Also, the Marines discovered the 88th NVA Field Hospital which had been abandoned only the day before. This facility consisted of eight large permanent buildings with a capacity for 160 patients. In their haste to leave, the Communists had left behind large quantities of Russian-made medicines and stainless steel operating instruments.

On February 2, the Communists shelled Fire Support Base (FSB) Cunningham with approximately 40 rounds of artillery fire from their big 122-mm field guns located safely to the west in Laos beyond the range of the Marines' howitzers. Five Marines were killed and another five wounded. The Marines requested permission to enter Laos and destroy the guns, which threatened them, but permission was not granted. Given the rules of engagement, such permission seemed most unlikely.[5]

Bad weather closed in for the next nine days, preventing the Marines from further developing their attack. Weather was so bad that aerial resupply was limited to parachute drops directed by radar. On February 10, the weather cleared sufficiently for the Marines to helicopter to FSB Erskine in preparation for their push southward across the Da Krong.

On February 11, the 3rd Battalion, 9th Marines, crossed the shallow Song Da Krong and proceeded along a series of ridgelines south-southwest into the enemy's redoubt, Base Area 611. The next day, they were joined by the 1st Battalion moving along a ridgeline further to the west and by the 2nd Battalion, moving through a valley that straddled the Laotian border.

First Lieutenant Wesley L. Fox, commander of Alpha Company (1/9), observed that, "This was the first time that U.S. or South Vietnamese ground

NVA artillerymen firing their Soviet-made field guns. The NVA sited these weapons, which could shoot further than the Marines' howitzers, in "neutral" Laos and out of range of the Americans' artillery.
Credit: Democratic Republic of Vietnam

forces had been in the Da Krong Valley and the northern part of the A Shau." Lieutenant Fox, who had served 16 years as an enlisted Marine, rising to the rank of staff sergeant before receiving his commission three years before, noted with some anticipation that, ". . . the hunting should be good."[6]

The NVA resistance to this entry into their base camp, snuggled up against the Laotian border, was fierce. By day, the Marines attacked fortified positions within their path, and the NVA defended resolutely. By night, the NVA probed the Marine positions, looking for a weak point to attack. NVA soldiers tied themselves into the treetops to fire and throw grenades down at the Marines.

On February 18, the hundred or so Marines of Lieutenant Fox's Alpha Company, preceded by airstrikes, assaulted an NVA position five kilometers southeast of FSB Erskine. The NVA held tenaciously, losing 30 soldiers before the Marines managed to overrun their position. The next day, Charlie Company continued the attack against the hilltop position, killing another 30 NVA. On the following day, Charlie Company again made contact with the enemy and used napalm strikes within 50 meters of their own positions to eventually rout the NVA, who suffered 71 killed in the action. Alpha Company continued the attack, killing another 17 of the enemy. In addition to the casualties they inflicted on the enemy, the Marines also captured a large quantity of equipment, including two Russian-made 122-mm field guns and a five-ton, tracked prime mover used to haul them. The operation was proving to be very successful, so much so that the NVA were beginning to move their artillery further away to again be out of reach of the Marines' smaller howitzers.

On February 20, the hundred or so Marines of Captain Winecoff's Hotel Company occupied a ridgeline looking onto the Laotian border and Route 922, which lay just beyond it. The Marines observed helplessly from their vantage point as heavy trucks and tracked vehicles slowly clambered westward; the NVA were retreating deeper into Laos and further away from them. The Marines called fire missions onto the enemy but, observing from a distance of almost two kilometers and firing at moving targets, the results were questionable. Radio intercepts confirmed that the Communists were withdrawing their heavy artillery out of the range of the Marines' guns.

It was the same old story for the Marines. Once again, the battered NVA troops were withdrawing into "neutral" Laos; and the Marines, prevented from pursuing them, were being denied the final kill. They watched helplessly as the NVA withdrew their big guns to safety. By the afternoon of February 21, Colonel Barrow had had enough. As he would later relate, "I did not wait for approval when I ordered Hotel Company into Laos—it was a 'done deal'—and approval or no approval, Hotel Company would conduct an ambush." He relayed a hand-coded message to Captain Winecoff, ordering him to move his Marines into Laos and establish a night ambush on Route 922 that very same evening . They were instructed to be back inside South Vietnam no later than 6:30 A.M. the next morning.[7]

Captain Winecoff sought to have the action deferred for 24 hours to allow his exhausted men to get some much-needed rest. But Colonel Barrow denied this request, seeing the urgency of the action. Captain Winecoff, two of his platoons out on patrol, hurriedly drew up a plan in consultation with his one available platoon commander, Lieutenant Al D. Guins.[8]

Captain Winecoff quickly radioed an order to the commander of his 2nd Platoon, Lieutenant Dick Vercauteren, already out on patrol near the Laotian border. Lieutenant Vercauteren, who had celebrated his twenty-fourth birthday only days before, was simply told to halt in place and await further instructions. Meanwhile, Lieutenant Guins advised his Marines of 1st Platoon that they would move out in a few hours, together with Captain Winecoff. 3rd Platoon, commanded by Lieutenant Pete Robertson, was on a patrol in the opposite direction and was advised to return to the company position. Their job would be to remain behind, manning the company's defenses. Because the enemy periodically sent small reconnaissance units to probe the Marines' position, Captain Winecoff wanted to deceive the NVA into thinking that his company had not shifted.

The thirty or so Marines of Lieutenant Guins' 1st Platoon, together with a machine gun team, a mortar team, and Captain Winecoff himself, moved out of the perimeter at 4:00 P.M. and linked up with 2nd Platoon at 5:30 P.M. While Captain Winecoff and his two platoon commanders reconnoitered the proposed ambush site with two Marine riflemen as security, the bulk of the Marines ate their rations cold.

Just before darkness, Captain Winecoff and his officers briefed the men on the plan of attack and, eventually, in the total darkness of a moonless night, the Marines set off for the ambush site. With clouds and tall trees preventing even the faint illumination of the stars from penetrating, the Marines literally could not see their hands in front of their faces and had to grab hold of the man in front of them to avoid being separated. Moving in single file along a creek bed in the pitch dark at first, the Marines tripped and fell repeatedly and noisily on the slippery rocks. Eventually, they were forced to abandon the creek bed. Relying on their compasses and previous reconnaissance, the Marines' navigational skills were sorely tested and, fortunately, proved equal to the task. As they shifted onto a ridgeline paralleling the creek, they emerged from the foliage and were met with a dramatic sight. Below them off to the west, they could see the dimmed lights of a column of trucks, inching its way along the road as it approached them.

The point element of the Marine column progressed until it was within 30 meters of the road, separated from it by a small stream that ran parallel. Suddenly, a Soviet-built truck, perhaps 200 meters to the right, switched on its dimmed lights and started its engine. The Marines remained motionless. When the truck was only meters away from the Marine at the head of the column, the driver coasted to a halt and then switched off his motor and lights. The silence was broken only by the steady background chirping of crickets. The NVA driver cautiously watched and waited for several long moments before again switching his motor and lights on and then proceeding along a short distance and repeating the process.

It was now 8:30 P.M. A Marine scouting party, made up of Lieutenant Guins and a sergeant, was sent across the stream to check out the far side of the road as a possible ambush site. While they were doing so, the truck traffic continued its start-stop movement along the road in front of them. From further to their right, Vietnamese voices could be heard. A moment later, the Marines were startled to hear an enemy tank start its motor and clank noisily in their direction. It stopped twice, using the pause to direct a powerful searchlight along the roadside, trying to locate any ambushers. The tank rumbled to a halt directly in front of the Marines and shone its searchlight directly where they lay, but to their great relief, the tank failed to spot them and eventually rumbled off, deeper into Laos.

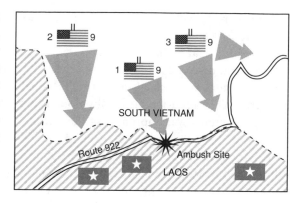

The two-man scouting party eventually returned at 10:15 P.M. When asked why they had taken so long, the two Marines half-joked that, "Every fallen tree looked like an enemy soldier. We pounced upon one log with drawn knives because we were so sure."[9]

Within moments, the Marines splashed across the stream and then filed across the road and up the gentle slope on its far side. The two platoons of Marines stretched out alongside the road, lying in the darkness, awaiting the enemy. The three officers went forward, placing claymore mines in position and, in so doing, discovered an unoccupied bunker, no doubt used by truck drivers to shelter from air attacks. Knowing it made an ideal observation point, Captain Winecoff asked for volunteers, and two Marines quickly stepped forward. They took a radio, a red-lensed flashlight, and a LAAW antitank weapon. Then they settled into the enemy bunker.

While the Marines waited, they could hear shots being fired from a short distance further into Laos where the enemy tank had stopped. An NVA infantry patrol approached down the road, firing their weapons into likely ambush sites. Captain Winecoff quickly briefed his men that they were not to return fire should the NVA fire in their direction. As luck would have it, though, the enemy patrol turned back into Laos before reaching the Marines' ambush site.

At 2:00 A.M. on the morning of February 22, a single truck entered the ambush zone but was allowed to pass through. The Marines broke radio silence for the first time, describing the nature of the truck and its cargo. For the American high command monitoring the radio waves, this report was the first received about the ambush team. On the scrambled radio nets of military high command there was much surprise and consternation about the Marines' presence in Laos. However, Colonel Barrow knew he had leverage: his men were already in place and ready to do what the Marines had requested for so long.[10]

Suddenly, at 2:30 A.M., several truck engines roared into life. The Marines could see a convoy of trucks, their lights dimmed, approaching. Thirty minutes later, exactly as instructed, the two Marines in the enemy bunker blinked a red-lensed flashlight back at their fellow Marines, indicating the enemy was approaching the ambush zone. Captain Winecoff waited until three trucks had entered and then fired the first claymore mine, destroying one of the trucks and setting it on fire. The second claymore mine failed to stop the lead truck, but a quick-thinking Marine in the bunker fired a LAAW antitank rocket at it, scoring a direct hit. The two platoons of Marines opened up with their M-16s, and within 30 seconds, the artillery observer had rounds landing to the left and right of the ambush zone, causing panicked NVA drivers to crash and capsize their loads. With the trucks burning and their ammunition exploding, the Marines assaulted through the zone, and then recrossing the creek bed, climbed the opposite slope and proceeded back into South Vietnam, but still in a position to observe the road below.

From their vantage point, the Marines could see the burning trucks and the rest of the convoy hastily moving off the now-blocked road, trying to camouflage their vehicles from possible air strikes. But Colonel Barrow was not finished yet. Knowing he now had the necessary leverage, he sent a request to higher headquarters for a continuation of operations over the border into Laos. He ended his request with the comment, "Put another way, my forces should not be here if ground interdiction of Route 922 is not authorized." Faced with a *fait accompli,* General Abrams approved the request on February 24, with the proviso that the operation be kept as secret as possible. Even the American ambassador in Laos was not to be informed until it was well underway.[11]

Colonel Barrow then ordered the rest of the battalion, minus one company, to join Captain Winecoff's company back down onto the road. For the next several days, the Marines proceeded along the road through the convoy's camouflaged positions, taking the fight to the enemy. Along the way eastward on Route 922, the Marines of Captain Winecoff's Company captured another three of the enemy's 122-mm Soviet field guns and, a short distance up the road, a complete four-gun 85-mm artillery battery. A number of other weapons were captured, including mortars and antiaircraft weapons. The other companies were having similar successes.

Further east, inside South Vietnam's border, the other battalions were clearing out the valleys and ridges associated with Route 548. In one par-

Captain Thomas Hinkle of Wilmington Delaware examines a 122-mm field gun destroyed on Operation Dewey Canyon. These Russian-made guns (the barrel lies in the foreground) easily outdistanced the Marines' howitzers.
Credit: National Archives and Records Administration

ticularly fierce engagement, the Marines of Lieutenant Wesley Fox's Alpha Company (1/9) fought an NVA unit dug in on a ridgeline. Because of the steep hills, tall trees, and poor weather, the Marines were unable to use artillery or air support. The Marines had little choice except to form up "on line" and assault the enemy. All three of his subordinate officers were killed or wounded in the fighting but, as Lieutenant Fox later commented, "In Marine tradition, the platoon sergeants knew what had to be done, and their Marines were already doing it—moving to the sound of the enemy's guns." Eventually, the Marines took the hill, killing 105 NVA soldiers in the process. The Marines noted that the NVA were wearing new uniforms and that several of them were officers, highly decorated veterans of other campaigns. The Marines of Alpha Company lost ten killed; almost everyone else in the company was wounded at least once. Lieutenant Fox noted that, ". . . but if they were conscious, they almost to a man refused the medevac. Each Marine would mumble something like: 'My squad is short; I'll stay until some replacements come in.' " Fifty-two badly wounded Marines were given no choice and were ordered to be evacuated on February 23, when the weather cleared enough for helicopters to operate.[12]

Operation Dewey Canyon ceased on March 19, 1969. During this operation, 130 Marines were killed and 920 wounded. North Vietnamese losses included 1,617 killed and five captured; 1,223 individual weapons were captured, along with 16 artillery pieces, 73 antiaircraft guns, 26 mor-

PFC Bernardo Blazek of Wisconsin stands atop a prime mover, a tracked vehicle for towing a 122-mm field gun, destroyed by the 9th Marine Regiment on Operation Dewey Canyon.

Credit: National Archives and Records Administration

tars, 104 machine guns, 92 trucks, over 807,000 rounds of ammunition, and over 220,000 pounds of rice.

When Laotian Prime Minister Souvanna Phouma was eventually told of the incursion into Laos, he ". . . expressed understanding of the action" and said "the essential element was to keep the matter secret." On March 9, the *New York Times*, in spite of the military's requests for secrecy, published an account of the raid in its Sunday edition. Later, the American ambassador would publicly apologize to the Laotian premier and the matter would be argued heatedly in Congress in 1970 and again in 1973. Colonel Barrow, the Commander of the 9th Marine Regiment, who ordered the raid, would remain unmoved. Twenty-five years later, he remarked, "I never gave 'what if' a second thought. I was *there*—to do what I as commander believed to be the right thing to do."[13]

Operation Dewey Canyon, and the raid into Laos that was a part of it, was so successful that, for the first time in the war, the NVA were unable to launch a spring offensive in I Corps. The spring of 1969 passed peacefully in Hue and Da Nang in sharp contrast to the bloodshed of previous years, no doubt confirming to Colonel Barrow that his decision had been, indeed, the right one.

15

Securing the Western Borders

While the Marines were clearing out the border areas near Laos, the U.S. Army's attention was focused further south, along the Cambodian border. The Ben Het Special Forces Camp was one of numerous outposts intended to detect enemy intrusions along South Vietnam's 800-mile western border. Located in the Central Highlands where the borders of South Vietnam, Cambodia and Laos meet, the Ben Het Camp directly overlooked the Ho Chi Minh Trail.[1]

At the camp itself were the 300 or so men of three South Vietnamese infantry companies and their American Special Forces advisers. Also located in the camp were a battery of American 155-mm artillery and two M-42 "dusters," tank-like vehicles mounting twin 40-mm antiaircraft guns, originally intended for air defense but used in Vietnam against massed infantry attacks.

The Communists wanted to remove this obstacle to their infiltration plans and knock out the 155-mm artillery battery. They would attempt to do so by throwing elements of the 16th Company, 4th Battalion, 202nd NVA Armored Regiment, into the attack. In February

1969, they commenced shelling the camp to mask their troop movements. The Americans responded by reinforcing the Ben Het Camp with tanks from the 1st Battalion, 69th Armored Regiment, and deployed them to positions on a hillside facing into Cambodia. The American tankers soon began trading shots with North Vietnamese soldiers in bunkers on the rugged slopes opposite them.

By March, the continuing enemy buildup led to a decision to move the American tanks to the defense of the camp itself. After a three-day respite from the shelling, the NVA hit the camp with a barrage of artillery and mortar fire at 9:00 P.M. on March 3.

Sergeant First Class Hugh Havermale and Staff Sergeant Jerry Jones, commanders of two M-48 tanks deployed to the southwestern area of the sprawling camp, both heard the distant rumbling and clanking sounds of tanks over the crashing and booming of the incoming artillery. Knowing there were no "friendly" tanks to the west, they quickly loaded their 90-mm main guns with high explosive antitank (HEAT) rounds and strained their eyes into the darkness. Sergeant Havermale's tank was equipped with an infrared searchlight that allowed him to scan the area in front of him. He could see nothing for the area's clinging fog. Sergeant Jones's tank faced the direction from which the tank sounds emanated but, because his tank was not equipped with infrared equipment, he was unable to see anything in the darkness to his front.

Within moments, an antitank mine exploded in the darkness, about 1,100 meters to the southwest, disabling a North Vietnamese PT76 tank and giving the enemy's position away. The enemy immediately commenced firing, and Ben Het's defenders could see the muzzle flashes of eight different tanks firing at them from out of the darkness. The American tankers quickly returned fire, gunner Specialist Fourth Class Frank Hembree scoring a direct hit with his second shot, turning a North Vietnamese tank into a fireball.

The American defenders soon illuminated the battlefield with flares fired by the base's mortar section. Moments later, an NVA tank scored a hit on an American tank. While the damage to the tank was relatively light, the round had hit the loader's hatch and the concussion killed the tank's loader and driver. In the eerie light of the descending parachute flares, Sergeant Jones clambered out of his tank and dashed over to another nearby tank, situated so that it couldn't get a clear shot at the enemy. As enemy shells landed around him, Sergeant Jones directed the tank to a better firing position. His actions were quickly rewarded as the tank was now able to spot another PT76 beside the burning hulk of one already hit and opened

fire on it. Sergeant Jones and the tank's gunner, Specialist Fourth Class
Eddie Davis, watched the enemy tank explode a second later.

Having used up all their antitank ammunition, the American tankers
loaded their guns with shells intended to penetrate concrete and continued firing. The enemy firing slowly dissipated and the NVA survivors withdrew into the darkness. The NVA attack had failed and Ben Het's 155-mm
artillery continued to fire at Hanoi's infiltrators. In the only head-to-head
encounter between American and North Vietnamese armor, the Americans were the clear victors, turning back the attack and forcing the enemy to
leave three burned-out hulks behind.

Shortly after this, continuing operations in the A Shau Valley by the
101st Airborne Division cleared out a traditional enemy base camp near the
Laotian border. For the first time ever, American and South Vietnamese
armored forces entered the valley, following on the heels of the paratroopers. Task Force Remagen, an armored force under the command of the 5th
Infantry Division, operated for 43 days along the Laotian border further
north in Quang Tri, cleaning out enemy base camps. Operation Montana

**A Soviet-supplied PT-76 tank of the NVA's 202nd Armored Regiment, destroyed by
American M48 tanks at Ben Het. In the only tank-to-tank battle between the NVA
and the Americans, the NVA were soundly defeated in this night-time battle.**
Credit: US Army

PFC Robert Geirley of Dillon South Carolina—a paratrooper of the 101st Airborne—guarding one of ninety-five NVA soldiers who surrendered when the Americans attacked their base camp.
Credit: U.S. Military History Institute

Raider, under the command of the 11th Armored Cavalry, took the fight to Communist base camps in III Corps Tactical Zone and cleaned out base camps along the Cambodian border near Tay Ninh City.

With American and South Vietnamese forces operating freely in their old base camps, the North Vietnamese Army had no choice but to pull back to their bases in Cambodia and Laos. By the middle of 1969, it was clear that the war was winding down. General Giap would not challenge the Americans in a face-to-face battle again and had withdrawn from the battlefield.[2]

The first of the American troop withdrawals were soon announced in response to Giap's withdrawal from the fight. By August 31, 1969, 25,000 American servicemen would be withdrawn. Of these, 8,388 were to be Marines, drawn coincidentally from the very same 9th Marine Regiment that had successfully invaded the enemy base camp in Operation Dewey Canyon only months ago. Others to be withdrawn were the paratroopers of the 173rd Airborne Brigade, the first Army ground unit to arrive in Vietnam and the heroes of Dak To and numerous other battles. On September 16, the next stage was announced: 45,000 Americans were to return to the United States. Of these, 18,483 were to be Marines, essentially the rest of the entire 3rd Marine Division.

Although many troops were being withdrawn, there was still work to be done by the remaining forces. Now that the North Vietnamese Army had been evicted, American forces turned their attention to securing the borders. Rather than attempting to defend the entire 800-mile stretch with static defenses, it would use highly mobile armored and airmobile units to strike at the enemy whenever they dared to cross into South Vietnam. In order to spot them, it augmented its previous sprinkling of Special Forces camps with electronic sensing devices. Also in many areas, American troops plowed 500-meter-wide stretches of open ground, much like fire breaks in the forest, along the border to better visually observe from the air.

Typical of the encounters was one that took place on January 21, 1970. The 1st Squadron, 11th Armored Cavalry, was operating in a Loc Ninh rubber plantation when it intercepted two North Vietnamese battalions. With their fellow armored cavalrymen from the 2nd and 3rd Squadrons racing to join the fight and arriving within hours, the combined force dealt the NVA a severe blow and sent them reeling back to the Cambodian border. In their haste to leave, they failed to remove the mapcase from their dead commander and the Americans, upon locating it, discovered that the NVA had marked the map with their emergency escape plan. Tactical airstrikes and artillery were immediately called on to these routes with devastating effect on the fleeing NVA soldiers.[3]

In March 1970, Captain John Caldwell's cavalry troop from the 3rd Squadron killed more than 200 soldiers of the 209th NVA Regiment in a one-sided battle near the same area. In April, the 95C North Vietnamese Regiment tried crossing in this area, but was met by Lieutenant Colonel James Reed's 1st Squadron. While two NVA battalions fought it out with the Americans, the third NVA battalion attempted to escape to the north. The American cavalry and tanks were joined by elements of the 2nd Squadron. When the NVA commander realized his situation, he panicked and began issuing immediate withdrawal orders to his men in uncoded radio broadcasts. American forces immediately intercepted these broadcasts and passed them on to the cavalry, who placed a squadron in the path of the enemy and destroyed two entire North Vietnamese Army battalions. Infiltrating their troops over the borders of South Vietnam had proven a very costly exercise to the North Vietnamese Army.[4]

16

The Incursions
No More Sanctuaries

Events had changed dramatically by 1970. The Viet Cong had been destroyed and the North Vietnamese had withdrawn from the battlefield. American troops were on their way home, but they were determined to leave only after they had given South Vietnam every chance for a continued existence.

Having defeated the enemy time and again and successfully sealing the border, American troops now attacked the enemy's Cambodian weapons depots. Even though the North Vietnamese might recruit another generation into their army, they would have no weapons with which to wage war. With luck, the Americans might even capture some of the enemy's leadership.

Two such headquarters and weapons depots presented continuing problems. In the jungles far to the west of Saigon, the irregular twists and turns of the Cambodian border formed two salients that protruded deeply into what would otherwise have been South Vietnamese territory. Surrounded on three sides by South Vietnam, Americans referred to these features as the Fish Hook and the Parrot's Beak.

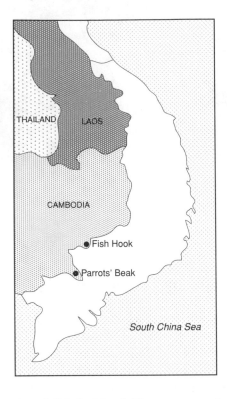

Having been preceded two days earlier by a South Vietnamese attack into the Parrot's Beak, American troops launched their own daring raid into the Fish Hook on May 1, 1970. This portion of Cambodia, jutting into South Vietnam, was being used as a safe sanctuary by the enemy. That safety ended when the armored personnel carriers and tanks of the 11th Armored Cavalry and the 2nd Battalion, 34th Armored, swept into the attack. They were soon joined by units from the 25th Infantry Division, the 4th Infantry Division, and the 1st Air Cavalry.[1]

The NVA grudgingly fell back further into Cambodia, fighting delaying actions as they withdrew. Only when the American armor reached the Cambodian town of Snuol did the North Vietnamese resistance stiffen. Dug in around the outskirts of the town, the NVA forced the American tanks to grind to a halt. After knocking out the NVA's larger weapons with cannon fire, the tanks again pressed forward. Joined by more than 100 Sheridan light tanks, the Americans pushed the NVA out of the town building by building.

After the battle, when American soldiers questioned nearby villagers, they learned why the resistance had been so strong. The villagers told of massive NVA storage compounds nearby. Scout helicopters were sent to investigate and, before long, a sharp-eyed pilot found a well-camouflaged hut. The 100 infantrymen sent in found the area to be well guarded, but they managed to eliminate the guards with a series of ambushes once night had fallen. The next day, the Americans discovered what they came to call the "city," a complex of 400 buildings, complete with bunkers, dining facilities, a rifle range, even a swimming pool under the concealment of a heavy jungle canopy. Well laid out with pathways and street signs, the "city" yielded enormous tonnages of weapons and equipment. When helicopters spotted four trucks some distance away two days later, the infantry was again sent in. There was a brief but savage battle before the NVA were forced to again admit defeat and withdraw. The Americans seized yet another huge complex and called this one "Rock Island East" after the American Rock Island Arsenal in Illinois. This cache included telephone switchboards, several trucks, millions of rounds of ammunition, and thousands of rockets. It was the biggest single cache ever captured. Within two weeks, American troops had seized 124 trucks and enormous stores of food, ammunition, and weapons, stores that would take the Communists years to replace.

With the fighting over, the Americans settled into the drudgery of emptying the enemy's warehouses of their war material and carting it off. In that two-week period ending on June 30, 1970, the allies captured:

- 124 trucks
- 23,000 rifles, enough to equip 74 battalions
- 2,500 machine guns, mortars, and antitank weapons, enough to equip 25 battalions

Troopers of the 1st Cavalry Division (Airmobile) uncover a 37-mm anti-aircraft gun. Its origin is clear from the Soviet flag found alongside their booty.
Credit: US Army Military History Institute

- 16,700,000 rounds of ammunition, as much ammunition as the Communists expended annually
- 200,000 rounds of antiaircraft ammunition
- 143,000 rounds of mortar, rocket, and recoilless rifle ammunition
- 14,000,000 pounds of rice.

In attacking these well-defended and long-held enemy base camps, the South Vietnamese Army suffered 638 of its troops killed, while Americans losses were listed as 338. Once again, Communist losses were heavy: approximately 11,000 of their troops were killed and another 2,500 were captured. The loss of these troops and the massive quantities of supplies was a severe setback to Hanoi. Perhaps of even more concern to the Communists was the solid performance of the South Vietnamese troops.[2]

These operations in 1970 were so successful that, on February 8, 1971, the South Vietnamese Army launched an attack deep into Laos using only its own troops. South Vietnamese forces attacked westward from Khe Sanh just south of the DMZ, attempting to sever NVA supply lines indefinitely. They were forced to do so alone because the United States Congress's Cooper-Church Amendment in December 1970 prevented U.S. ground troops from operating outside South Vietnamese borders. General Westmoreland had previously calculated that it would require 60,000 American troops to perform a similar operation into Laos and, lacking that number of spare troops, he had rejected the plan to attack. Now, in early 1971, South Vietnam was so full of confidence that it launched the attack with only 25,000 men.[3]

The attack proceeded well for the first four days, but then the NVA hurled 36,000 men, including two armored divisions, at the narrow corridor of attacking South Vietnamese troops. The South Vietnamese troops lacked effective antitank weapons and were hit hard by Hanoi's Soviet-built heavy tanks. Regardless, they fought on for a month until, on March 10, a withdrawal was ordered which, in some instances, became a rout. But the South Vietnamese had indeed met tough resistance, something often not credited to them. They were attempting one of the most difficult of military maneuvers: withdrawal while under enemy attack. Some suggestion of this resistance is the fact that American forces lost 107 helicopters in supporting the Southern troops.

As it turned out, General Westmoreland's estimate about the difficulty of the task was proven correct, and the South Vietnamese found out that they had bitten off more than they could chew. One cannot help but be impressed, however, at their new-found confidence and the fact that they launched the attack at all, an attack that even the Americans had never dared.

17

Vietnamization Is Tested
North Vietnam's Spring Offensive, 1972

Quiet had come to South Vietnam by the spring of 1972. The old battlegrounds in South Vietnam's northernmost provinces, known to the Americans as I Corps, were now thriving civilian communities. Having believed Hanoi's assurance, given in return for the November 1968 cessation of American bombing attacks on North Vietnam—that they would not blatantly invade through the DMZ, South Vietnam had emplaced only one relatively poor-quality division of troops in the area. Previously defended by 80,000 of America's best troops, the defense of I Corps was now in the hands of less than 9,000 South Vietnamese troops, which they themselves regarded as green.[1]

America had been successfully pursuing its "Vietnamization" plan to turn the war over to the South Vietnamese people themselves since the late 1960s. America also pursued a vigorous diplomatic effort to enlist the help of China and the Soviet Union in forcing Hanoi to give up its attempt to take over the southern republic by force. Much had changed in the world since America first sent its troops to South Vietnam some 11 years previously. Great cracks had appeared in what had then been seen as a rock-solid alliance between China and the Soviet Union. Border clashes between the two Communist superpowers were not uncommon. They were both losing interest in the war in South Vietnam as they grew increasingly concerned about each other.

In late February 1972, President Richard Nixon made his historic trip to China, a trip which would have been unthinkable only a few years before. This trip, which changed world politics forever, saw President Richard Nixon meeting cordially with America's old cold war adversaries, Mao Zedong and Premier Zhou Enlai.

Nixon was successful in enlisting Chinese help. The Chinese deemed the Soviets an even greater threat to their security than the Americans. They also feared that Hanoi would one day seize Laos and Cambodia and pose a threat to their southern border. China continued to give small arms and ammunition to the now-ineffectual Viet Cong, but they pointedly tried to minimize Hanoi's influence by reducing aid to North Vietnam, especially in heavy weapons and the transportation facilities needed to wage offensive war against South Vietnam.[2]

Hanoi, always skillful at playing the two Communist superpowers against each other, had already begun courting the Soviets. In early spring 1971, Le Duan went to Moscow, seeking massive aid, including hundreds of T-34 and T-54 tanks, scores of long-range artillery pieces, sophisticated antiaircraft missiles, and tons of fuel, spare parts and ammunition. All of this aid was necessary for an invasion of South Vietnam. Shortly after his return, in June/July 1971, the Politburo met and decided to proceed with plans for an invasion.[3]

President Richard Nixon, however, was about to stage another diplomatic coup, a summit meeting with Soviet Premier Brezhnev. Hanoi became increasingly concerned that its arms supplies would soon stop entirely as a result of a United States/Soviet Union agreement. His supply of weapons threatened by détente, Defense Minister Giap decided he must act quickly.

North Vietnam launched its attacks beginning at 12:00 noon on March 30, 1972. Attacking through the DMZ with over 45,000 troops and 200 Soviet-made tanks and supported by heavy 122-mm and 130-mm field guns, Hanoi broke its November 1968 promise about the sanctity of the DMZ. Its troops poured southward. Before long, the old combat bases, such as Camp Carroll and Con Thien, so familiar to Americans from previous times, began to fall. The green troops of South Vietnam's Third Army Division reeled back, attempting to establish a new defensive line along the Cua Viet River, which runs roughly east to west.

South Vietnamese Marines were rushed northward from their Dong Ha base to counter the invasion. They established themselves on the southern end of the the Dong Ha bridge, main bridge spanning the Cua Viet River. They could see an

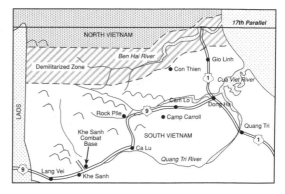

NVA flag already flying from the bridge's northern end. South Vietnamese Marine Sergeant Luom was the leader of a six-man antitank squad that took up positions on the bridge's southern end. Armed only with one-shot, disposable LAAW antitank rockets, Sergeant Luom deployed one two-man team on each side of the highway bridge abutment. Then he and his assistant took up a middle position on the bridge's southern tip. While fleeing refugees and South Vietnamese Army soldiers from the 3rd Division streamed past, Sergeant Luom and his assistant crouched behind two dirt-filled ammunition boxes, which afforded only 12 inches of dirt protection from the invasion force headed his way. When the 95-pound South Vietnamese Marine spotted a 40-ton, Soviet-made T-54 crashing down the road in his direction, he calmly fired the tiny LAAW rocket at the approaching behemoth. The first round sailed harmlessly over the top of the tank's turret, but the little Vietnamese Marine quickly fired a second rocket, this time scoring a hit at that point where the tank's turret joins its chassis. The hit appeared to affect the tank's ability to traverse its main gun. Although still perfectly capable of firing and attacking, the NVA tank ground to a halt. The tank's hatch then opened, and the puzzled NVA tank commander peered across the bridge. Rather than resume the attack, he instead reversed his tank back down off the bridge. The Communist offensive momentarily came to a halt. The little Marine had done the unimaginable.[4]

Using the time Sergeant Luom had thus gained, two American advisers, Marine Captain John W. Ripley and Army Major James E. Smock, placed explosive charges on the Dong Ha bridge and at the nearby railway bridge. Dangling precariously from the bridge's structure, they lugged the heavy boxes of explosives into position. While fully exposed to the NVA on the bridge's northern end, the Communists never made a concerted effort to stop the two Americans. Captain Ripley remembers the NVA watching him, instead, with humor and amazement. Captain Ripley states that, "In my judgment, they knew their massive assault would be successful and whatever I happened to be doing was relatively inconsequential; besides, I was providing them amusement." No doubt their amusement ceased when, shortly before 4:30 P.M. on April 2, 1972, the two bridges were totally destroyed by the Americans' explosive charges. Frustrated in their attempt to cross the Dong Ha bridge, the NVA moved westward, hoping to cross further inland at Cam Lo. They were stopped in their movement by naval gunfire from the USS *Bachanian, Strauss,* and *Weddell* lying offshore.[5]

Attacks Through Cambodia

The North Vietnamese attacks on the central part of South Vietnam began on April 2 with diversionary attacks near the Cambodian border. Three reinforced Communist divisions began the main thrust by attacking Loc Ninh on April 4. Although the defenders successfully beat back several attacks, the town had fallen to yet another assault by April 6, this one supported by 25 to 30 tanks.[6]

The next target was the town of An Loc, which the Communists hoped to establish as seat of the Provisional Revolutionary Government, much as they had previously sought to do at Hue during the 1968 Tet Offensive. Emboldened by their early successes, they moved south to the town. On April 7, they reached An Loc's outskirts and quickly captured the airfield, which not only isolated the town but also allowed its occupiers to look down onto the city from its dominating high ground.[7]

Defended by only one South Vietnamese Army regiment and two battalions of Rangers (perhaps 2,500 troops), the town's defenses had little chance against the two Communist divisions (20,000 troops) that besieged it. Then, in the words of General Phillip Davidson, there occurred ". . . one of those 'foulups' which makes war the unpredictable and dicey business it is." Instead of attacking immediately, the Communists' 9th Division, scheduled for the main attack, just remained in place and did nothing for a week. Their inadequate and inflexible logistic system had failed to keep pace with them, and they had to wait for their needed supplies.[8]

The South Vietnamese Army used the time to rush reinforcements to An Loc. When the Communists attacked on April 13, they hit the town with an artillery barrage and then with an attack by tanks. This assault was followed later by an infantry attack. The South Vietnamese Army troops stopped the tank attack, largely with hand-held LAAW antitank weapons. The Communists attacked again and again until the fighting eventually slackened off on April 16.

On April 18, the South Vietnamese Army captured a document from the political officer of the Communists' 9th Division. The document was described as "one of those priceless windfalls which win battles." Written to COSVN high command, the document gave detailed plans for the next attack. The next day, the attack occurred just as predicted. Although suffering heavy casualties, the forewarned and prepared South Vietnamese Army managed to stop the Communists from taking An Loc.[9]

The Attack Through the DMZ

Although one thrust of the attack southward through the DMZ was halted at the Cua Viet River, a separate thrust through the western portion of the DMZ, mainly by the NVA 304th Division, was having more success. With no natural obstacles blocking them, the Soviet-made T-54 tanks were able to breach the perimeter of Fire Support Base Pedro, just west of Quang Tri. Using their weight to crush the defenders' bunkers, 16 NVA tanks were soon closing in on the city. South Vietnamese armor, in the form of American-made M-48 tanks, was thrown into the counterattack and, with the support of South Vietnamese Air Force propeller-driven fighter/bombers, 13 of the 16 NVA tanks were destroyed within the next two hours. Of the remaining three, one NVA tank managed to withdraw to safety, while the other two were abandoned by their crews who chose to flee on foot. A three-day battle ensued before the NVA pulled back, leaving 368 bodies on the battlefield.

The NVA eventually managed to move troops and tanks across the Cam Lo bridge complex to the west and then turn to attack Dong Ha. On April 28, the South Vietnamese troops were ordered to withdraw further south, falling back to a defensive line centering on Quang Tri City. By May 1, the authorities decided that Quang Tri would need to be evacuated and South Vietnam's troops fell back further southward, some of their units in full rout, others maintaining good order in their withdrawal. The new line of defense was to be the My Chanh River, the next natural obstacle to the NVA juggernaut some seven kilometers south of Quang Tri. With South Vietnamese Marines defending the vital bridges over the river, South Vietnamese troops and civilians fled southward. South Vietnamese Marines destroyed 17 NVA tanks and killed hundreds of NVA infantry in their successful defense of those bridgeheads. Meanwhile, the NVA seized the abandoned Quang Tri City, proclaiming it their "Provincial Capital in the South."

America Responds

By early 1972, America had already withdrawn virtually all of its ground combat forces from South Vietnam. Total troop strength was less than 70,000, almost entirely made up of technicians and support staff. America could still, however, deliver a powerful punch from the air.

Poor weather over South Vietnam initially prevented effective use of American air power. At a meeting in the Oval Office at the White House, the President of the United States asked his aides to pray for fair weather, noting that, "The bastards have never been bombed like they're going to be bombed this time." He then paused momentarily before adding ". . . but you've got to have the weather."[10]

On April 1, President Nixon ordered the bombing of the most southern portion of North Vietnam, that is the area within 25 miles of the DMZ. Within two weeks, he extended this order to bombing up to the 20th parallel, about 250 miles north of the DMZ.

Henry Kissinger arrived in Moscow on April 20, while American bombers were hitting military targets in the southern part of North Vietnam for the first time since 1968. He participated in a five-day meeting to make arrangements for the upcoming summit, scheduled for May 22. Antiwar protesters back in America were hopeful that the Soviets would cancel the summit in protest, but they did not.

On May 8, President Nixon went on television to announce the resumption of bombing attacks on military targets throughout North Vietnam. For the first time, American aircraft used the new "smart bombs" that were guided to their targets by laser beams. One of the targets was the massive Thanh Hoa bridge which spanned the Song Mai River 80 miles south of Hanoi. In the raids of 1965-1968, the bridge had been attacked over one hundred times with conventional bombs, but despite being hit several times, only its paintwork had been scratched. Now, on May 13, F-4 Phantom jets from the 8th Tactical Fighter Wing attacked the bridge with the new laser-guided 2,000-pound and 3,000-pound bombs, scoring 15 direct hits and totally collapsing the structure. President Nixon also announced the mining of Haiphong harbor, a direct slap at the Soviets who supplied the North Vietnamese mainly by ship. Still there was no cancellation of the summit. The message to Hanoi was clear. The summit meeting proceeded and was attended by Soviet leaders Brezhnev, Kosygin, and Podgorny, and by President Nixon from May 22 to June 1. A new era in east-west relations was emerging. It promised to permanently "turn off the tap" of military supplies to Hanoi.[11]

Another Attempt to Seize An Loc

The thrust from Cambodia, aimed at the city of An Loc, had stalled after the city's successful defense in April. On May 5, a Communist officer defected and told his interrogators that the Communists' 9th Division had been reprimanded for its failure. The Commanding General of the Communists' 5th Division boasted that his troops could take the town in two days, and he was given the opportunity to do so. The Communist officer gave detailed information about the plan of attack and said it would come before May 12. The attack against An Loc came on May 11, 1972, as warned. At exactly 9:00 A.M., acting on the information provided, preplanned concentrations of B-52 attacks began hitting the enemy assault troops. Twenty-four B-52 strikes hit the enemy within the day. General Phillip Davidson described how, ". . . in one area, the B-52s struck an NVA regiment [1500 troops] in the open, and when the smoke and dust had settled, the regiment had simply vanished." The attacking enemy forces were being obliterated from the air by a combination of the B-52s' massive bomb tonnages, their precise accuracy, and the detailed information provided by the Communist defector.[12]

South Vietnam Counterattacks

By May, a new spirit began to be instilled in the South Vietnamese Army. Orders were given that restructured their forces and made them more combat-capable. Ominously for Hanoi's troops, a new "Order of the Day" was issued: "There would be no further withdrawals." Throughout the month of May, Hanoi threw its troops at the My Chanh defensive line but failed to crack it. Both the NVA 66th and 88th Regiments were forced to retire temporarily from the battlefield as casualties mounted. Communist forces in May suffered almost 3,000 killed and lost 64 armored vehicles.

During June, the South Vietnamese seized the initiative and launched a series of amphibious operations, preceded by B-52 strikes, against the NVA supply lines. They managed to push the NVA back four kilometers from their My Chanh line. On June 28, the South Vietnamese began Operation Sont Than 9-72, intended to defeat the NVA and recapture Quang Tri City. After much bitter fighting, South Vietnamese troops achieved their objective and, at 12:00 noon on September 16, the South Vietnamese hoisted their flag over Quang Tri City. The provincial capital was back in Southern hands.

The Process Continues

With the defeat of Hanoi's Easter Offensive, and as a result of discussions with the Soviets at the summit, Vietnamization continued at an even brisker pace. In mid-June 1972, Soviet Union President Podgorny visited Hanoi and bluntly told the North Vietnamese that it was time to negotiate. At about the same time, Chairman Mao similarly urged North Vietnam to be more flexible.[13]

Hanoi could see it had little choice left. Communist General Tra Van Tra wrote that, "If in 1972, at Shanghai, they [the Chinese] had not promised to save Thieu and South Vietnam for the United States . . . the United States would not have boldly withdrawn its troops from Vietnam and changed its strategy." General Tra lamented, ". . . that meant that whether the United States remained in Vietnam or left Vietnam it had the assurance, ironically, of its gigantic friend to the north, a country bordering ours."[14]

In August, Nixon announced yet another round of withdrawals, leaving only 27,000 men of a force that had numbered over 500,000 only three years before. Vietnamization was proceeding at such a brisk pace that Henry Kissinger became increasingly concerned that the United States would have unilaterally withdrawn even before the peace accords were finalized. Nixon wasn't concerned; he calculated that he had won the war. Senator and former presidential candidate Eugene McCarthy confirmed this, saying, ". . . [Nixon] and Rusk had in fact thought they had won, and they thought they might de-escalate because of the victory."[15]

Continuing the process begun in 1969 with the withdrawal of America's elite units, the conventional combat units, the regular infantry and artillery units of the U.S. Army had also been gradually withdrawn throughout the early 1970s. The process was completed on August 12, 1972, with the withdrawal of the 3rd Battalion, 21st Infantry and G Battery, 29th Field Artillery. The United States was left with *no combat forces whatsoever* in South Vietnam.[16]

Believing that the long-awaited signing of a cease-fire was imminent, the United States halted all bombing north of the 20th parallel on October 23, effectively ending the attacks on North Vietnam.

Hanoi may not have given up on its hopes to take over South Vietnam, but it had been consistently thwarted on the battlefield. Now, with the agreement of China and the Soviet Union, their ability to wage war would be severely limited. Only the formal agreement needed to be signed.

18

Linebacker II
A Farewell Knockout Blow

Aware that America had defeated North Vietnam time and again on the battlefield, President Richard Nixon was increasingly annoyed during the closing months of 1972 at the intransigence of the Communists at the peace negotiations. He was especially concerned that this intransigence was delaying the much-awaited release of American prisoners of war (POWs).

On December 14, President Nixon called the Chairman of the Joint Chiefs of Staff, Admiral Thomas Moorer. President Nixon made it clear that the "gloves" were now off on the use of American aircraft. He was tired of hearing which targets could and could not be hit. "This is your chance," he said, "to use military power effectively to win this war . . ."[1]

A plan was drawn up to destroy all military installations in the Hanoi/Hai Phong area as well as all other facilities, such as railroad yards, bridges, roads, electric power plants, and steel works, which supported North Vietnam's war efforts. Originally planned to be a three-day campaign, it was later decided to run indefinitely until all targets had been destroyed or North Vietnam returned to the peace talks, whichever came first.[2]

On December 18, 1972, the United States resumed its air attacks on North Vietnam. For seven days, the United States pummeled Northern targets, then unilaterally declared a cease-fire for Christmas Day. The air attacks began again on December 26 and continued for a further four days. In 11 days in total, the United States dropped 20,370 tons of bombs on military targets in the Haiphong-Hanoi area. With 724 B-52 sorties against larger targets in the cities' outskirts and 640 strikes by more accurate fighter-bombers equipped with the new "smart bombs" against targets that posed risks of civilian casualties, the attacks can be compared to some of the biggest of World War II.[3]

U.S. Air Force Captain Frank D. Lewis was in a Hanoi POW camp at the time of the attacks. He was awakened by the sound of air raid sirens and then, moments later, by the sonic boom of an F-111 passing low overhead at supersonic speed. A few seconds later, he heard the F-111's string of bombs detonating in the distance. "I couldn't keep quiet," he recalls, "and danced around my cell like a fool, yelling and cheering." All was quiet for a moment but Captain Lewis correctly guessed that the F-111's mission was merely to prepare the way for the main attack. After about ten minutes of silence, the air raid sirens began wailing again, and he could hear heavy-caliber antiaircraft guns firing into the sky and the occasional "whooshing" sound as a surface-to-air missile (SAM) was launched against the approaching American aircraft. Moments later, he could hear a distant rumbling as the B-52s hit their targets on the city's outskirts. Then the rumblings grew louder as the B-52s walked their strings of bombs across their targets. Captain Lewis thought that, "It sounded like Godzilla was crunching around the city." The overlapping explosions shook the ground beneath him and caused plaster to fall from the walls of his cell, but throughout the whole attack, he jumped and yelled with delight. "Never again in the next three months would I ever feel alone," Captain Lewis recalls. "I prayed for the men, the crews, and the aircraft they flew. To me they had become the hand of God that had reached out to bring me an inner peace and strength with which I could endure this cruel land."[4]

The North Vietnamese fired an estimated 1,242 SAMs at American aircraft. The huge majority missed their targets entirely and fell back onto North Vietnam, many with their warheads still intact. Even with this added element of "friendly fire" damage, the relatively small number of civilian casualties is amazing. *Even at the time*, when wartime propaganda tended to exaggerate civilian casualties and minimize military ones, Hanoi estimated

North Vietnamese pilots scramble to their MiG-21PF fighters. No MiG managed to shoot down a B-52. All B-52 losses were due to Soviet-supplied ground-to-air missiles.
Credit: Democratic Republic of Vietnam

civilian casualties from the Christmas 1972 bombings at between 1300 and 1600, amazingly low in comparison to the hundreds of thousands of civilian casualties inflicted by raids of smaller bomb-tonnages against Tokyo, Berlin, or Dresden less than 30 years previously.[5]

Fearful of the U.S. Air Force's F-105 Wild Weasel aircraft, whose specific mission was to monitor the antiaircraft missiles' radars and then attack the launch sites, many of the North Vietnamese chose to fire their missiles "blind," their radars turned off and missiles simply unleashed in hopeful volleys. Not surprisingly, most of them missed.

During these "Christmas" bombings (Nixon objected to the press referring to them in these words because, as he pointed out, none of them occurred on Christmas), the North Vietnamese shot down a total of 26 American planes, including 15 B-52s, brought down by SAMs. During the battle, the North Vietnamese were continuously resupplied with SAMs by Soviet ships anchored close offshore. The missile components were brought in on small boats, then trucked to a small assembly plant located in heavily populated southeast Hanoi, where they were assembled and readied for the launchers by nighttime when the Americans struck. General Meyers sought permission to attack this assembly plant but permission was denied to use B-52s for fear of civilian casualties, even though the North Vietnamese had knowingly placed the facility in a civilian area and the SAMs were killing many Americans. Eventually, permission was granted to attack the site with the smaller, more accurate F-4 Phantoms. The plant was destroyed and the North Vietnamese soon had no more SAMs to fire. Further, the North Vietnamese wouldn't be getting any more missile components. The U.S. Navy now cruised off the coast, having established a blockade of North Vietnam's coastline.[6]

A B-52 bomber of the type used in Operation Linebacker II. Note the 'sting in the tail' supplied by the four .50 caliber machine guns. B-52 tail gunners accounted for two of the eight MiG fighters shot down during the eleven day battle.
Credit: United States Air Force

Eight North Vietnamese fighters were shot down during the campaign, including two by B-52 tail gunners. For the final three days of the raids, the Americans roamed the skies of North Vietnam with virtual impunity; little or no fire was being directed at them. By December 29, the bombing was complete. The United States had achieved complete domination over North Vietnam's skies and, as former Intelligence Chief, Lieutenant General Phillip Davidson, would later write, "North Vietnam's military potential, its industry, and economy lay in ruins. In fact, there were no more legitimate military targets in North Vietnam to strike." Its antiaircraft system shattered, North Vietnam now lay defenseless to the American bombers, but the United States stopped the attack because there was nothing left worth attacking. Later, accounts began to surface from those with relatives in North Vietnam who told them that, "They were preparing white flags to surrender" because they were convinced they were losing the war badly. [7]

North Vietnam quickly returned to the peace talks, signing the accords within a few days and releasing America's POWs shortly thereafter. North Vietnam also dropped its requirement that President Thieu step down from power in South Vietnam, but there was a more important change. Something else was now added to the formula through which the United States hoped that South Vietnam might survive: North Vietnam had lost its internal communications system, electrical power grid, and its entire air force.

In the words of one who was generally a critic of American war policies, Sir Robert Thompson (credited with having defeated the Communist insurgency in Malaya): "In my view, on December 30, 1972, after eleven days of those B-52 attacks on the Hanoi area, you had won the war. It was over! They had fired 1,242 SAMs; they had none left, and what would come in overland from China would be a mere trickle. They and their whole rear base were at your mercy."[8]

Perhaps one of the more eloquent testimonials is that of Colonel Fred Cherry, a U.S. Air Force pilot shot down in 1965 and held captive, and repeatedly tortured, until his release in February 1973: "We could hear the B-52s." he reported. "And we knew they were going to solve it. When the bombing stopped, we knew they didn't have any more missiles. And that the agreements were going to be signed."[9]

19

Defeat of the North Vietnamese Army

As far back as May 1968, General Westmoreland had asked retired General S.L.A. Marshal to return to South Vietnam for an independent assessment of the situation. At that time, combat had been at a very high level with four hundred Americans per week being killed. Even at this level of combat, General Marshal's observations were very positive.[1]

Because of the change in command (General Westmoreland was replaced by General Creighton Abrams), Marshal found himself reporting to General Abrams about what he had seen. "I said I was certain that the Army of North Vietnam was all but washed up," he later wrote. "The old combat cleverness was gone; there was no longer effective deception. Combat fields were littered with weapons and dead bodies. Camouflage was not even attempted. These signs indicated that the enemy had to be just about scraping the bottom of the barrel."[2]

To replace their horrendous losses during Tet, the North Vietnamese had rushed 80,000 to 90,000 replacements into the battlefields of South Vietnam between January 1 and May 5, 1968. Before the offensive, 82% of Communist prisoners revealed they had more than six months of

NVA soldiers surrender *en masse* after a four-day battle with American paratroopers of the 101st Airborne. The quality and training of the NVA deteriorated badly as result of the heavy casualties they suffered and of the need to quickly replace these lost troops.
Credit: US Army Military History Institute

military service. By May 1968, only 40% had that much service and 50% had less than three months service, including the time traveling south.[3]

Lieutenant Colonel Justin Martin had a unique perspective of the war and a clear view of the North Vietnamese Army's deteriorating quality. As a young first lieutenant, he commanded a U.S. Marine rifle company in 1968 and fought North Vietnamese Army troops in the Khe Sanh area before later taking on duties as an aerial observer. By the middle of 1969, he was flying in an OV-10 reconnaissance aircraft. A slow-moving plane, the OV-10 was only lightly armed and intended primarily to observe enemy movements. Colonel Martin distinctly recalls a day in mid-March 1969, when he sighted 60 NVA troops crossing into South Vietnam from Laos. He recalls, "These men literally stood and stared up at us as we rolled in on them, guns and rockets blazing." Thirty-seven of the enemy were killed before they finally reacted and ran for cover. "Not the normal reaction that I had encountered in 1968" from the better-trained troops encountered earlier in the war, Colonel Martin concludes. As the training and quality of the North Vietnamese Army declined, their casualties soared.[4]

North Vietnamese Army Casualties

Le Thanh, who was a university student in Hai Phong, remembers a slogan that his generation of North Vietnamese adopted. It was a slogan they even tattooed on their bodies: "Born in the North to die in the South." During 1966, the North Vietnamese Army suffered approximately 93,000 killed. In 1967, the casualty figure climbed to over 145,000. By the early 1970s General Giap was publicly admitting that his forces had suffered at least 500,000 killed during the war. In April 1995, Hanoi finally admitted that they had kept their heavy losses a secret and had consistently lied about their own casualties. The actual number of Communist soldiers killed during the war: 1.1 million![5]

NVA Private Nguyen Van Hung was 28 years old when he was drafted into the army in April 1968. Previously exempted, the big battles such as Khe Sanh and Hue had wrought such heavy casualties that virtually everyone from age 18 to 35 was called up. He remembers: "When I got the draft notice I knew I was destined to go South. And I knew the chances of coming back were very slim. About a hundred from my village had gone, starting in 1962, and none had returned." From April to August (four months), he did his military training, half of which was political in nature.[6]

The Viet Cong losses during Tet also had ramifications for the North Vietnamese Army. In addition to replacing their own losses, the NVA were forced to fill the role of the annihilated Viet Cong units. The situation was so bad after Tet that General Tran Van Tra had no choice but to fill the vacuum created by the loss of the Viet Cong guerrilla units with regular army NVA units, split up into companies, platoons, and even squads. The NVA 320th Regiment was sent in to operate in Long An Province after Tet. "Sending a concentrated main-force unit to operate in such a dispersed manner, so that it could be said to be no longer a main-force unit, was a reluctant necessity under those circumstances and at that time," General Tra observed. But he was forced to do so because ". . . the guerrillas and local troops in that area had been worn down . . ." But the NVA replacements, too, would suffer badly. In battles of 1969 and 1970, the 320th's regimental commander (Nguyen Duc Khoi), the political officer (Le Van Minh), and both deputy regimental commanders (Hong Hai and Trinh Ngoc Cham) were all killed.[7]

NVA 2nd Lieutenant Tran Xuan Niem proceeded south via the Ho Chi Minh Trail after completing basic training. "At places along the sides of the trail were the hulks of military vehicles and graves, graves of dead NVA soldiers. . . . There were graves all over in some areas," he would later remember. Near Kontum, his unit passed groups of soldiers going north, back home. Those walking had mutilated arms. Those who had lost their legs were allowed to ride in the camouflaged trucks. [8]

Morale of North Vietnam and Its Army

Predictably, the North Vietnamese Army's repeated defeats and heavy casualties had its effects on those being asked to fight the war. Hanoi was very concerned about this effect and later, in April 1995, admitted that they had publicly under-stated their losses throughout the war, specifically because of their concerns about morale. Captain Tran Dinh Thong, a North Vietnamese Army regular soldier was typical. He felt "depressed and worried about the future" after the abortive attacks and defeats of early 1968.[9]

Han Vi was the political officer for the Vietnamese School of Music (later renamed Vietnamese Conservatory of Music and renowned as its leading musical institute). He recalls that wounded soldiers were kept isolated when they returned to North Vietnam. "These soldiers were a real threat. They had sacrificed a lot, and they couldn't see that it had been for anything. They talked a lot against the government. They had big mouths and they weren't afraid to use them. One of the things they were angriest about was that the university kids and the children of high cadres didn't have to go. So they were kept in special camps."[10]

University student, Le Thanh, later recalled that, "Many parents tried to keep their sons out of the army. They would hide them when they were called up to the recruiting center. Other draftees mutilated themselves or managed to find other ways to fail the physical. People with money were able to pay doctors to disqualify their children."[11]

This same North Vietnamese student noted that draft resistance, including bribery, feigning illnesses, and going into hiding, was easier in the big cities of Hanoi, Haiphong, and Nam Dinh where the Communist Party officials and government workers lived. He also noted that, because of this, the large majority of the army were recruited from the countryside. Of his own three brothers, one dropped iodine into his eyes before going for his induction medical examination, the other managed to bribe the doctor, and the third tried to hide but was caught and put in jail.[12]

Political officer, Han Vi, recalls that early in the war ". . . most conservatory students weren't too worried. They had their exemptions. But later on in the war the students in general began to get very scared. That was especially true after the 1972 bombings. They scared everybody."[13]

The Progress of the War

The concern about the progress of the war was widespread. Peking, especially, was highly critical of the way the North Vietnamese waged the war. To a lesser extent, such criticism also came from the Kremlin. Stunned at the heavy losses their forces were suffering in South Vietnam, one senior Hanoi official declared in spring 1967, "If we keep fighting five more years, all that will be left of Vietnam will be a desert." Soon after, a secret delegation of Communist military experts from North Korea, China, and Cuba visited the war theater, reporting back that the North Vietnamese and Viet Cong forces could not hold out many months longer against the United States and its allies.[14]

The situation continued to worsen until, by 1972, General Tran Van Tra reluctantly observed: ". . . there were continual reports about the difficulties, the shortages of troops, food, and ammunition, and especially the fatigue of the cadres and men. The Military Region 9 Command (Western Nam Bo) sent a message recommending straightforwardly that the Regional Command order an immediate cessation of hostilities so that we could reorganize our forces. The troops were no longer capable of fighting!"[15]

The North Vietnamese Army, after years of head-to-head battles with the Americans and their allies, and the additional drain on its manpower of providing replacements for the Viet Cong, was a spent force. It had been defeated again and again. All that was now necessary was the signing of the Paris Peace Accords, and that would occur in January 1973.

20

The End of the War
The Paris Peace Accords Are Signed

On January 23, 1973, the Paris Peace Accords were signed to come into effect at 2400 Greenwich Mean Time, four days hence.

While twenty-twenty hindsight and the prevailing cynicism of the time have made it fashionable to believe otherwise, America had every reason at the time of their signing to believe that the Paris Peace Accords held the promise of a genuine peace. It appeared to many Americans to be at least as good as the cease-fire that had ended the shooting in the Korean War and, with continuing American military support, had allowed the nation of South Korea to continue to survive.

Three factors supported the belief that the Paris Peace Accords would end the fighting and allow the continuing survival of South Vietnam. First, the indigenous South Vietnamese Viet Cong force no longer existed as a viable threat. Second, a rough military parity now existed between North and South Vietnam. Finally, America believed it had an agreement with both the Chinese and the Soviets to limit their arms shipments to North Vietnam, shipments without which Hanoi could not wage offensive warfare.

No More Indigenous Viet Cong

Years of minor skirmishes, search-and-clear operations, and cordon-and-search operations had taken their toll on the Viet Cong. Further, the Phung Hoang program had been enormously successful in eliminating the key "cadre" personnel. The disastrous Tet Offensive, perhaps more than any other one single factor, however, was responsible for the demise of the Viet Cong. Not only did they suffer enormous losses in the Tet battles but also, even those who had survived had "blown their cover." New recruits for the Viet Cong had proven impossible to provide. A combination of factors, including the increasing urbanization of South Vietnam, which reduced their traditional rural/peasant recruiting base, was at work here. Finally, the brief example of what the Viet Cong might do if they achieved control, as they had done briefly in Hue, clearly terrified the South Vietnamese people and suggested that the Saigon government, with all of its problems and shortcomings, was still a preferable alternative.

As they grew weaker, the Viet Cong found it more and more difficult precisely because of that weakness. While service in the South Vietnamese Armed Forces may have been dangerous, service in the Viet Cong was increasingly proving to be suicidal. Southern reinforcements became impossible to recruit and, by the 1970s, so-called "Viet Cong" units consisted overwhelmingly of North Vietnamese troops.

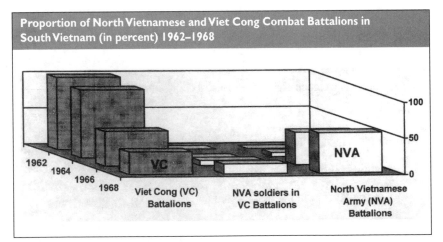

Source: General William Westmoreland, "Report on Operations in South Vietnam January 1964–June 1968," in Admiral U.S.G. Sharp, *Report on the War in Vietnam (As of 30 June 1968)*, (Washington, D.C.: U.S. Government Printing Office, 1969), Chart 3, 195

As their casualties continued to mount, the situation deteriorated even further for the Viet Cong. Typical of this was the 273rd Viet Cong Regiment of the 9th Viet Cong Division, which, despite its name, was eventually not really Viet Cong at all. By May 1969, fully 80% of its manpower were soldiers of the NVA. [1]

Just how weak the Viet Cong had become by the early 1970s is suggested by the official bargaining position of the Communists in Paris. The American peace proposal, suggesting mutual withdrawal of both American and North Vietnamese forces from South Vietnam, was consistently rejected by the North Vietnamese because they realized that the Viet Cong were no longer any match for the South Vietnamese Army, so successful had been the campaigns against them. [2]

Rough Military Parity

A rough military parity had been created between North and South Vietnam. The Armed Forces of South Vietnam were among the best equipped and most modern in the world. The last-minute Operation Enhance and Operation Enhance Plus had seen a massive effort to ensure that, at the time of the signing of the accords, South Vietnam would have more than enough equipment. Since the accords allowed this equipment to be replaced on a piece-for-piece basis, its continuing strength seemed guaranteed.

Even Communist General Tran Van Tra admitted the operation's success. He described it as, "Providing additional equipment, weapons, and modern technical equipment in order to transform the [South Vietnamese] army into a strong force capable of annihilating the liberation armed forces." [3]

When the agreement had been signed and the last of the American technicians were preparing to leave, the Communists complained that the Americans had not dismantled their bases as required by the accords. But the Americans had planned ahead, hoping to give South Vietnam every chance of surviving. American Major General Woodward solemnly replied, "We are authorized to reply to you that at present we have no bases in South Vietnam. All of them were turned over to the Republic of South Vietnam prior to the signing of the agreement. The American troops are now stationed in camps temporarily borrowed from the Republic of South Vietnam." [4]

Relative Weakness of the Communist Army

In contrast to the freshly supplied South Vietnamese Army, Hanoi's troops were debilitated from their recent Easter Offensive losses and the drubbing they had taken in the Linebacker I bombings. General Tran Van Tra, soon after the signing of the accords, noted that the South Vietnamese battalions numbered, ". . . between 400 and 550 men, with ample food and ammunition, while our main-force battalions had not yet been augmented and totaled at most 200 men, with insufficient ammunition and food."[5]

In the closing days of the war, the United States then unleashed the devastating series of bombing raids, known as Linebacker II, that dealt a knockout blow to North Vietnam's war-making capacity just before the final bell. President Nixon confirmed the intention and the success of these efforts. "Our bombing achieved its purposes," he said. "Militarily, we had shattered North Vietnam's war-making capacity."[6]

The North Vietnamese agreed, later admitting that the bombing had destroyed virtually all industrial, transportation and communications facilities built since 1954 and had blotted out 10 to 15 years' *potential* economic growth.[7]

Agreement with China and the Soviet Union

The plan to enlist the support of China and the Soviet Union in order to stop Hanoi had proceeded for years. Dean Rusk, after lengthy discussions with the Soviets, Gromyko and Dobrynin, in early 1966, was convinced that the Soviets were trying to help and had little interest in seeing a continuation of American involvement in Vietnam. Gromyko and Dobrynin blamed the Chinese and said that, at least temporarily, their hands were tied because they had to provide aid to North Vietnam lest it fall into the Chinese camp. In 1966, the terror of the Chinese cultural revolution began, confirming Rusk's fears.[8]

Dean Rusk argued, during the early 1960s, that Haiphong should be left alone. He believed that if the port city was destroyed, the Soviets, who provided their aid mainly by sea, would lose influence and the more dangerous Chinese would take their place. By the beginning of 1972, however, China's cultural revolution was over and the country was courting better ties with America. Chinese supplies to Hanoi began drying up. The Soviet Union stepped in to fill the gap but, in May 1972, they agreed to reduce their aid in return for trade concessions from the United States. The supply line was effectively stopped.[9]

Tran Van Lam, South Vietnam's Foreign Minister, was in Paris when, after 11 days of American bombings, the Communists agreed to return to the peace talks. Henry Kissinger told Lam, "Don't worry. I have a deal with the Soviet Union and China. From now on they will stop supplying all offensive arms to North Vietnam." This deal was confirmed by NVA General Tran Van Tra. He noted the American plan to win peace by, "Using the policy of U.S.-style détente on a worldwide basis to create pressure and limit the aid of the socialist bloc for both the north and the south, in hopes of strangling our ability to fight." He also noted the success of this policy adding, "In fact, after reaching agreement at Shanghai to retain Thieu and keep South Vietnam in the U.S. orbit, China limited its aid to Vietnam, especially with regard to large weapons and transportation facilities."[10]

Central Committee member, To Huu, and Army Chief of Staff General Van Tien Dung toured the battlefront immediately before the cease-fire to assess the relative strengths of the opposing forces. They visited the headquarters of all the major areas, from military region Tri-Thien Hue near the DMZ all the way down to COSVN in the delta. At the end of that time they reached what must have been a depressing conclusion for them. To Huu told COSVN staff that no large-scale offensive could be launched for at least three years to five years because of the détente occurring between the big powers and also because of the military weakness of Communist forces.[11]

North Vietnam reacted angrily to its abandonment by its long-time benefactors. Hanoi's Communist Party newspaper, *Nhan Dan,* denounced the Russians and Chinese for ". . . throwing a life buoy to a drowning pirate" and being ". . . mired on the dark and muddy road of unprincipled compromise."[12]

Paris Peace Accords Signed

The Paris Peace Accords went into effect at midnight on January 27, 1973. They essentially called for a halt to all hostilities, for the return of all prisoners of war, for America to withdraw its military forces from Vietnam (which was something of a hollow concession given that all American combat troops were long-since gone) and for Hanoi to henceforth honor the border between North and South Vietnam. A genuine American concession, and one heatedly debated at the time, was that Hanoi's troops would remain in the most northern parts of South Vietnam in that land they still held from their Easter Offensive four months before. Hanoi still preposterously, though stubbornly, refused to admit that their troops had ever fought in South Vietnam. This lie was actively abetted by a vocal antiwar minority in America itself. President Nixon was prepared to tacitly concede these troops' continued presence in South Vietnam, though not their legitimacy. He believed they would soon "wither on the vine" and leave of their own volition once supplies could no longer reach them through the DMZ. While not a perfect agreement, the Paris Peace Accords appeared to hold the promise that America's *military* victory over the Viet Cong and the North Vietnamese Army would now result in the *political* survival of the Republic of South Vietnam.[13]

The End of the War: Mission Accomplished

On March 29, 1973, General Frederick C. Weyand, U.S. Commander in South Vietnam, spoke at formal ceremonies noting the departure of U.S. troops. Speaking in Vietnamese, he said that, "Our mission has been accomplished. I depart with a strong feeling of pride in what we've achieved, and in what our achievement represents." Following these ceremonies, he and the last 2,500 American troops departed from Saigon and from Da Nang. America's war in Vietnam was over.[14]

21

Epilogue

Within the next few months after signing the Paris Peace Accords in January 1973, events occurred that could not have been predicted when the accords were signed. These events had disastrous results for the South Vietnamese and would culminate two years later in their defeat at the hands of Hanoi. The 1973 Arab-Israeli War caused oil prices to skyrocket and inflation to soar throughout the world. This event had terrible consequences for the South Vietnamese economy, an effect exacerbated by the U.S. Congress' dramatic reduction of aid to South Vietnam. When the United States urgently supplied the Israelis with military equipment from their own American stocks to replace Israeli losses, arms and equipment, which might have gone to the South Vietnamese, were severely depleted and no funds were available for restocking. The return of cold war hostilities between the Soviet Union and America saw the U.S. Congress revoke Russia's most favored trading nation status, removing the 1972 trade concessions that had enticed them to reduce aid to Hanoi.[1]

The Soviet Union responded to American actions by once again pouring money and equipment into North Vietnam. On March 1, 1975, the NVA, fully rebuilt and reequipped by Moscow, launched an offensive that marked the beginning of yet another war in that area of Southeast Asia. With Hanoi's Soviet-equipped juggernaut closing in, South Vietnamese Army soldiers, invariably with their wives and children living nearby and with fearful memories of Hue in their minds, chose en masse to save their families. A mad scramble south took place. With only a handful of notable exceptions, such as the stout defense of Xuan Loc, the North Vietnamese were not forced to defeat the South Vietnamese Army; it collapsed in front of them. The main hindrance to the Communists' progress was the mass of fleeing South Vietnamese who blocked the roads, the start of an exodus that would later culminate in the "boat people" phenomenon. [2]

When Hanoi's troops neared Saigon at 11:08 A.M. on April 29, a force of 865 U.S. Marines was helicoptered into the city from American ships offshore. They quickly secured a landing zone at Tan Son Nhut Airport, and a fleet of American helicopters began ferrying out American and South Vietnamese evacuees. By 6:30 P.M. that day, the Marines had completed the evacuation, except for that being conducted from the roof of the American embassy, which continued throughout the night. A total of 1,373 Americans and 5,595 South Vietnamese were evacuated. At 7:53 A.M. on April 30, the last American helicopter took off from the U.S. Embassy. Onboard were the last eleven of the Marine security force, carrying the embassy's flag with them as they departed.[3]

At 11:00 A.M., April 30, 1975, a Soviet-made T-54 tank crashed through the gates of the South Vietnamese Presidential Palace. Soon the flag of North Vietnam flew over the former Southern Republic, and fresh-faced Northern soldiers marched in a victory parade through the streets of Saigon. However, these young troops were clearly not the veterans of Ia Drang, of Long Tan, of Khe Sanh . . . or of those thousand other battles. The veterans of those actions, the fathers, cousins, and older brothers of these marching youngsters, lay in cemeteries and unmarked graves the length and breadth of South Vietnam. American troops and their allies, in their unheralded victory of that previous war, had seen to that.

PART III

THE DICH VAN PROGRAM: ORCHESTRATED MYTHS, FALSEHOODS, AND LIES

22

The *Dich Van* Program

Why is it that most accounts of the Vietnam War to this day portray the American involvement in such a negative light? Why is it that the American troops were so maligned at the time? Why was acknowledgment of their victories denied them; instead, why were every tiny fault and mistake magnified until those negative images still dominate in most of the world?

The Communists developed a highly complex plan to dominate South Vietnam one day. Direct armed conflict was obviously a major part of that plan and, in the end, it sent their Soviet-made tanks crashing through the South Vietnamese Presidential Palace. Their plan involved much more than the simple use of armed force, however. Crucial to their plan was a psychological warfare program they called *dich van* (action among the enemy). Specifically, *dich van* referred to nonmilitary programs aimed at the civilian populations of their South Vietnamese and American enemy.[1]

While psychological warfare is nothing new, the *dich van* program added some unique and sophisticated elements. Central to this was the

Communists' claim that the American people were not their enemy; instead, they said their enemy were the soldiers who fought the war and the politicians who sent them there. By claiming this, the Communists sought to drive a wedge between those doing the fighting and those back home.

No Opposition

One of the reasons for the *dich van* program's success was the simple fact that it faced no organized opposition. As Secretary of State Dean Rusk explained, unlike the Communists, America "never made any effort to create a war psychology in the United States" during the Vietnam War. Because of the American government's decision to fight the war in Vietnam without going on a "war footing," Washington specifically avoided the sort of drum-beating, war bond drives, parades, etc., used in previous conflicts. It never attempted a strong propaganda campaign of its own.[2]

Second, with the memory of Chinese intervention in the Korean War very fresh in their minds, American politicians took great care to avoid antagonizing China and the Soviet Union. Although the South Vietnamese government was keen to talk about "unifying" both Vietnams under its non-Communist rule, America prevented it from doing so, leaving Hanoi a monopoly on the unification issue. Similarly, although American generals were keen on taking the war to North Vietnam, they were consistently prevented from raising the matter publicly. So, unlike previous wars, American policy allowed the enemy to have a monopoly on the psychological warfare battlefield.[3]

Strategic and Tactical

The Communists' *dich van* program operated against the American people at two levels: strategic and tactical. At the strategic level, it sought to undermine the American war effort by convincing the American people that the war was unwinnable and immoral. At the tactical level, it used what the Communists referred to as "power nullification," whereby it sought to prevent America from using its battlefield strengths and instead fighting on terms dictated by the Communists themselves.[4]

Strategic: The War Is Unwinnable

The *dich van* program sought to present a very idealized image of North Vietnam. Sociologist Douglas Pike summarized this idealized self-description as ". . . a tough, perhaps sometimes ruthless, but essentially attractive society, peopled by highly motivated, incorruptible nationalists dedicated to a cause of justice, peace, democracy, and possible unification, a cause entirely domestic and defensive, threatening no one, certainly no one outside of Vietnam's borders."[5]

In contrast to this idealized image, it sought to point out every flaw and fault on the American and South Vietnamese side. Problems of morale among the troops, failure to support the troops by the Americans back home, and military blunders and mistakes were all highlighted as a way of suggesting that the war was unwinnable and should therefore be abandoned.

Observers of the Vietnam War were presented with this carefully constructed, ideal notion of the Communists with no opportunity to assess it objectively. In contrast, the Communists loudly proclaimed every shortcoming, both real and imagined, of the American side.

The American government made no concerted effort to counter these claims with its own propaganda. Reporting of the war from the western side was almost entirely a function of the commercial media. In this, the open nature of American society made the *dich van* program's task all the easier. While hundreds of journalists daily reported every mistake and failure in the American effort, the Communists were able to prevent similar scrutiny.

Tactical: Power Nullification

The Communists sought to limit America's ability to wage the war successfully by limiting the weapons and actions available to it. They sought the freedom to keep their own troops operating in Laos and Cambodia, while preventing American troops from doing the same by claiming that America must recognize these countries' "neutrality." The Communists used the simple expedient of holding to the lie that their troops weren't there. Similarly, they sought to impose restrictions on the use of American strengths, such as airpower, through claims that American bombing of military targets in North Vietnam was somehow immoral. However, the Communists retained their own "right" to attack similar targets in South Vietnam. It sought to depict itself as a "barefoot army," armed with only primitive weapons while waging war against a military Goliath.

By claiming that the struggle in Vietnam was purely political in nature, Hanoi argued that any attempt to resist it by military force was, therefore, by definition "terror, repression, or war crime." The *dich van* program sought to create the perception that the South Vietnamese government should use only political means to defend itself and that to defend itself by military means, including the legitimate request for support from its various allies, was illegitimate.[6]

Semantics

The *dich van* program used great finesse in its techniques. It consciously and systematically used semantics to redefine words in order to make its argument more plausible. It cleverly redefined the word, *enemy,* so that they could claim that the enemy was not the American people but rather those who would pursue the war. Similarly, it redefined the word, *antiwar,* so that those who were on the Communists' side, and therefore sought the armed takeover of South Vietnam, did so under the mantle of the *antiwar* movement; meanwhile, those who sought to end the fighting with a negotiated settlement found themselves labeled as *prowar* or *hawks.* In the same way, those Americans who flew aircraft against legitimate military targets in North Vietnam suddenly became *pirates* in Hanoi's Orwellian newspeak. Before long, it became impossible to discuss the war rationally because the meanings of words were not those ordinarily used in the English language but, rather, those that were dictated and created by Hanoi.

Success of Dich Van

The Communists were aware of the *dich van* program's successes from an early time. A Hanoi radio broadcast in June 1967, announced that the U.S. Air Force ". . . has many weaknesses. Its basic weakness lies in the fact that it cannot freely develop its strength, which is really restricted because [they] are highly isolated politically." Radio Hanoi described the success of their program in influencing popular opinion by stating that: "The worldwide people's struggle to compel the U.S. imperialists to stop bombing the North has become a more and more comprehensive mass movement."[7]

The success of the *dich van* program is also evident in that the myths created by the Communists for psychological warfare purposes still remain as the dominant discourses of the Vietnam War. Unfortunately for those who seek the truth, they form the basis for most "histories" of the conflict.

Difficult to Undo, Even for Hanoi

During the war, Hanoi consistently claimed that its troops were not involved in the fighting in South Vietnam; rather, they stated that it was purely an internal domestic struggle within South Vietnam. While this claim was patently and obviously false, it was steadfastly maintained by Hanoi and supported by scores of antiwar celebrities. Throughout the war, they proclaimed Hanoi's innocence and, therefore, the immorality of any attacks upon North Vietnam itself. The Communists were so successful in this part of their program that, after their successes in 1975, Hanoi had hard work to counter their previous lie and claim the "credit" they believe they deserve. Hanoi now openly and loudly boasts that they controlled the war from its beginning.[8]

An analysis of the various *dich van* claims, that is, the bombing of North Vietnam, the David-versus-Goliath nature of the struggle, the morale of American troops, etc., is necessary to get a more accurate view of the Vietnam War.

23

The Bombings

North Vietnamese dich van efforts were especially active in respect to America's use of its air power. It sought to establish the belief that America was immoral in its use of aircraft to attack military targets in North Vietnam. Simultaneously, the Communists argued that its own rocket and artillery attacks on targets in South Vietnam were entirely legitimate. In doing so, it sought to deny to America one of the best weapons in its arsenal and to limit America to fighting a war on terms dictated by the Communists.

At its most extreme hyperbole, the antiwar movement's "Russell Tribunal" (a mock "war crimes" tribunal held in Stockholm during the war) claimed at the time that the United States was guilty of ". . . the systematic destruction of hospitals, schools, sanatoria, dams, dikes, churches and pagodas . . . [and that] . . . the cultural remains of a rich and complex civilization had been smashed in a terror of five million pounds of high explosive daily." Further, it claimed that, "It is as if the Louvre and the cathedrals of Italy had been doused in napalm and pulverized by 1,000-pound bombs." The taint left by this lie has two legacies. The first is that the

United States was the "moral villain" by occasionally using its strength in the air in the Vietnam War. The second legacy is the notion that the United States fully utilized its military resources and yet was unable to destroy North Vietnam. Neither of these statements is true.[1]

The United States did indeed drop enormous tonnages of bombs during the Vietnam War, but not on populated areas. This crucial fact is often ignored by writers who make simple comparisons such as, "More bombs were dropped in the Vietnam War than on Nazi Germany in World War II." This kind of statement fails to note that the allies specifically targeted enemy population centers in World War II, whereas such centers were specifically avoided in Vietnam. Severe limitations were placed on the use of American air power against North Vietnam itself, with most key military facilities and cities "off limits" right up until the closing days of the war in 1972. Also, for most of the war, no serious effort was made to interdict the flow of supplies from North Vietnam. An example of the limitations placed on American air power was the entirely arbitrary and self-imposed rule that U.S. aircraft were not permitted to knock out enemy interceptors on the ground, but had to wait until the enemy aircraft were in the air before they could become engaged.[2]

Unpopulated Areas Bombed

The overwhelming majority of bombs were targeted and dropped on the virtually unpopulated stretches of countryside that made up the Ho Chi Minh Trail. From 1965 to 1971, over 2,235,918 tons of bombs were dropped over these Laotian infiltration routes. One of the main targets within South Vietnam was the unpopulated (except for NVA troops) Ashau Valley. From April 1, 1968, to April 19, 1968, for example, B-52s dropped over 9,000 tons of bombs on the valley. Major General John R. Tolson, Commander of the 1st Cavalry Division (Airmobile), described the valley as one of the enemy's "top logistical support bases, as important to him as Camranh Bay is to us."[3]

One reason for the U.S. decision to defend the Khe Sanh Combat Base was that it allowed the battle to be fought in an unpopulated area. The Marines' tight defense required the NVA to mass its troops in order to assault in sufficient numbers; whenever they did so, they allowed the Americans B-52s to attack them effectively. Thus, Khe Sanh was a "bait," drawing the NVA into a position for obliteration from the air, far from any populated areas. In this way, American policy specifically attempted to fight any battles away from population centers.[4]

Not Intended to Stop Infiltration

There is a popular misconception that the United States went "all out" to stop infiltration down the Ho Chi Minh Trail with the use of its airpower. In fact, Colonel D. Frizzell (Chief of Strategic Concept Studies at the Air War College) points out that, up until 1972, the bombing campaign ". . . was not conceived as part of a comprehensive interdiction campaign but was a highly restricted and selective program that was designed gradually, and in a very controlled manner, to apply increasing pressure on the North Vietnamese."[5]

The bombing campaign was largely a result of the "tit-for-tat" policy whereby the United States retaliated for an ever-escalating series of military actions on the part of the North Vietnamese. From the first bombings in retaliation for the attack on the USS *Maddox*, these raids were primarily intended to send a political signal, not to achieve some particularly military goal. Throughout the war, pauses in the bombing were initiated, regardless of their military consequences, in an effort to "get the North Vietnamese to the conference table." The North Vietnamese boasted of their success in limiting American use of its airpower over Radio Hanoi, saying that because of their ". . . political isolation . . . the U.S. Air Force is compelled to escalate step by step, and cannot attack the North massively and swiftly" but instead must attack targets of "minor importance."[6]

A concerted attempt to stop infiltration into South Vietnam would not have simply hit the routes; it would have struck at the sources as well. Further, it would not have left untouched the harbor facilities at Haiphong. Though the *numbers* of these raids increased up until 1968, the *range* remained minimal in scope up until the final days. A serious effort to use airpower to inflict damage on North Vietnam was not attempted until the last six months of the war, well into the Nixon presidency. Not until Operation Linebacker and then again Linebacker II, both in 1972, was the U.S. Air Force allowed to play a decisive part in the war. Until then, the brunt of the war was carried by the American infantryman fighting in South Vietnam. American air strikes against North Vietnam were used only occasionally, and sparingly, in attempts to coerce Hanoi to sit down at the negotiation table.

North Vietnam Bombed

While often criticized by the antiwar movement for its bombing of North Vietnam, the United States, in fact, exercised extreme restraint in carrying the war to the North. If anything, it could be argued that the United States failed to properly acknowledge North Vietnam's role as aggressor in the war and deal directly with it. A complaint often heard from the military is that the various restrictions placed on them, and specifically on their actions against the aggressor in North Vietnam, were at the core of American problems in achieving a decisive "victory" earlier in the war.

In spite of the popular image to the contrary, only 6% of all B-52 sorties were flown against targets in North Vietnam; two-thirds of *these sorties* were flown in 1972. Further, except for those sorties flown in 1972, B-52 strikes were limited to the relatively unpopulated areas within a few miles of the demilitarized zone separating North and South Vietnam.[7]

Limitations and restrictions placed on the U.S. Air Force bombing of North Vietnam were extensive. Even during the years 1965-1968, theses restrictions included:[8]

- No bombing within 10 miles of Haiphong (even though North Vietnam received 85% of its aid from China and the Soviet Union from this port)
- No bombing within 30 miles of Hanoi
- No bombing within 30 miles of the Chinese border

From 1968 until 1972, there was a total halt to the bombing of North Vietnam above the 19th parallel. Bombings were not resumed until 1972 when, in ". . . the first twenty-five days of October, the United States dropped 31,600 tons on [North Vietnam], making this the most intense period of daily bombing of the north until then."[9]

American efforts to avoid civilian casualties were Herculean, routinely putting their own pilots at risk in the process. The job was made even more difficult by the number of targets attacked and the enemy's unconcern

TABLE III-I B-52 Sorties by Year and Target								
Targets	1965	1966	1967	1968	1969	1970	1971	1972
South Vietnam	1,320	4,290	6,609	16,505	11,494	3,697	2,386	19,289
North Vietnam*	0	280	1,364	686	0	0	0	4,440
Laos	18	647	1,713	3,377	5,567	8,500	8,850	2,799
Cambodia	0	0	0	0	2,437	2,906	1,319	1,855

*With severe limitations, until 1972, as described in the text.
Source: Thomas C. Thayer, *War Without Fronts: The American Experience in Vietnam.* (Boulder, Colorado: Westview Press, 1985), 84.

about placing military facilities in close proximity to civilian areas. Le Thanh was a university student in Hai Phong and remembers seeing anti-aircraft guns established right next to the pagodas and the schools. "The official explanation was that they had to protect these places," he recalled. "But it didn't take too long to realize that the U.S. planes were dropping bombs where they saw the guns firing."[10]

Also, the North Vietnamese added their own "friendly fire" casualties to the toll from surface-to-air missiles (SAMs), which missed their target and then plummeted back to earth. In late 1967, the ratio of SAMs fired to aircraft shot down was 67:1. During the 1972 "Christmas bombings," the North Vietnamese fired an estimated 1,242 SAMs at American aircraft and, again, the huge majority missed their targets entirely and fell back onto North Vietnam soil, many with their warheads still intact. Even with this added element, the relatively small number of civilian casualties is amazing.[11]

Malcolm Browne of the *New York Times*, described as "a confirmed critic of the Nixon administration's conduct of the war," filed a report from Hanoi in late March that, "The damage caused by American bombing was grossly overstated by North Vietnamese propaganda." Similarly, Stanley Karnow, having heard the claims of bombing damage, returned to Vietnam in 1981, expecting to see devastation. He stated, "I expected to observe ruins everywhere. But Hanoi and Haiphong are almost completely unscathed, and the surrounding countryside appears to have been barely touched."[12]

The relatively light "collateral" damage and civilian casualties can be attributed to three factors. First, B-52s were assigned to targets only in outlying areas away from population centers. More accurate fighter-bombers equipped with laser-guided bombs were assigned targets where civilians might be at risk. Second, B-52s delivered their bombs in much tighter "packages" than when they were hitting area targets such as in the area around Khe Sanh. They were ordered, at the risk of court martial, to fly straight at the target without taking evasive maneuvers in order to be more accurate in spite of the SAMs being fired at them. Third, the North Vietnamese themselves can take some large measure of credit because they put into place very good civil defense measures. When the first bomb fell, they had already evacuated two-thirds of the cities' population into the countryside. By the end of December, three-fourths of the population had been evacuated.[13]

While a persistent legacy of the Vietnam War appears to be the notion that America unleashed a wild torrent of bombs onto the people of North

Vietnam, the facts clearly contradict this. Instead, America can be shown to have exercised incredible, some would even say foolish, restraint on its use of airpower. Only in 1972 in the closing days of the war, when America had already withdrawn its ground combat troops, did the United States use its strategic airpower in a concentrated attack on the enemy's military forces and capabilities in North Vietnam. Even then, it went to extraordinary lengths, even risking its own pilots and aircrew, to avoid civilian casualties. Those involved have every right to be proud of their actions.

24

Civilian Deaths and Atrocities

"On 18 September [1961] a guerrilla force seized the city of Phuoc Vinh, capital of Phuoc Long Province, [and] publicly beheaded the province chief . . ."[1]

Terrorist acts, such as this beheading, intended to shake the people's trust in existing institutions and thereby make change more palatable, were routinely conducted by the Viet Cong. In spite of this, the *dich van* program sought to portray the American conduct of the war as immoral. The Viet Cong therefore denied its own activities and spread false propaganda about the activities of the Americans.

My Lai provided the Communists with the exception upon which to weave their myth. The tragic story of My Lai is well known, a black event in America's military history. What is rarely acknowledged, however, is that it is the only recorded incident of its kind. The military careers of those who participated were ended; the occurrence eventually came to light because it was pursued by a soldier of the U.S. Army who witnessed it. And yet, to many, it is the archetypal example of atrocities committed by Americans during the Vietnam War. It is indeed a rare popular history of the war that does not emphasize this singular event, making it seem that such events were commonplace. At the same time, these histories totally ignore or make only passing reference to the routine and systematic civilian murders and atrocities committed by the Communists.

Thomas Thayer served as the Director of Southeast Asia (SEA) Intelligence and Force Effectiveness Division of the SEA Program Office under the Assistant Secretary of Defense for Systems Analysis from 1967 through 1975. Ten years after the war, he re-visited this issue of civilian casualties. After a thorough analysis of the data, Thayer concluded that most civilian casualties in Vietnam were the result, not of allied forces and their firepower, but of the systematic and intentional attack on civilians by the Communist forces.[2]

The Systematic Killing of Civilians: The Example of Hue

During the battle of Hue, Communist forces took over portions of the city during the Tet Offensive of 1968 and held onto control in some areas for three weeks. The worst of Communist atrocities became an everyday affair at that time. A total of 2,810 bodies were eventually found in shallow mass graves by the mid-1970s. Also, 1,946 people remained unaccounted for. A Communist document, captured April 25, 1968, but not made public until November 24, 1969, reported that in Hue, "We eliminated 1,892 administrative personnel, 38 policemen, 790 tyrants, 6 captains, 2 first lieutenants, 20 2d lieutenants and many noncommissioned officers."[3]

For many years after the Hue killings, apologists for the Viet Cong attempted to claim that these killings didn't occur, or that these killings were committed by the South Vietnamese army. No doubt remained, however, after the publication of the former NLF Justice Minister's memoirs, in which he admits that, "Large numbers of people had been executed, most of them associated with the government or opponents of the revolution. But others had been killed as well, including some captured American soldiers and several other foreigners who were not combatants." Huynh Tan Phat, the most senior of Viet Cong officials, later expressed sorrow and regret for these atrocities, saying that ". . . the discipline in Hue had been seriously inadequate. Fanatic young soldiers had indiscriminately shot people. . . ."[4]

TABLE III-2 Village Officials and Civil Servants Killed by the Viet Cong									
Year	1965	1966	1967	1968	1969	1970	1971	1972	Total
Number Killed by VC	1,900	1,732	3,706	5,389	6,202	5,947	3,771	4,405	33,052

Source: Thomas C. Thayer, *War Without Fronts: The American Experience in Vietnam.* (Boulder, Colorado: Westview Press, 1985), 51.

Lieutenant-Colonel George R. Christmas, who commanded Hotel Company, Second Battalion, Fifth Marines, during the battle of Hue, points out the differences between the Viet Cong and the North Vietnamese. He reported that the Viet Cong formed "goon squads," which dealt with those who may have worked for the government among others. He noted, however, that, "The North Vietnamese commander did put a stop to this eventually when he found out about it."[5]

Stockholm War Crimes Tribunal

The Stockholm War Crimes Tribunal, as its self-appointed leadership chose to name it, was held in Stockholm in 1967 under the auspices of the Bertrand Russell Peace Foundation. Its executive president was Jean Paul Sartre, who had been denied permission to hold the "tribunal" in France by President Charles de Gaulle. Discredited even before it began, this organ of left-wing propaganda "passed verdicts" that continue to be quoted. "Two anticivilian weapons were particularly condemned [by the tribunal]: napalm and CBUs (cluster bomb units)," one author quoted nearly two decades later. The use of the word, "anticivilian," in the preceding quote is typical of the dich van program's creative and manipulative use of semantics. Objective observers would note that napalm and CBUs are "antipersonnel" weapons, which means they are intended to kill enemy troops as distinct from being intended to knock out enemy armor or penetrate concrete bunkers, for instance. They are **not** "anticivilian." Such statements were typical of the tribunal's bias and perfidy and its misleading use of language to reinforce its myths. David Horowitz, former editor of the New Left magazine, *Ramparts,* in the 1960s, now decries his previous support for that tribunal, which he admits brought possible American wrongdoings ". . . under intense and damning scrutiny but ignored atrocities committed by the Communist forces in Vietnam."[6]

"Body Counts" and Myths

While the whole notion and accuracy of the "body count," that is, the tallying up of enemy casualties after a battle, is much maligned in the popular histories of the Vietnam War, its reality is somewhat different. The myth, which attempts to denigrate American battlefield successes and taint the morality of the war, would have U.S. troops falsifying their body counts for extra kudos from their senior officers. The myth also portrayed U.S. troops as routinely murdering civilians and claiming them as enemy dead. This myth, however, fails to hold up under closer scrutiny.

Accurate body counts were necessary to assess the enemy's fighting capabilities. Falsely stating that one's own unit had inflicted a grievous loss on the enemy when it hadn't actually done so would be to endanger that unit's future survival. In 1968, when the Marines at Khe Sanh knew they were facing three enemy divisions, it was absolutely vital that they accurately measure the enemy's losses to better plan their own future defense. American units were so fully aware of the need for accuracy that infantry units were routinely placed into areas recently hit by artillery or aircraft to get an accurate "on-the-ground" count of enemy casualties. The Marines, in making these counts, needed to be especially careful about NVA attempts to conceal the number of casualties they'd received. Often the enemy stacked their bodies one on top of the other in a single grave, hoping thereby to mislead the Americans about the number of corpses contained. Standard American policy countered this by requiring troops to exhume the bodies and then dig deeper to check for other bodies. As American infantry troops can attest, the "body count" was not only as accurate as possible, but also often painstakingly and ghoulishly tallied.

No doubt there was scope for the occasional claim that, "I think I hit him," in some isolated encounter with a sniper. Multiplied thousands of times over, such claims added to the degree of uncertainty of the total figure. By and large, though, the body count was more accurate than not. When asked by an interviewer about American estimates that his troops had suffered 500,000 killed, Giap is reported to have nodded his agreement. On the 20th anniversary of their successful 1975 invasion, Hanoi finally admitted that the figure was actually more than double that: 1,100,000 troops killed! As it turned out, American body count figures actually underestimated Communist losses![7]

Hanoi not only saw the value of the body count, they also even awarded medals based on these figures. Former NVA Lieutenant Colonel Nguyen Van Tich stated that, "It was decreed that those who killed at least five Americans would be nominated as Valiant Heroes Third Class. Those who killed ten would be awarded Second Class, and those who killed more than ten would be First Class Heroes."[8]

The NVA "body count" claims were really far-fetched. In Operation Junction City in 1967, for instance, official North Vietnamese reports claimed 13,500 allied soldiers killed, 800 tanks and 119 artillery pieces destroyed. In fact, there were 289 allied troops killed, three tanks and five artillery pieces destroyed. Some of this gross exaggeration may have been related to simple propaganda; some of it may have been related to the Communist system of awarding medals based on the number of Americans killed, with every soldier's accounts thus inflated.[9]

The Treatment of Prisoners of War

The topic of atrocities would not be complete without making mention of the treatment of prisoners of war (POWs). Colonel Fred Cherry, a U.S. Air Force pilot, shot down in October 1965, is typical. He tells of his mistreatment while in captivity. American aircrew were referred to as "pirates" by their captors, who denied they deserved treatment as prisoners of war (POWs) under the Geneva Convention. They were routinely tortured and mistreated. Colonel Cherry describes the routine torture and beatings while they tried, especially in his own case as an African-American officer, to get him to denounce the American war effort.[10]

The International Committee of the Red Cross (ICRC) constantly encouraged North Vietnam to comply with the Geneva Convention regarding treatment of prisoners, relief packages, mail, repatriation of sick and wounded, and exchange of prisoner lists. South Vietnam, which maintained custody of Viet Cong and North Vietnamese prisoners, fully complied. The North Vietnamese consistently refused.[11]

The POWs were cynically exploited by the North Vietnamese and by the American antiwar movement, when they were forced to parade themselves before antiwar activists visiting Hanoi. The courage and discipline of the POWs was noted by CIA Executive Director William Colby as he described one prisoner blinking out the Morse code letters to T-O-R-T-U-R-E with his eyelids while the television cameras recorded one such meeting. He also describes another group of prisoners giving a "rude hand signal" to the still photographers, which *LIFE* magazine chose to publish regardless, "thus ensuring punishment for the captives."[12]

In spite of *dich van* myths to the contrary, American involvement in the war was *not* notable for its misuse of power. The forces that joined the South Vietnamese Army in its struggle performed their mission with a professionalism that stands in stark contrast to the Viet Cong's terrorism and the NVA's careless brutality.

25

No 'David-Versus-Goliath' Struggle

Those who watch the popular media would be forgiven for thinking that the war was fought entirely by opposing forces silently creeping through the jungle, by death from punji traps and devious spiked flails whipping out from the trail, and by the inability to tell friend from foe. One would conclude from this that the Communists were poorly armed and equipped in comparison to the Americans, that action raged throughout the country, and that a handful of barefoot soldiers fought a numerically superior American force. In essence, one would believe the war was a David-versus-Goliath struggle. The reality is quite different.

North Vietnam hoped to achieve a political advantage by portraying the American war effort as a David-versus-Goliath struggle, and therefore implicitly immoral and unfair. It also hoped to achieve a tactical advantage in doing so by preventing America from using its full military strength for fear of negative world reaction.

Weaponry

The North Vietnamese Army was well-equipped for ground combat and had several tactical and strategic advantages. Its infantry units had modern Soviet-built weaponry, the AK47 assault rifle, the RPD machine gun, the RPG7 antitank weapon, which were more than a match for anything the Americans had. Military experts at the time noted that, ". . . weapon for weapon, a regular NVA unit outguns a US infantry unit in organic firepower [i.e., those weapons actually carried with them into battle], due primarily to the enemy RPG [Rocket Propelled Grenade] weapon family." Lacking the NVA's firepower, American infantry units were forced to rely instead upon *external* firepower in the form of artillery and air support. The same experts noted that, "This situation in turn gives rise to the standard [American] infantry tactic of pulling back on contact, bringing fire to bear, then moving back into the contact area." The aggressive Americans, although outgunned by the NVA, used this "attack, withdraw, call in artillery and then attack again" tactic to defeat their Communist foes in battle after battle despite their lesser firepower.[1]

In addition to the organic weapons available to NVA infantry units, their artillery units were equipped with heavy Soviet-made weaponry, such as the 130-mm field gun that could hurl a 73.6-lb (33.4-kg) shell a distance of 33,900 yards (a little over 31 kilometers). These field guns outdistanced anything the Americans possessed, "allowing," in the words of one authority, "the NVA gunners to operate almost with impunity" against the Americans.[2]

As well as supplying most of this weaponry, the Soviets also helped Hanoi in other ways. Among their contributions was the provision of intelligence. Soviet trawlers cruising off the coast of Guam monitored B-52 takeoffs from Anderson Air Force Base and informed Hanoi. As former National

An NVA soldier prepares to fire a Rocket Propelled Grenade from an RPG-7 launcher while his AK47-armed comrades look on. These Soviet-designed weapons gave the NVA a firepower advantage over the Americans and forced US troops to depend upon artillery and airstrikes to tip the balance in their favor.
Credit: Democratic Republic of Vietnam

Liberation Front Minister Truong Nhu Tang pointed out: "The planes' headings and air speed would be computed and relayed to COSVN headquarters, which would then order NLF or Northern elements in the anticipated target zones to move away perpendicularly to the attack trajectory." Since this 2650-mile flight from Anderson Air Force Base to the Vietnam war zone took about nine hours, there was usually ample time for the Communists to disperse or at least to seek shelter. If the attacks were directed against North Vietnam, they would be met by one of the most sophisticated air defense systems in the world. Their surface-to-air missile (SAM) sites were equipped with Soviet missiles and, for the first years of the war, actually *commanded* by Soviet Air Force technicians. The North Vietnamese Air Force was equipped with advanced MiG-19 and MiG-21 aircraft; their pilots trained in the Soviet Union and China. In addition, Soviet advisers also took to the air, occasionally tangling in dogfights with their American opponents.[3]

The Communist Chinese, meanwhile, also supplied huge quantities of weapons and ammunition. In addition, the Chinese "netted in" their own early warning radar network to that of Hanoi, thus providing the North Vietnamese with their own electronic warning of impending American attacks. The Chinese Air Force positioned its best units on their southern border and often clashed directly with American planes. Ten American planes were shot down by the Communist Chinese Air Force in support of North Vietnam.[4]

Comparative Strengths of Forces

While America as a country was indeed a Goliath compared to the country of North Vietnam, its strength and size did not directly equate to dominance on the faraway battlefield. America's troops enjoyed a tremendous training and technology advantage, but the Communists maintained a numerical and geopolitical advantage throughout the war. That American troops were able to defeat the North Vietnamese Army under those conditions is a feat about which it should feel some large measure of pride.

Numerical Advantage

To begin with, of course, America continued to have enormous military obligations *elsewhere* throughout the war. The cold war was then at its peak and the threat of a Soviet armored invasion of Europe was very real. In contrast, North Vietnam was able to deploy virtually its entire army to

South Vietnam. Of those American forces actually deployed to South Vietnam, only a small percentage were available for direct combat. Because of the need for security functions and other duties, the number of allied maneuver battalions available to fight the enemy maneuver battalions was never large. A thorough analysis later concluded that the "force ratio" ranged from an allied (including South Vietnamese, Australians, etc.) advantage of 1.2 to 1 to an allied *disadvantage* of 0.7 to 1. In other words, the VC/NVA potential sometimes outnumbered the allied maneuver forces by 1.4 to 1. Regarding purely *American* forces, it has been estimated that there were never more than approximately 80,000 American combat troops actually ranged against over 400,000 VC/NVA. Casualties in these handfuls of American maneuver battalions accounted for 80% of total American casualties. American combat troops in Vietnam were locked in a bitter struggle against Hanoi's numerically superior combat forces.[5]

Geopolitical Advantage

Because Hanoi was allowed safe sanctuaries in Cambodia and Laos, the Americans and the South Vietnamese were forced to defend 800 miles of border, all along the western frontier of the country in addition to defending the DMZ in its north. With insufficient troops to defend all this vulnerable border area, General Westmoreland was forced to establish a "picket line" of Special Forces bases, manned by mountain tribesman, along its western borders. These outposts were like tripwires, alerting him of enemy intrusions. Westmoreland would then use his handful of combat battalions as mobile "fire brigades," rushing to attack the Communists whenever they appeared.

Where did the Fighting Actually Occur?

Of South Vietnam's 44 provinces, the two most northern provinces that Hanoi controlled directly as its Tri-Thien-Hue front accounted for 24% of American combat deaths.

The five most northern of the 44 provinces, all located in I Corps, accounted for 53% of American combat deaths. In contrast, the various provinces in Military Region IV, the Mekong Delta area just south of Saigon, accounted for in total for only 5% of American combat deaths.[6]

In the provinces where the NVA regular battalions routinely operated, the heaviest American casualties occurred.

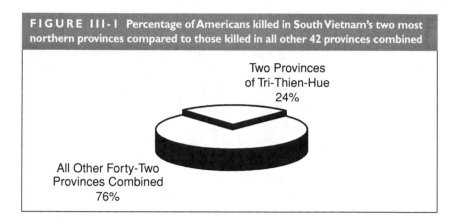

FIGURE III-1 Percentage of Americans killed in South Vietnam's two most northern provinces compared to those killed in all other 42 provinces combined

Two Provinces
of Tri-Thien-Hue
24%

All Other Forty-Two
Provinces Combined
76%

"Captured" Weapons

Many photos, especially those from the 1950s but often used to illustrate "typical" enemy troops, show Viet Cong soldiers with American-made weapons. These weapons are often described as "captured American weapons." In fact, however, many of them were captured from the South *Korean* Army by the Chinese fighting in the Korean War and then later handed on to their Vietnamese Communist allies.

The distinction between "*American* equipment" and "*American-made* equipment" is an important one. At no time during the war did the Communists capture significant quantities of weapons from American troops. But, interestingly, quite the opposite is true of the Americans. While American combat troops were involved in the war (from 1961–1972) truly enor-

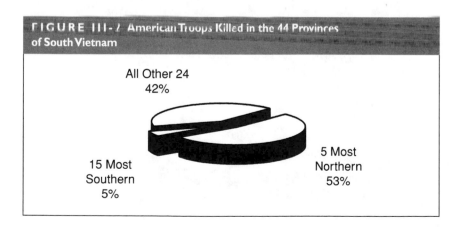

FIGURE III-2 American Troops Killed in the 44 Provinces of South Vietnam

All Other 24
42%

15 Most
Southern
5%

5 Most
Northern
53%

mous stockpiles of weapons and equipment were captured from the Viet-Cong and from the North Vietnamese Army. In one two-week period, for instance, 4,793 rifles and machine guns, 730 mortars, three million rounds of ammunition, 7285 rockets, and 124 trucks were captured from the Communists. This action alone required more than 6,436 helicopter cargo flights to remove the captured material.[7]

By the mid-1960s, all main force Communist units were armed with the AK47 (or the Chinese-manufactured copy) assault rifle and had little use for American weapons, even if they could capture them. The notion that the Communists armed themselves with weapons taken from their enemies is romantic, but untrue. They armed themselves with weapons given them by their allies, the Chinese and the Soviets.

Punjis and Booby Traps

The *dich van* myth of the Vietnam War would have people believe that the Communists fought the war with crude weapons like booby traps made from sharpened bamboo stakes, known as *punjis*. In fact, an analysis of U.S. Army casualties shows that *punjis* accounted for only 2% of wounds inflicted and *not a single death*. In contrast, rifle and machine gun fire accounted for 51% of U.S. Army deaths. Grenades, mortars, and artillery accounted for 36% of deaths; and mines and booby traps, often employing jerry-rigged hand grenades, accounted for 11%.[8]

Overwhelmingly, Americans died as a result of fire from Soviet- and Chinese-supplied rifles, machine guns, mortars, artillery, and rockets. They

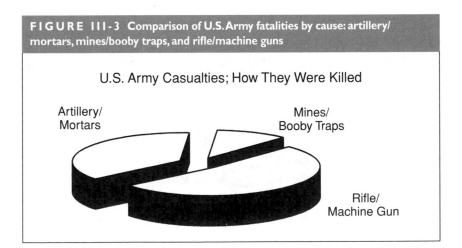

FIGURE III-3 Comparison of U.S. Army fatalities by cause: artillery/mortars, mines/booby traps, and rifle/machine guns

U.S. Army Casualties; How They Were Killed

Artillery/Mortars

Mines/Booby Traps

Rifle/Machine Gun

were killed in those provinces adjoining North Vietnam, whose troops had the advantage of nearby safe sanctuaries for most of the war and whose combat forces routinely outnumbered the American forces pitted against them. One only needs to look at the various battles, Hue, Khe Sanh, Ia Drang, to be reminded of the numerical advantage of the Communist combat troops.

That North Vietnam's struggle, massively supported by China and the Soviet Union at its peak, to seize power in South Vietnam should be cast as "David-versus-Goliath" perhaps says more about the success of their *dich van* program than it does about the historical realities.

26

The Home Front
Attitude of the American People

The *dich van* program sought to create the belief that the American people did not support America's actions in South Vietnam. In doing so, it sought to change American foreign policy. Also, Hanoi sought to create the belief that the American people did not support the soldiers who were doing the fighting. Hanoi hoped to make a direct attack on the troops' morale and their ability to wage war.

Diminishing Support for the War

A *dich van* "truism" about the Vietnam War, rarely if ever even questioned, is that of diminishing support for those fighting the war as the years went by. One needs to be very careful, however, of the surveys that purport to show diminishing support. Often these are based on questions that asked respondents whether they define themselves as "hawks" or "doves" on the war issue. The actual, full question that formed the basis of this survey was: "*People are called 'hawks' if they want to step up our military effort in Vietnam. They are called 'doves' if they want to reduce our military effort. How would you describe yourself—as a 'hawk' or as a 'dove'?"*[1]

The question thus did not measure support for those troops involved in the fighting ("Do you support the troops there?") or even for the moral right or wrong of the war. Rather, the question simply measured beliefs about desirable levels of military effort. Especially toward the end of the war, when Vietnamization sought increasingly to turn the military effort over to the South Vietnamese Army, those people in support of Nixon's policies could well have described themselves as "doves" according to the wording of that question.

Also, while it is often said that people's responses to the opinion polls changed during the course of the war, few realize that the *questions themselves*, asked by the pollsters, changed during that time. Prior to 1966, for instance, the American Gallup poll asked whether the United States should *"have become involved with our military forces in Southeast Asia?"* Beginning in May 1966, however, the line of questioning was changed: *"In view of developments since we entered the fighting in Vietnam [has America] made a mistake sending troops to fight?"* [2]

Pollster Roy Morgan was sufficiently concerned about the misleading nature of this line of questioning in 1970 that, he wrote to the Gallup organization's head, George Gallup, outlining his concerns. Essentially, he felt that the wording of this "mistake" question was biased and tended to elicit "yes" answers. He contended that the question appeared "to suggest that the interviewer is implying that all developments had been adverse." Morgan also felt that the wording of the question implied "that the US did make a mistake." Finally, he objected to the black-or-white response required in this "yes" or "no" question whereas previous questions allowed shades of agreement/disagreement.[3]

Speaking on the "Meet the Press" television show on April 16, 1968, Secretary of State Dean Rusk, asked to comment on the size of the antiwar protest demonstrations, put the matter into perspective by reminding the interviewer that, "We have a population of almost 200 million people and those who speak for the 200 million Americans are the President and the Congress on these issues." The wider community, Secretary Rusk firmly believed, supported American actions.[4]

In May 1970, four student protesters at Kent State University were killed by National Guardsmen. Students at some 500 college campuses went on strike in protest over their deaths and at the Cambodian incursion. Shortly thereafter, antiwar demonstrators held a rally in the financial district of New York City. Two hundred "hard hat" construction workers left their nearby building sites and, chanting, "All the way USA," pushed their way through the police ranks and confronted the antiwar demonstrators. The construction workers then moved on to City Hall, their ranks swelling to more than 500. They demanded that the American flag, flying at half-mast in memory of the Kent State students at Mayor John Lindsay's order, be raised to the top of the mast. When it was raised, they sang the national anthem. Concerned at the negative publicity they had received from their attacks on the demonstrators, a peaceful rally was organized two weeks later. *Time* magazine wrote: "Callused hands gripped tiny flags. Weathered faces shone with sweat. . . . For three hours, 100,000 members of New York's brawniest unions marched and shouted . . . in a massive display of gleeful patriotism and muscular pride." *Time* described it as "a kind of workers' Woodstock."[5]

In his 1985 study of the American people's views on the war, analyst Randall M. Fisher concluded that, "A great many of those who believed that American involvement had been unfortunate also believed that once committed we should take whatever steps necessary to secure the surrender of the enemy. Any position based on the claim that the American public 'turned against the war' needs careful qualification."[6]

While in late 1971 various polls showed that the majority of Americans now wanted its troops withdrawn from Vietnam by the end of the year, a thorough analysis found that, "That majority fell apart if it was suggested that withdrawal would mean a Communist takeover in South Vietnam, and the support utterly disintegrated if withdrawal would threaten the lives or safety of United States prisoners of war."[7]

On May 13, 1972, Louis Harris reported that 59% of Americans supported the recent mining of Haiphong, while only 24% opposed it. Measures such as this suggest that, in many ways, support for the war remained strong even throughout its final years.[8]

Socioeconomic Class and the War

One of the fascinating anomalies of the Vietnam War is that it was supported most by those most likely to be directly involved themselves. Conversely, its most outspoken opponents faced little prospect of having to go to Vietnam.

Seventy-six percent of the men who went to Vietnam were from lower middle/working class backgrounds. In one very specific example, an extensive study of casualties from the state of Illinois found that men from neighborhoods with median family income of $5,000 were four times more likely to die in Vietnam than men from neighborhoods with median family incomes above $15,000. Christian Appey, as part of his doctorol studies at Harvard, compared the total number of casualties from the working class suburb of Dorchester, Massachusetts, with those of nearby affluent suburbs. Appey found that Dorchester (population 100,000) lost 42 of its sons in Vietnam. The wealthy suburbs of Andover, Lincoln, Sudbury, Weston, Dover, Amherst, and Longmeadow (*combined* total population also 100,000) lost ten.[9]

In 1969, "Newsday" looked at the family backgrounds of 400 young men from Long Island who had been killed in the war. The newspaper concluded that, "As a group, Long Island's war dead have been overwhelmingly white, working-class men. Their parents were typically blue collar or clerical workers, mailmen, factory workers, building tradesmen, and so on."[10]

The military, especially the ground forces of the Army and Marine Corps, have always been drawn largely from the working classes. This continued to be the case in the Vietnam War. In its early years, when the war was being fought mainly by elite volunteer units, there was some concern that casualties among racial minorities were disproportionate. The figures eventually leveled out as the elite units were later withdrawn and replaced by non-elite units made up of conscripted troops. Even then, however, conscripted troops were predominantly drawn from the working class.

Several reasons are cited for the overrepresentation of the working class among those conscripted. In previous wars, the selective service or "draft" system cast a much larger net. In World War II, virtually all able-bodied young men entered the service, some 12 million. This process continued during the Korean War and afterward, when approximately 70% of draft-age men in the population served in the military in some form. Later, during the Vietnam War, this proportion dropped to 40%, with the majority of this figure serving in places other than Vietnam, such as Germany, Korea, and countless "stateside" postings. Thus, the troops bound for Vietnam, 10% of the draft-age male population, were a distinct minority.[11]

The student deferment system clearly favored the wealthy. Young people from families with incomes between $7,500 and $10,000 were two and one-half times more likely to attend college than those from families earning under $5,000. Also, working-class young men, who did attend college, were far more likely to do so on a part-time basis, while working; but part-time studies did not qualify the individual for deferment.[12]

Another exemption offered by the selective service system was through membership in stateside-based Reserve or National Guard units.

While over one million men served in these part-time forces during the war years, only 15,000 of them were sent to Vietnam. Studies showed that this safest form of military service almost entirely excluded African-Americans and was most open to middle-class whites.[13]

General William Westmoreland described the situation thus: "Contrary to Mr. Kennedy's charge, 'we'll bear any burden, pay any price,' the only ones that bore a burden, paid a price and made a sacrifice were those on the battlefields, who were mainly the poor man's sons, and their loved ones at home."[14]

The Antiwar Movement

Radical antiwar activity was consistently centered in the elite, prestigious universities where students were overwhelmingly drawn from well-to-do and politically liberal families. Studies have shown a direct link: the more prestigious the university, the more likely it was that the students would support militant antiwar protest. Wisconsin University radicals, protesting Dow Chemical personnel recruiting on campus in 1967, threatened their staff with clubs while smashing windows and destroying property. The majority of these activists were identified as the children of lawyers, doctors, academics, and corporate executives.[15]

It should be clearly noted here that it was the nature of the prestigious universities, with their emphasis on liberal arts studies and their upper-class patronage that was at the root of their radical antiwar bias. It was *not* that their students were any more intelligent than their less radical fellow students who attended other universities. Various writers during the war claimed that left-wing activists were superior academically to those who supported the war. It was subsequently discovered, however, that their supposed superiority was based on their "*self-reported grade point averages*." When later studies looked at their "*actual*" grades, there was no difference between the two groups in intelligence or academic success. The antiwar activists weren't smarter; they just claimed to be.[16]

General Westmoreland was later to concede that, although he had supported the notion of a one-year tour of duty in Vietnam, he had done so in the belief that the burden of the war should be shared by a cross section of American youth. "I did not anticipate that numbers of our young men would be allowed by national policy to defer service by going to a college campus," he noted. Some observers were more blunt, stating that, ". . . in affluent white suburbs, the sons of the well-off could easily get a deferment by staying on at college, getting married, feigning homosexuality, or faking medical conditions."[17]

The socioeconomic division is perhaps summed up by the comments of Marian Goodman, a student at Tufts during the Vietnam War. She, like so many of her student friends, said she ". . . didn't know anyone who served in Vietnam, so sharp was the class line separating the campus from the battlefield."[18]

Because the war in Vietnam was being fought mainly by the sons, brothers, husbands, and friends of the working class, their support for "our" troops could be taken quite literally. It was this support that never wavered. On the other hand, the radical opposition to the war by the privileged classes in America always maintained an aloof, detached, very cognitive style. It could be impersonal because, for them, it really was detached in the sense that they had so little to do with the "persons" fighting it.

Some Did Seek an American Defeat

David Horowitz, an editor of the radical antiwar movement's journal, *Ramparts,* during those years, later acknowledged: "Let me make this perfectly clear. Those of us, who inspired and then led the antiwar movement did not want just to stop the killing as so many veterans of those domestic battles now claim. We wanted the Communists to win."[19]

Carl Davidson, while a student at Pennsylvania State University, joined the antiwar movement. Davidson, the son of an auto mechanic and the first in his family to go to college, discovered profound differences between his belief and those of the radical pro-NLF types. He viewed these "upper-middle-class" radicals as "elitists" and "fanatics" and observed that they had a strong "contempt for ordinary people."[20]

A Harris poll of American students taken in the spring of 1968 estimated that radical activists accounted for less than 2% of the college population. Seymour Lipset, Professor of Sociology and Government at Harvard, explains the strong impact of this minority by noting that, while conservative students may have felt strongly about their views, they believed that the university should be an apolitical "house of study"; conversely, the left-wing radicals believed that the university should be an agency for social change. Professor Lipset refers to these handful of radical left-wing activists as "the powerful 2 per cent."[21]

While very small in numbers and not representative of America, one should not underestimate the impact of this vocal minority, especially when it was able to commandeer an existing protest and with its display of NLF flags give the impression that the crowd shared their anti-U.S. feelings. Such protests had a dramatic media impact. Dean Rusk, long after the war, remained convinced that "the machinations of the press," the "foolish" protests, and all the demonstrations convinced the North Vietnamese that they should persevere in the war in spite of their horrendous casualties.[22]

Decision-Makers Swayed

While the general public had not turned against the war and still continued to support the troops in Vietnam, the elite universities continued to be the seat of radical antiwar and even pro-NLF activism. Not only did this minority capture a disproportionate amount of media time and space, but also they had direct access to their well-to-do and influential parents.

During the late 1960s and early 1970s, senior bureaucrats in the U.S. Department of Defense would arrive home to be harangued by their college-age sons and daughters who had attended "teach-ins," demonstrations, and antiwar rallies. Dinner conversation was poisoned by the disputes that ensued. Leslie Gelb, a Pentagon analyst, remembers arriving home to his wife, who had been watching the television coverage of the war before his arrival. As he walked in the door, she greeted him with the angry question, "What are you guys doing out there?"[23]

Other events involving family members of senior government and military officials include the following:

- Three of the four children of senior Pentagon official Paul Nitze took part in "Confrontation with the Warmakers" demonstration at the Pentagon in October 1967.[24]
- Representative Thomas T. (Tip) O'Neil, who enjoyed close ties with President Johnson, was nightly bombarded with questions from his 20-year-old daughter and 22-year-old son, both students at Boston College.[25]
- Secretary of State Dean Rusk, who resolutely stood by his convictions that the war was correct, was nonetheless reputedly "devastated" when his son Rich, a student at Cornell University, telephoned him in tears and begged him not to increase the troop levels in Vietnam.[26]
- Secretary of Defense Robert McNamara's son, Craig, a Stanford University student by 1969, had placed an NLF flag on the wall of his bedroom as a symbol of his views as early as 1966. "It must have just really hurt my folks," he would realize years later. "It must have

been devastating." Paul Warnke agreed, adding that, "I'm quite sure that the strong opposition of his [McNamara's] own children to the war had a very definite impact on him." This strong impact of his children's antiwar views (even though, at the time, 67% of the American people supported the bombing of North Vietnam) was confirmed by a tearful Robert McNamara in a 1995 interview.[27]

Thus, those civilians who directly advised President Johnson about the war were perhaps among those most directly affected by this vocal minority. Hence, Johnson may have given it more currency than it deserved. The proof of this came on March 25, 1968, when President Johnson called together 14 of such advisers, whom he referred to as his "wise men," for dinner and then met, one by one, with each of them the next afternoon. Their tone was overwhelmingly negative. "If they had been so deeply influenced by the reports of the Tet Offensive," he wrote, "what must the average citizen in the country be thinking?"[28]

Support for the troops in Vietnam, contrary to media impressions, may not have collapsed. However, the media's focus on those acts of opposition gave an impression to Johnson and selected influential others that support for the troops had collapsed. So, at the very moment when perhaps President Johnson could have won the war and then gone on to focus upon his beloved Great Society social reforms, he decided to take the military pressure off the Communists and abdicate his presidency.

General Westmoreland and many others blame the media for the problems of Vietnam. President Johnson, however, put the blame directly on the American public itself. Thus, it may be that Johnson blamed the public because he falsely believed their support had diminished, while Westmoreland simply blamed the media for falsely claiming it.

Avoiding the Draft

Many popular writers claim that the war was so unpopular that the majority of American youth turned away from it, refusing to register for the draft or burning their draft cards. While the visual imagery of a small group of men publicly burning their draft cards is emotionally evocative, it really means very little if it is a relatively isolated event.

The fact is that, by and large, people not only accepted their responsibility in the way of the draft, but also preemptively volunteered for service in Vietnam. Over two-thirds of the troops serving in Vietnam were there voluntarily. It has been estimated that approximately 50,000 men broke the law by evading the draft or deserting between 1964 and 1972. An interesting historical comparison is drawn by looking at an August 1917 issue of the *New York Herald,* which reported that ". . . in New York City ninety out of the first hundred draftees claimed exemption" and noting that the War Department listed 337,649 draft evaders in World War I."[29]

Canada

The relative handful of draft evaders who fled to Canada always received much publicity. Their number was often cited as some measure of the war's unpopularity. However, the flow of traffic wasn't all in one direction. An even larger number of young men flooded *into* America to voluntarily join the U.S military effort in Vietnam.

It is estimated that 20,000 American draft dodgers took refuge by fleeing into Canada. Another 12,000 members of the American armed forces deserted and went to Canada. Few people realize, however, that 40,000 Canadians voluntarily joined the American military in that same period and that 12,000 Canadians served in Vietnam with American troops. Official figures cite 106 Canadians killed while serving in Vietnam but estimates place the true figure as closer to 400 because many Canadians gave American addresses when they enlisted. Contrary to the myth, the net flow *out of Canada* to fight the Communists in South Vietnam was well in excess of the net flow *into Canada* to escape serving in the war.[30]

Hostile Reaction

In June 1966, the Commanding Officer of the returning 1st Battalion Royal Australian Regiment, marching at the head of his troops through the streets of Sydney, was splattered with red paint by an antiwar demonstrator. What is most interesting about this event is not that it happened, but rather, that it was the only incident of its kind throughout the whole war. *Despite the fact that the event was an entirely unique incident*, an Australian historian notes that, "the collective memory of the veterans and of many of the antiwar movement, and of subsequent popular historians, focuses on that incident as typical of the hostile reception of the veterans."[31]

Similarly, the image of returning American veterans being spat upon has also become part of the Vietnam mythology. (Even the cartoon series, "The Simpsons," has its resident Vietnam veteran, Principal Skinner, angrily reminiscing about being spat upon.) It is interesting, however, to actually ask a veteran of his own personal experiences. When General Norman

Schwartzkopf was asked about this type of experience, he angrily exclaimed, "Nobody spat on *me*," suggesting that the perpetrator wouldn't have walked away lightly from the incident. Like Schwartzkopf, veterans should ask themselves if they had actually been recipients of that hostility, or had they simply been informed that it existed.

In the late 1980s, journalist Bob Greene, writing in his syndicated newspaper column, asked if returning veterans really were spat upon by hippies and protesters. He received over a thousand replies. About one-third of these replies claimed it had happened to them. Greene concluded that, while this action most likely had indeed occurred, there was an "apparent sameness" to the responses, which cast doubts on the literal truthfulness of many of those who had written in. The vast majority of those who replied were either highly skeptical about the claims or else believed it was a very rare occurrence. Many of them offered accounts of the warm reception they had received.[32]

Vietnam veteran and author, Charles Anderson, remembers the rumors circulating about people's hostility to returning veterans. He wondered: "Was it true all the girls thought the veterans were babykillers and would have nothing to do with them?" Of course that was nonsense, but one should never underestimate the lingering consequences of such a potentially devastating possibility. In the words of Anderson, "When the veteran learned those rumors were not true, his suspicion still remained."[33]

Like their Australian counterparts who now believe that returning troops were often splattered with paint, so too have American veterans come to believe that unusual acts of hostility were commonplace. They have come to believe that their own personal experiences were atypical and that the hostility they had probably only heard about was, on the contrary, typical.

A further exacerbating factor is that many Americans' first stop on arrival back in America was in San Francisco, a seat of the radical antiwar movement. A relative handful of "regular" protesters staked out the airport there and gave the returning troops the impression of wide-spread rejection.

Also, it may well be that it was in the interests of those few who *did* act with hostility to believe, and convince others, that those feelings and actions were typical of their time. In their own consciences it permits them in a way to "dilute" the severity of their crime. "If you get shot, you will have deserved it," Boston writer, Carl Nagin, remembers telling a friend who had decided to volunteer for Vietnam duty. "It's a statement I'm not proud of," he now admits. He goes on to quickly justify it by adding, ". . . but it was an indication of a very unconscious, programmed response, an arrogance that was part of politics then."[34]

The Welcome Home Parade

The "welcome home parade," or the lack of one, has come to symbolize the initial failure of those back home to properly honor their returning soldiers. Two inconsistencies stand out.

The Australian Example

Interestingly, the Australian army, unlike the Americans, did not operate on an "individual replacement" basis. That is, an Australian soldier was posted to a unit, which then trained and deployed to Vietnam as a unit. After its tour of duty, the entire unit was then posted back to Australia. Because of this, Australian units *did* typically "parade" through either Sydney, Adelaide, Brisbane, or Townsville before leaving for Vietnam and also *did* typically "receive a parade" upon their arrival back in Australia. Australian sociologist, Jane Ross, who has made a particular study of Vietnam veterans, states categorically that, "All of the battalions marched in capital cities when they returned to their home bases—sixteen marches in all." They were welcomed as heroes, even in the 1970s, when the antiwar movement was at its peak. An Australian newspaper described the final parade just before Christmas in 1971 as the last of the Australian battalions arrived home from Vietnam and marched through Townsville: "Thousands of Townsville people turned on a rousing heroes welcome. Cheering drowned the sounds of marching feet for three city blocks as Townsville made the most of the last major parade by troops from Vietnam. The marchers were swamped with ticker-tape thrown from balconies and roadside vantage points." The cheering crowd was described as having "packed the Flinders Street footpaths to capacity."[35]

If they had received so many "welcome home parades" already, why then did Australian veterans feel the need for their 1987 Vietnam Veterans parade? One reason may have to do with a feeling that, while they may have been paraded, their parade had not been warmly received. In this regard, many veterans refer to the paint-splattering incident that occurred in June 1966. Yet, the evidence overwhelmingly shows that this was the only incident of its kind and that, by and large, Australian troops were met by cheering crowds.

This paint-splattering incident is perhaps another example of an isolated instance, which selectively played again and again in the media, has led many, even the veterans themselves, to believe that it was a typical response. The evidence overwhelmingly shows it was not.

The American Example

Because of the "individual replacement" policy of the United States, troops bound for Vietnam generally did not proceed to Vietnam as an organized military unit. (Exceptions include the initial deployment of the various units in 1965 and 1966 and the deployment of the 27th Marines and the 82nd Airborne in 1968.) Instead, American troops were sent as a group of replacements who were assigned to their particular unit only after arrival in Vietnam. For the vast majority of American troops, there was no parade associated with their going to Vietnam . . . *and no particular expectation or desire for one upon their return.*[36]

Even in the early days of the Vietnam War, when even the left-wing writers acknowledge public support was with the troops, there were no ticker-tape "welcome home parades" while the war was continuing, just as such parades had not occurred during World War II. The absence of such parades back then did not indicate a lack of support from the American people. That was true also during the Vietnam War.

Yet, by the late 1970s, various "spokesmen" for the veterans began to focus on their lack of a "welcome home parade" as symbolic of the failure of society to properly support them. While often heralded as a success, the 1982 parade for Vietnam Veterans, held in Washington D.C, attracted only about 20,000 of the *two and one-half million* veterans of that war, less than 1% of them. Overwhelmingly, veterans ignored it. The figures suggest a profound disinterest in a "welcome home parade," albeit a very belated one.[37]

Perhaps the veterans feel a disappointment, not at their failure to receive a "welcome home parade" that they had never expected in the first place (or, in the case of the Australians, had already received), but rather, that *they've never received the "victory parade" they felt they had ultimately earned.*

What may have been missing for both the Americans and the Australians, therefore, was not a "welcome home parade," but perhaps, instead, some acknowledgment of the victory they had achieved over the Viet Cong and the North Vietnamese Army.

All-in-all, the popular notion that those who fought in Vietnam were not supported by those back at home needs to be seriously questioned. While a vocal minority certainly opposed them, and certainly had an effect out of all proportion to their numbers, it can be argued that the American people overwhelmingly kept faith with its young troops throughout the conflict.

27

The Myth of Poor Morale

Unsupported statements like the following are found in numerous histories of the war: "Most infantrymen were drafted into an unpopular war, against their will, and their main interest was simply to survive the year's tour of duty they had to serve in Vietnam."[1]

One of the many injustices perpetrated on the veterans of the Vietnam War is the myth of their poor morale. This particular myth is related to two orchestrated *dich van* myths: the war's immorality and the inevitability of American defeat. The Communists needed to "prove" poor American morale in order to support their claim of the war's immorality. What better proof could there be if even America's own troops turned against it? Second, poor morale, and its relationship to combat efficiency, was a key plank in the Communists' claim that they held a battlefield edge that would lead to a certain victory.

Volunteers

Contrary to popular belief, volunteers provided the bulk of the manpower to U.S. forces throughout the Vietnam War. Only 25% (648,500) of total U.S. forces were draftees; in comparison, 66% of U.S. troops were draftees during World War II. Further, the units most heavily engaged in actually fighting the Vietnam War tended to be almost exclusively composed of volunteers (1st

233

Marine Division, 3rd Marine Division, Army Special Forces, 173rd Airborne Brigade, 101st Airborne Division, Army Rangers, Special Forces, Navy SEALs, etc.). Only later in the war, when the elite troops were withdrawn and replaced by units with significant numbers of draftees, did the percentage of conscripted casualties rise to their ultimate figure of approximately one-third of the total.[2]

Blue Collar Troops, Blue Collar Work Ethic

While the topic of whether America should have become involved in Vietnam in the first place was a hot topic on the college campuses and the newspapers back in America, it was of remarkably little interest to the troops themselves. Most of the troops in Vietnam were of working-class backgrounds. Their parents were largely factory workers, tradespeople, and unskilled workers. The esoteric interest in the "meaningfulness" of their work was a luxury simply not afforded them. While the privileged could dreamily aspire to being "fulfilled" in their work, the families of those who fought in Vietnam generally had to content themselves with having honest jobs that put meals on the table and a roof over their families' heads. They tended, as a result, to take pride in the *manner* in which they did their job, no matter how distasteful, menial, or even apparently meaningless that job happened to be. This attitude, that is, the importance of doing a job, *any job*, well, was passed on to those who would fight the war in Vietnam. As a result, they tended to be more interested in being the best soldier (or Marine or sailor or airman) they could be, not in any philosophical debates about the war's "meaning."[3]

Also, for many of these troops, the war was more personal; older brothers, cousins, and friends had already fought there. Many had already died there. Regardless of how the fight had started, they felt an obligation to win it.[4]

Drugs

Drug usage is often cited unquestioningly as one example of deteriorating morale. While a 1971 survey found that 50.9% of U.S. troops smoked marijuana and that 28.5% had tried "hard" drugs like opium, a similar survey in 1968 found that 75% of Harvard College students had smoked marijuana or tried hard drugs.[5]

Routine urinalysis, designed to identify those men using hard drugs such as heroin, amphetamines, and barbiturates, was initiated in Vietnam in

June 1971. At its peak, drug usage was identified in 4.2% of service personnel. A combination of rehabilitation programs and education about the dangers of drugs brought this figure down to 2.5% by the end of 1971.[6]

One reason for the sudden rise in reported drug usage was that, reflecting changes in American social attitudes of that same era, military attitudes to drug use also changed. Beginning in late 1970, drug abuse increasingly became seen as a "treatable" condition, and users were encouraged to seek professional treatment. So, while previously soldiers would have hidden a drug problem from authorities, by late 1970, they confessed their dependency to obtain punishment-free treatment.[7]

Marijuana, although illegal, was easily available and was no doubt a very tempting diversion to some young Americans whenever their units passed through rear base camp areas to rest or reequip. The young people who served in Vietnam were very much like the young people of the 1960's American society from which they were drawn. They generally had a far more tolerant view about marijuana than that of their parents. But even marijuana was rarely used in the field. Soldiers and Marines in combat areas had a better sense of personal survival, and, if they didn't, their buddies did. Robert Julian, who served in one of the so-called "draftee divisions," the 25th Infantry, during 1971, when drug use was supposed to have been epidemic, recalls, "There weren't any drugs in my platoon out in the field. It just did not happen, and we wouldn't have let it happen if a new guy had brought drugs with him."[8]

This prohibition on using drugs while in combat situations was conversely often ignored by Communist troops. Several times American commanders noted the drugged state of Communist attackers. During the battle of Hue City in February 1968, American Marines were startled by the sight of an NVA soldier, lying among the rubble, one hand on his rifle, dreamily staring up into space. The Marines fired quickly and then marveled at their luck of having survived. Then they noticed there were numerous enemy foxholes in the area, many occupied by dead NVA, killed by Marine bullets. When they searched through their equipment, the Marines found quantities of heroin, syringes, matches, and bent spoons with scorch marks on the bottom. The Marines described the enemy as looking like ". . . a bunch of urban junkies."[9]

Fraggings

The term, "fragging," used to describe the murder of one's own leader by the use of a hand grenade, was largely a media invention. Troops themselves used the term "fragging" more generally, simply as a verb to describe the act of throwing a fragmentation grenade. Hence, to "frag" a VC tunnel meant "to throw a grenade" into the tunnel. The word itself carried no particular connotation about the intended target of the grenade and would, therefore, be followed by a verbal description of that target.

It appears to have entered the lexicon with its new meaning (not requiring a description of the target) sometime in the late 1960s. Interestingly, some writers therefore assert that, prior to 1968, fraggings did not exist. While this is technically true (the term fragging was not used in this manner), the surreptitious murder of disliked leaders in battle is as old as history itself.

One of the many myths surrounding the Vietnam War is the one that goes something like this: "In the final years of the War, the American army was an undisciplined rabble, refusing to go into combat and even murdering its own officers." Interestingly, the reputation of the Australian forces in Vietnam was not similarly tainted; they maintained a good reputation for discipline and effective combat performance. A total of 46,852 Australians served in Vietnam; 494 died there; and 2 of these deaths were "fragging" murders. A total of 2,594,000 Americans served in Vietnam; 58,183 died there; and 86 of these were "fragging" murders. These figures translate to an Australian "fragging ratio" of 4.0 per 100,000 troops and a smaller American "fragging ratio" of 3.4 per 100,000 troops.[10]

Thus, the data show that there were actually more Australian fragging homicides, in proportion to the size of their force, than among the Americans. This observation is not offered in order to question the reputation of the Australians, who deservedly were and still are regarded as a superb fighting force, but rather, to point out the dual standard by which the American force is judged. The fact of the matter is that the "homicide by fragging rate" for both forces was so low as to be insignificant. Among Australian forces in Vietnam, for example, while indeed two soldiers were killed by "fragging," that same number were killed by being struck by lightning, which speaks profoundly for the rarity of the event.[11]

The rarity of "fraggings" in Vietnam is suggested by comparing it to the homicide rate in modern America (see table 111-3).

While the *dich van* myth would malign American troops for their supposedly commonplace fragging of their own leaders, the reality is quite different. The homicide rate for these predominantly 19-year-old males, each armed with an assault rifle and with easy access to fragmentation grenades, was less than one-tenth the homicide rate of the citizens of our nation's capital.[12]

TABLE III-3 1990 Homicide Rate per 100,000 Population in Five American Cities	
City	**Homicides per 100,000 pop.**
Washington, D.C.	80.1
Detroit	59.3
Los Angeles	28.9
New York	29.3
Atlanta	50.9

Source: U.S. Bureau of the Census, *Statistical Abstract of the United States;* 1993 (113th Edition), (Washington D.C.: U.S. Govt. Printing, 1993), 194.

Combat Refusals

A popular notion is that troops routinely refused to go into combat in the later years of the war. In fact, this occurrence rarely happened (as it has also rarely happened in every other war) and it would appear that combat refusal remained a most rare and punishable action. Even the term, "combat refusal," is misleading since no such offense actually exists in the Uniform Code of Military Justice under which the armed forces operate. Such an action would be punishable under the general charge, "Insubordination, mutiny, and other acts involving willful refusal of a lawful order."[13]

In Vietnam, however, it was quite possible to receive a conviction for "willful refusal to carry out a lawful order" for very minor infractions of rules, which in no way reflected the person's state of morale or their enthusiasm to pursue the enemy. In the 1st Cavalry Division's base camp at An Khe, for example, it was a standing order that all personnel sleep inside a mosquito net, no matter how hot the weather. It was an automatic Article 15 (Uniform Code of Military Justice) offense, therefore, to be caught failing to do so, as this constituted the refusal to carry out a lawful order. Service at these base camps was noted for the adherence to the "rules and regulations," the violation of which would quickly lead to a formal charge.[14]

The Australians conducted a study that found that behavioral disturbances were 18 times greater among their support troops than their combat troops. Similar figures were also reported for American troops. These figures suggest the disciplinary problems inherent in a support assignment to one of the sprawling bases. Not surprisingly, as the war wound down and the combat troops were withdrawn, greater and greater percentages of troops were "support" troops posted to these bases; the percentage of disciplinary infractions increased proportionally. It must be remembered, however, that such infractions, even in the base camps, remained relatively rare events.[15]

No statistics exist about the frequency of the so-called "combat refusals" themselves. The statistics that do exist on the more general "insubordination" charge unfortunately don't help to shed light on the question. These figures are very open to interpretation. In order to support a thesis of lowering of discipline, some writers may choose to argue a simple linear relationship: more charges means more acts of insubordination. Alternatively, others may view the same figures and reach a contradictory conclusion. They may argue that a higher level of charges indicates tougher discipline, citing units where violations are *punished* instead of *overlooked*. The reader must maintain a skeptical perspective. The raw figures for "insubordination" cases were 94 in 1968, 128 in 1969, and 152 in 1970. These figures represent approximately *two* such cases for every *ten thousand* troops in 1968, "climbing" to approximately *four* such cases for every *ten thousand* troops in 1970. From this perspective, it appears that "insubordination" remained a most rare occurrence.

Robert Julian, who served with the 25th Infantry Division in 1971, recalls, "People were reading about insubordination, mutiny, and failure to obey orders. It's true that no infantryman looked forward to or enjoyed combat: I certainly didn't. But we gave better than we got whenever it happened. It's true that the joke was—and I want to emphasize it was a joke—that rather than on search and destroy missions, we were on search and avoid missions. The fact is, we never refused an order or refused a fight."[16]

A parallel to the "combat refusal" is sometimes quoted in regard to the U.S. Navy. One often reads, for example, of Navy ships that "voted" not to participate in the war. The most celebrated case is that of the USS *Constellation* where, it is sometimes claimed, the crew voted "five to one against a return to the war." This case is based on an incident that actually occurred on the *Constellation* in October 1971. The ship was preparing to go to Vietnam when two antiwar groups tried to persuade the sailors to refuse. A poll was then taken by the antiwar groups. Even according to the groups' own figures, 90% of the ships company ignored the poll. Of the 10% who responded, 292 sailors voted that they wished to go to Vietnam; 354 sailors (out of a crew more than 5,000) voted that they preferred to stay with their wives and girlfriends in San Diego. These numbers were hardly a resounding "antiwar" vote, but this incident is routinely cited as an example of troops "turning against the war."[17]

"Disciplinary" Versus "Medical" Reasons for Discharges

Another area of doubt exists in the supposedly higher ratio of disciplinary problems in the Vietnam War. This doubt is related to changing definitions and practices within the field of military psychiatry and of what constituted the grounds for a *medical* discharge.

Doctor Raymond M. Scurfield served as a U.S. Army psychiatrist during the Vietnam War and then went on to work with the Department of Veterans Affairs. He has noted the "unprecedented utilization of administrative channels" during the Vietnam War to give soldiers *other than honorable* discharges instead of *medical* discharges. He observes that, "In contrast to other war veterans, the acute psychiatric casualty rate in Vietnam was significantly less than half that of Korea, which, in turn, was about half that of World War II." During the Vietnam War, behaviors that would previously have been labeled as "psychiatric" in nature were instead labeled as "disciplinary" in nature and punished accordingly.[18]

Thus, there is reason to believe that *disciplinary problems* may have been over-reported during the Vietnam War when such problems are compared to previous wars and because of changes in the practice of military psychiatry. These changes in practice further skewed the facts and contributed to the myth of poor morale.

American Military Culture

America has a rich democratic tradition: its soldiers question and contribute to their battle plans. American troops are not trained to be mindless automatons; they are encouraged to be flexible, read the situation, and make judgments on the spot. American troops in World War II were amazed at the inflexibility of Japanese troops, who continued to carry out attack orders that were patently flawed. Similarly, in Vietnam, Communist troops continued with preplanned attacks even when circumstances had changed and alternative plans might have led to victories. While some of this inflexibility can be attributed to their poor communications, much of it is related to their unquestioning military culture.

One aspect of American military culture is that it may be seen as less disciplined than other armies whose notion of discipline is based on inflexibility. U.S. Army Medic Lee Reynolds, who served with the 25th Division, makes the point that, "Much of what uninformed and hostile observers took to be a lack of discipline and a lack of spirit was, instead, a reflection of the skills of the American soldier in the bush." They had enough combat savvy and good sense to question orders that were patently ill-considered.[19]

Perhaps a more balanced picture of American troops' ability to wage aggressive warfare is maintained if one remembers that, in April 1970, U.S. troops launched the daring attacks into the Communist strongholds of Cambodia with the subsequent capture of enormous stockpiles of weapons and ammunition. Similarly, in November 1970, American troops launched the commando raid deep into North Vietnam in an attempt to rescue POWs in the Song Tay raid.

Communist General Tran Van Tra admitted to more serious problems: "Of course, it was unavoidable that certain backward elements would violate discipline in a cowardly manner," he would say of his own troops. "Some were afraid of dying and sought ways to avoid going to the front." General Tra realized, though, that these "cowards" were an insignificant minority. So, too, were they among the Americans.[20]

AWOLs, Deserters, and Defectors

In commenting on the "collapse" of morale as the war progressed, many histories of the Vietnam War naively treat these three categories of offense as equal. This treatment, however, is most misleading. AWOL (absence without leave) is a relatively minor crime and occurs when a person is absent from where he or she is supposed to be without authorized permission. Examples of AWOL could include actions like arriving late to work or going off base without permission. *Desertion* is the unlawful quitting of ones duties with an intention not to return. *Defection* is the act of voluntarily turning oneself over to the enemy and is by far the most serious of these three offenses.

While AWOL rates rose throughout the war years, it is interesting to note that the AWOL rate in the Marines was actually higher *after* they had pulled out of Vietnam and returned to the United States than while they were involved in the war. (Worldwide U.S. AWOL rates were 112.3 per 1000 in 1969 and 177 per 1000 in 1971. U.S. Marine AWOLs were 234 per 1000 in 1973.) So, the notion that the war's "unpopularity" is somehow reflected in AWOL statistics is suspect from the beginning. Other, more complicated, societal factors were apparently at play.[21]

Desertion rates were very high among South Vietnamese Army troops, who often were unable to provide for their families with their meager salaries, and so returned to their farms. It is claimed that desertion rates among U.S. forces worldwide rose throughout the 1960s and early 1970s (21 per 1000 in 1967; 42.4 per 1000 in 1969; 74 per 1000 in 1971). As with AWOL rates, one must be very cautious about making conclusions in using these rates as a simple one-to-one metaphor about the war's "unpopularity."[22]

A far more interesting figure is that of defections, that is, voluntarily turning oneself over to the enemy. Most experts agree that there was only one or perhaps no American defectors depending on one's point of view. Meanwhile, over 200,000 Viet Cong and North Vietnamese troops had gone over to the South Vietnamese forces from the beginning of the Chieu Hoi (Open Arms) Program in 1963. More than 172,000 troops came over after 1966; the great majority of these were in III and IV Corps, the center of the indigenous Viet Cong insurgency. Approximately 200 of these defectors were described as "high-level officers," and approximately 1,000 were "middle-level" personnel. In many of the key battles in the Vietnam War, Communist defectors willingly defected to the Americans and then voluntarily revealed all they knew of their own side's dispositions and plans. Yet, for some unexplained reason, Communist troops are described as remaining highly motivated to their cause throughout the war, while the popular histories describe American morale as declining. The facts suggest otherwise. Especially in the war's later years following the Tet Offensive. Comparatively, American morale can be shown to have remained high throughout the later years.[23]

Withdrawal of Elite Troops First

One of the major factors that led to an increase in the number of various types of minor offenses in the latter periods of the war is directly related to the nature of the troops and where they were based at the time. In the early years, through 1969, when combat was heaviest, a higher proportion of American "elite" units and a higher proportion of combat troops served in Vietnam. By their very nature, these troops spent large proportions of their time in unpopulated regions seeking out the enemy. These combat troops were well removed from the various temptations available to those posted to the base camps, often in or near cities. Further, combat units were well known to have a relaxed attitude toward some of the petty aspects of military discipline, such as "proper" wearing of the uniform, haircuts, shaving, etc. These same minor infractions, however, would quickly warrant a charge in rear areas and base camps.

A look at the composition of U.S. military forces in Vietnam shows this marked change as the war progressed.

TABLE III-4 U.S. Army and Marine Corps Troop Numbers Compared							
U.S. Military Forces in Vietnam (End of Year Strength in Thousands)							
Targets	1965	1966	1967	1968	1969	1970	1971
US Army	117	239	320	360	331	251	120
US Marines	38	69	78	81	55	25	0.6

Source: Table 103, Southeast Asia Statistical Summary, Office of the Assistant Secretary of Defense (Comptroller) February 7, 1973 cited in Thomas C. Thayer, War Without Fronts, The American Experience in Vietnam. (Boulder, Colorado: Westview Press, 1985), 37.

As the "elite" volunteer units were withdrawn from Vietnam (the entire 3rd Marine Division withdrew in 1969), the percentage of conscripted soldiers in Vietnam grew as a consequence. A measure of this is the ratio of troops of the U.S. Army (a mix of volunteers and conscripts) to those of the U.S. Marines (essentially an all-volunteer force).

A further reflection of this ratio can be seen in the casualty figures. In 1966, only 21% of those Americans killed that year had been conscripted. By 1970, this figure for that year had risen to 43%. By U.S. government policy, the military forces were increasingly a conscripted, nonprofessional, noncombat force serving in Vietnam.[24]

Much of what is now alleged about the decline of morale traces its roots to an article by Colonel Robert D. Heinl, Jr., (Ret.) a Marine Corps historian, whose June 7, 1971, article in *Armed Forces Journal*, claimed that

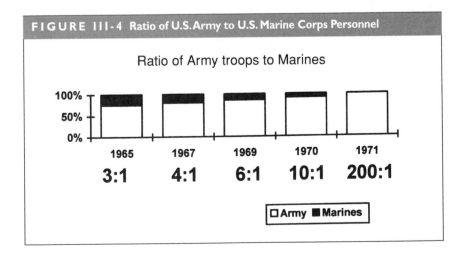

FIGURE III-4 Ratio of U.S. Army to U.S. Marine Corps Personnel

the American Army troops in Vietnam had a serious crisis of morale. More knowledgeable and impartial observers could dismiss much of this as yet another example of interservice rivalry: the Marines telling the Army how bad they are in comparison.[25]

Fewer Combat Troops

As America withdrew its elite troops, it also dramatically altered the proportion of "combat" troops in its ranks. "Combat" troops (even according to the generous official definition of "combat") accounted for 28% of the American force in July 1969; two years later, the figure was 21%. On August 12, 1972, *some five months before the war's end* at the Paris Accords, America withdrew the 3rd Battalion, 21st Infantry and G Battery, 29th Field Artillery, leaving the United States with *no combat forces whatsoever* in South Vietnam; the remaining 43,500 were entirely made up of support personnel. Thus, the composition of the American force altered dramatically in the final years. It changed from a combat force, which spent a good deal of its time in unpopulated areas, to one that was overwhelmingly noncombat, consisting of that myriad of truck drivers, mechanics, typists, technicians, and clerks assigned to the big bases situated in or near the major cities.[26]

Further compounding the matter and as a consequence of the policy of Vietnamization of the war and beginning as early as the late 1960s, American combat units increasingly handed over their previous aggressive search-and-destroy combat assignments to the South Vietnamese Armed Forces. What few combat troops the United States did deploy to Vietnam in the 1970s were themselves increasingly spending time in a defensive posture at their base camps out of combat. (On a man-for-man basis, the casualty rate in 1971 was less than 10% of the 1968 rate.)

The troops of the 1970s were probably not the "hard-charging" troops of the 1960s, but they weren't asked to be and didn't need to be. The hard chargers had completed their mission and were back at their Fort Braggs and their Camp Pendletons. The remaining task was to equip the South Vietnamese so that they could maintain the relative security they now enjoyed and deal with occasional brushfire outbreaks.

The troops of the 1970s worked long and grueling hours, thousands of miles from family and friends. They worked at their thankless tasks: repairing and servicing equipment, dealing with the reams of necessary "paperwork," firing artillery barrages, standing long and boring guard details at their base camps, and rarely engaging in combat with the enemy. They did these tasks often without any sense of "contributing" to the war's goals in the way an infantry soldier could. Theirs was not a particularly glamorous job, but full credit should be given for them performing the job so well under such negative circumstances. They can take pride in the part they played. As Major General Robert Barrow (USMC) remarked about the "support troops" involved in Operation Dewey Canyon, "I don't draw any fine distinction between those supporting and those supported. If you had anything to do with the operation, you were a part of it." The same could be said for those who supported the war's effort in its closing days.[27]

African-American Troops; Not Fools, Dupes, or Victims

One of the most patronizing of the claims made by members of the privileged antiwar movement has to do with African-American troops in Vietnam. In 1965, when it was discovered that African-Americans were suffering a disproportionately high casualty rate, the privileged group immediately perceived this in terms of their own stereotypes. They assumed African-American troops were being victimized. It apparently didn't occur to them that their casualties might be higher because African-Americans knowingly and proudly volunteered to fight in the war and chose to do so in the elite units most likely to see combat. Their casualties were highest precisely at that time when the war was being fought by the professionals and the volunteers.

Thomas Johnson, writing in *Ebony* magazine in 1968, described the large numbers of African-American troops proudly serving in the Marines and the paratroops. A desire for "status, a proof of manhood and a youthful pursuit of excitement" could be seen driving the young African-Americans of the Marines and paratroopers, he wrote. Whitney Young of the Urban League, writing in *Harper's* magazine, justified disproportionate casualties in the early years of the war not as a result of discrimination, but rather ". . . the simple fact that a higher proportion [of African-Americans] volunteer for hazardous duty"[28]

"The brother does all right here," an African-American army officer remarked to an *Ebony* magazine correspondent. "You see it's just about the first time in his life that he finds he can really compete with whites on an equal—or very close to equal—basis. He tries hard in this kind of situation and he does well."[29]

Colonel Fred Cherry, an Air Force pilot captured in 1965, was routinely tortured by the North Vietnamese and kept in solitary confinement for 700 days to force him to make propaganda-type tapes wherein he'd say that African-Americans didn't belong in Vietnam. He remembers with considerable pride that, "By this time, our black guys are doing good work, hurtin' 'em down South." Colonel Cherry didn't break. "They never got to home plate," he recalls. "Just like when they beat me, I always kept in mind I was representing 24 million black Americans. If they are going to kill me, they are going to have to kill me. I'm just not going to denounce my government or shame my people."[30]

Many writers suggest that serious racial tensions existed in Vietnam. Once again, it is yet another way to slight and demean the contribution and morale of those troops sent to fight the war in Vietnam. First, it must be noted that any racial tensions were very much a function of life at the base camps, not out in the field where combat took place. Second, while racial taunts and threats were indeed occasionally hurled back at base camp areas, such events must be kept in perspective. Eric Bergerud, who extensively interviewed a range of veterans in his research on the war, concluded, "Aloofness or dislike is not the same thing as hatred. Indeed, it may well be that racial relations in the 25th Division were better than they were in the United States."[31]

Ulysee Williams, Jr., of Miami, Florida, served in the U.S. Air Force in South Vietnam in the early 1970's. When he returned to the United States, he recalled that "Compared to the racial prejudice which existed at home, Vietnam had been easier to cope with. I had experienced little racial prejudice in Vietnam, but here it was everywhere."[32]

Medals

It is sometimes claimed that medals were handed out at prodigious rates in the closing years of the Vietnam War "in an attempt to keep up morale." Not only does this claim falsely appear to "prove" a lowering of morale, but also it denigrates every American who was so decorated, suggesting that their awards weren't duly earned. Former Secretary of the Navy James Webb points out that these false allegations invariably include in their totals the Air Medal, which was never intended, nor claimed to be, a medal of bravery. On the contrary, the Air Medal was awarded on a points basis for the number of missions flown and is therefore simply a measure of the widespread use of helicopters in the war. U.S. Army soldiers were awarded more than a million of these medals throughout the war, with many pilots chalking up scores of them. Secretary Webb states "If we compare actual gallantry awards, the Army awarded 289 Medals of Honor in World War II and 155 in Vietnam, 4,434 Distinguished Service Crosses in World War II and 846 in Vietnam, and 73,651 Silver Stars in World War II as against 21,630 in Vietnam. The Marine Corps, which lost 102,000 killed or wounded out of some 400,000 sent to Vietnam, awarded 47 Medals of Honor (34 posthumously), 362 Navy Crosses (139 posthumously) and 2,592 Silver Star Medals." The United States was not overly generous in its awarding of medals in Vietnam.[33]

The Veterans

The *dich van* propaganda claim that the war was immoral was often translated into "American soldiers are rapists and baby killers" by antiwar activists of the time. Similarly, antiwar leaders' claims that *avoidance* of the draft was just and honorable had as its corollary that "military service is either dishonorable or stupid." This kind of thinking, together with the *dich van* claims about American mistakes and defeats, sowed the seeds for the later claim that those who fought in the war would of necessity be troubled forever by their complicity in it.[34]

The media helped to reinforce this false impression by portraying Vietnam veterans as mentally deranged, psychotic killers in scores of films in the 1970s and 1980s. A *Washington Post*/ABC news poll taken in 1986 found that, contrary to the myth, Vietnam veterans were by then more likely to have a college education, more likely to own their own home, and more likely to earn above-average incomes than their nonveteran peers.[35]

Similarly, Dr. Robert Fleming, writing in *Psychiatry*, noted that the number of actual cases of posttraumatic stress disorder was "astonishingly low, given the publicity that the media and mental health professionals have placed on this diagnosis." Perhaps in no other war has the focus been so much on the veterans' ills and so little on the positive side of their service.[36]

Remembering

No doubt the best judges of their morale were the troops themselves. How did they feel about the war? A 1980 Veterans Administration study found that, looking back, 71% of veterans were "glad" to have gone to Vietnam and 66% expressed a willingness to serve again, even knowing the 1975 outcome. An Australian historian could also have been describing many Americans when he noted: "Australian soldiers who fought in Vietnam were imbued with a notion of serving an honorable cause at the nation's behest. For most, this seems not to have changed."[37]

QUESTIONING THE CREDIBILITY OF THE WITNESSES

*Gaining
a Fairer Verdict
by History*

28

The "Narrow Sample" Problem
Combat Veterans as Eyewitnesses

An old Buddhist fable tells of three blind men coming upon an elephant in the jungle. One reaches out, and grasping the elephant's leg, tells his friends that it's built like a massive tree. Another, reaching out, grasps the elephant's trunk, and declares that, no, it's more like a snake. The third . .

The individual American fighting man in Vietnam had a very limited, very narrow, very personal view of the war. Even though one might expect him to have the most accurate view of the war, in fact, his view was often flawed by this limited perspective. Interestingly, his view routinely caused him to overestimate his enemy and underestimate his own performance, thereby not refuting the *dich van* myths about which he might have expertise.

Two aspects of American actions contributed most to this biased and often blatantly inaccurate assessment of the situation by the ground troops. It appears that these aspects may have led American troops to rate the enemy more highly than more objective measures. These aspects include: (a) the fact that American combat troops were routinely outnumbered by the enemy and (b) the fact that American troops actively sought to engage the enemy and were prepared give the enemy the initial advantage, if necessary, just in order to start the battle.

Combat Numbers

U.S. combat troops aggressively attempted to locate and destroy the enemy's main force units operating within the boundaries of South Vietnam. This fact itself suggests something of the relative military merits and strengths of the opposing forces. The makeup of the opposing forces, however, was quite different. The American force was modern and technological, fighting 10,000 miles from home. It had an enormous administrative and support "tail" necessary to support its combat troops. In addition, a large part of its efforts went into the construction of facilities that previously did not exist, such as the huge sea port facilities at Camranh Bay. In contrast, the Viet Cong and NVA in South Vietnam were comparatively "in their own back-yard" and with safe sanctuaries, which remained until very late in the war. Virtually all their troops were available for combat.

Even when the huge South Vietnamese Army and "Free World Forces," such as those of South Korea and Australia, are included, the number of troops available for combat against the Communists was always relatively small. Thomas Thayer studied troop numbers and concluded that, "Given the commitment of regular forces to security missions for much of the war, the remaining allied force held no significant advantage over the VC/NVA forces that could potentially be committed against them." Thayer went on to conclude that, in many situations, Communist combat forces outnumbered American and allied troops by a ratio of about 3:2.[1]

The situation "in the field" was often much worse than official fig-ures would suggest. Lieutenant Colonel Carl Neilson, who served with the 25th Infantry Division, noted that, while on paper, the division was always "up to strength," the reality was somewhat different. Because of the ongoing need to service the administrative needs of the division, of troops away on R&R, and the various "standing details of various and sundry types," the number of troops available for combat was significantly less than reported. "According to my records," he observed, "although the rifle company was authorized 188 personnel, . . . when we actually got out in the field with our company, we were lucky to have 100. Looking at my records, I find that rarely in a combat situation operating out of a firebase was our strength more than 350 out of a total of 907." Similarly, when the 1st Brigade of the 7th Cavalry launched their attack into Ia Drang in 1966, their com-pany strengths were: Alpha Company 115 men (49 short), Bravo 114 (50 short), Charlie 106 (58 short), and the weapons company only 76 (42 short).[2]

Engage the Enemy—at Any Price

The problem of the small number of American combat troops was exacerbated by the need to first locate the enemy who, in spite of their greater numbers, avoided standup battles with the better trained and equipped Americans. This task required American troops to split their forces into much smaller scouting and patrolling units. Just how commonplace this situation was in Vietnam is suggested by the following, blandly-reported official communiqué from 1968: *"The U.S. command May 21 announced the start of 2 offensives to safeguard Quangtri and Hue from North Vietnamese attack. The largest of the operations was being carried out near Hue, where about 1,500 men of the 101st Airborne were seeking out 2 North Vietnamese divisions totaling about 20,000 men. 92 North Vietnamese were reported killed in the 2 drives so far."* Fifteen hundred American troops were seeking twenty thousand enemy soldiers! Little wonder they had an enormous respect for the enemy.[3]

In the battles around Khe Sahn in May/June 1968, for another example, the Third Marine Division was pitted against three NVA Divisions, the 320th, 304th, and 308th. In order to locate an enemy division and bring it to battle, the Marines spread out in units no larger than company (100-men) in size. Thus, each Marine was in a *100-man* unit, which sought to locate one of the *10,000-man* NVA divisions. The Marines all realized the consequences to their unit if they were the ones to locate the sought-after enemy.

General William DePuy (U.S. Army) described this situation by saying that American forces were able "to put very small units, platoons and companies, sometimes smaller patrols, out into the jungle to find and fight. And then from the first shot and every minute thereafter the advantage turned in our favor because the Viet Cong or the NVA were seldom able to reinforce. They started the battle with whatever they had. But every minute we were able to bring in fighters, attack helicopters, artillery and then additional troops by helicopter. So it reversed what was an exclusive advantage to the guerrilla and when used well it resulted in frustration for the guerrilla and victory for our own army."[4]

As a tactic, this action was very effective, but for the individual soldier or Marine involved in these patrols, the experience was certainly unnerving. There was the constant sense of searching for an enemy unit, which was much larger and stronger than one's own. This sense contributed to the myth of the invincible enemy.

In the effort leading up to the battle of Ia Drang in 1966, a platoon of 27 men from the 1st Air Cavalry Division was helicoptered into what turned out to be position defended by an NVA force of several hundred. As they unloaded from their helicopters, 22 of the 27 men were killed on the spot. The survivors called in artillery and air support. Major Joe Anderson (U.S. Army), then a platoon commander in a relief force, struggled for the rest of the day and into the night to get to their beleaguered colleagues. An historic battle ensued: the first clash of arms between an NVA unit and the Americans. "We looked on it as a victory," Major Anderson recalls, "but it was a very tragic loss for the platoon that we went to rescue."[5]

Perhaps the most succinct account of this tactic, referred to as "dangling the bait," is that of Lieutenant James Webb (U.S. Marines). "We would dive into an area, set up as a company [approximately one hundred men], and platoons [approximately thirty men] would patrol out from the company operation base, hoping to make contact. It was almost like seducing the enemy into making contact with you. Then you could fix the position and bring in other units and supporting arms—and destroy, which is very nice when you start tallying numbers on a tote board but which can be really devastating for the smaller units." The oft-quoted statistic, stating that most contacts with the enemy were initiated by the Communists, needs to be seen in the context of this "dangling the bait" tactic. Nonetheless, intentional or not, "leading with the chin" no doubt tended to encourage exaggerated assessments of enemy capabilities.[6]

Early in the war, when the Australian troops first had occasion to work with the paratroopers of the 173rd Airborne Brigade, they were stunned. They noted that the 173rd deliberately made noise and in other ways provoked the Viet Cong to attack. For a small country like Australia, which could only muster one regiment to fight outside its national borders, the prospect of actively inviting the sort of attack which their Yank "mates" seemed to hope for, was untenable. If the United States lost a battalion, it would be bad, but if the Australians lost a battalion, it would be a national catastrophe. It was henceforth decided that the Australians would work independently, playing more of a pacification role, like that allocated to the South Vietnamese Army. American troops would continue to go after the Main Force Communist units.[7]

While they chose not to adopt American tactics, the Australians appreciated their value. In May 1968, the Australians fought their biggest battle of the war. They had established a fire support base (Coral) deep in enemy-held territory. The NVA attempted to attack it at that time. The Australians received air support from American helicopters who used a variation of the "dangling the bait" tactic. When an NVA antiaircraft machine gun fired on the American helicopters during the nighttime battle, the

American flight leader deliberately drew enemy fire by leaving his lights on. With his helicopter "lit up like a Christmas tree," other blacked-out helicopters hovered nearby, hidden in the darkness. The Australians watched in awe as the NVA antiaircraft gun fired up at the illuminated "sitting duck," only to be instantly destroyed by the blacked-out ships' rocket salvoes in return. Australian Captain Bob Hennessy recalled, "This was typical [of] American bravery, courage and their gung-ho approach to war." Captain Hennessy summarized by saying, "I admired the Americans."[8]

So the American fighting man routinely found himself in a unit searching for, and willingly offering itself up as bait to, an enemy force several times its superior, both in numbers and firepower. Often, the particular unit that located the enemy was thus severely mauled; ultimately, however, the enemy unit would suffer even greater casualties.

Also, because the American troops were on the offensive, the enemy usually had the advantage of fighting from well-concealed and protected positions. Some of these, such as those in the "hill fights" of 1967, had protective roofs several feet thick and were impervious to all but direct hits with the heaviest of bombs. Meanwhile, the American troops attacked in the open, proceeding at a crouch up the barren hillsides, clearly visible in the gunsights of the well-concealed NVA. American combat troops, knowing that they would be initially outnumbered and outgunned, and faced by a well-concealed and often entrenched enemy until help could eventually arrive in the form of artillery or reinforcements, therefore developed a respect for the enemy bordering on the epic.

This "narrow sample" problem was exacerbated by the way in which troops perceived and explained their firefights. In Vietnam, the use of the word, "ambush," was routinely overused and misused. One former Special Forces sergeant, for instance, commented on the fact that an American infantryman would probably report *any* contact as an ambush ". . . even if his unit had been sent to the location on hard intelligence" and was tactically deployed for the attack. Because American troops were so thoroughly trained and indoctrinated in the dangers of an ambush that the possibility of an ambush was always present in their minds, American troops tended to call *any* contact an ambush if the enemy fired from concealed positions. Hence, they tended to describe their battle experiences in terms of the number of times they had been "ambushed." The Americans felt and so conveyed a false impression of the enemy's skills and their own vulnerability.[9]

In fact, throughout the war, the U.S. troops were the ones trying to locate and destroy the enemy; the VC/NVA were almost always attempting to hide, except in those few instances when they held a local tactical advantage and would inflict whatever casualties they could before withdrawing. Similarly, while the odd handful of specialized Viet Cong "sapper" troops would occasionally launch a commando attack on a U.S. air base, it must be remembered that tens of thousands of U.S. combat troops routinely operated in the heart of so-called "enemy areas" seeking out and destroying the enemy.

It must also be remembered that, while American units were routinely outnumbered by the Communist forces they faced, it was nonetheless a very aggressive American strategy that placed these units into locations where the Communists might be. American policy actively sought pitched battles with the enemy while, generally, the enemy attempted to avoid them. The matter of who fired first is often irrelevant. More important is the question of who forced the action to occur. Many texts still miss this vital point. One popular text, for example, in describing Operation Junction City, in which the U.S. parachuted a whole battalion of paratroopers into the midst of the suspected COSVN headquarters and then quickly followed up with a large-scale ground attack, demonstrates the pervasiveness of this error. When the trapped VC attempted to break out to safety and were eliminated by the U.S. troops in a lopsided victory to the Americans, this text describes the action by concluding that, ". . . more significant was that once again the action had been initiated by the VC." The authors of these texts, noting that the Viet Cong fired first, credit them with "initiating the action." They fail to recognize that the Viet Cong did so only because they were on the receiving end of aggressive American actions which had the clear intention of forcing them "into a corner," in which they had no other choice but to fight.[10]

Last, the battle conditions themselves, sometimes fighting in deep jungle cover, sometimes fighting in the narrow streets of Hue, or often fighting in the pitch black of night, made it physically impossible to get any sort of "big picture" with their own eyes. The commander of the Australian force, which fought the battle of Long Tan, was reputedly "ashen-faced and almost speechless" the night after the battle because he thought his men had taken heavy casualties with nothing to show for it. The Australians thought they'd suffered a major defeat. The next day, when they went back into the battlefield, they discovered the bodies of 245 enemy troops killed in the battle. They took three wounded Communists prisoner and subsequently captured the enemy commander's diary, which indicated that total killed had been 500. Only then did the Australian discover that, rather than suffering a defeat as he had imagined, his forces had achieved one of the great victories of the war.[11]

Ordinarily, the individual soldier or Marine had very little, if any, real notion of what was taking place only a few hundred meters away. He, just like everyone else, relied on other sources for perspective. This was true of most veterans, and not just the troops, even their officers. Colonel Gordon Batcheller USMC (Retired) had led the first relief force as a captain through to Hue during that city's 1968 Tet battle. As the commander of a U.S. Marine infantry company at the height of the war and as a recipient of the Navy Cross he could fairly lay claim to being an eyewitness to the combat there. However, in questioning him about the battle at Hue, even he observes that his opinions are "based more on secondary information than on firsthand experience."[12]

The very nature of combat precluded combat veterans from gaining a full and accurate assessment based on their own firsthand observations. They, like everyone else, were dependent on other sources for their overall understanding. And many of those sources were badly flawed and sometimes even openly hostile.

Talking About the War

Often, combat veterans themselves, naively believing some of the falsehoods they'd heard, have helped to perpetuate the various myths. Joseph Galloway (a UPI correspondent and veteran of the Ia Drang battle), who spends time on the CompuServe military forum's Vietnam section, observes that he often finds individuals who were actual combat soldiers themselves "retelling latrine rumors about actions they never saw as if they were the gospel truth." Galloway notes that, when challenged with the facts, "They invariably retreat with a lame: 'Well that's what I heard up in II Corps' or 'Well I heard that from a Huey pilot who knew a guy up there.'"[13]

Finally, one must be cautious about the literal truth of many veterans' accounts of what they did in the war. Observers like Christian Appey have noted the discomfort that some veterans felt when discussing their combat experiences with nonveterans. Assuming that nonveterans would be unable to understand properly and relate to the truth of their combat experiences, veterans learned to fob off such inquiries with an evasive answer, which, while effective in evading further interrogation, no doubt served to reinforce some of the misperceptions. "If asked directly," Appey noted, "they might reveal a piece of their experience, some stock anecdote they had practiced enough to feel comfortable telling; an amusing story about some crazy GI who booby-trapped the shitter. . . ." Unfortunately, those hearing these carefully selected, diversionary stories may falsely believe they are privy to the reality of that veteran's experience.[14]

In summary, most combat veterans saw only a narrow little slice of the war, too small a slice to make any overall assessments. For the "big picture" about what took place, they were as dependent upon secondary sources, newspapers, television and radio, as anyone else. But how accurate and how unbiased were those sources?

29

Not Expert Witnesses

Many of the "expert" witnesses and chroniclers of the Vietnam War in the western world were not really experts at all. They were as vulnerable to the *dich van* program as anyone else, and hence, to misreading and misreporting the situation. The American people, though, were hungry for some authoritative view or opinion; they wanted someone who could explain the war to them. Sadly, during the Vietnam War, many people stepped forward claiming to be experts when, in truth, they were not.

Journalists as "Expert" Witnesses

David Hallin noted that, "One consequence of the expansion of American involvement was that, after mid-1965, Vietnam was no longer covered by the Collingwoods, foreign correspondents with long experience in Asia, but by young reporters who, like the soldiers, would be rotated out of their dangerous assignments in six months or a year." The turnover was so great that Associated Press went through 300 Saigon reporters in the course of the conflict. In addition, many reporters simply visited Vietnam for a few weeks on their way to Singapore, Tokyo or Hong Kong. [1]

Australian journalist, Denis Warner, noted: "The Vietnam War threw up more impostors and charlatans in the name of war correspondents than I can remember in all the other wars I covered put together." Pulitzer prize winner, Eddie Adams, was more blunt: "Some of the press corps," he said, "were real assholes. You had a lot of adventure seekers, little rich kids who had never taken a picture in their lives, and writers the same way."[2]

Peter Braestrup, who covered the war for the *Washington Post*, agreed that "the 'learning curve' was flattened by the short tour of most American newsman." Braestrup is particularly critical of the electronic media: "In 1966-69, the television networks were perhaps the least 'serious' in this respect. Their bureau chiefs were assigned to Vietnam for one year; the reporters came and went on tours varying from one to six months."[3]

Although most viewers might have reasonably assumed that the "expert opinion" they heard on the television was that of a knowledgeable expert, they would have been very wrong. A CBS reporter summed it up by saying, "There was no premium on experience or expertise in our business. The networks see no harm in running a standup piece on the war's progress by a guy who has just come in the country two day's earlier."[4]

The civilian journalists who covered the Vietnam war for their brief "tour" generally had a very poor knowledge of, and background in, military matters. Peter Braestrup noted this "blank spot" in the experience of American newsmen in Vietnam. "Few, for example," he wrote, "knew the difference between, say, a mortar and a howitzer, battalions and divisions, logistics and tactics, or between overall U.S. personnel strength in Vietnam . . . and the relatively small number of men actually firing weapons at the enemy."[5]

One reporter, asked to comment on Braestrup's charges that his fellow journalists turned the Communist defeat at Tet into a victory, excused it by suggesting that, "Braestrup was basically a war correspondent. I was a political reporter." The problem in Vietnam was that this group of politically-focused reporters nonetheless also reported on the military aspects of the war, making "sage" pronouncements on the progress of battles and the outcomes of firefights. [6]

"To many newsmen," Peter Braestrup would later write, "the outcome of a skirmish or even of a major action seemed irrelevant amid the shock of seeing Americans die or Vietnamese peasants huddled beside their ruined huts. To many, the difference between braving a dozen noisy rounds of [relatively harmless] enemy mortar fire and seeing a 200-round barrage accompanied by a 300-man assault was imperceptible: it was all equally important, impressive and terrifying, . . ."[7]

One can see the terror and the confusion they felt in the photographs they took: the *Newsweek* story on Khe Sanh in which 18 of the 29 photos showed men either wounded, dead, or huddled under fire. None of the photographs showed Marines firing back, in spite of the fact that Marine artillery fired ten rounds at the enemy for every one Khe Sanh received. That became the perspective of the battle that the American people back home saw.[8]

Don Oberdorfer of the *Washington Post* agrees, citing the specific example of Khe Sanh where because "most correspondents and camera crews did not remain at Khe Sanh for more than a day or two—there was a waiting list of journalists requesting visits to the base—a sense of continuity about the battle was difficult and the sense of danger and impending disaster was more intense among the newsmen than among the Marines who were accustomed to living under the enemy's guns." [9]

"The Khe Sanh garrison," Braestrup observes, "comes through on TV film as an assemblage of apprehensive, unorganized, even hapless individuals—like the exhausted reporters—not as a group of trained soldiers, organized into fighting units, with friends, local knowledge, training, and a special esprit de corps to sustain them . . ." Further, he adds, "Unconveyed on TV was the crazy gallows humor, considerable professionalism, and camaraderie of the Marines."[10]

Many journalists began to believe their own publicity and, indeed, they not only proclaimed themselves as experts to the public but also to the real experts. Secretary of State Dean Rusk was reputedly outraged when journalists Walter Lippman and Arthur Krock sent him messages that, if Rusk would like to avail himself of their advice, *they were prepared to see him*.[11]

Saigon and Tet (1968)

Journalists themselves were often scathing in evaluating their own kind. Michael Herr (*Esquire*) described the range of journalists who covered the war: Everything from ". . . Vietnamese who took up combat photography to avoid the draft, [to] Americans who spent all their days in Saigon drinking at the bar of L'Admiral Restaurant . . ."[12]

The main theme of Peter Braestrup's critical analysis of the media's performance during the Tet Offensive of 1968 is that the war was brought to the doorstep of these militarily naive journalists in Saigon and that they reported *the panic they felt*, rather than *the events that occurred*. This attitude was especially evident in the firefight that occurred on the front lawn of the American Embassy. The terrified reporters crouched behind the cover of the high wall that surrounded the embassy compound. Prevented from seeing any of the action, they nonetheless filed colorful, wildly inaccurate, and totally fabricated stories, claiming that the Viet Cong had occupied the first five floors. This claim was made despite the fact that the Viet Cong failed to even enter the building. As General Bruce Clark (U.S. Army Ret.) commented after visiting Vietnam during the Tet Offensive: "[The enemy] took the battle down around the Caravelle Hotel and, so, from the standpoint of the average reporter over there, it was the acorn that fell on the chicken's head and it said 'The sky is falling!' "[13]

Journalistic expertise was put into clear perspective in the 1968 battle for the city of Hue. A provincial capital, Hue was a city of some 140,000 residents and hence large enough to offer the kinds of facilities that journalists found attractive. Further, the battle raged for some 28 days, allowing sufficient time for the media to actually be in the vicinity of a continuing battle. As the U.S. media reported on the progress of the battle, U.S. Army officials became concerned that journalists were broadcasting very accurate and specific details of troops movements (down to 100-man, company-sized units) and locations that could endanger American lives. After reflecting on the matter, however, U.S. Army officers concluded that American journalists were so lacking in credibility, even in Hanoi's eyes, that their reports of troop movements, although accurate in this particular case, posed no threat to American safety.[14]

Civilian "Experts"

Sadly, some of the civilian leaders of the war also often showed a marked lack of expertise on military matters. Clark Clifford was appointed Secretary of Defense to take up duties on March 1, 1968. Clifford was described as ". . . not a career politician, he was a tough corporation lawyer who had given up a $500,000 practice for a $35,000 job." Secretary of State Dean Rusk, a career diplomat, had not been impressed with Clifford prior to his appointment. He believed Clifford to be ill-informed and that his advice, given knowing that he would suffer no consequence if it were wrong, was of little value.[15]

When Clifford questioned the Pentagon generals after his appointment, he recalled one of them remarking about the difficulty in getting the enemy to engage in the sort of "stand-up battle" in which American firepower could prevail. Clifford later showed a remarkably superficial and fanciful notion of the reasons for the American victory over the British in the Revolutionary War when he remarked that, "It reminded me of the complaint by the British general in the revolutionary war that the American troops wouldn't come out and fight. We hung behind brick fences, rocks and trees and knocked off those red coats. And this was the same kind of problem."[16]

This fancifully simplistic notion of combat in the Vietnam War is often perpetuated in the various popular histories of the war. One often reads in these accounts that American troops were too burdened with equipment (helmets, flak jackets, ammunition), for instance, to catch the lightly equipped Viet Cong. Authors of this sort of "analysis" presumably believe that combat is something like a footrace where the two opposing forces sprint after each other.

Similarly, Clifford is often quoted as being amazed that, when he asked the Joint Chiefs of Staff at the Pentagon in early March, 1968, "What is the plan for victory?", the response given was, "There is no plan." What is usually not reported, though, is that the Joint Chiefs continued by explaining, "Because American forces operate under three major restrictions; the President has forbidden them to invade the North, . . . he has forbidden the mining of Haiphong Harbor, . . . he has forbidden pursuing the enemy into Laos and Cambodia." Plans did exist to "win" the war, including detailed plans for an amphibious-airborne invasion of North Vietnam and the bombing of military targets in Hanoi and Haiphong. However, these plans had been consistently rejected by McNamara since 1966.[17]

The lack of insight suggested by these comments would not augur well for Clifford's later analysis of military aspects of the Vietnam War. It was largely on his advice that, after the resounding American victories of the Tet Offensive, Lyndon Johnson began to think he could not win the war and so chose to stop bombing North Vietnam, a move that would delay the defeat of the North Vietnamese Army by five years. Clifford's influence is confirmed by social historian Professor Tod Gitlin, who claims that Clifford was ". . . the decisive agent who lost faith in the war effort and set out to mobilize influential opposition within the highest political-economic circles of Washington and New York."[18]

Perhaps the final word is best given by a real expert on the situation. General Phillip Davidson, intelligence chief to General Westmoreland during the war, recalls the frustration of seeing often well-meaning, but inexpert, civilians acting as "experts." "To see [them] huddled over maps and aerial photographs, planning air strikes would have been ludicrous," he would later write, "had the consequences not been so serious." What all these reports suggest is that the "expert opinions" of the war's progress were often not expert at all. Real experts would have been able to counter many of the dich van myths [19]

30

Storytellers, Not Witnesses

Many chroniclers of the war, perhaps without intentional malice, nonetheless created a very biased and negative account of the American effort in the Vietnam War. In contrast to this focus on the negative, the tightly controlled Hanoi machinery orchestrated a very positive image of its own effort. The myths thus created still abound.

Looking for Stories

Western journalists were required by their editors and publishers to do more than simply *report facts*; they were required to write and photograph *stories,* to use the language of journalism. In balancing these requirements, some journalists felt their primary responsibility was to tell "the news" and, secondarily, to tell that news within an interesting storyline. Not all journalists agreed, however. According to fellow photojournalist Susan Moeller, some journalists "felt even less of a responsibility . . . to tell just the 'news'; they primarily wanted to tell stories."[1]

Peter Braestrup observed this tendency to produce or "create" stories that were often contrary to the facts firsthand, while covering the war for the *Washington Post*. He cites one such example: the Marines' defense of Khe Sanh. The media elected to portray the battle with the dramatic touch of "beleaguered Marines," of the "agony of Khe Sanh," and of the "Marines under siege," and then proceeded to illustrate their stories with photos that supported this theme.

Braestrup notes that *Newsweek* devoted 29 of its 59 action photos to the battle of Khe Sanh during Tet 1968. Further, he notes that "18 of the 29 showed Americans or South Vietnamese troops either wounded or dead or huddled under fire. None showed allied troops at Khe Sanh firing back." This report was published despite the fact that, throughout the battle, the defenders fired many times more "outgoing" rounds than they received in "incoming." Also, if one counts the tonnages of bombs dropped by B-52s and tactical airstrikes on the enemy and directed by the defenders from Khe Sanh, the count becomes even more one-sided.[2]

How these "stories" came to be created is suggested by a telex sent by the executive producer of ABC news to his Saigon bureau in March 1969. "I think the time has come," he wrote them, "to shift our focus from the battlefield, or more specifically American military involvement with the enemy, to themes and stories under the general heading: We Are on Our Way Out of Vietnam..." For the next two months, the Saigon bureau continued to send the same amount of combat footage, but it was shown in the United States on only three occasions. Previously such footage was shown 25 to 30 times for every two-month period. The executive producer decided the "story" they wished to tell had changed, regardless of the facts being filmed. The American public therefore saw little of the action film and much more of the *"we're pulling out"* film.[3]

Looking for the Sensational

General William Westmoreland, who grew to feel that the media were his worst enemies in the war, summed up the situation as he saw it: "At one time in Vietnam we had 700 accredited reporters—all practicing, seeking and reporting news as they were accustomed to in the United States, all looking for the sensational stories." General Westmoreland also noted that the American news media "tended to report the war like crime on a police beat, [or a] no-holds-barred political campaign. What is news? News is most often the sensational, the bizarre, the offbeat."[4]

Secretary of State Dean Rusk believed that the press was not concerned with the best interests of the country; rather, they saw their sole business as making headlines and selling newspapers. When Rusk took his 15-year-old daughter to see the singing group, Peter, Paul and Mary, at a Washington hotel, he later complained that the only thing the muck-raking journalists at the State Department were asking the next day was, "Who was that chick the Secretary was out with last night?"[5]

Several commentators have noted the tendency, especially of the wire services, to send their reports before the "fog of war" had cleared and, where necessary, to "needle up" their stories in order to catch the attention of their editors. Jack Raymond of the *New York Times* wrote, "The correspondent is almost compelled to play up the sights and sounds of battle. It takes only a few casualties in any skirmish to generate descriptions worthy of the battle of Iwo Jima."[6]

Many commentators support this belief, adding that, "In addition to the more professional journalists, there were many young and experienced observers overly susceptible to the sensational." When there was no "big story" to report, they naturally turned to the sensational, the unusual, events such as "friendly fire" deaths, "fragging" murders, and tragic accidents.[7]

What made this particularly confusing for the public was that it relied on the media for *facts* about the war as well as *stories* about it. Often, however, it was impossible for them to distinguish one from the other. Further, very few of its audience had the personal experience of war necessary to put the stories into perspective. When they read or saw pictures of an accidental civilian death caused by an American air strike, they were unable to place it in any context. While undeniably tragic, they weren't told, and so had no way of knowing, that an incident like that was indeed rare. They also weren't told of the circumstances, such as an attempt to rescue fellow South Vietnamese from almost certain destruction at the hands of the Viet Cong.

Precisely because American forces were such superbly trained and equipped warriors, they were able to bring into action very close use of supporting arms, artillery and airstrikes. They were able to routinely bring in devastating B-52 strikes within 500 meters of Khe Sanh, for instance. On the assault, they would saturate the enemy with bombs and shells and then, before the enemy could recover and reorganize their defenses, assault with ground troops before the smoke had cleared. Lesser armies were, and still are, unable to do so; they pay the costs in the lives of their own troops. But, as with everything, there is a consequence: U.S. troops will occasionally suffer "friendly fire."

Again, the facts of these incidents do not make for "the big story." So journalists sought out and focused on, the unusual, the tragic, the lurid. They gave an audience that was unable to put their stories into perspective the impression that those events were not only true but also somehow typical.

General Westmoreland would one day say that it was the "doom and gloom reporting [which] gave the American people the impression that the Americans were being defeated on the battlefield." This kind of thinking led to political decisions to reduce the very pressure on the enemy, which was proving so successful.[8]

Photojournalist Susan Moeller acknowledges that, "The individual photographs, as well as the photographic essays published during the Vietnam conflict, were not representative of the war; the images overemphasized some aspects of the war and minimized others." She also notes that, in particular, the "atrocity" pictures are most remembered. "These images," she writes, "such as Brown's burning monk, Adams's Tet execution, and Haeberle's My Lai villagers, overwhelmed the photographers' intent and willy-nilly defined as well as described the conflict." Finally, she admits that, "In the media and in the memory, photography, intentionally or not, selectively paraphrased the war."[9]

Pulitzer Prize winning photojournalist Eddie Adams agrees. Adams took the infamous photo of General Loan killing the Viet Cong officer who had just murdered the entire family of his best friend. But when the general died in America in 1998, Adams observed about that photo: "The General killed the Viet Cong; I killed the General. Still photographs are the most powerful weapon in the world. People believe them, but photographs do lie, even without manipulation. They are only half truths." Adams then went on to comment about the death of General Loan and the disservice he'd done to him: "I'm sorry. There are tears in my eyes." Regardless, though, the photograph will continue to be printed in books about the war; Adams' comments about regret will not.[10]

In their eagerness to tell stories, these journalists helped, often unwittingly, to create a very false notion about the realities of the Vietnam War. Their reports and photographs, which so selectively paraphrased the war, were not at all representative or typical of the conflict at large. Overwhelmingly, those false impressions were negative ones, reflecting poorly on America's fighting troops and how they conducted the war.

31

The Hostile Witness

Marguerite Higgins, a journalist herself, who had covered both World War II and the Korean War, said of Vietnam, "Reporters here would like us to lose the war to prove they're right."[1]

The strategic *dich van* objective of convincing the American people that the war was immoral and unwinnable received active support from many Americans for various reasons. For one, it was eagerly embraced by those Americans who could easily avoid military service and who selfishly preferred not to serve. General Westmoreland regretted the policy of college deferments, noting that, "The policy contributed to antiwar militancy on college campuses in that young men feeling twinges of conscience because they sat out a war while others fought could appease their conscience if they convinced themselves the war was immoral."

For understandable reasons of wanting to validate their own sense of "self worth" at the time and—all these years later—to validate their actions back then in the eyes of their children, these people could assuage those "twinges of conscience" by damning the war and those who fought it. Former Secretary of the Navy James Webb, Jr., points out that their ". . . fear of judgment of history on their acts . . . still persists today, hurting the chances of a more equitable analysis of what we did and why we did it."[2]

Antiwar Elements Within the Government

General Phillip Davidson, chief intelligence officer in Vietnam, claims that the systems analysis group within the Office of the Secretary of Defense as well as the CIA misled incoming Secretary of State Clark Clifford about the results of the Tet Offensive in 1968, failing to tell him of the American successes. General Davidson claims that this failure wasn't because they ignored available intelligence but, rather, "because their deep-seated liberal and antiwar bias distorted their judgment." General Davidson adds that, "They wanted to see the bleakest picture, and from it to extrapolate the gloomiest forecast of future events in Vietnam." Upon their advice and counsel, Clifford argued against the war and eventually convinced President Johnson that the American people had turned against it as well.[3]

The Antiwar Media

General S.L.A. Marshall, on a mission to South Vietnam in the war's early years, was among the first to note the growing antiwar stance of the media. He wrote that, "Especially alarming to me was the group attitude in the U.S. press corps." He observed that, ". . . without exception, they were bitterly hostile to the [Saigon] Government and hardly less so to the U.S. Embassy and the military command."[4]

This hostility also resonates in the words of David Halbertson, who reported on the war for the *New York Times*. Halbertson recalls that, "The journalists very quickly came to the conclusion that the top people in the embassy were either fools or liars or both."[5]

The old caveat needs to be inserted here. No, not all reporters and journalists were openly hostile to those in the military. However it nonetheless is clear that there was a growing antiwar bias in the media. This bias was most pronounced in the bigger circulation "prestige press" and the television news elite.

Generational Change Occurring With Journalists

A factor possibly contributing to the growing antiwar stance of the media was the "generational change" of the correspondent corps as the media increasingly turned its attention to the war. It has already been noted that, as the war increased in tempo and more and more correspondents were assigned to Vietnam, the age and experience of the correspondents fell enormously.

These "baby boomers" were of a different generation from the generals and colonels who directed the Vietnam War. Many brought with them an ideological bias: "Never trust anyone over thirty." This attitude made them hostile to these military leaders from the outset. At a more personal level, this age difference and perceived "generation gap" made interpersonal and social relationships between them uncomfortable and further contributed to mistrust or misunderstandings. By the late-1960s, rare was the journalist and battalion commander, for instance, who viewed each other as peers and who would routinely sit down and enjoy a social drink or chat together.

While for most Americans, young soldier and young civilian alike, the rebelliousness of the 1960s was nothing more than preference for rock and roll music and longer hair, a handful in that generation were indeed affected more fundamentally. Journalism provided many of them with a public forum. Their suspicious and cynical view of those in command and of their traditional ethics and codes, which motivated them, immediately flavored their reporting and cast a negative interpretation of events unfolding in Vietnam.

This situation soon had predictable consequences. By the late 1960s, according to Todd Gitlin, "the television news elite" had begun to "destabilize American politics around a moderate antiwar consensus." By late 1970, truly unbiased reporting would be almost impossible as "most of the correspondents and news executives personally opposed the war."[6]

Journalists from the Privileged Class; Working-Class Troops

Other factors also contributed to the antiwar/antiauthority bias of American journalists. In many cases, journalists were trained at those same prestigious institutions of higher education that formed the seat of the radical antiwar movement. Often, these journalists, voicing the gulf created by their own privileged, educated backgrounds and the working class roots of the combat troops, totally failed to identify with the young men of their own generation who were actually fighting the war. Michael Herr, who covered the war for *Esquire* magazine, later wrote of the many journalists ". . . who would ask us what we ever found to talk to grunts about, who said they never heard a grunt talk about anything except cars, football, and [sex]." Similarly, when Herr refers to the combat troops of the U.S. Marine Corps, he remarks that ". . . a lot of correspondents privately felt that [they were just] . . . a bunch of dumb, brutal killer kids." The American officials and troops weren't blind to the hostility felt toward them by the media people. They fully sensed this and reacted with equal dislike. A 1965 memorandum from American officials in Vietnam to President Johnson voiced these complaints in claiming that most of these correspondents in Vietnam ". . . are strictly third class . . . [and] cover the war from the bars in Saigon."[7]

Journalists who actually had face-to-face contact with the combat troops heard a more visceral dislike and distrust. Michael Herr noted that many troops believed that, as a journalist, you "took your living from their deaths" and that journalists are all "traitors and liars and the creepiest kinds of parasites."[8]

The Salisbury Reports

Late in December 1966, Harrison E. Salisbury, assistant managing editor of the *New York Times,* arrived in Hanoi, his request for a visa having been granted earlier that same month. Before leaving in early January, North Vietnamese officials conducted him on tours of Hanoi and surrounding areas. Based both on his own observations as well *as information supplied him by the North Vietnamese,* he wrote a series of 14 reports. Without initially citing their source, his articles quoted the Communist-supplied "statistics" about civilian casualties and damage to nonmilitary structures and of seeing "block after block of utter destruction." The White House and the Pentagon, given no advance warning of the various reports' allegations, were placed on the defensive, each time having to react to Salisbury's claims.[9]

Deputy Assistant Secretary of Defense for Public Affairs, Phil Goulding, noted that intelligence analysts were eventually able to chip away at the articles "line by line," but not before immense public relations damage had been done. Goulding's boss, Arthur Sylvester, henceforth referred to the *Times* as "The New Hanoi *Times.*" Even other members of the press were concerned. ABC's Howard K. Smith noted that, "The *Times'* carelessness about the simple basic practices of fair and accurate reporting has become suspicious." Even within the *Times'* organization, there were concerns. Hanson Baldwin observed that the articles "seem to put Mr Salisbury and the *Times* squarely on the side of North Vietnam." Eventually, the *Times* acknowledged that the reports were "grossly exaggerated" but, regardless of their inaccuracy, *Newsweek* described them as "easily the biggest news beat of 1966."[10]

Even by late 1972, little appeared to have changed. On December 21, the *New York Times* carried on its front page a report from the Soviet news agency, Tass, which claimed that the "Christmas" bombings of Hanoi had caused "heavy" civilian casualties and damaged "thousands" of homes. To many readers, familiar with the 100,000 Germans killed in a single raid on Dresden, those words, "heavy casualties," no doubt conjured images of mass destruction on a similar scale. Buried on page 16 was an inconspicuous Associated Press report that Hanoi itself claimed only 260 deaths in Hanoi and Haiphong.[11]

The "Prestige Press"

The Ethics and Public Policy Center in Washington, D.C., undertook a study to investigate the reporting of the "Christmas Bombings" of 1972 in the country's prestige press. As a part of this study, they tallied the number of lines of text that tended to describe the bombing campaign as (a) a "legitimate military operation" versus (b) that which suggested that the bombing was indiscriminate, killing civilians and therefore "reprehensible" (Table IV-1).

Ambassador Graham Martin, who replaced Ellsworth Bunker in August 1973, summed up his assessment of the situation when he noted that, "The editorial page of the *New York Times* . . . has long been generally regarded as having a deep emotional involvement in the success of North Vietnam's attempt to take over South Vietnam by force of arms."[12]

Not Just the American Press

Of course, the problem was not limited to the *New York Times,* nor even to American newspapers. Much the same occurred in Australia. In 1966, at the Battle of Long Tan, a 108-man Australian company fought and defeated a Communist regiment. The following day, when the Australian troops

TABLE IV-1 Reported Legitimacy of the Bombing of North Vietnam		
Bombing of North Vietnam: December 1972 **Number of Lines of Reporting**		
	Military Damage (Legitimate)	**Civilian Damage (Reprehensible)**
New York Times	525	1,070
Washington Post	225	610
Time	21	133
Newsweek	20	70
CBS	24	91

Source: Martin F. Herz, The Prestige Press and the Christmas Bombing, 1972. (Washington, D.C.: Ethics and Public Policy Center, 1980), 29.

returned to the battlefield to recover the bodies of their dead comrades, they also came upon a handful of surviving Communist troops. Three wounded Communists surrendered, but others, although wounded, preferred to retain their weapons and continue the fight. The Australians took them under fire and killed them. Two years later, in 1968, as antiwar hysteria mounted in the press, a journalist published a book citing a "witness" (who later admitted he'd merely heard the story from someone else) claiming to have seen an Australian soldier after the battle ". . . shooting any wounded he could find." As if that weren't misleading enough, the leading Australian newspaper the *Melbourne Age*, in writing about the book's claims, went even further by unilaterally inserting the word "civilian" into the allegation. Its March 9, 1968, edition thus claimed that the witness had seen an Australian soldier ". . . shooting any wounded *civilian* he could find."[13]

The Antiwar Entertainment Media

A number of popular television shows, which portrayed American soldiers in a favorable light: honest, brave, well-meaning, were summarily canceled by network executives in the mid-1960s. Shows, such as "Combat!" (about an American infantry squad in World War II), "12 O'clock High" (about an American bomber group in England in World War II), and "Convoy" (about the U.S. Navy in the Battle of the Atlantic) were all canceled by 1967. "Combat!" was canceled at the end of the 1966 season in spite of "substantial numbers" of viewers. Its star, Vic Morrow, would later claim that the show's cancellation was directly related to negative attitudes about the Vietnam War.[14]

A strong antiwar/antiauthority theme soon ran through many of the popular films, television shows, and written fiction of the time. "Rowan and Martin's Laugh-In," "All In The Family," the "Smothers Brothers" were all outspokenly antiauthority in general but also very specifically against the war being fought in Vietnam. The question of course is whether these shows simply *reflected* the attitudes of their audience or did they also help *shape* those attitudes? And, if they did shape public attitudes, how much of that was intentional?

The cancellation of "Combat!", while its ratings were still strong, raises suspicions. Real concerns are raised by the antiwar beliefs of those in charge and the instructions given to shows that survived. One such example is Barry Rosenzweig, who supervised the writers on "Daniel Boone," which ran on television from 1964–1970. Rosenzweig demanded that the scripts portray the American Revolutionary War as "England's Vietnam," with the colonists appearing like the Viet Cong and the British redcoats appearing like the Americans in Vietnam.[15]

Regardless of whether it was intended to change attitudes, the fact is that those who entertained America did so with antiwar messages. Researchers have noted that, by 1970, films and television routinely portrayed the American military as a "corrupt, bloodthirsty institution." Military officers were invariably shown to be "incompetent, self-serving, and destructive."[16]

That *dich van* myths, including those relating to American military incompetence and the insurgent nature of Hanoi's war, came to be accepted is little wonder. In many cases, they were aided, consciously or not, by the world's best myth-makers: those who controlled the American entertainment media.

Later, after the war, this same popular media would routinely portray the Vietnam veteran as a deranged killer. On "Kojak," a popular detective show which premiered in 1973, for example, Lieutenant Kojak would routinely request that "all Vietnam vets be brought in for questioning" as a matter of course whenever a murder had been committed. Little wonder that, for many years, the term "Vietnam veteran" should conjure the most negative of images.[17]

The Military Finally Get Fed Up

General Phillip Davidson described watching ". . . the news media consistently, and often villainously, savage General Westmoreland. The more General Westmoreland tried to cooperate with the reporters, the more they attacked his policies and his veracity." When General Creighton Abrams took over for Westmoreland, having also witnessed these attacks as Westmoreland's deputy, he immediately and abruptly announced that there would be no more press conferences; and he stuck to his word for his entire tenure. For the next five years in Vietnam he never held one.[18]

When United Press International (UPI) correspondents claimed in the early 1970s that they were unable to speak to the troops or get accommodation, an American colonel told UPI's Kenneth Braddick and Stewart Kellerman, "You guys have been shafting us for years so now we're shafting you right back."[19]

It wasn't just the American troops who'd had enough of the American media's bias. The South Vietnamese themselves shared these feelings. Malcolm Browne of the *New York Times* told of a South Vietnamese Army captain who said to him, ". . . the press is the agent of the Vietcong, so don't be surprised by what happens to newsmen here." He also told of an artillery officer who deliberately gave him misleading directions, which would have resulted in Browne's capture by the NVA. Bob Jones of NBC reports asking a South Vietnamese Army officer for directions to the citadel in Quang Tri in the closing moments of battle there. The officer smiled and, pointing to an open field that was under artillery bombardment, said, "Just walk across that field, and someone will show you the way." Still smiling, the officer added, "You go. I'll stay here."[20]

Continuing Bias

It should be noted that bias continues to affect the perception and reporting of those events, now termed "history." Kenneth J. Heineman has observed that, "Contemporary journalists, activists turned memoir writers, and present-day scholars were generally trained at prestigious institutions of higher education. Such writers and elite-university educated activists shared school ties and high social-class origins which have colored their perceptions of events in the 1960s."[21]

Typical of this biased perception is a recent book: *Vietnam and America: A Documented History.* The book presents various documents and articles related to the Vietnam War and purports to "provide a true documentary history" of the conflict. When it presents an article sympathetic to the Communists, "Remembering the Tet Offensive," it does so totally uncritically; the reader is presented its content and opinion as fact. But when this "history" presents Westmoreland's article, "The Year of Decision—1968," it picks away with 24 footnoted complaints and "corrections" that are factually wrong. One "correction" claims that the murder of civilians at Hue was an American fabrication despite later admissions by the Communists.[22]

Other examples include the following:

- The author of *Vietnam: Anatomy of a War, 1940–1975*, Gabriel Kolko, describes himself thus: "In my case, I was from its inception totally opposed to all American involvement in Vietnam . . . and I fully welcomed the Vietnamese Communist Party's success over the French and American alternatives to it."[23]
- Frank Snepp, author of *Decent Interval*, alludes to his biases as he writes that, "I had joined the CIA back in 1968 to avoid the Vietnam War, and that I should be part of the governments warmaking machinery there was a token of both my utter lack of conniving and the weakness of the system."[24]

■ Daniel Ellsberg, who went on to fame with the publication of "The Pentagon Papers" presents a particularly fascinating case. A former officer who never got his chance at combat, it is alleged that Ellsberg turned against the war after his personal life fell into disarray and his divorce became complicated by a romance with journalist Patricia Marx who violently opposed the war. Tom Wells recounts that Ellsberg, in the spring of 1969, began undergoing pschoanalysis. This analysis, and his growing indulgence in hallucinogenic drugs, provoked severe self-questioning. When, in the summer of 1969, he began participating in Los Angeles' swinging singles scene (under the alias of Don Hunter), he became further exposed to anti-establishment views.[25]

Whose Side Are You On?

An event in 1975, when U.S. Marines returned to help in the evacuation of Saigon, illustrates something about the relationship between the troops and the media. Helicopters, using the American Embassy roof, were evacuating allied officials and troops while U.S. Marines guarded the premises from the mob, many of whom had dubious claim on their "right" to evacuation. An American television crew was filming the scene when they noticed a young Vietnamese man bringing a rifle to his shoulder and taking aim at a group of U.S. Marines at the gate. Rather than shout out a warning, the television crew instead panned over to the Marines in preparation for filming the bullets' impact. Before the weapon could be fired, though, other Marines rushed to their comrades' aid by knocking the rifleman to the ground and seizing his weapon. Demonstrating what could be judged remarkable restraint under the circumstances, one of the Marines then grabbed the camera and smashed it to pieces on the ground.[26]

Perhaps, though, there is something timeless in this mutual mistrust and dislike. During the battle of Cold Harbor in the American Civil War, Edward Crapsey of the *Philadelphia Inquirer,* reported something he'd heard about the advice General Meade had given to General Grant. But Meade took exception to this reporting and forced the journalist to ride under armed escort along the entire line of Union troops for all to see with a large placard fastened to his back reading, "Libeler of the Press." A witness noted that "The wish to tear him limb from limb and strew him over the ground was fiercely expressed." Later, General Meade commented on how much this action had delighted his troops, ". . . for the race of newspaper correspondents is universally despised by the soldiers."[27]

In Vietnam, unfortunately, the feeling was often mutual.

32

Not Eyewitnesses At All

O ne of the factors contributing to the continuing failure to refute the *dich van* myths was the scarcity of western eye witnesses. Many of those who reported on the war never saw it themselves; they relied entirely on "second-hand" accounts, which themselves may have been tainted.

Journalists Not "Eye-Witnesses"

Peter Braestrup calculated that only about 40 journalists out of the 354 (181 American, 11 Vietnamese, and 162 other journalists reporting the war at its height) observed any combat action at battalion (approximately 500 men) or smaller unit level prior to the Tet Offensive. Fellow journalist Joseph Galloway (United Press International) confirms this, observing that, "I had the distinct feeling that I saw the same 6 or 8 or a dozen [correspondents] at every major fight, and on every major operation." The huge majority, Galloway notes, ". . . seemed content to cover the [Saigon Press Briefings] and occasionally take a day trip . . . into the aftermath of a battle." Rather than admit that they simply missed the story, they often invented one. David Halberstam observed that, "Journalists so rarely caught sight of the actual battles that the camera crews assigned most of their film to a category they entitled 'the wily VC got away again.' "[1]

Even when journalists, again with some notable exceptions, accompanied the troops into a combat zone, it must be remembered that they only did so for very brief periods, possibly three hours to four hours at a time. Peter Braestrup recalls that, "In late 1967, it was rare for newsmen to spend the night with a U.S. company or battalion in the field, or to live with a division, as journalists did in World War II, long enough to see the struggle as the troops or their leaders saw it."[2]

General Hal Moore of the 1st Cavalry Division agreed, observing that most reporters didn't spend the night with the troops but instead were noted for "scrambling on a supply Huey and heading back to a warm bunk and a hot meal in the rear." General Moore would also note that there were three exceptions to this in his experience: Joseph Galloway, Bob Poos, and Charlie Black.[3]

Because of these factors, on those rare occasions when they did go into the field, reporters and photographers were, in the words of journalist Peter Braestrup, ". . . plunged alongside uniformed strangers in a remote, often dangerous locale for a brief time, and then whisked away, often with 'good-film' but without any notion of either why the fight started or its 'before' and 'after.' "[4]

In addition, although television footage had the greatest impact on the American public, it must be remembered that, in the 1960s, television cameras were heavy, bulky, and unable to film at night. Where they went and what they filmed were very limited.

Based in Saigon

Primarily, journalists covering the war in Vietnam operated out of Saigon. Throughout the war, though, the majority of the "action" took place in the northernmost five provinces known as I Corps. To get a story from that location, the Saigon-based journalists would need to rise before dawn to get a C-130 cargo plane flight up to the big Marine base at Da Nang. They would then spend the night at the press center, hoping to get an early morning flight to the Marines' "divisional rear" area of Dong Ha and then a helicopter flight out to the battalion in question. After a few hours of filming, the journalists would hope to retrace their steps to Dong Ha and then on to Da Nang where they'd again stay at the press center while phoning their story down to Saigon. Because of these difficulties, it is perhaps little wonder that the journalists so rarely witnessed the war firsthand. And even more so, it's little wonder that they failed to witness the brief, violent firefights—at company, platoon, and even squad level—which were so typical of the war.[5]

Pieced Together in New York

Very little of what the American people were told about a given battle on the nightly television news actually came from one of their reporters "on the spot." During the Khe Sanh action, for instance, reports about this battle accounted for 25% of all television reports; but the vast majority (80 out of 110) of these reports were written in the United States from a variety of "wire service" reports and then spoken on-air by the news presenter. Only 30 came from reporters actually in Vietnam. Similarly, during the battle of Hue, 18 reports came from reporters on the scene while 44 were synthesized in New York from that same variety of wire service reports. Reporting on the firefight that took place on the front lawn of the American Embassy in Saigon in 1968, one of these synthesized reports announced, quite incorrectly, that "19 VC bodies lay inside the embassy."[6]

Although based on material from Vietnam, these synthesized reports were put together by people far removed from the scene. The media were not concerned by this distance. Australian journalist, Denis Warner, recalls, for instance, that he had just left Vietnam on one occasion when he received a request from *Look*, enclosing some sketchy news clippings, to write a story about the damage cause by defoliation on Route 1, running north from Saigon to Xuan Loc. The magazine wanted an article describing the crime. " 'Don't bother to go back to Vietnam, of course,' Warner was told, 'but just use the clips and your own knowledge.' " To his credit, Warner declined the job.[7]

This situation, where reports were written by those not on the scene, was inherently more vulnerable to bias. Rather than being *eyewitness* accounts, they were instead *interpretations* of eyewitness accounts, adding one more layer of possible misreporting. In a court of law, these accounts are referred to as "hearsay" and are ordinarily inadmissible as evidence, which suggests something of the credibility they should have been given.

A War Zone, Not a Combat Zone

One of the many *dich van* myths had to do with the danger inherent in South Vietnam. To this day, a casual observer would be forgiven for thinking that cinemas and bars were routinely bombed and that life in the cities was very dangerous. Hanoi was very keen on promoting this myth because it suggested that the government of the Republic of South Vietnam was incapable of providing security and hence unfit to rule. In comparison, the Viet Cong appeared to be a strong and viable force.

Understandably, many returning troops did not actively discount this myth of danger in South Vietnam. When friends and relatives lavished praise and respect upon them for having endured such hardship and danger, one can sympathize with their failure to "burst the bubble" in regard to the nature of the service. However, it remains clear that the country of Vietnam was not a "combat zone"; rather, it was a "war zone." Although everyone who served in Vietnam received "hostile fire pay," it was a political decision that did not reflect the reality. A combat zone, by definition, is "contested territory" and is not characterized by isolated incidents in secured areas. While the image of Saigon is often based on what emerged from the handful of days of fighting during the Tet Offensive of 1968, in fact, Saigon was for the most part a very safe and secure area. Some measure of this safety is that U.S. personnel were not allowed to wear their combat fatigues in Saigon , but rather, were required to wear their dress uniforms just as they would have done in the United States. Similarly, the carrying of weapons on the streets of Saigon was illegal. The streets were guarded by military policemen who, just like a stateside base, were armed only with pistols and nightsticks; their main function was to keep the Americans from getting out of order in the many bars and massage parlors. Even on most of the sprawling military bases, the carrying of weapons was limited to those actually performing some sort of guard duty.

Service in Saigon during the Vietnam War has been compared to service in London during World War II, that is, not totally without threat but far removed from the combat. Just as one would not expect an informed firsthand appraisal about the Battle of the Bulge (for instance) from someone who was sitting in London in 1944, neither does service in Vietnam by itself confer upon the person any "eyewitness" or "expert" status. One must therefore be very careful about people claiming expert knowledge of the Vietnam War because they had "been there themselves." Often, their location was itself far removed from the action and provided little opportunity for assessing the war's progress directly.[8]

Not Combat Troops

The great majority of troops in Vietnam were not combat troops with any firsthand view of the war. It has been estimated that perhaps one in five

American troops serving in Vietnam were involved in firing weapons at the enemy, including those men assigned to artillery units, aircrews, and tank units. The largest single major command in Vietnam during the height of the war was not the 1st Infantry Division or the 3rd Marine Division; it was the 1st Logistical Command, which had 55,000 men, mostly clerks, cooks, truck drivers, and other support personnel.[9]

Thus, the "typical" veteran of Vietnam was assigned to one of the sprawling American bases, which were the size of cities. (In 1968, the three air bases of Bien Hoa, Da Nang, and Ton Son Nhut, *each* had more takeoffs and landings than O'Hare International Airport in Chicago.) The typical veteran worked in an office, storehouse, or mechanical workshop and ate his meals in large "mess halls."[10]

While they performed their jobs magnificently, the overwhelming majority of Vietnam veterans had no direct, personal way of discerning the progress of the war. They were as dependent on the media accounts as was the American public back home. What about the journalists who wrote those media accounts? Except for a handful of noteworthy exceptions, the journalists in Vietnam rarely went into the field, where the war was actually being fought. Further, many of the American accounts were based on journalists' reports conceived in the safety of Saigon and then written by those even further removed from the battlefield in New York. In hindsight, it seems little wonder that the reporting was so open to bias and inaccuracy and that the veterans' own perceptions of the war could be so flawed.

33

False Witnesses
The Phonies and Liars

The story of Robert Fife appeared to be a classic Vietnam veteran tragedy: a decorated Navy pilot during the Vietnam War, shot down over enemy territory and captured by the Viet Cong. After the war, things just never seemed right again and he spent his life in and out of therapy. He seemed a living example of that "Vietnam veteran syndrome" and proof of the terrible consequences of that war. Finally, he became yet another Viet-vet statistic: he committed suicide.[1]

Only after Robert Fife's death did his wife of 22 years discover the truth. In spite of his stories, Robert Fife had never been to Vietnam. True, he had enlisted in the Navy as a young man, but he had been discharged after only eight months because of medical problems. Robert Fife, like many other troubled people, was unhappy with the realities of his life and so instead acted out a fantasy. He pretended to be the veteran he never was.

Unfortunately, these "phonies" abound. Some, no doubt, simply act out a fantasy life in preference to the mundane reality. Others perhaps through fantasy may be attempting to deal with their guilt about not having served. Claiming to be veterans with a knowledge of what actually took place during the war, the lies and fabrications of these men feed and nurture the various myths about the war.

Dr. Robert Fleming, writing in *Psychiatry*, observed that this same phenomenon had also occurred in previous wars in which, ". . . non-combatants and those who did not go overseas would sometimes try to imitate what they perceived to be the combat veteran's behavior to gain attention." These imitators acted out what they believed to be the attitudes and behaviors of the real veterans. A complicating factor, however, was added in the Vietnam War. Hanoi's successful *dich van* program provided these phonies with a "script," which they believed was genuine but wasn't. Thus, these phonies naively tell their stories about fraggings, rapes, and murders in their attempts at passing themselves off as genuine combat veterans.[2]

At Pepperdine University in 1970, a burly dark-haired student named Tom, usually seen wearing an olive-green field jacket, routinely spoke to his fellow students about the horrors of war he had seen during his tour of duty in Vietnam as an Army medic. One day Tom was in conversation with a new student. When asked why he had taken a three-year break from his studies, the student explained that he had been in the Marines for those years. Tom asked the new student what he'd done in the Corps and if he had been to Vietnam. When the new student responded that he'd been a grunt in Vietnam, Tom patronizingly put his arm on the new student, saying, "Yeah, I was a medic there, patching you guys up." The new student shrugged off Tom's arm while saying, "No medic ever patched *us* up," referring to the fact that the Marines' medical needs were provided by Navy hospital corpsman, not Army medics. Accusingly looking into Tom's face, the new student began asking where Tom had trained and where he had served in Vietnam. Tom hesitated momentarily, then sheepishly admitted, "Well I was *going* to be a medic but I had to leave the Army after two weeks because they discovered I had asthma."[3]

A number of other stories told by phonies include the following:

- The 1971 Executive Director of Vietnam Veterans Against the War, Al Hubbard, claimed to have been an Air Force captain with two tours of Vietnam. He also claimed to have received a Purple Heart medal for wounds received there. In fact, Hubbard had never been in combat and of course was never wounded either. During the war, he had served as a staff sergeant stationed at Tacoma, Washington.[4]
- The former president of the Vietnam Veterans of America chapter in Morrisville, New York, was David Goff. Goff not only claimed to have posttraumatic stress disorder (PTSD) from his Vietnam experiences as a CIA assassin, but also used these experiences to counsel "other" vets. Hailed by the press as a hero, Goff even persuaded Representative James Walsh (R. New York) to pin a number of combat medals on his chest during an April 1989 ceremony. Subsequent investigations showed Goff was a clerk in Okinawa and

had never been to Vietnam. To his credit, Representative Walsh called for a criminal investigation.[5]

- Massachusetts State Representative Royall H. Switzler (Republican), when running for Governor in 1986, claimed to have served with the Special Forces in Vietnam. In fact, he had served a peacetime tour of duty with the Army in Korea.[6]

- Iowa Senator Tom Harkin (Democrat) claimed to have been a fighter pilot in Vietnam with numerous combat missions to his credit. He also intimated that he had seen something of the war on the ground as well. Eventually, he was unmasked by Senator Barry Goldwater (a genuine major general in the Air Force Reserve) as having been a ferry pilot, flying planes from Saigon to repair facilities in Japan.[7]

- Darrow Tully was the publisher of the *Arizona Republic* and the *Phoenix Gazette*. Claiming to have been a combat pilot in Vietnam, Tully resigned when it was learned he had never served in any branch of the military.[8]

- Kenneth Bonner and Gaylord Stevens claimed to be Vietnam veterans who sought to ease the plight of other veterans. They opened the Vietnam War Museum in San Antonio, Texas. A few months after the museum's opening, it was discovered that neither had been to Vietnam. Stevens was a veteran, but of three years of stateside duty in the Coast Guard.[9]

- The Executive Director of the Vietnam Veterans Resource and Service Center in Dallas, Texas, John Woods claimed to have served a tour of duty in Vietnam. Later, it was discovered that he had served in the Coast Guard but had never been to Vietnam. He had been discharged from the Coast Guard early because of repeated drug use.[10]

- Dallas' Vietnam Veterans of America chapter president, Joe Testa, often spoke of the anguish of seeing buddies killed in the war as well as seeing returning veterans mistreated by people in the antiwar movement. He was often seen wearing a uniform with sergeant's stripes and adorned with the Silver Star medal. It turned out that Testa had never been to Vietnam. He had served 21 months of stateside duty, been AWOL repeatedly (resulting in his spending a total of nine months in the stockade) and never rose above the rank of private.[11]

- Barton Osborn testified before both the Senate Committee on Armed Services in July, 1973, and earlier, the House Committee on Government Operations in August 1971. Barton claimed to have been a part of the Phoenix program and claimed to have witnessed a number of murders. Further, days of testimony by other witnesses had clearly established that the Program's aim of "neutralizing" the enemy meant doing so by either imprisoning, "turning" them onto the government's side, or killing them. Osborn alleged the term, "neutralize," meant simply to kill. Questioned by committee members with an eye to the sensational, Osborn gave lengthy testimony. His full account was accepted and publicized in the media in spite of the fact that the long-haired Osborn had never, in fact, been associated with Phoenix. He had indeed served in Vietnam, but in I Corps (where the Marines were waging a conventional war against the NVA) and a time (1967–68) when the Phoenix Program was hardly off the ground. Further, he was unable to provide a shred of evidence, names or any documentation, to support his claims.[12]

- Lieutenant Francis T. Reitmeyer claimed in a proffer filed by the American Civil Liberties Union in February 1969 that he'd been assigned to the Phoenix program and that he had a "kill quota of fifty Viet Cong a month." Much publicity was generated by this claim, and some of the current myth is an outgrowth of this. This publicity was widespread in spite of the fact that Reitmeyer had never been to Vietnam. In 1967, Reitmeyer had been studying for the priesthood at Immaculate Conception Seminary when he suddenly decided to join the Army. While it was true that he had received his commission and had been trained in Maryland to one day become a Phoenix adviser, Reitmeyer requested and received a discharge as a conscientious objector *prior to going to Vietnam.* Further, when the Army became aware that he was telling his girlfriend that he was "being trained to murder," Reitmeyer willingly stated for the record that he was not being trained in assassination and also denied having made the claim to his girlfriend.[13]

- The Veterans Administration Medical Center in Reno, Nevada, has a 20-bed psychiatric unit and a significant interest in Vietnam veterans suffering from PTSD, a supposedly common complaint among veterans. Dr. Edward Lynn, Chief Psychiatrist at the center, describes how, in one four-month period (November 1982–March 1983), it was discovered that seven of those twenty patients claiming PTSD from their Vietnam experiences had never been to Vietnam. One of them was so convincing in his lies that he got a job as a counselor at a Veteran's Center, "counseling" real veterans. Another patient had acted out his lies for several years and had been an active participant in the "Vietnam Veterans Against the War" movement in the 1970s.[14]

■ The Veterans Administration Medical Center at Portland, Oregon, reported treating a number of "veterans" who turned out to be phonies. A report in the *American Journal of Psychiatry* discussed five of these. One of them, "Mr. A," had even convinced his wife of six months that he was having nightmares and flashbacks because of his Vietnam service. In fact, it was eventually discovered that he'd never been in the military. "Mr. B," claimed to have been a POW, still suffering painful wounds from the torture he'd endured. He was eventually discharged when it was discovered he'd never been in the military either. "Mr. E" was admitted when his wife became concerned about his behavior and the belief that it was caused by the horrors he'd endured in his Vietnam service. Psychiatrists noted that he "described buddies being killed and maimed, sudden ambushes, and suffocating heat and humidity." He also spoke of his "gradual disenchantment with the war and his cynicism upon returning home." It was subsequently discovered that he also had never been to Vietnam and that his fabricated descriptions were drawn from a *fictional* war novel he'd read.[15]

Continuing the Dich Van Myths

In a CBS documentary entitled, "The Wall Within," first broadcast in 1988, Dan Rather presented the stories of several traumatized Vietnam veterans so deeply disturbed by their war actions that they were living in the wilderness of Washington state. They were described as "outcasts, broken spirits" who came "out of hiding" in order to tell their story. One of the scenes showed one of these men howling at the moon. "Steve" claimed to be a former SEAL who left Vietnam in a straitjacket, addicted to drugs and alcohol. An investigator later discovered Steve's real name was Steven Ernest Southards and that he was never a SEAL; he was an apprentice fireman who had spent all his time in rear area bases. Another "veteran" was Terry Bradley, who, it was claimed, skinned alive up to 50 Vietnamese people in an hour. In fact, Steve Bradley spent his tour in Vietnam in an artillery unit near Saigon and amassed a total of over 300 days either AWOL or in confinement in his three years in the army. Even though diagnosed as schizophrenic, his claims in the documentary were aired without challenge. Two of the "combat veterans" interviewed were later discovered to have actually worked as security guards. The fifth, who claimed to have been traumatized by an event in Vietnam, was shown later to have indeed been traumatized, but by an accident that occurred during training off the coast of California.[16]

In spite of its blatant fiction, the documentary, "The Wall Within," is currently being shown in schools across the United States. The myths of the Vietnam war continue to be taught and promoted. The real story of America's actions in Vietnam, as it successfully defeated the Viet Cong and the North Vietnamese Army, remains largely untold.

Final

34

Summing Up

n the 1950s and 1960s, the United States had been involved in a worldwide struggle with the Soviet Union and Communist China. The United States had fought the Chinese in a bloody war in Korea in the early 1950s. Soviet tanks maintained Communist rule throughout eastern Europe and posed a real threat to western Europe.

It was in these circumstances that America became heavily involved in Southeast Asia. At first, the United States merely relieved some of the pressure on the French by providing financial backing to their anti-Communist war in Indochina. But when the French withdrew, America filled the vacuum thus created and provided direct support to the Republic of South Vietnam. In order to give credibility to its many defense pacts with anti-Communist states, it had little choice but to do so. Even if it failed to stop the Communists, America believed that it must send the clear message throughout the world that it would honor its agreements. While it may not be able to stave off every attack against its various allies, it would give notice that it would at least bloody the nose of any would-be attacker.

America countered North Vietnamese assistance to the Viet Cong with assistance of its own to the South Vietnamese forces. Northern military aid continued to grow, including the dispatch of its infantry battalions into the southern war zone. By 1965, America was countering with the dispatch of its own combat battalions, beginning with its Marine and airborne battalions.

America initially sent its best troops to fight against the Communists. Serving in Vietnam became a rite of passage among working class American boys of the time. Service in the Marines, the Army paratroopers, or the Rangers gained the sort of status and peer approval that some years before they might have gained on the high school football field. Hundreds of thousands of young men volunteered to serve during the conflict. These volunteers would one day make up the majority of the names inscribed in granite on the memorial in Washington, D.C. These volunteers scored stunning victories over the Communists, who lost a whole generation of men fighting against them.

While the working class boys were locked in battle with the North Vietnamese Army, the children of America's rich and privileged went about their lives as usual. By and large they avoided the war, continuing with their university studies and their careers. The Vietnam War is remarkably devoid of tales of the wealthy, quite unlike the accounts of John F. Kennedy at the helm of PT 109 or his brother, Joseph, killed in a B-24 over Europe in World War II.

Regardless of the failure by some to contribute to the war effort, by 1969 the North Vietnamese were forced to accept that they could not defeat America's troops and they grudgingly withdrew from the southern battlefield. America responded by withdrawing its own troops, starting with its elite units, who were then followed by the regular combat troops and, last, by the technicians and support troops. With *détente* about to cut off their supplies from the Soviets and Chinese, the North Vietnamese made a last-minute attempt to win the war outright in 1972 but were stopped by a combination of American airpower and South Vietnamese resolve.

The Paris Peace Accords were signed in January 1973, an agreement that held good prospects for future peace. Unfortunately, those good prospects didn't hold. Two years later, Hanoi attacked again, this time successfully.

While the Communists had been big losers on the battlefield throughout the war with the Americans, their *dich van* propaganda effort was an easy winner, pitted as it was against an American policy that chose to fight the war in its "business as usual" mode. The American people relied on the commercial media for their progress reports and understanding of the war. It soon developed that the media were both unfair and unkind to America's efforts in Vietnam. History has been equally unfair. In many cases, the writers of the histories are still being drawn from that rich and privileged group who sometimes opposed American war efforts and failed always to participate.

America's victories on the battlefield up until 1973 were overwhelmed by later events, and the sad fact is that Communist North Vietnam did later invade and conquer its southern neighbor. Those who predicted that the surrounding countries would fall like dominoes were proven wrong, but the world will never know if they might have fallen if America had not acted when it did. In 1994, Singapore's President Lee Kwan Yew noted that America's actions in Vietnam had given his country ten years to strengthen itself against the Communists, ten years without which Singapore might well have fallen. One can only speculate on how many other then-vulnerable states could also be added to this list.

Was it right that America became involved in the war in the first place? Even years after the war's end, the various politicians and their civilian appointees continue to disagree about whether America's forces should ever have been sent to fight alongside the South Vietnamese. To most veterans of the war, though, it really makes little difference. Their blue collar upbringing had instilled in them the belief that merit lay in doing a job well, no matter how difficult or thankless that job may be.

For many of those who fought in the Vietnam War, theirs was the simple but honest pride they felt in doing their job well. Regardless of the war's rights or wrongs, full credit must be given them for their magnificent performance under those difficult circumstances. In their victory, which to this day remains unheralded, they annihilated forever the Viet Cong and soundly defeated the North Vietnamese Army.

Notes

Preface

1. Memo of March, 1965, cited in Neil Sheehan et al., *The Pentagon Papers*, (New York: Quadrangle Books, 1971), 448.

I

Two Different Countries

1. For early history, see George M. Watson and Richard O'Neil, "The End of French Rule in Indochina," in Ray Bonds ed., *The Vietnam War: The Illustrated History of the Conflict in Southeast Asia*, (New York: Military Press, 1979), 46–55. Also see Edward Doyle, Samual Lippman, and the Editors of Boston Publishing Company, *The Vietnam Experience: Setting the Stage*, (Boston: Boston Publishing Company, 1981), 48–93.

2. Michael Charlton and Anthony Moncreiff, *Many Reasons Why: The American Involvement in Vietnam*, (New York: Hill and Wang, 1989), 41.

3. Michael Maclear, *Vietnam: The Ten Thousand Day War*, (London: Thames Methuen, 1981), 51.

4. Maclear, *Vietnam: The Ten Thousand Day War*, 55. For details of North Vietnam's role in the war, see Part II: Defeat of the North Vietnamese Army.

5. Truong quote from Nhu Trang Truong, David Chanoff, and Van Toai Doan, *A Vietcong Memoir*, (San Diego: Harcourt Brace Jovanovich, 1985), 36. While technically a Minister in the PRG, Truong describes himself in this autobiography as a "Viet Cong."

2

The Advisor Period

1. Regarding the NLF/PLAF describing themselves as Viet Cong, see for instance the NLF Radio Broadcast of 18 Feb 1968 cited in Bernard Weinraub, "Viet Cong Indicate Giap Heads Offensive in South," *New York Times*, 27 February 1968, 3. Also, note that Nhu Tang Truong, a Minister in the National Liberation Front, refers to himself as a Viet Cong Minister in his memoirs (Truong, Chanoff, and Taoi, *A Vietcong Memoir*).

2. Details of early period from William Michael Hammond, "U.S. Intervention and the Fall of Diem," in Bonds, *The Vietnam War*, 64–71.

3. Numbers of advisers from General William Westmoreland, "Report on Operations in South Vietnam January 1964–June 1968," in U.S.G. Sharp and W.C. Westmoreland, *Report on the War in Vietnam (As of 30 June 1968)*, (Washington D.C.: U.S. Government Printing Office, 1969), 77.

4. From 1981 interview with NVA General Tran Do by Karnow in Stanley Karnow, *Vietnam: A History*, (Middlesex: Penguin, 1983), 400–401.

5. For re-equipping with AK-47s, see Westmoreland, "Report on Operations," 84.

6. For formation of first division-sized unit see Lieutenant General Philip Davidson, *Vietnam At War*, (London: Sidgwick & Jackson, 1988), 313.

3

Fighting the VC Main Force

1. Described in detail in Part II.

2. Details of rules of engagement and area of responsibility from Tom Bartlett, "Operation Starlite," *Leatherneck*, August 1985, 19.

3. Details of the loss of one ARVN Battalion and mauling of another from General William C. Westmoreland, *A Soldier Reports*, (Garden City, New York: Doubleday,1976), 136.

4. Details of Marine movements in Operation Starlite from Brig. Gen. Edwin H. Simmons, "Marine Corps Operations in Vietnam, 1965–1966," *Naval Review*, (Annapolis: U.S. Naval Institute, 1968), 18–19. Additional information on Operation Starlite is from Tim Page and John Pimlott eds., *Nam: The Vietnam Experience, 1965–1975*, (London: Hamlin, 1990), 9–13.

5. Muir quote from Bartlett, "Operation Starlite" 20–21.

6. Ian McNeil, *To Long Tan: The Australian Army and the Vietnam War, 1950–1966*, (St Leonards, Australia: Allen & Unwin, 1993), 101.

7. McNeil, *To Long Tan*, 104.

8. General Sir John Wilton said that Americans were, ". . . flung around and accepted enormous casualties." From an interview, page 30 AHQ FILE 707/r2/38 (5) held in the Australian War Memorial (series AWM 107), cited in McNeil, *To Long Tan*, 98.

9. McNeil, *To Long Tan*, 118–120.

10. 6RAR was intentionally kept under strength by about 100 so that it could absorb that number of men who had come over as individual replacements to 1RAR (but who had been in Vietnam for less than six months) and so did not return to Australia with the unit. McNeil, *To Long Tan*, 193.

11. Wilton interview, p. 30., AHQ file 707/R2/38(5), AWM 107, cited in McNeil, *To Long Tan*, 201. Being allowed to conduct pacification efforts like the South Vietnamese noted in McNeil, *To Long Tan*, 428

12. McNeil, *To Long Tan*, 222.

13. Trin Duc quote ("The Australians . . .) from David Chanoff and Doan Van Toai, *Portrait of the Enemy*, (London: I.B. Taurus, 1987),108.

14. McNeil, *To Long Tan*, 222.

15. Terry Burstall, *The Soldiers Story: The Battle of Xa Long Tan Vietnam, 18 August 1966*, (St Lucia, Australia: University of Queensland, 1986), 57. Terry Burstall fought with 12 Platoon at the Battle of Long Tan.

16. Lieutenant. Sharp quote ("It's bigger . . .) from Geoffrey Kendall interview, pp. 9–10, November 1984, Official Historian's Collection, Australian War Memorial cited in McNeil, *To Long Tan*, 318.

17. Most texts quote the battalion after-action report, which says that B Company was advised to return at 4:30. B Company's radio operator, Corporal Robin Jones, however, claims they were not advised to do so until 5:30 P.M., which would explain the time taken to travel the short distance. Cited in Burstall, *The Soldiers Story*, 70.

18. LZ requirement ("Relatively secure . . .") from Department of Air Organisation Directive No. 9/66. Reformation and Deployment of No. 9 Sqn to Vietnam, 18 April 1966, p. 2 Air Force Office File 566/2/215, copy OHC, AWM, cited in McNeil, *To Long Tan*, 322. The matter of the resupply is covered well in McNeil, *To Long Tan*, 322.

19. McNeil, *To Long Tan*, 327.

20. McNeil, *To Long Tan*, 322.

21. Interview with either McCauley or Dr Bruce Horsfield (La Trobe University) cited in Lex McAuley, *The Battle of Long Tan*, (Melbourne: Century Hutchinson Australia, 1986), 98.

22 McAuley, *The Battle of Long Tan*, 100.

23. McAuley, *The Battle of Long Tan*, p. 140.

24. See the Chapter "Demise of the Viet Cong" and also "Twofold Invasion" (Part II) for a more complete description of this.

4

TET

1. For the necessity of action, see Lieutenant General Dave Richard Palmer, *Summons of the Trumpet: U.S.—Vietnam in Perspective*, (California: Presidio, 1978),174. In regard to planning and preparation behind the Tet Offensive, see Don Oberdorfer, *Tet!*, (New York: Da Capo, 1984), 42–76; James J. Wirtz, "Deception and the Tet Offensive," *Journal of Strategic Studies*, 13, (June 1990): 82–98; and Ronnie Ford, "Tet Revisited: The Strategy of the Communist Vietnamese," *Intelligence and National Security*, 9, no. 2 (April 1994): 242–286.

2. While Peter Macdonald, in *Giap: The Victor in Vietnam* (London: Warner, 1994), 262–291, and others have described this three-phase plan, I am indebted to

General Philip Davidson for a lengthy and insightful exposition in his letter to author of 28 February 1995.

3. For the linking into "spontaneous" public demonstrations, see Ford, "Tet Revisited," 269–273.

4. Ford, "Tet Revisited," 272.

5. Oberdorfer, *Tet!*, 126.

6. Oberdorfer, *Tet!*, 137

7. Ford, "Tet Revisited," 270.

8. Neil Sheehan, *A Bright Shining Lie: John Paul Vann and America in Vietnam*, (London, Pan: 1990), 713–714.

9. Ford, "Tet Revisited," 272–273.

10. Oberdorfer, *Tet!*, 2–40.

11. UPI report and dispatch both cited in Oberdorfer, *Tet!*, 31.

12. Oberdorfer, *Tet!*, 144–145.

13. Oberdorfer, *Tet!*, 150.

14. Sydney Stone, 25th Division's historian in an interview with Bergerud in Eric M. Bergerud, *Red Thunder, Tropic Lightning: The World of a Combat Division in Vietnam*, (St Leonards, Australia: Allen & Unwin, 1993), 167.

15. Colonel Otis, interviewed by Bergerud in Bergerud, *Red Thunder*, 171.

16. Oberdorfer, *Tet!*, p. 148.

17. Oberdorfer, *Tet!*, p. 143

18. For an account of the battle in Widow's Village, see SFC Robert E. Jones ed., *Redcatcher's Yearbook*, (APO San Francisco: Information Office, 199th Light Infantry Brigade, 1969) 16. See also Oberdorfer, *Tet!*, 145 and Sheehan, *A Bright Shining Lie*, 713–714

19. Oberdorfer, *Tet!*, 145

20. Oberdorfer, *Tet!*, 142.

21. Oberdorfer, *Tet!*, 150–151.

22. For the role of the pagoda, see Stanley Millet, *South Vietnam: U.S.-Communist Confrontation in Southeast Asia*, vol. 3, 1968, (New York: Facts on File, 1974) 36. For details of the execution, see Tim Bowden, *One Crowded Hour: Neil Davis, Combat Cameraman 1934–1985*, (Australia: Angus & Robertson, 1988), 160.

23. Troop numbers and dispositions from Brig. Gen. Edwin H. Simmons, "Marine Corps Operations in Vietnam, 1968", (Annapolis: *Naval Review*, 1973), 99–101; and from Westmoreland, "Report on Operations," 159–160; as well as "Fighting For the Citadel," in Page and Pimlott, *Nam*, 369.

24. Krainick quote from Oberdorfer, *Tet!*, 214.

25. Millet, *South Vietnam*, 124.

26. The NVA commander putting a stop to it cited in MacLear, *Vietnam: The Ten Thousand Day War*, 211. Casualty figures from Peter Braestrup, *Big Story: How the American Press and Television Reported and Interpreted the Crisis of Tet 1968 in Vietnam and Washington*, (Boulder, Colorado: Westview, 1977), 284.

27. Giap admission of military defeat in "How North Vietnam Won the War," *Wall Street Journal*, 3 August 1995, 4. Viet Cong casualty figures from Charles B. MacDonald, "Communist Thrust—The Tet Offensive of 1968," in Bonds, *The Vietnam War*, 152.

5

The End of the VC

1. Information on this action from Command Chronology, Second Battalion, Third Marine Regiment, May 1968, (Washington, D.C.: Headquarters, United States Marine Corps), and author's own personal recollections.

2. Trin Duc interview in Chanoff and Toai, *Portrait of the Enemy*, 107.

3. Battle account from Dale Andrade, *Ashes to Ashes: The Phoenix Program and the Vietnam War*, (Lexington, Mass: Lexington, 1990), 78–80.

4. Vietnamese interpreters quote ("the confused . . .) cited in Andrade, *Ashes to Ashes*, 79.

5. Estimate of length of tunnels from Nguyen Thgi Dinh, described as a 'Military Official' in "The Cu Chi Tunnels," (Ho Chi Minh City: Gia Phong Studios,1995)

6. Weyand quote from interview with Mangold in Tom Mangold and John Pennycate, *The Tunnels of Cu Chi*, 241.

7. Mai Chi Tho quote ("They were especially . . .") and Nguyen Thnah Linh quote ("When the Americans . . .") from interview with Mangold in Mangold and Pennycate, *The Tunnels of Cu Chi*, 257 and 259, respectively.

8. Account of post-Tet action in Mangold and Pennycate, *The Tunnels of Cu Chi*, 262–263.

9. Nguyen Thnah Linh quote ("They had two . . .") in Mangold and Pennycate, *The Tunnels of Cu Chi*, 260.

10. Tran Nhu quote from "The Cu Chi Tunnels."

11. Major Quot quote ("A five metre . . .") in Mangold and Pennycate, *The Tunnels of Cu Chi*, 264.

12. Vien Phuong quote ("There were only . . .") in Mangold and Pennycate, *The Tunnels of Cu Chi*, 260.

13. Thomas C. Thayer, *War Without Fronts: The American Experience in Vietnam*, (Boulder, Colorado: Westview, 1985), 208.

14. Andrade, *Ashes to Ashes*, 73.

15. Ralph W Johnson, "Phoenix/ Phung Hoang: A Study of Wartime Intelligence Management," Ph.D. Dissertation, The American University, Washington, D.C., 1983, 213–214, cited in Andrade, *Ashes to Ashes*, 83.

16. Komer quote in W. Scott Thompson and Donald D. Frizzel eds., *The Lessons of Vietnam*, (New York: Crane, Russack & Company, 1977), 217. Beginning of Phoenix from Andrade, *Ashes To Ashes*, 72.

17. Thayer, *War Without Fronts*, 208.

18. Gabriel Kolko, *Vietnam: Anatomy of A War, 1940–1975*, (London: Allen & Unwin, 1986), 330.

19. Truong, Chanoff, and Toai, *A Viet Cong Memoir*, 201

20. Statement that hamlets were controlled by only a handful of Viet Cong from Sheehan, *A Bright Shining Lie*, 733.

21. Truong, Chanoff, and Toai, *A Viet Cong Memoir*, 169.

22. Description of first attack on "Breakfast" from Walter Isaacson, *Kissinger: A Biography*, (New York: Simon & Schuster, 1992), 175–177. Patrol leader quote ("Like somebody had kicked . . .") and Davidson quote ("Is precisely . . .") from Davidson, *Vietnam at War*, 595. Bomb tonnages from Isaacson, *Kissinger*, 175–177.

23. Truong, Chanoff, and Toai, *A Viet Cong Memoir*, 168.

24. Truong, Chanoff, and Toai, *A Viet Cong Memoir*, 168.

25. Truong, Chanoff, and Toai, *A Viet Cong Memoir*, 168–170.

26. The official Hanoi news release at the time claimed he had suffered a severe heart attack and was flown to Hanoi where he died on 6 July. British researchers Mangold and Pennycate went to Vietnam in 1978 and were told by Communist officials that Thanh had died of "cancer", Mangold and Pennycate, *The Tunnels of Cu Chi*, 256. In 1990 British researcher Peter Macdonald went to Hanoi where he was told that Thanh had died of "heart disease", Macdonald, *Giap*, 208. General Philip Davidson, chief of U.S. Intelligence, discovered from defectors that Thanh had been hit in the chest by bomb fragments from a B-52 raid, flown to a Hanoi hospital, where he died of wounds, Davidson, *Vietnam At War*, 442.

27. Truong, Chanoff, and Toai, *A Viet Cong Memoir*, 179–182.

28. Cited in Karnow, *Vietnam: A History*, 544–545.

29. The reference to "Gironde Battalion" and its leader later being killed, as well as the direct quote, is from Colonel General Tran Van Tra, *Vietnam: History of the Bulwark B2 Theatre Vol. 5: Concluding the 30-Years War*, (Ho Chi Minh City: Van Nghe, 1982), 220. The numerical designation is from Dr William Michael Hammond, "U.S. Intervention and the Fall of Diem," in Bonds, *The Vietnam War*, 68.

30. Tra, *Vietnam: History of the Bulwark B2*, 39.

31. Both VC officers were interrogated by General Davidson when they defected. Davidson, *Vietnam At War*, 542.

32. Trin Duc quote in Chanoff and Toai, *Portrait of the Enemy*, 108.

33. Cited in Braestrup, *Big Story*, xxi–xxii.

34. Tra, *Vietnam: History of the Bulwark B2*, 35.

35. Sheehan, *A Bright Shining Lie*, 724.

36. Battalion strengths from Thayer, *War Without Fronts*, 33. Strength of VC 316 Company and description as "a first class unit" from Sir Robert Thompson, "Vietnam," in Sir Robert Thompson ed., *War In Peace: An Analysis of Warfare to the Present Day*, (London: Macdonald & Co., 1988), 187.

37. Security of Route 15 from interview with General Dunstan cited in Peter Peirce, Jeffrey Grey, and Jeff Doyle eds, *Vietnam Days: Australia and the Impact of*

Vietnam, (Australia: Penguin, 1991), 59. Battalion strength and activities of D445 in 1971 from McAuley, *The Battle of Long Tan,* 152.

38. Dr. Duong Quynh Hoa interview with Karnow in Karnow, *Vietnam: A History,* 534.

39. Truong quote ("the Vietcong units . . .") from Truong, Chanoff, and Toai, *A Viet Cong Memoir,* 264

40. Truong's reference ("sleazy former . . .") from Truong, Chanoff, and Toai, *A Viet Cong Memoir,* 270.

6

A Different Struggle

1. In February, 1962 American military strength in South Vietnam reached 4,000. In November, 1963 there were 15,000 American advisers. By the end of December, 1964, total U.S. strength in South Vietnam was 23,000. By contrast, hundreds of thousands of U.S. troops were stationed in Korea and throughout Europe. Figures from Bonds, *The Vietnam War,* 12.

2. Rusk quotes cited in Maclear, *Vietnam: The Ten Thousand Day War,* 124.

3. For an explanation of the point of international law, under the Hague Convention, which permits such actions, see Colonel Harry G. Summers, *On Strategy: A Critical Analysis of the Vietnam War,* (Novato, California: Presidio, 1982), 98.

4. Regarding the date of the decision, see Sheehan et al., *Pentagon Papers,* 72. For Tra quote, see Tra, *Vietnam: History of the Bulwark B2,* 103.

5. Interview with Tran Do in Hanoi in 1981 with Karnow in Karnow, *Vietnam; A History,* 400–401.

6. For Ba quotes, see Chanoff and Taoi, *Portrait of the Enemy,* 152–153. For percentage of Northerners in VC units, see Major General R. Wetherill, "Debriefing of Senior and Designated Key Officers Returning From Field Assignments, Report of," (U.S. Department of the Army, 25 February 1970), 72. See also Sheehan, *A Bright Shining Lie,* 724.

7. Davidson, *Vietnam At War,* 313.

8. McAuley, *The Battle of Long Tan,* 152.

9. Chanoff and Taoi, *Portrait of the Enemy,* 148.

10. The original quote specifies the "Provisional Revolutionary Government" and has been replaced by "Viet Cong" in brackets. Similarly, the original quote used the term "DRV" [Democratic Republic of Vietnam] and has been replaced by the bracketed word "Hanoi." These changes, it is hoped, keep the essence of the quote while maintaining consistency of terminology used throughout this text. Interview from Vietnam Press, Foreign Language Publishing House, Hanoi, 1978, cited in Truong, Chanoff, and Toai, *A Vietcong Memoir,* 269. Note also recently released documents which confirm the Northern involvement, cited in Stephan B.Young, "Vietnam War: Washington Was Right," *Wall Street Journal,* 7 November 1995, 5.

11. Interview with Karnow in Hanoi, February, 1981, in Karnow, *Vietnam; A History,* 330–334.

12. Troop movements from Westmoreland, "Report on Operations," 107. Westmoreland does not refer to the 808th as its purpose was not primarily combat.

13. Dennis Warner, *Not With Guns Alone*, (Melbourne: Hutchinson, 1977), 153.

14. Davidson, *Vietnam At War*, 403.

15. Described in detail in Chapter Seven.

7

Ia Drang

1. I unapologetically draw heavily upon Lieutenant General Harold G. Moore and Joseph L. Galloway, *We Were Soldiers Once . . . And Young: Ia Drang, The Battle That Changed the War in Vietnam*, (New York: Random House, 1992). The combination of their own first-hand accounts, added to interviews with their former enemies, and a thorough survey of related documents is the outstanding reference to this key battle. Additionally, General Moore was kind enough to meticulously read through the draft manuscript of this chapter, offering clarifications and changes where necessary.

2. For NVA plan to seize Plei Me and South Vietnamese intelligence deciphering, see Si Dunn, *The History of the 1st Cavalry Division*, (Texas: 1st Cavalry Division Assoc., 1984), 138–139.

3. The nature of Stockton's mission in letter to author from General Moore of 23 August 1995.

4. Quotes from Brown and Moore in Moore and Galloway, *We Were Soldiers Once*, 33.

5. Quote from Chu Hut Man in Moore and Galloway, *We Were Soldiers Once*, 51.

6. Quote from prisoner in Moore and Galloway, *We Were Soldiers Once*, 63.

7. Herren quote in Moore and Galloway, *We Were Soldiers Once*, 69.

8. Savage quote in Moore and Galloway, *We Were Soldiers Once*, 71.

9. Nadal quote in Moore and Galloway, *We Were Soldiers Once*, 79.

10. Nadal and Staley quotes in Moore and Galloway, *We Were Soldiers Once*, 81.

11. Herrick quote in Moore and Galloway, *We Were Soldiers Once*, 88.

12. Patterson quote in Moore and Galloway, *We Were Soldiers Once*, 89.

13. Moore quote in Moore and Galloway, *We Were Soldiers Once*, 105.

14. Nadal quote in Moore and Galloway, *We Were Soldiers Once*, 121.

15. Deal and Beck quotes in Moore and Galloway, *We Were Soldiers Once*, 122.

16. Setelin quote in Moore and Galloway, *We Were Soldiers Once*, 126.

17. Diduryk quote in Moore and Galloway, *We Were Soldiers Once*, 126.

18. Bungum quote in Moore and Galloway, *We Were Soldiers Once*, 141.

19. Unsourced quote in Moore and Galloway, *We Were Soldiers Once*, 145. Nature and unit designation of patrols in letter from Moore of 23 August 1995.

20. Viera quote in Moore and Galloway, *We Were Soldiers Once*, 7. Casualties among command group in letter from Moore of 23 August 1995.

21. Hastings quote in Moore and Galloway, *We Were Soldiers Once*, 7.

22. Moore notes that, had the NVA attacked his Command Post, he would have "called air and artillery right on top of the melee." While he thus may have been able to beat back the attack, he concedes that the NVA may have been able to wipe out his CP. Details in letter from Moore of 23 August 1995.

23. Setelin quote in Moore and Galloway, *We Were Soldiers Once*, 188.

24. Martin quote in Moore and Galloway, *We Were Soldiers Once*, 189.

25. Details of extraction from LZ X-Ray in letter from Moore, 23 August 1995.

26. Cornet quote in Moore and Galloway, *We Were Soldiers Once*, 240.

27. Nguyen Huu An quote in Moore and Galloway, *We Were Soldiers Once*, 250.

28. Wayne quote in Moore and Galloway, *We Were Soldiers Once*, 260.

29. Schwarzkopf quote in Moore and Galloway, *We Were Soldiers Once*, 314.

30. Kinnard quote in Moore and Galloway, *We Were Soldiers Once*, 315.

31. Kinnard quote in Moore and Galloway, *We Were Soldiers Once*, 341.

32. Davidson, *Vietnam At War*, 364–365.

33. For description of Westmoreland's thinking on this, see Brigadier General S.L.A. Marshall, *Battles in the Monsoon*, (Nashville: Battery, 1967), 259–261.

34. For Westmoreland's plan, see Marshall, *Battles in the Monsoon*, 259–261. For number of manoeuvre battalions, see Westmoreland, "Report on Operations," 176–180.

35. Casualty figures from these battles from Westmoreland, "Report on Operations," 123–129.

8

Battles Along the Borders

1. Unless otherwise credited, for facts/dates/etc., see Captain S. Shore II, *The Battle for Khe Sanh*, (Washington D.C.: History and Museums Division, Headquarters United States Marine Corps, 1969).

2. For details of Dak To, see John Steer, "True Valor At Hill 875," *Vietnam*, June 1990, 38–40.

3. PFC Lozada would receive a posthumous Medal of Honor; Spec4 Steer who lost an arm in the battle, received the Silver Star.

4. Quote "talked eagerly" from Peter Arnett, "The Taking of Hill 875" in Page and Pimlott, *Nam*, 295.

5. Officers and medics casualty figures from Peter Arnett, "The Taking of Hill 875" in Page and Pimlott, *Nam*, 290. Westmoreland quote ("exceeding . . . 1965) from Westmoreland, "Report On Operations," 139.

6. Colonel Tran Van Doc quote from interrogation by Davidson in April, 1968 cited in Davidson, *Vietnam At War*, 469.

9

Generals

1. Davidson, *Vietnam At War*, 287–289.

2. Davidson, *Vietnam At War*, 289.

3. "Cuu Long " quotes from *Cuu Long on New Developments in the Guerrilla War in South Vietnam*, broadcast by Liberation Radio on November 13, 1966, in Patrick J. McGarvey, *Visions of Victory: Selected Vietnamese Communist Military Writings, 1964–1968*, (Stanford, California: Hoover Institution on War, Revolution and Peace, Stanford University, 1969) 101–113. "Truong Son" quote from *Truong Son on the 1965–66 Dry Season*, broadcast by Radio Hanoi July 4–7, 1966, in McGarvey, *Visions of Victory*, 82.

4. Chanoff and Toai, *Portrait of the Enemy*, 155.

5. Giap, Vo Nguyen, *May Van De Ve Duong Loi Quan Su Cua Dang Ta* [Some Problems of our Party's Military Line], Truth Publishing House, Hanoi, 1970, pp 325–384, cited in Ford, "Tet Revisited," 253.

6. Figures on Marine amphibious operations from Brigadier General Edwin H. Simmons, "Marine Operation in Vietnam, 1967," *Naval Review* (Annapolis: U.S. Naval Institute, 1973), 117–118. U.S. Marine Colonel's comments ("Landing . . .") from Colonel Gordon Batcheller, letter to the author of 22 November 1994.

7. Lieutenant General Willard Pearson, *The War in the Northern Provinces: 1966–1968*, (Washington D.C.: Department of the Army, 1975), 9. See also, Westmoreland, "Report on Operations," 116 and William S. Turley, *The Second IndoChina War: A Short Political and Military History, 1954–1975*, (Boulder, Colorado: Westview, 1986), 77.

8. Quote from Vu Ky Lan ("Near the . . .") cited in Macdonald, *Giap*, 213.

9. For the reasons—including the cooling of "international revolutionary fervor"—behind the decison, see Ford, "Tet Revisited," 253.

10. John Keegan, "Vietnam," in John Keegan ed., *The World Armies (Second Edition)*, London: MacMillan, 1983), 652.

11. For Giap's opposition to the plan and for his modifying it after Thanh's death, see Turley, *The Second Indochina War*, 99–100 and 114.

12. For the "scaling down of the plan" see Turley, *The Second Indochina War*, 114 and 100. Giap quotes cited in Macdonald, *Giap*, 269; For details about "Second Wave" also see Douglas Pike, *PAVN: People's Army of Vietnam*, (New York: Da Capo, 1991), 232. General Philip Davidson recounts a MACV study in late 1967 which had come to the same conclusion as Giap. This study concluded his best chance of success would be to attack the two northern provinces with four or five divisions while

mounting diversionary attacks against the cities, and seize Hue. The MACV study pointed out that if the plan failed, Giap had a relatively short distance to retreat back to the north. Davidson, *Vietnam at War*, 480–481.

13. Official History ("Those that . . .") cited in Mcdonald, *Giap*, 266. Tran Bach Dang is presumeably referring to the NVA Regiments at Hue beginning their *movement* phase 18 hours prematurely, which would explain why they were fully in position by the early hours of January 31st when the actual attack on the MACV compound was launched. Tran Bach Dang quote ("got Hue to jump the gun . . .") from Tran Bach Dang, *'Nhat Ky Mau Than'* ['Mau Than Diary'] *in Mau Than Saigon* (Ho Chi Minh City; Nha Xuat Ben Tre Publishers, 1986), 35. in Ford, "Tet Revisited," 273.

14. General Davidson points out that American firebases which defended the DMZ provided only a very "porous" defence; one which the NVA *infantry units* could go around, using the miles of jungled hills and valleys which separated these bases (Davidson letter to author of 28 February 1995). But the Marine firebases were able to prevent Giap's movement of artillery and armor through the DMZ and for this reason, Giap needed to take Khe Sanh.

10

Khe Sanh

1. Unless otherwise credited, facts/dates/etc are from the definitive history, Shore, *The Battle for Khe Sanh*.

2. Regarding the upgrading of the airstrip in preparation for a future attack, see Davidson, *Vietnam At War*, 554.

3. Pearson, *The War in the Northern Provinces*, 29–30 and 95–96.

4. Colonel Lownds' belief that the seniority of these officers precluded a "mere diversion" in letter from Colonel Lownds to author 22 February 1995.

5. Throughout most of the ensuing battles, his order of battle for the hill outposts was: Defending Hill 881S, he had emplaced Company I, with an additional two platoons and a command group from M/2/26, as well as a three-gun detachment of 105mm howitzers (from C/1/13). On Hill 861, he had Company K (3/26), an additional two platoons from Company A (1/26), as well as two 4.2 inch mortars. On Hill 861A, he had Company E (2/26). On Hill 558 he had three companies of Marines (F, G, and H, 2/26). On Hill 950, defending the radio-relay site, he had one platoon from the 1st Battalion. These deployments left Colonel Lownds with three companies from the 1st Battalion, as well as one company (L) plus one platoon (from M/3/26) from the Third Battalion for the defense of the base itself. In addition, he had under his command an Army Special Forces group and their indigenous troops which were allocated to a sector of the base's perimeter.

6. Westmoreland quote (". . . emergence from hiding . . .") from Westmoreland, "A Military War of Attrition," in Thompson and Frizzel, *The Lessons of Vietnam*, 65.

7. Bruce E. Jones, *War without Windows*, (New York: Berkely Books, 1987), 170.

8. Account of Lieutenant Colonel Schungel from Page and Pimlott, *Nam*, 342–343.

9. Quote from the US Marine Colonel cited in Braestrup, *Big Story*, Vol. 2, 237.

10. Davidson, *Vietnam At War*, 562–563.

11. Several historians have doubted this but Davidson remains adamant and was in the best position to have known. It is believed that Giap wanted to be close to the site so that, once seized, he would be able to take full propaganda advantage. Davidson, *Vietnam At War*, 563. See also Bernard Weinraub, "Vietcong Indicate Giap Heads Offensive in South," *New York Times*, February 27, 1968, 3.

12. Dabney quote from William H. Dabney, "Dabney's Hill," in Page and Pimlott, *Nam*, 336–337.

13. Lownds interview on Khe Sanh, in *Vietnam: Ten Thousand Day War*, Television series.

14. Description of closure of Khe Sanh and quote from Colonel Marion C. Dalby, "Task Force Hotel's Inland Beachheads," *Marine Corps Gazette*, v. 53, no. 10, October 1969, 35–38.

I I

Hue

1. For an outstanding account of this battle, see Keith William Nolan, *Battle for Hue: Tet, 1968*, (Novato, California: Presidio, 1983).

2. Description of being in civilian clothes and of institutions seized from Simmons, "Marine Corps Operations in Vietnam, 1968," 300.

3. Troop reinforcement designations from Nolan, *Battle for Hue*, 29

4. NVA rocket hitting own troops in Oberdorfer, *Tet!*, 220. NVA units identified from Pearson, *The War in the Northern Provinces*, 41.

5. Captain Batcheller simply being told that "something was up" in letter from Colonel Gordon Batcheller to author of 8 January 1995.

6. Captain Christmas's observations about the NVA defences as well as the use of recoilless rifles to screen movements from Captain G.R. Christmas, "A Company Commander Reflects on Operation Hue City," *Marine Corps Gazette*, April 1971, 36–37.

7. Description of cavalry action in Nolan, *Battle for Hue*, 28.

8. Account of artillery observer in Warner, *Not With Guns Alone*, 56.

9. Major Swenson quote ("Although many . . .") cited in Nolan, *Battle for Hue*, 120.

10. Two battalions were from the 29th Regiment (325C NVA Division) and three from the 24th Regiment (304th NVA Division) in Pearson, *The War in the Northern Provinces*, 72; and Macdonald, *Giap*, 288. See also Davidson, *Vietnam At*

War, 560–561. These lightly-armed troops were a far cry from those with which Giap had hoped to reinforce Hue. Their removal from the battle taking place at Khe Sanh had made no discernable difference to the enemy strength there. This was confirmed by both the Commanding Officer, and the Logistics Officer at Khe Sanh at the time. Letter from Lownds to author of 22 February 1995; and letter from Colonel Roger Hagerty to author of 16 December 1994.

11. Request to withdraw cited in Oberdorfer, *Tet!*, 221.

12. NVA Commander putting a stop to killings cited in MacLear, *Vietnam: The Ten Thousand Day War*, 211.

13. Casualties from Pearson, *The War in the Northern Provinces*, 48.

12

Offensive is Stopped

1. Number of attackers cited in Nolan, *Battle for Hue*, xii–xiii.

2. Statement that a "platoon" occupied Hue from I Corps Commander, Lt Gen Hoang Xuan Lam, cited in Oberdorfer, *Tet!*, 217.

3. For speculation about "Second Wave" see Pike, *PAVN*, 232. Regarding Westmoreland's concerns, see Westmoreland, "Report on the War," 115–116. Quote from Col. Mai The Chinh in Macdonald, *Giap*, 270. The Politburo Order is known as the Quang Tin Document. The wording states "Region 5" because at that stage of the war Hanoi was not admitting to direct administrative control of Tri-Thien-Hue. Quang Tin document cited in Ford, "Tet Revisited," 268.

4. Abrams quote in Braestrup, *Big Story*, 351.

5. Quote from Col. Mai The Chinh in Macdonald, *Giap*, 270.

6. McCarthy's statement was reported in the *New York Times* of February 4, 1968. (cited in Oberdorfer, *Tet!*, 174). Cronkite broadcast cited in Oberdorfer, *Tet!*, 250–251.

7. For a discussion of the effect of the antiwar movement, including Senator McCarthy's campaign, see Jon M. Van Dyke, *North Vietnam's Strategy for Survival*, (Palo Alto, California: Pacific, 1972), 31–32.

8. Thayer studied casualties in the war and notes the "intentional concentration on Americans to keep U.S. casualty rates as high as possible". For discussion on increasing targeting of Americans in the late 1960s, see Thayer, *War Without Fronts*, 51–53.

13

Foxtrot Ridge

1. I am indebted to Major General (now General) James Jones, USMC, for studying a draft copy of this chapter and offering his detailed comments in Major General Jones, letter to author of 19 December 1995. Details of F2/3 from Command Chronology, 2nd Battalion, 3rd Marine Regiment, May, 1968. NVA troop movements from Simmons, "Marine Corps Operations in Vietnam," 1968, 309. Ref-

erence to being new troops, freshly equipped from interview with Lt James Jones Jr Interview at LZ Hawk, May 28–29 [1968], Tape #2745, Oral History, Headquarters USMC.

2. Details of F2/3 from Command Chronology, 2nd Battalion, 3rd Marine Regiment, May, 1968.

3. Precise number of Marines from General Jones, letter to the author of 19 December 1995.

4. Comments from Jones interview at LZ Hawk.

5. Account of PFC Lawrence Kenneth Arthur taken from his Silver Star Medal (posthumous) file.

6. First Sergeant USMC (Ret) Kevin Howell, letter to the author of 1 February 1999.

7. Account of HM Sarwicki from HM2 Emanuel Layos Interview at LZ Hawk May 28–29 [1968], Tape #2745, Oral History, Headquarters USMC.

8. Jones quote ("Just think . . .") cited in letter from Foxtrot Ridge veteran in author's collection

9. Enemy casualty figures for May 30 and 31 from Navy Cross Citation of Captain William E. Russell USMC.

10. For Australians at Fire Support Bases Coral and Balmoral, see Lex McAulay, *The Battle of Coral*, (Melbourne: Century Hutchinson, 1988).

11. Thanh's reproach from McGarvey, *Visions of Victory*, 9.

12. Westmoreland, "Report on Operations," 281–289.

13. For discussion of Hanoi's reading of the decline of the antiwar movement in the U.S. and the decision in late 1968 to shift goals, see Van Dyke, *North Vietnam's Strategy for Survival*, 32.

14. While the news media immediately began to push the story that Gen Abrams was abandoning Westmoreland's previous large-unit search and destroy tactics in favor of smaller-unit tactics, General Philip Davidson, chief of intelligence for both generals, patently denies this. What actually occurred, he insists, was that the situation itself dramatically changed. After their massive defeats on the battlefield, the Communists were forced to return to hit-and-run guerrilla tactics and the U.S. simply responded appropriately. For discussion on changing nature of Communist tactics and Abrams' reaction, see Davidson, *Vietnam at War*, 571–572.

14

Dewey Canyon

1. Details of this action are taken from "Combat Leadership Symposium: 'Dewey Canyon,' Selected Readings and Advance Sheet," Quantico Virginia: Command and Staff College, USMC, June 1994, unless otherwise referenced.

2. For Hanoi's promise to honor the DMZ (other concessions include stopping the shelling of South Vietnamese cities and agreeing to allow the government in Saigon to participate in the Paris talks), see Van Dyke, *North Vietnam's Strategy for Survival*, 22.

3. Charles R. Smith, *U.S. Marines in Vietnam: High Mobility and Standown, 1969,* (Washington D.C.: History and Museums Division, Headquarters USMC, 1988), 18.

4. Martin account in letter from Lieutenant Colonel Justin M. Martin to author of 6 March 1995.

5. Following the artillery attack on Fire Support Base Cunningham on February 2nd, Major General Raymond Davis (USMC) requested permission to send the 9th Marine Regiment into Laos to destroy artillery and other forces which threatened the Marines. Lt General Stilwell subsequently recommended a raid to a depth of five kilometres and passed this on to Lt General Cushman who in turn recommended the attack to General Abrams, the commander of all U.S. forces in South Vietnam. Smith, *U.S. Marines in Vietnam,* 21.

6. Fox quotes from Colonel Wesley L. Fox, "Moving to the Sound of the Enemy's Guns," *Marine Corps Gazette,* November 1989, 64.

7. Barrow quote ("I did not . . .") in letter from General Barrow to author of 12 September 1994.

8. Details of Hotel Company's actions, including names of platoon commanders, from interview with Brigadier General Vercauteren by author on 5 June 1996.

9. Quote from anonymous Marine ("Every fallen . . .") cited in Lieutenant Colonel Dave Winecoff, "Night Ambush!," *Marine Corps Gazette,* January 1984, 50.

10. Reference to necessary "leverage" in letter from General Barrow to author of 12 September 1994.

11. Barrow request in Smith, *U.S. Marines in Vietnam,* 45.

12. Fox quotes in Fox, "Moving to the Sound of the Enemy's Guns," 71–72.

13. Souvanna Phouma comments cited in Smith, *U.S. Marines in Vietnam,* 45. Barrow quote in letter from General Barrow to author of 12 September 1994.

15

Securing the Borders

1. For account of the Ben Het battle see Major General Donn R. Pepke, "Debriefing of Senior and Designated Key Officers Returning From Field Assignments: Report of," Assistant Chief of Staff for Force Development, U.S. Department of the Army, June 12, 1970, 8–9 and 73. See also Simon Dunstan, *Vietnam Tracks: Armor in Battle, 1945–1975,* (London: Osprey, 1982), 182–183, and General Donn A. Starry, *Armored Combat in Vietnam,* (Indianapolis: Bobbs-Merril, 1980), 149–153.

2. U.S. combat deaths in 1968 were 14,592; for 1969 they were 9,414; for 1970 they were 4,221; for 1971 they were 1,380. It wasn't just United States casualties which were decreasing. Combined US/South Vietnamese/3rd Nation casualties were 43,000 for 1969; 28,000 for 1970; 25,000 for 1971, a steady downward trend. From Southeast Asia Statistical Summary, Office of the Assistant Secretary of Defence (Comptroller), April 1973, pp. 1–9 cited in Thayer, *War Without Fronts,* 20.

3. Starry, *Armored Combat*, 153–161.

4. Starry, *Armored Combat*, 153–161.

16

Incursions

1. For operations in the Kingdom of Cambodia, see Starry, "Debriefing Report," 121–123. See also "Extending the War," in Page and Pimlott, *Nam*, 449–452.

2. Amount of material captured and casualties from Davidson, *Vietnam At War*, 627.

3. Nguyen Tien Hung and Jerrold L. Schecter, *The Palace File: Vietnam Secret Documents*, (New York: Harper and Row, 1986), 42–44.

17

Vietnamization Tested

1. For troop displacements and numbers, see Lieutenant Colonel G.H. Turley and Captain M.R. Wells, "Easter Invasion 1972," *Marine Corps Gazette*, March 1973, 18–19. For Hanoi's promise regarding the DMZ, see Van Dyke, *North Vietnam's Strategy for Survival*, 22, and also the specific comments of Secretary of Defense Melvin Laird on April 18th, 1972 cited in Allen, William L., "Spring 1972: Northern Invasion Repulsed," in Bonds, *The Vietnam War*, 224.

2. Tra, *Vietnam: History of the Bulwark B2*, 79.

3. Davidson, *Vietnam At War*, 675.

4. Account of Sergeant Luom from Colonel Gerald H. Turley, *The Easter Offensive*: Vietnam 1972, (Novato, California: Presidio, 1985), 130–135.

5. Ripley quote cited in Turley, *The Easter Offensive*, 157. For descriptions and analysis of battles in I Corps see Turley and Wells, "Easter Invasion 1972", as well as Turley, *The Easter Offensive*.

6. Davidson, *Vietnam At War*, 695–696.

7. Davidson, *Vietnam At War*, 696.

8. While nominally a "VC" Division, by this time in the war it was VC in name only, being manned, led and equipped by the NVA; hence the reference to "Communists' 9th Division" instead of "9th VC Division". Davidson quote ("one of those . . .") in Davidson, *Vietnam At War*, 696.

9. Davidson quote in Davidson, *Vietnam At War*, 697.

10. From a tape recording made public during the impeachment hearings, quoted in Hersh, Seymour M., *The Price of Power*, (New York: Summit Books, 1983), 506, cited in Hung and Schecter, *The Palace File*, 55.

11. Account of attack on Thanh Hoa Bridge from "Smart Bombs," in Page and Pimlott, *Nam*, 518–521.

12. Davidson quote in Davidson, *Vietnam At War*, 699.

13. Podgorny statement from Davidson, *Vietnam At War*, 714. Chairman Mao statement to Hanoi from Tuchman, Barbara W., *The March of Folly, from Troy to*

Vietnam, (New York: Alfred A Knopf, 1984), 371, cited in Davidson, *Vietnam At War*, 714.

14. Tra, *Vietnam: History of the Bulwark B2,* 81.

15. Kissinger's concerns in Kolko, *Vietnam; Anatomy of a War,* 436. McCarthy quote in Charlton and Moncrieff, *Many Reasons Why,* 166.

16. There still remained 43,500 support personnel. See Edward W. Knappman ed., *South Vietnam, Volume 7, U.S.-Communist Confrontation in Southeast Asia, 1972–1973,* (New York: Facts on File, 1973), 157.

18

Linebacker II

1. Richard Nixon, *The Memoirs of Richard Nixon,* (New York: Grosset and Dunlap, 1983), 734.

2. Davidson, *Vietnam At War,* 727.

3. Martine F. Herz, *The Prestige Press and the Christmas Bombing, 1972,* (Washington D.C.: Ethics and Policy Center, 1980), 54.

4. Account of Captain Lewis and his direct quotes of same are cited in Macdonald, *Giap,* 319–320.

5. Number of missiles fired given by General John W. Vogt, Seventh U.S. Air Force commander, who also notes that there were an estimated 884 surface-to-air missiles launched against the B-52s. Only 24 found their targets and, of these, 15 resulted in a downed B-52. Thus only 1.7% of the missiles fired resulted in a downed B-52. The B-52s themselves had a loss rate of 4%, cited in Hung and Schecter, *The Palace File,* 502. Casualty figures from Richard Nixon, *No More Vietnams,* (New York: Arbor House, 1985), 158. A more precise accounting is offered in Herz, *The Prestige Press,* in which he cites the official North Vietnamese account of January 4, 1973 stating that 1,318 were killed in the Hanoi area and 305 in the Haiphong area.

6. Hung and Schecter, *The Palace File,* 141–142.

7. Davidson quote from Davidson, *Vietnam At War,* 727. "Preparing white flags" quote from Hung and Schecter, *The Palace File,* 142.

8. Sir Robert Thompson, "Rear Bases and Sanctuaries," in Thompson and Frizzel, *The Lessons of Vietnam,* 105.

9. Wallace Terry, *Bloods: An Oral History of the Vietnam War by Black Veterans,* (New York: Random House, 1984), 296.

19

Defeat of the NVA

1. General S.L.A. Marshall "Thoughts on Vietnam," in Thompson and Frizzel, *The Lessons of Vietnam,* 53–54.

2. General S.L.A. Marshall "Thoughts on Vietnam," in Thompson and Frizzel, *The Lessons of Vietnam,* 54.

3. Davidson, *Vietnam At War,* 542.

4. Colonel Martin quotes in letter from Martin to author of 6 March 1995.

5. Le Thanh quote from Chanoff and Taoi, *Portrait of the Enemy*, 63. 1966/1967 casualty figures in Pearson, *The War in the Northern Provinces*, 95. Giap estimate from interview with Giap in Fallaci, Oriana, *Interview With History*, 1974 Trans. by John Shipley. (Milan: Liveright, 1976), 82, cited in Davidson, *Vietnam At War*, 402. Later admissions of 1.1 million killed from Agence France Presse release of April 4, 1995, Hanoi.

6. Chanoff and Taoi, *Portrait of the Enemy*, 48.

7. Tra quote ("Sending a concentrated . . .") from Tra, *Vietnam: History of the Bulwark B2*, 40. Deaths of 320th's leaders in Tra, *Vietnam: History of the Bulwark B2*, 41.

8. Chanoff and Taoi, *Portrait of the Enemy*, 67.

9. Morale concerns from Agence France Presse release of April 4, 1995. Thong quote from Karnow, *Vietnam; A History*, 545.

10. Chanoff and Taoi, *Portrait of the Enemy*, 120.

11. Chanoff and Taoi, *Portrait of the Enemy*, 64–65.

12. Chanoff and Taoi, *Portrait of the Enemy*, 65.

13. Chanoff and Taoi, *Portrait of the Enemy*, 120.

14. Soviet and Chinese criticism in Douglas Pike, "Giap Offensive Aims At War's End By Midyear," *Washington Post*, February 25, 1968, cited in Braestrup, *Big Story*, Vol 2, 168. The Tet Offensive: Senior official quote in "How They Did It," *Newsweek*, March 11, 1968.

15. Tra, *Vietnam: History of the Bulwark B2*, 6.

20

Paris Accords

1 For percentage of NVA in VC units—and especially in the 273 VC Regiment—see Wetherill, Debriefing Report, 8–9 and also Sheehan, *A Bright Shining Lie*, 724.

2. Daniel C. Hallin, *The Uncensored War: The Media and Vietnam*, (New York: Oxford, 1986), 189.

3. The Tra quote refers to the "puppet army" and, for consistency in the text, this has been replaced by "[South Vietnamese] army". Tra, *Vietnam: History of the Bulwark B2*, 79.

4. Tra, *Vietnam: History of the Bulwark B2*, 21.

5. Tra, *Vietnam: History of the Bulwark B2*, 34.

6. Nixon, *No More Vietnams*, 158.

7. Vietnam Communist Party, Central Committee Political Report, Fourth Party Congress, December, 1976; and *Vietnam: Destruction, War Damage* (Hanoi: Foreign Languages Publishing House, 1977), 28, cited in Turley, *The Second Indochina War*, 95.

8. Thomas J. Schoenbaum, *Waging Peace and War: Dean Rusk in the Truman, Kennedy & Johnson Years*, (New York: Siman and Schuster, 1988), 453.

9. Schoenbaum, *Waging Peace and War*, 452.

10. Interview with Tran Van Lam in Warner, *Not With Guns Alone*, 5. Tra quote from Tra, *Vietnam: History of the Bulwark B2*, 79.

11. Frank Snepp, *Decent Interval*, (Middlesex: Penguin, 1980), 54

12. Isaacson, *Kissinger*, 438.

13. For his decision to allow Hanoi's troops to remain in South Vietnam, see Nixon, *No More Vietnams*, 152–153.

14. Knappman, *South Vietnam*, 288–289.

21

Epilogue

1. Former Ambassador Graham Martin, in a BBC radio interview with Anthony Moncrieff in Charlton and Moncrieff, *Many Reasons Why*, 231–232.

All of this had, by late 1974, made South Vietnam so desperate for arms and fuel supplies that Saigon was preparing to use its precious gold reserves to buy arms from a source other than America. The Soviet Union got wind of this, according to "impeccable intelligence sources" and advised Hanoi to "go for broke" before Saigon could do so. See Warner, *Not With Guns Alone*, 9.

2. Colonel Harry Summers, who studied the war at length, observed that "contrary to the accepted wisdom, we did not create South Vietnamese regular units in our own image. With the exception of their marine and airborne units, the South Vietnamese Army was much like the American militia at the beginning of the republic."

Like those early American colonists, they were stationed in their home areas and had their families with them. This gave them great stability in counter-guerrilla operations and, just like early militia did a good job of protecting settlers from Indians, so too did the South Vietnamese successfully defeat the Viet Cong.

With the exception of the Airborne and Marine Division, each ARVN Division was located in its "home area." It recruited locally, was given conscripts who lived locally, and statically defended its area. Families tended to congregate in shanty towns nearby. Fleeing families would clog avenues of retreat and soldiers would desert their post to save their families living nearby. See Colonel Harry G. Summers, *On Strategy; The Vietnam War In Context* (Pennsylvania: Strategic Studies Institute, U.S. Army War College, 1981), 85.

3. "Frequent Wind" figures from "Operation Frequent Wind," in Page and Pimlott, *Nam*, 563.

22

Dich Van

1. For a description of *dich van*, see Pike, *PAVN*, 236–244 and Macdonald, *Giap*, 83.

2. Rusk quote in Charlton and Moncrieff, *Many Reasons Why*, 115.

3. Dean Rusk alludes to the dangers in his interview with Michael Charlton in Charlton and Moncrieff, *Many Reasons Why*, 115. For South Vietnamese enthusiasm to attack North Vietnam, and American restraints on them, see Dr William Michael Hammond, "Communist Aggression Provokes US Retaliation," in Bonds, *The Vietnam War*, 72–74.

4. Pike, *PAVN*, 239.

5. Pike quote from Pike, *PAVN*, 240.

6. "Terror . . ." quote from Pike, *PAVN*, 240.

7. Broadcasts by Radio Hanoi Domestic Service to South Vietnam, June 13–16, 1967, and published in *Quan Doi Nhan Dan* (Hanoi), June, 1967, cited in McGarvey, *Visions of Victory*, 156 and 153.

8. For Hanoi now boasting of its role in the war, see Pike, *PAVN*, 47–48.

23

The Bombings

1. Russell Tribunal quote in Jhn Duffet ed., *Against the Crime of Silence*, (New York: Simon & Schuster [Touchstone-Clarion], 1970), 8, cited in Nancy Zaroulis and Gerald Sullivan, *Who Spoke Up? American Protest Against the War in Vietnam, 1961–1975*, (New York: Doubleday, 1984), 351.

2. This was the reason for elaborate plans such as "Operation Bolo" in January 1967, to lure the enemy into the air, in Bernard C. Nalty, "The Air War Against North Vietnam," in Bonds, *The Vietnam War*, 90.

3. 1965–71 tonnages from Maclear, *Vietnam; The Ten Thousand Day War*, 185. 1968 tonnages and Tolsen's quote cited in Millet, *South Vietnam*, 119.

4. Braestrup, *Big Story, Vol. 2*, 141.

5. Thompson and Frizzel, *The Lessons of Vietnam*, 154.

6. Radio Hanoi quote in Broadcast by Radio Hanoi Domestic Service to South Vietnam, June 13–16, 1967, and published in *Quan Doi Nhan Dan* (Hanoi), June, 1967, cited in McGarvey, *Visions of Victory*, 156.

7. Percentage of B-52 sorties flown against North Vietnam from Thayer, *War Without Fronts*, 83.

8. Nixon, *No More Vietnams*, 87–88.

9. Kolko, *Vietnam; Anatomy Of A War*, 434.

10. Chanoff and Taoi, *Portrait of the Enemy*, 63.

11. From Admiral U.S.G. Sharp, "Report on Air and Naval Campaigns Against North Vietnam and Pacific-Wide Suport of the War, June 1964–July 1968," in U.S.G. Sharp and W.C. Westmoreland, *Report on the War in Vietnam (As of 30 June 1968)*, (Washington D.C.: U.S. Government Printing Office, 1969), 48.

12. Malcolm Browne description from Herz, *The Prestige Press*, 58. His report from *New York Times* March 31, 1973. cited in Herz, *The Prestige Press*, 58. Karnow quote from Karnow, *Vietnam; A History*, 41.

13. Herz, *The Prestige Press*, 55–56. Herz also notes that there may have been one exception to the B-52 targetting, with B-52s having been assigned the Hanoi communications facility.

24

Civilians Deaths/Atrocities

1. Kevin M. Generous, *Vietnam; The Secret War*, (London: Bison, 1985), 124.

2. Cited in Thayer, *War Without Fronts*, 129.

3. Total number of killed and unaccounted for in Braestrup, *Big Story*, 284. Communist document of April 25, 1968, in Millet, *South Vietnam*, 123.

4. NLF minister's comments ("Large numbers . . .") fromTruong, Chanoff, and Taoi, *A Vietcong Memoir*, 154. Phat conversation with Truong ("the discipline . . .") cited in Truong, Chanoff, and Taoi, *A Vietcong Memoir*, 154. In the same conversation, Phat (first vice president of the NLF and, later, president of the PRG) also claims that the massacre was the result of local Viet Cong commanders, not from orders issued by NLF central command.

5. Cited in MacLear, *Vietnam; The Ten Thousand Day War*, 211.

6. Tribunal quote ("Two anticivilian . . .") cited in Zaroulis and Sullivan, *Who Spoke Up?*, 351. Horowitz quote (". . . under intense . . .") from Peter Collier and David Horowitz, *Deconstructing the Left: FromVietnam to the Persian Gulf*, (Maryland: Second Thoughts, 1991), 79.

7. Casualty figures from Agence France Press release of April 4, 1995.

8. Tich quote in Macdonald, *Giap*, 223.

9. Communist claims in Westmoreland, "Report on Operations," 137.

10. Terry, *Bloods*, 274–300.

11. Sharp, "Report on Air and Naval Campaigns," 68.

12. William Colby with James McCarger, *Lost Victory: A Firsthand Account of America's Sixteen-Year Involvement in Vietnam*, (Chicago: Contemporary, 1989), 337–338.

25

David & Goliath

1. Expert quotes ("weapon for weapon . . ." and "this situation . . .") from Colonel Donn A. Starry, "Debriefing of Senior and Designated Officers Returning From Field Assignments, Report of," Assistant Chief of Staff for Force Development, U.S. Department of the Army [12 June 1970], 6.

2. Technical data on 130mm field gun and "impunity" quote from Lieutenant Colonel David Miller, "Weapons and Warfare Techniques Used in Vietnam," in Bonds, *The Vietnam War*, 24.

3. For warnings to COSVN see Truong, Chanoff, and Taoi, *A Vietcong Memoir*, 168. For Soviet Air Force commanding SAM sites and flying missions, see David C. Isby, *Fighter Combat in the Jet Age (Jane's Air War 1)*, (Great Britain: Harper Collins, 1997), 72–73.

4. Number of planes shot down by China from Isby, *Fighter Combat*, 75.

5. Analysis on force ratio from Thomas C. Thayer, "We Could Not Win the War of Attrition We Tried to Fight," in Thompson and Frizzel, *The Lessons of Vietnam*, 91. For this estimate of total number of American troops, see (for example) Charles C. Anderson, *The Grunts*, (New York: Berkely, 1984), xiv. Casualty figure of 80% cited in Thayer, *War Without Fronts*, 109.

6. Figures on where American combat deaths occurred is from Office of the Assistant Secretary of Defence, (Comptroller), Directorate for Information Operations, cited in Thayer, *War Without Fronts*, 116.

7. Captured material figures from Page and Pimlott, *Nam*, 452.

8. These are Army figures. Marine casualties, due to the area in which they fought, would no doubt have even fewer *punji* casualties. U.S. Army casualties, January 1965–June, 1970, cited in Lt Col. David Miller, "Weapons and Warfare Techniques Used in Vietnam," in Bonds, *The Vietnam War*, 23.

26

The Home Front

1. Seymour Martin Lipset, *Rebellion in the University: A History of Student Activism in America*, (London: Routledge & Kegan Paul,1972), 43.

2. Cited in Peter King ed., *Australia's Vietnam*, (Sydney: Allan & Unwin, 1983), 137.

3. Cited in King, *Australia's Vietnam*, 137.

4. Rusk quote cited in Fred Halstead, *Out Now! A Participants Account of the American Movement Against the Vietnam War*, (New York: Monad Press, 1978), 298–299.

5. *Time*, 1 June, 1970, 12.

6. Randall M. Fisher, *Rhetoric and American Democracy: Black Protest Through Vietnam Dissent*, (Lanham: University Press of America, 1985), 240.

7. John E. Mueller, *War Presidents and Public Opinion*, (New York: John Wiley, 1973), 100.

8. *New York Times* May 14, 1972, cited in Tom Wells, *The War Within: America's Battle Over Vietnam*, (Berkely: University of California Press, 1994), 545.

9. 76% figure from "Vietnam", *VFW*, March 1993, 20. Casualties by town were provided by Friends of the Vietnam Memorial (Wash DC) from software derived from the Vietnam Veterans Memorial Directory of Names; the Illinois study is Willis, John Martin, "Who Died in Vietnam: An Analysis of the Social Background of Vietnam War Casualties." Ph.D. diss. Purdue University, 1975, cited in Christian

G. Appey, *Working Class War: American Combat Soldiers and Vietnam*, (Chapel Hill: University of North Carolina, 1993), 12.

10. The *Newsday* quote is from Michael Useem, *Conscription, Protest, and Social Conflict: The Life and Death of a Draft Resistance Movement*, (New York: Wiley, 1973), 83. cited in Appey, *Working Class War*, 14.

11. John Helmer, *Bringing the War Home: The American Soldier in Vietnam and After*, (New York: Free Press, 1974), 4–5, cited in Appey, *Working Class War*, 18.

12. James W. Davis and Kenneth M Dolbeare, *Little Groups of Neighbors: The Selective Service System*, (Chicago: Markham Publishing, 1968), 137, cited in Appey, *Working Class War*, 35.

13. Lawrence M Baskir and William A., Strauss, *Chance and Circumstance: The Draft, the War, and the Vietnam Generation*, (New York: Knopf, 1978), 48–52, cited in Appey, *Working Class War*, 37.

14. Westmoreland, interviewed on BBC radio by Anthony Moncrief in Charlton and Moncrief, *Many Reasons Why*, 137.

15. Prestige-militancy link in Lipset, *Rebellion in the University*, 109. Wisconsin University example in Irwin Unger, *The Movement: A History of the American Left, 1959–72*, (New York: Dodd, Mead & Company,1975), 103.

16. Lipset, *Rebellion in the University*, 109.

17. Westmoreland quote in Thompson and Frizzel, *The Lessons of Vietnam*, p. 60. Un-referenced quote ("in affluent . . .") in Page and Pimlott, *Nam*, 54.

18. Annie Gotleib, *Do You Believe in Magic?*, (New York: Fireside, 1987), 67.

19. Collier and Horowitz, *Deconstructing the Left*, 79–80.

20. Davidson quote in Kenneth J. Heineman, *Campus Wars: The Peace Movement at American State Universities in the Vietnam Era*, (New York: New York Press, 1993), 97.

21. Discussion of nature of left-wing radicalism in Seymour Martin Lipset, "The Activists: A Profile," in Daniel Bell and Irving Kristol eds., *Confrontation: The Student Rebellion and the Universities*, New York: Basic Books, 1969). Harris Poll cited in Lipset, "The Activists: A Profile," 51. Quote ("powerful 2 per cent") from Lipset, "The Activists: A Profile," 51.

22. Schoenbaum, *Waging Peace and War*, 496.

23. Karnow, *Vietnam; A History*, 506.

24. Wells, *The War Within*, 107.

25. Oberdorfer, *Tet!*, 85

26. Schoenbaum, *Waging Peace and War*, 472.

27. Warnke and McNamara quotes in Wells, *The War Within*, 111 and 108. The 1995 interview was by Dianne Sawyer of ABC, shown on "Sunday", on the Nine Network, Australia, April 16, 1995. In this same interview Diane Sawyer notes that, while his children were amongst the protesters, "67% of the people in the country still supported the bombing" of North Vietnam at that time.

28. Karnow, *Vietnam; A History*, 562.

29. 1964–1972 figures from Knappman, *South Vietnam*, 301. *New York Herald* quote cited in Lipset, *Rebellion in the University*, 13.

30. Canadian figures from Al Hemingway, "Perspectives," *Vietnam*, June, 1996, 58–60.

31. Peirce, Grey, and Doyle, *Vietnam Days*, 137.

32. Bob Greene, *Homecoming: When the Soldiers Returned from Vietnam*, (New York: G.P. Putnam's Sons, 1989), 62, cited in Appey, *Working Class War*, 304.

33. Anderson, *The Grunts*, 177.

34. Gotleib, *Do You Believe in Magic?*, 65.

35. Ross quote and newspaper quote from *Daily Bulletin (Townsville)*, 18 December, 1971, from Jane Ross, "Veterans in Australia: The Search For Integration," in Jeff Doyle and Jeffrey Grey eds., *Australia R & R: Representations and Reinterpretations of Australia's War in Vietnam*, (Chevy Chase Maryland: Vietnam Generation, 1991), 66.

36. Author's assessment based on his own personal experience as well as countless interviews with fellow Vietnam veterans.

37. Estimate of number of veterans who took part in the march from Mike Feinsilber of The Associated Press, in his article, "Day of Emotion for Vietnam Vets," which appeared in newspapers throughout the United States on 14 November, 1982.

27

Morale

1. Philip Katcher, *Armies of the Vietnam War, 1962–75*, (London: Osprey, 1980), 16.

2. Percentage of conscripted troops in "Vietnam Warriors: A Statistical Profile," *VFW* , March 1993, 20.

3. For a discussion of the working class nature of troops in Vietnam, see Appey, *Working Class War*.

4. For the importance of completing the job regardless of how it had started, see Fisher, *Rhetoric and American Democracy*, 240.

5. Cited in Nixon, *No More Vietnams*, 129.

6. Knappman, *South Vietnam*, 331.

7. Davidson, *Vietnam At War*, 662.

8. Interview with Bergerud cited in Bergerud, *Red Thunder*, 285.

9. Nolan, *Battle For Hue*, 137.

10. Number of U.S. fragging homicides from BDM Corporation, *The Strategic Lessons Learned in Vietnam, Vol VII, The Soldier*, (Carlisle, PA: Strategic Studies Institute, U.S. Army War College, 1980), Table 4-3, 4-17. Australian fraggings from "500: The Australians Who Died in Vietnam," *The Weekend Australian Special Edition*, October 3–4, 1992, 1–20.

11. Details of how casualties were killed is from "500: The Australians Who Died in Vietnam," 1–20.

12. A total of 190 "intentional homicides" occurred among American troops in Vietnam out of almost 2,600,000 who served there, for a *total* homicide rate of 7.3

per 100,000. Figures from Office of the Assistant Secretary of Defense (Comptroller) cited in Thayer, *War Without Fronts*, 118.

13. In one of the more celebrated cases, a B-52 pilot refused to fly during Linebacker II. A veteran of 175 missions, 30 year old Captain Michael Heck, sought an honorable discharge on the basis of conscientious objection to the war. The Air Force, considering a court martial, rejected this request, eventually permitting him a discharge on "other than honorable grounds." (Knappman, *South Vietnam*, 257–257).

14. Moore and Galloway, *We Were Soldiers Once*, 27.

15. Australian figures from Boman, "The Vietnam Veteran Ten Years On," *Australian & New Zealand Journal of Psychiatry*, Vol. 16, 107–127. "Similar figures from American troops" quote from Jones, "Medical and Psychiatric Policy and Practice in Vietnam," *Journal of Social Issues*, Vol. 31, 1975, 49–65, both cited in Bruce Boman, "Are All Vietnam Veterans Like John Rambo?" in Marion Wolf and Aron Mosnaim, eds., *Posttraumatic Stress Disorder: Etiology, Phenomenology, and Treatment*, (Washington D.C.: American Psychiatric Press, 1990), 84–85.

16. Interview with Bergerud cited in Bergerud, *Red Thunder*, 285.

17. Examples of the claim that sailors voted not to sail abound; for example see Jacob Neufeld, "Disengagement Abroad—Disenchantment at Home," in Bonds, *The Vietnam War*, p.214. Actual poll figures in Halstead, *Out Now!*, 640–641.

18. "In contrast to . . . World War II" and "unprecedented utilization . . ." quotes from Raymond Monsour Scurfield, "Posttraumatic Stress Disorder in Vietnam Veterans," in John P. Wilson and Beverley Raphael, *International Handbook of Traumatic Stress Syndromes*, (New York: Plenum, 1993), 288 and 289 respectively.

19. Reynolds quote in Bergerud, *Red Thunder*, 307.

20. Tra realised, accurately, that this was simply a regrettable fact of life. He noted that these "cowards" were "a small, insignificant minority." Unlike the U.S., however, there was no Hanoi media intent on blowing this out of proportion. Tra quotes from Tra, *Vietnam: History of the Bulwark B2*, 49.

21. AWOL rates cited in Page and Pimlott, *Nam*, 403.

22. AWOL rates cited in Page and Pimlott, *Nam*, 403.

23. Chieu Hoi figures from Komer, in Thompson and Frizzel, *The Lessons of Vietnam*, 220. Numbers of high and middle level defectors cited in Kolko, *Vietnam: Anatomy of a War*, 259.

24. Percentage killed is from US Bureau of Census, 1971, 253, cited in Appey, *Working Class War*, 29.

25. Heinl is cited in this regard in Halstead, Fred, *Out Now!*, 637–639.

26. Percentage of "combat" troops in Thayer, *War Without Fronts*, 120. Details on last combat troops in Vietnam in Knappman, *South Vietnam*, Volume 7, 157.

27. Barrow quote from, Maj General Robert H. Barrow, "Operation Dewey Canyon," *Marine Corps Gazette*, November, 1981, 84.

28. Thomas A. Johnson, "Negroes in 'the Nam,' " *Ebony*, August 1968, p. 32. Whitney Young, "When the Negroes In Vietnam Come Home," *Harper's*, June 1967, p. 63 cited in Appey, *Working Class War*, 21.

29. Johnson, "Negroes in 'the Nam'", 31.

30. Interview with Terry cited in Terry, *Bloods*, 290–291.

31. Bergerud, *Red Thunder*, 290.

32. Williams quote from autobiographical account in Glen D. Edwards, *Vietnam; The War Within*, (South Australia: Glen D. Edwards, 1992), 153.

33. Reference to need to keep up morale in Macdonald, *Giap*, 304. Webb quote in James H. Webb Jr, "Military Incompetence," *Defense Issues*, Vol. 1, No. 61, 1986, 3.

34. See James Webb, "Viet Vets Didn't Kill Babies and They Aren't Suicidal," *Washington Post*, April 6, 1986, Outlook, C1-C2.

35. *Washington Post/ABC News* poll cited in Webb, "Viet Vets Didn't Kill Babies," C2.

36. Dr. Robert Fleming, "Post Vietnam Syndrome: Neurosis or Sociosis?," *Psychiatry*, Vol. 48., May 1985, 122.

37. VA study cited in Karnow, *Vietnam; A History*, 465–466. Australian historian in Peirce, Grey, and Doyle, *Vietnam Days*, 61.

28

Narrow Sample

1. Thayer specifies an advantage of "1.4 to 1." I've taken the liberty of restating this in the more readable form of 3:2. Thomas C Thayer,"We Could Not Win the War of Attrition We Tried to Fight," in Thompson and Frizzel, *The Lessons of Vietnam*, 91.

2. Neilson quote from Bergerud, *Red Thunder*, 114. Company strengths from Moore and Galloway, *We Were Soldiers Once*, 39.

3. Report on 101st Airborne in Millet, *South Vietnam*, 133.

4. DePuy quote cited in Maclear, *Vietnam: The Ten Thousand Day War*, 159.

5. Anderson quote cited in MacLear, *Vietnam: The Ten Thousand Day War*, 159–160.

6. Webb quote cited in MacLear, *Vietnam: The Ten Thousand Day War*, 159. Regarding the "oft-quoted statistic" see for example Page and Pimlott, *Nam*, 109.

7. McNeil, *To Long Tan*, 92.

8. Description and Hennessy quote from McCaulay, *The Battle of Coral*, 169.

9. "Even if" quote from Page and Pimlott, *Nam*, 56.

10. "More significant" quote from Page and Pimlott, *Nam*, 192.

11. Reference to the Australians having thought they'd suffered a defeat from McNeil, *To Long Tan*, 341–342. Enemy diary information from McNeil, *To Long Tan*, 351.

12. Batcheller quote from letter from Colonel Batcheller to author of 23 August 1994.

13. Galloway quote from letter from Joseph Galloway of 14 August 1995.

14. Appey quote from Appey, *Working Class War*, 307.

29

Not Expert Witnesses

1. Hallin quote in Hallin, *The Uncensored War,* 135. "Turnover" figures in Susan D. Moeller, *Shooting War: Photography and the American Experience of Combat,* (New York: Basic Books, 1989), 382.

2. Warner quote in Warner, *Not With Guns Alone,* 201–202. Adams quote in Moeller, *Shooting War,* 380.

3. Braestrup quotes from Braestrup, *Big Story,* 14–15. In regards Braestrup's thesis of Press failings, Noam Chomsky's concerns (Chomsky, "10 Years After Tet: The Big Story That Got Away," *More,* Vol. 8., June 1978, 16–23) are of interest but are refuted by subsequent admissions by North Vietnam.

4. Cited in Braestrup, *Big Story,*. 14–15.

5. Braestrup, *Big Story,* 14.

6. Hallin, *The Uncensored War,* 173.

7. Braestrup, *Big Story,* 26.

8. *Newsweek's* photo count in Braestrup, *Big Story,* Vol 2., 323.

9. Oberdorfer, *TET!,* 241.

10. Braestrup, *Big Story,* 384.

11. Schoenbaum, *Waging Peace and War,* 443.

12. Michael Herr, *Dispatches,* (London: Pan, 1979), 178.

13. False report of first five floors being occupied cited in Oberdorfer, *Tet!,* 31. General Bruce Clarke quote cited in Braestrup, *Big Story,* 141.

14. Braestrup, *Big Story,* 201.

15. Description of Cliiford in MacLear, *Vietnam: The Ten Thousand Day War,* p. 216. Dean Rusk beliefs in Schoenbaum, *Waging Peace and War,* 415.

16. Cited in MacLear, *Vietnam: The Ten Thousand Day War,* 216.

17. JCS quote ("Because the American . . .") cited in Davidson, *Vietnam At War,* 514. Rejection of invasion plan from Davidson, *Vietnam At War,* 515.

18. Todd Gitlin, *The Whole World Is Watching: Mass Media in the Making & Unmaking of the New Left,* (Berkeley: University of California, 1980), 207.

19. Davidson, *Vietnam At War,* 341.

30

Storytellers

1. Moeller, *Shooting War,* 404.

2. Braestrup quote in Braestrup, *Big Story,* Vol. 2, 323.

3. ABC telex cited in King, *Australia's Vietnam,* 178.

4. Westmoreland quote ("At one time . . .") cited in MacLear, *Vietnam: The Ten Thousand Day War,* 220. Westmoreland quote ("tended to report . . .") in Charlton and Moncrieff, *Many Reasons Why,* 151–152.

5. Schoenbaum, *Waging Peace and War,* 443.

6. Jack Raymond, "It's a Dirty War for Correspondents, Too," *New York Times Magazine*, February 23, 1966, 92, cited in Clarence R. Wyatt, *Paper Soldiers: The American Press and the Vietnam War*, (New York: W.W. Norton, 1993), 138–139.

7. Anderson quote in Anderson, *The Grunts*, 222.

8. Westmoreland quote cited in MacLear, *Vietnam: The Ten Thousand Day War*, 220.

9. Moeller, *Shooting War*, 379.

10. Eddie Adams, "Eulogy," *Time*, July 27, 1998, 17.

31

Hostile Witnesses

1. Marguerite Higgins, "Foreign Correspondents: The Saigon Story," *Time*, October 11, 1963, 55.

2. Westmoreland quote in Westmoreland, *A Soldier Reports*, 297. Webb quote from letter from James Webb, Jr. to author of 30 August 1994.

3. Davidson quotes from Davidson, *Vietnam At War*, 512.

4. Cited in Thompson and Frizzel, *The Lessons of Vietnam*, 49.

5. Cited in Hallin, *The Uncensored War*, 5–6.

6. "Antiwar consensus" and "personally opposed the war" quotes in Gitlin, *The Whole World Is Watching*, 216 and 218, respectively.

7. Herr quotes ("who would . . .) and ("a lot of correspondents . . .") from Herr, *Dispatches*, 31 and 167, respectively. Memo to President Johnson cited in Kathleen J. Turner, *Lyndon Johnson's Dual War*, (Chicago: University of Chicago, 1985), 151.

8. Herr, *Dispatches*, 168.

9. The general account of this is from Harrison E. Salisbury, *Behind the Lines—Hanoi: December 23, 1966—January 7, 1967*, (London: Secker & Warburg, 1967). Two examples of the reporting are to be found in Harrison E. Salisbury, "US Raids Batter 2 Towns; Supply Route is Little Hurt," *New York Times*, December 27, 1966, 1 and Harrison E. Salisbury, "No Military Targets, Namdinh Insists," *New York Times*, December 31, 1966, 3.

10. Goulding actions and Sylvester comment from Phil Goulding, *Confirm or Deny: Informing the People on National Security*, (New York: Harper & Row, 1970), 52–92, cited in Wyatt, *Paper Soldiers*, 154. Smith quote ("The Times' . . .") from Howard K. Smith, "Credibility and the Times," *National Review*, January 24, 1967, 73–74, cited in Wyatt, *Paper Soldiers*, 155. Baldwin quote ("seem to put . . .") from Baldwin to Daniel, December 27, 1966, box 11; Hanson Baldwin Papers, Yale University Library, Hanson Baldwin "Bombing the North", *New York Times*, December 30, 1966, p 1 cited in Wyatt, *Paper Soldiers*, 155–156.

11. *New York Times* Dec 21, 1972, cited in Herz, *The Prestige Press*, 54–55.

12. Cited in Wyatt, *Paper Soldiers*, 213

13. The witness was subsequently interviewed and it turned out he was driving one of the APCs and his account was based on an infantryman telling him that two wounded communists had been killed. Mr M. L. Nicholson, quoted in letter AG 28/68, Major General C.E. Long, to Secretary Department of the Army, 22 March 1968; both in Director of Army Legal Services (DALS) file 'Allegations of Torture in SVN', part 1 (no registry number), DD (copy OHC, AWM) cited in McNeil, *To Long Tan*, 345. The book is Ian Mackay, *Australians in Vietnam*, (Adelaide: Rigby, 1968), 199–200. The Newspaper account is from "Digger Shot Wounded Viets—Book", *The Melbourne Age*, March 9, 1968, 1.

14. Reference to war-based TV shows and, especially "Combat!," its "substantial viewers" and Morrow's claims in Sarah Farenick, "Television and the Vietnam War" in James S. Olson, *The Vietnam War: Handbook of the Literature and Research*, (Connecticut: Greenwood, 1993), 365.

15. Reference to "Daniel Boone" writers from Todd Gitlin, *Inside Prime Time*, (New York: Pantheon, 1983, 1985), 89–90.

16. Quotes from Olson, *The Vietnam War*, 370.

17. Reference to Kojak and quote ("All Vietnam vets . . .") from Sarah Farenick, "Television and the Vietnam War," in Olson, *The Vietnam War*, 370.

18. Davidson, *Vietnam At War*, 579. (including the direct quote).

19. Arthur Higbee, UPI cable, December 17, 1971, Robert Shaplen Papers, Mass Communications History Collection, Wisconsin State Historical Society, box 30, cited in Wyatt, *Paper Soldiers*, 202.

20. Malcolm W. Browne, "Saigon Officers' Hostility to Foreign Newsmen at Peak," *New York Times*, July 13, 1972, 2, and "Viet Nam: New Dangers Covering an Old Story," *Time* (Australian Edition), August 14, 1972, 36.

21. Heineman, *Campus Wars*, 3.

22. Marvin Gettleman et al, *Vietnam and America: A Documented History*, (New York: Grove, 1985), 339–354 and 355–372.

23. Kolko, *Vietnam; Anatomy of a War*, xiv.

24. Snepp, *Decent Interval*, 30.

25. Reasons for Ellsberg turning against the war from Sheehan, *A Bright Shining Lie*, 666. Ellsberg and the "swinging singles" from Wells, *The War Within*, 360.

26. Cited in Wyatt, *Paper Soldiers*, 215.

27. Account of Crapsey as well as Meade quote ("for the race of . . .") cited in Frank Wilkeson, "243," in Max Hastings ed., *The Oxford Book of Military Anecdotes*, (Oxford: Oxford University, 1985, 1989), 277.

32

Not Eyewitnesses

1. Braestrup calculations from Braestrup, *Big Story*, 25–26. Galloway quotes from Galloway letter to author of 14 August 1995. Halberstam cited in Turner, *Lyndon Johnson's Dual War*, 217.

2. Braestrup, *Big Story*, 26.

3. Moore's statement about exceptions from Moore and Galloway, *We Were Soldiers Once*, 134.

4. Braestrup, *Big Story*, 25–26.

5. Description of difficulties in getting to and from I Corps from Braestrup, *Big Story*, 23.

6. Number of synthesised reports from Braestrup, *Big Story*, 42. Details about the embassy cited in Oberdorfer, *Tet!*, 31.

7. Warner, *Not With Guns Alone*, 201–202

8. For similarity of service in London, see Fleming, "Post Vietnam Syndrome, Neurosis or Sociosis?", 124–125.

9. Page and Pimlott, *Nam*, 83.

10. Takeoff-and-landing figures cited in Oberdorfer, *Tet!*, 139.

33

False Witnesses

1. Susan Katz Keating, "Only the Phony," *Soldier Of Fortune*, October, 1991 64–67.

2. Fleming quote from Fleming, "Post Vietnam Syndrome, Neurosis or Sociosis?", 135.

3. "Tom" is a fictitious name but the account is true; based on author's own experience.

4. Keating, "Only the Phony," 64–67.

5. Malcolm McConnell, "True Faces of the Vietnam Vet," *Readers Digest*, May, 1994, 126–130.

6. Keating, "Only the Phony," 64–67.

7. Keating, "Only the Phony," 64–67.

8. Keating, "Only the Phony," 64–67.

9. Keating, "Only the Phony," 64–67.

10. Keating, "Only the Phony," 64–67.

11. Keating, "Only the Phony," 64–67.

12. Andrade, *Ashes to Ashes*, xv–xviii.

13. Andrade, *Ashes to Ashes*, 211–213.

14. Edward J. Lynn and Mark Belza, "Factitious Posttraumatic Stress Disorder: The Veteran Who Never Got to Vietnam," *Hospital and Community Psychiatry*, Vol. 35, No. 7, July 1984, 697–701.

15. Landy Sparr and Loren Pankrantz, "Factitious Posttraumatic Disorder," *American Journal of Psychiatry*, 140:8, August 1983, 1018.

16. McConnell, "True Faces of the Vietnam Vet," 126–130.

Bibliography

Interviews/Correspondence

Barrow, General Robert H. USMC (Ret), letter to the author, 12 September 1994.
Batcheller, Colonel Gordon, USMC (Ret), letters to the author, 23 August 1994, 24 September 1994, 22 November 1994, and 8 January 1995.
Davidson, General Philip B. Jr., USA (Ret) letter to the author, 28 February 1995.
Galloway, Joseph, letters to the author, 24 July 1995 and 14 August 1995.
Hagerty, Colonel Roger C., USMC (Ret), letter to the author, 16 December 1994.
Howell, 1st Sergeant Kevin, USMC (Ret), letter to the author, 1 February 1999.
Jones, Major General James J., USMC, letter to author, 19 December 1995.
Lownds, Colonel David E., USMC (Ret), letter to the author, 22 February 1995.
Martin, Lieutenant Colonel Justin M., USMC (Ret), letters to the author, 12 December 1994, 24 January 1995, 6 March 1995, and interview by author, 3 June 1996.
Moore, Lieutenant General Harold G., USA (Ret), letters to the author 23 August 1995 (including annotated draft manuscript) and 29 August 1995.
Vercauteren, Brigadier General Dick, USMC, interview by author, 5 June 1996.
Webb, Captain James H. Jr., USMC (Ret), letter to the author, 30 August 1994.

Documents

Command Chronology, 2nd Battalion, 3rd Marine Regiment, May 1968. Headquarters, United States Marine Corps.
"Combat Leadership Symposium; 'Dewey Canyon', Selected Readings and Advance Sheet." Quantico Virginia: Command and Staff College, United States Marine Corps, June 1994.
Jones, Lt James Jr interview at LZ Hawk, 28–29 May 1968, Tape #2745. Oral History, USMC.
Jones, SFC Robert E., ed. Redcatcher! Yearbook. APO San Francisco: Information Office, 199th Light Infantry Brigade, 1969.
Layos, HM2 Emanuel interview at LZ Hawk, 28–29 May, Tape # 2745. Oral History, USMC.
Patton, Colonel George S., Debriefing of Senior and Designated Key Officers Returning From Field Assignments; Report of, Assistant Chief of Staff for Force Development, U.S. Department of the Army [7 April 1969].

Pepke, Major General Donn R. "Debriefing of Senior and Designated Key Officers Returning From Field Assignments; Report of." Assistant Chief of Staff for Force Development, U.S. Department of the Army [12 June 1970].

Starry, Colonel Donn A. "Debriefing of Senior and Designated Key Officers Returning From Field Assignments; Report of." Assistant Chief of Staff for Force Development, U.S. Department of the Army [12 June 1970].

Wetherill, Major General R. "Debriefing of Senior and Designated Key Officers Returning From Field Assignments; Report of." Assistant Chief of Staff for Force Development, U.S. Department of the Army [25 February 1970].

Journals/Articles/Periodicals

Adams, Eddie. "Eulogy." *Time*, 27 July 1998.

Barrow, Major General Robert H. "Operation Dewey Canyon," *Marine Corps Gazette*, November 1981, 84–89.

Bartlett, Tom. "Operation Starlight," *Leatherneck*, August 1985, 18–23.

Boman, Bruce, Ph.D. "Are All Vietnam Veterans Like John Rambo?," in Wolf, Marion, M.D., and Aron Mosnaim, Ph.D. eds. *Posttraumatic Stess Disorder: Etiology, Phenomenology, and Treatment,* 80–93. Washington, D.C: American Psychiatric Press, Inc.1990.

Chomsky, Noam. "10 Years After Tet: The Big Story That Got Away." *More,* Vol. 8, June 1978, 16–23.

Christmas, Captain G. R.. "A Company Commander Reflects on Operation Hue City." *Marine Corps Gazette*, April 1971, 34– 39.

Dalby, Colonel M.C. "Task Force Hotel's Inland Beachheads." *Marine Corps Gazette*, October 1969, 35–38.

Fleming, Dr. Robert H. "Post Vietnam Syndrome: Neurosis or Sociosis?" *Psychiatry*, Vol. 48., May 1985, 122–139.

Ford, Ronnie. "Tet Revisited: The Strategy of the Communist Vietnamese." *Intelligence and National Security*, Vol. 9, No. 2 , April 1994, 242–286.

Fox, Colonel George C. "Recollections of Combat. " *Marine Corps Gazette*, June, 1984, 28–29.

Fox, Colonel Wesley L. "Moving to the Sound of the Enemy's Guns." *Marine Corps Gazette*, November, 1989, 63–75.

Grey, Jeffrey. "Lest We Forget the Facts." *The Bulletin*, 28 December 1993, 46–49.

Johnson, Thomas A. "Negroes in 'the Nam.'" *Ebony*, August 1968, 31–40.

Keating, Susan Katz. "Only the Phony." *Soldier of Fortune*, October 1991, 64–67.

Keegan, John. "Vietnam." in John Keegan ed. *World Armies* (Second Edition), 652–656. London: MacMillan Publishers, 1983.

Lipset, Seymour Martin. "The Activists: A Profile," in Daniel Bell and Irving Kristol, eds. *Confrontation: The Student Rebellion and the Universities.* New York: Basic Books, Inc.,1969.

Lynn, Edward J., M.D., and Mark Belza, M.D. "Factitious Posttraumatic Stress Disorder: The Veteran Who Never Got to Vietnam." *Hospital and Community Psychiatry*, Vol. 35, No. 7, July 1984, 697–701.

McConnell, Malcolm "True Faces of the Vietnam Vet." *Readers Digest*, May 1994, 126–130.

Scurfield, Raymond Monsour. "Posttraumatic Stress Disorder in Vietnam Veterans." in John P. Wilson and Beverley Raphael. *International Handbook of Traumatic Stress Syndromes*, 285–295. New York: Plenum Press, 1993.

Sharp, Admiral U.S.G. "Report on Air and Naval Campaigns Against North Vietnam and Pacific Command-Wide Report of the War, June 1964–July 1968," in Admiral U.S.G. Sharp and General W.C. Westmoreland. *Report on the War in Vietnam (As of 30 June 1968)*, 1–68. Washington D.C.: U.S. Government Printing Office, 1969.

Simmons, Brigadier General Edwin H. "Marine Corps Operations in Vietnam, 1965–1966." *Naval Review*, Annapolis:U.S. Naval Institute, 1968, 2–35.

————. "Marine Corps Operations in Vietnam, 1967." *Naval Review*. Annapolis: U.S. Naval Institute, 1969, 112–141.

————. "Marine Corps Operations in Vietnam, 1968," *Naval Review*, U.S. Naval Institute, Annapolis, 1970, pp. 289–320.

————. "Marine Corps Operations in Vietnam, 1969–1972." *Naval Review*. Annapolis: U.S. Naval Institute, 1973, 196–223.

Sparr, Landy, M.D., and Loren D. Pankratz, Ph.D. "Factitious Posttraumatic Stress Disorder." *American Journal of Psychiatry*, 140:8, August 1983, 1016–1019.

Steer, John. "True Valor At Hill 875." *Vietnam*, Volume 3, Number 1, June 1990, 38–44.

"The Tet Offensive: How They Did It." *Newsweek*, 11 March 11 1968.

Turley, Lieutenant Colonel G.H. and Captain M.R. Wells., "Easter Invasion 1972." *Marine Corps Gazette*, March 1973, 18–29.

"Viet Nam: New Dangers Covering an Old Story." *Time* (Australian Edition), 14 August 1972, 36.

Webb, James H. Jr. "Military Incompetence." *Defence Issues*, Vol.1, No. 61. Washington D.C: American Forces Information Service, 11 September 1986.

Westmoreland, General W.C. "Report on Operations in South Vietnam January 1964–June 1968," in Admiral U.S.G. Sharp and General W.C. Westmoreland. *Report on the War in Vietnam (As of 30 June 1968)*, 69–347. Washington D.C.: U.S. Government Printing Office, 1969.

Winecoff, Lieutenant Colonel Dave, USMC (Ret). "Night Ambush!" *Marine Corps Gazette*, January, 1984.

Wilkeson, Frank. "243," in Max Hastings ed. *The Oxford Book of Military Anecdotes*, 276–277. Oxford : Oxford University Press, 1985, 1989.

Wirtz, James J. "Deception and the Tet Offensive." *The Journal of Strategic Studies*, Volume 13, June 1990, 82–98.

Documentary Films

"The Cu Chi Tunnels." Ho Chi Minh City: Gia Phong Studios (Vietnam Friendship Run, Ltd.), 1995.

Books

Anderson, Charles R. *The Grunts*. New York: Berkely Books, 1984.

Andrade, Dale. *Ashes to Ashes: The Phoenix Program And the Vietnam War*. Lexington, Mass: Lexington Books, 1990.

Appy, Christian G. *Working Class War: American Combat Soldiers and Vietnam*. Chapel Hill: University of North Carolina Press, 1993.

BDM Corporation. *The Strategic Lessons Learned in Vietnam, Vol. VII, The Soldier*. Carlisle: Strategic Studies Institute, USAWC, 1980.

Bergerud, Eric M. *Red Thunder, Tropic Lightning: The World of a Combat Division in Vietnam*. St Leonards, Australia: Allen & Unwin, 1993.

Bonds, Ray ed. *The Vietnam War: The Illustrated History of the Conflict in Southeast Asia*. New York: Military Press, 1979.

Bowden, Tim. *One Crowded Hour: Neil Davis, Combat Cameraman 1934–1985*. Pymble, NSW Australia: Angus & Robertson Books, 1988.

Braestrup, Peter. *Big Story: How the American Press and Television Reported and Interpreted the Crisis of Tet 1968 in Vietnam and Washington*. Boulder, Colorado: Westview Press, 1977.

Burstall, Terry. *The Soldier's Story: The Battle of Xa Long Tan Vietnam, 18 August 1966*. St Lucia: University of Queensland Press, 1986.

Chanoff, David and Doan Van Toai. *Portrait of the Enemy*, London: I.B. Tauris & Co., 1987.

Charlton, Michael & Anthony Moncrieff. *Many Reasons Why: The American Involvement in Vietnam*. New York: Hill and Wang, 1989.

Colby, William with James McCargar. *Lost Victory: A Firsthand Account of America's Sixteen-Year Involvement in Vietnam*. Chicago: Contemporary Books, 1989.

Collier, Peter and David Horowitz. *Deconstructing the Left: From Vietnam to the Persian Gulf*. Maryland: Second Thoughts, 1991.

Davidson, Lt General Phillip B. *Secrets of the Vietnam War*. Novato, California: Presidio Press, 1990.

Davidson, Lt General Phillip B. *Vietnam At War*, London: Sidgwick & Jackson, 1988.

de St. Jorre, John. *The Marines*. New York: Doubleday, 1989.

Doyle, Edward, Samual Lipsman, and the Editors of Boston Publishing Company. *The Vietnam Experience: Setting the Stage*. Maryland: Boston Publishing Company, 1981.

Doyle, Jeff & Jeffrey Grey. *Australia's R&R: Representations and Reinterpretations of Australia's War in Vietnam*. Chevy Chase Maryland: Vietnam Generation Inc, 1991.

Duncan, David Douglas. *War Without Heroes.* New York and Evanston: Harper & Row, 1970.

Dunn, Si. *The History of the 1st Cavalry Division.* Texas: 1st Cavalry Division Association, 1984.

Dunstan, Simon. *Vietnam Tracks: Armor in Battle 1945–1975.* London: Osprey Publishing, 1982.

Edwards, Glen D. *Vietnam: The War Within.* South Australia: Glen D. Edwards, 1992.

Feuer, Lewis S. *The Conflict of Generations: The Character and Significance of Student Movement.* London: Heineman, 1969.

Fisher, Randall M. *Rhetoric and American Democracy: Black Protest Through Vietnam Dissent.* Lanham: University Press of America, 1985.

Ford, Ronnie E. *Tet 1968: Understanding the Surprise.* London: Frank Cass, 1995.

Fried, Morton, Marvin Harris, and Robert Murphy eds. *War.* Garden City: Doubleday, 1968.

Generous, Kevin M. *Vietnam: The Secret War.* London: Bison Books, 1985.

Gettleman, Marvin, Jane Franklyn, Marilyn Young, and H. Franklyn. *Vietnam and America: A Documented History.* New York: Grove Press, 1985.

Giap, General Vo Nguyen. *To Arm the Revolutionary Masses to Build the People's Army.* Hanoi: Foreign Languages Publishing House, 1975.

Giap, General Vo Nguyen. *People's War Against U.S. Aeronaval War*, Hanoi: Foreign Languages Publishing House, 1975.

Gitlin, Todd. *Inside Prime Time.* New York: Pantheon Books, 1983, 1985.

Gitlin, Todd. *The World Is Watching: Mass Media in the Making & Unmaking of the New Left.* Berkeley: University of California Press, 1980.

Gotleib, Annie. *Do You Believe in Magic?* New York: Fireside, 1987.

Greene, Bob. *Homecoming: When the Soldiers Returned from Vietnam.* New York: G.P. Putnam's Sons, 1989.

Grey, Jeffrey and Jeff Doyle. *Vietnam: War, Myth & Memory.* Australia: Allen & Unwin, 1992.

Hackworth, Colonel David H. and Julie Sherman. *About Face.* Sydney: Pan, 1989.

Halberstam, David. *The Powers That Be.* New York: Knopf, 1979.

Hallin, Daniel C. *The Uncensored War: The Media and Vietnam.* New York: Oxford University Press, 1986.

Halstead, Fred. *Out Now! A Participant's Account of the American Movement Against the Vietnam War.* New York: Monad Press, 1978.

Hammond, William M. *United States Army in Vietnam, Public Affairs: The Military and the Media, 1962–1968.* C Washington D.C.: Center of Military History United States Army, 1988.

Hasford, Gustav. *The Short Timers.* New York: Bantam, 1980.

Hatch, Gardiner ed. *The Blackhorse: 11th Armored Cavalry Regiment*, Kentucky: Turner Publishing, 1990.

Heineman, Kenneth J. *Campus Wars: The Peace Movement at American State Universities in the Vietnam Era.* New York: New York Press, 1993.

Herr, Michael. *Dispatches.* London: Pan Books, 1979.

Herz, Martin F. *The Prestige Press and the Christmas Bombing, 1972.* Washington D.C.: Ethics and Public Policy Center, 1980.

Hung, Nguyen Tien and Jerrold L Schecter, *The Palace File: Vietnam Secret Documents*, New York: Harper and Row, 1986.

Isaacson, Walter. *Kissinger: A Biography.* New York: Simon & Schuster, 1992.

Isby, David C. *Fighter Combat in the Jet Age (Jane's Air War* 1), Great Britain: Harper Collins, 1997.

Jensen-Stevenson, Monica and William Stevenson. *Kiss the Boys Goodbye: How the United States Betrayed Its Own POWs in Vietnam.* London: Bloomsbury Publishing, 1990.

Jones, Bruce E. *War Without Windows.* New York: Berkeley Books, 1987.

Karnow, Stanley. *Vietnam: A History.* Middlesex: Penguin, 1983.

Katcher, Philip. *Armies of the Vietnam War 1962–75.* London: Osprey, 1980.

King, Peter ed. *Australia's Vietnam.* Sydney: Allen & Unwin, 1983.

Knappman, Edward W. ed. *South Vietnam, Volume 7, U.S.-Communist Confrontation in Southeast Asia, 1972–1973.* New York: Facts on File, 1973.

Kolko, Gabriel. *Vietnam: Anatomy Of A War, 1940–197.* London: Allen & Unwin, 1986.

Lawliss, Chuck. *The Marine Book: A Portrait of America's Military Elite.* New York and London: Thames and Hudson, 1988.

Lipset, Seymour Martin. *Rebellion in the University: A History of Student Activism in America*, London: Routledge & Kegan Paul, 1972.

Macdonald, Peter. *Giap: The Victor in Vietnam.* London: Warner Books, 1994.

MacLear, Michael. *Vietnam: The Ten Thousand Day War.* London: Thames Methuen, 1981.

Mangold, Tom and John Penycate, *The Tunnels of Cu Chi.* London: Pan Books, 1986.

The Marines in Vietnam, 1954–73: An Anthology and Annotated Bibliography, Washington, D.C.: History and Museums Division, Headquarters, U.S. Marine Corps, 1974.

Marshall, S.L.A. *Battles in the Monsoons.* Nashville: The Battery Press, 1967.

McAulay, Lex, *The Battle of Coral.* Melbourne: Century Hutchinson Australia, 1988.

McAulay Lex. *The Battle of Long Tan*, Melbourne Century Hutchinson Australia, 1986.

McGarvey Patrick J. *Visions of Victory: Selected Vietnamese Communist Military Writings, 1964–1968.* Stanford California: Hoover Institution on War, Revolution and Peace, Stanford University, 1969.

McNeil, Ian. *To Long Tan: The Australian Army and the Vietnam War 1950–1966.* St Leonards NSW: Allen & Unwin, 1993.

Millet, Stanley ed. *South Vietnam: U.S.-Communist Confrontation in Southeast Asia, Vol 3, 1968.* New York: Facts on File, 1974.

Moeller, Susan D. *Shooting War: Photography and the American Experience of Combat.* New York: Basic Books, 1989.

Moore, Lt General Harold G., U.S.A. (Ret.) and Joseph L Galloway. *We Were Soldiers Once . . . And Young: Ia Drang, The Battle That Changed the War in Vietnam.* New York: Random House, 1992.

Mueller, John E. *War Presidents and Public Opinion*. New York: John Wiley and Sons, 1973.

Nixon, Richard. *No More Vietnams.* New York: Arbor House, 1985.

Nixon, Richard. *The Memoirs of Richard Nixon*. New York: Grosset and Dunlap, 1978.

Nolan, Keith William. *Battle for Hue: Tet, 1968,* Novato, California: Presidio, 1983.

Oberdorfer, Don. *Tet!* New York: Da Capo Press, 1984.

Olson, James S. *The Vietnam War: Handbook of the Literature and Research*. Connecticut: Greenwood Press, 1993.

Page, Tim, and John Pimlott eds. *Nam: The Vietnam Experience 1965–75*. London: Hamlyn, 1990.

Palmer, Lieutenant General Dave Richard, *Summons of the Trumpet; U.S.—Vietnam in Perspective,* Presidio Press, California, 1978.

Pearson, Lieutenant General Willard. *The War in the Northern Provinces; 1966–1968.* Washington D.C.: Department of the Army, 1975.

Pierce, Peter; Jeffrey Grey, and Jeff Doyle eds. *Vietnam Days: Australia and the impact of Vietnam*, Australia: Penguin, 1991.

Pike, Douglas. *PAVN: People's Army of Vietnam*. New York: Da Capo Press, 1991.

Salisbury, Harrison E. *Behind the Lines - Hanoi; December 23, 1966–January 7, 1967.* London: Secker & Warburg, 1967.

Schoenbaum, Thomas J. *Waging Peace and War: Dean Rusk in the Truman, Kennedy & Johnson Years'.* New York: Simon and Schuster, 1988.

Sharp, Admiral U.S.G. and General W.C. Westmoreland. *Report on the War in Vietnam (as of 30 June 1968)*, Washington D.C: U.S. Government Printing Office, 1968.

Sheehan, Neil. *A Bright Shining Lie: John Paul Vann and America in Vietnam*. London: Pan Books, 1990.

Sheehan, Neil, Hedrick Smith, E.W. Kenworth, and Fox Butterfield. *The Pentagon Papers*. New York: Quadrangle Books, 1971.

Shore, Captain Moyers S., II. *The Battle for Khe Sanh*. Washington D.C.: History and Museums Division, Headquarters, United States Marine Corps, 1969.

Smith, Charles R. *U.S. Marines in Vietnam: High Mobility and Standdown, 1969,* Washington, D.C.: History And Museums Division, Headquarters, U.S. Marine Corps, 1988.

Smith, R.B.. *An International History of the Vietnam War, Vol III, The Making of a Limited War, 1965–66.* London: MacMillan Academic and Professional, 1991.

Smith, Winnie. *Daughter Gone To War*, London: Warner Books,, 1994. First published by William Morrow and Company, 1992.

Snepp, Frank. *Decent Interval*. Middlesex, England: Penguin Books, 1980.

Starry, General Donn A. *Armored Combat in Vietnam*. Indianapolis: The Bobbs-Merril Company, 1980.

Summers, Colonel Harry G. *On Strategy: The Vietnam War In Context.* Pennsylvania: Strategic Studies Institute, USAWC, 1981.

Summers, Colonel Harry G. *On Strategy: A Critical Analysis of the Vietnam War.* Novato, California: Presidio Press, 1982.

Terry, Wallace. *Bloods: An Oral History of the Vietnam War by Black Veterans.* New York: Random House, 1984.

Thayer, Thomas C. *War Without Fronts: The American Experience in Vietnam.* Boulder, Colorado: Westview Press, 1985.

Thompson, Sir Robert and John Keegan eds, *War in Peace; An Analysis of Warfare to the Present Day.* London: Macdonald & Co., 1988.

Thompson, W. Scott, and Donald D. Frizzel eds. *The Lessons of Vietnam.* Crane, Russack & Company, 1977.

Tra, Colonel General Tran Van. *Vietnam: History of the Bulwark B2 Theatre, Vol. 5: Concluding the 30-Years War.* Ho Chi Minh City: Van Nghe Publishing House, 1982.

Truong, Nhu Tang; David Chanoff, and Van Toai Doan. *A Vietcong Memoir.* San Diego: Harcourt Brace Jovanovich, 1985.

Turley, Colonel Gerald H. *The Easter Offensive: Vietnam 1972.* Novato: Presidio Press, 1985.

Turley, William S. *The Second Indochina War: A Short Political and Military History, 1954-1975.* Boulder, Colorado: Westview Press, 1986.

Turner, Kathleen J. *Lyndon Johnson's Dual War.* Chicago: University of Chicago Press, 1985.

Unger, Irwin. *The Movement: A History of the American New Left, 1959–72,* New York: Dodd, Mead & Company, 1975.

VanDeMark, Brian. *Into the Quagmire: Lyndon Johnson and the Escalation of the Vietnam War.* New York: Oxford University Press, 1991.

Van Dyke, Jon M. *North Vietnams' Strategy For Survival.* , Palo Alto, California: Pacific Books, 1972.

Warner, Denis. *Not With Guns Alone.* Melbourne: Hutchinson of Australia, 1977.

Wells, Tom. *The War Within: America's Battle over Vietnam.* Berkeley: University of California Press, 1994.

Westmoreland, General William C. *A Soldier Reports.* , Garden City, New York: Doubleday, 1976.

Wyatt, Clarence R. *Paper Soldiers: The American Press and the Vietnam War.* New York: W.W. Norton & Company, 1993.

Young, Marilyn. *The Vietnam Wars 1945–1990.* New York: Harper Collins, 1991.

Zaroulis, Nancy and Gerald Sullivan. *Who Spoke Up? American Protest Against the War in Vietnam 1963–1975.* New York: Doubleday and Company, 1984.

Index